RE-THINKING MEN

For
Rowan and Gabriel
With Love

Re-Thinking Men
Heroes, Villains and Victims

ANTHONY SYNNOTT
Concordia University, Canada

ASHGATE

Published by
Ashgate Publishing Limited
Wey Court East
Union Road
Farnham
Surrey, GU9 7PT
England

Ashgate Publishing Company
Suite 420
101 Cherry Street
Burlington
VT 05401-4405
USA

www.ashgate.com

Reprinted 2010, 2011

British Library Cataloguing in Publication Data
Synnott, Anthony, 1940-
   Re-thinking men : heroes, villains and victims.
   1. Men. 2. Masculinity. 3. Man-woman relationships.
   I. Title
   305.3'1-dc22

Library of Congress Cataloging-in-Publication Data
Synnott, Anthony, 1940-
   Re-thinking men : heroes, villains and victims / by Anthony Synnott.
      p. cm.
   Includes bibliographical references and index.
   ISBN 978-0-7546-7709-3 (hardback) -- ISBN 978-0-7546-9422-9 (ebook)
   1. Sex discrimination against men. 2. Men--Social aspects. 3. Men in popular culture. 4.
Sexism. I. Title.
   HQ1090.S95 2009
   305.32--dc22

2009017571

ISBN: 978-0-7546-7709-3 (hbk)
ISBN: 978-0-7546-9422-9 (ebk)

Printed and bound in Great Britain by TJ International Ltd, Padstow, Cornwall

Contents

List of Tables

Introduction

Heroes or pigs? Villains or victims? Sex-objects, meal-tickets, deadbeats, in crisis or oppressive? all-powerful or mostly powerless? Men have been portrayed as the heroic sex, but also and more frequently as the suicide sex, the violent sex, the criminal sex, the death sex, the disposable sex – and as the enemy, misogynistic and morally inferior to women – and as soft, wimps, whiners, angry and most recently as stupid (Goldman, 2005), just boys (Cross, 2008) or simply unnecessary (Dowd, 2005). A more sympathetic portrait is of men as endangered (Parker, 2008). It is surely time to re-think men.

Love men or hate men, a storm of controversy surrounds men these days, much of it at the hate end of the continuum. Our cultural stereotypes of men, the majority in Euro-America being white, are reinforced by our stereotypes of the Other. Black men and Muslim men in particular, are victims of sexism and racism. Here racism and sexism reinforce each other. Faced with these negative portraits, men might say: "I am not who they say I am."

What does masculinity mean in the 21st century? Should we refer to "masculinity" or to "masculinities"? Are men "opposite" to women, as popular culture suggests, or 98% identical, as our chromosomes indicate? Are the ideals of masculinity so different from those for women? or can we refer to the masculinization of women and the feminization of men? Do men oppress women in Euro-American culture? or have they basically liberated women (and men) since the Enlightenment? These are some of the questions which we will address below. The answers vary however, depending on the theorist. Readers will have to make their own minds up, mindful of the evidence.

How men (or women) are defined is not just an academic matter, to be debated at leisure in coffee shops, on TV talk shows, in the press or in learned journals. These definitions, positive or negative, touch on the very heart of male identity and in turn define the patterns of relations between men and women, as well as between men and men.

Certainly the women's movements, the gay rights movement and the men's movements, whether pro-feminist or men's rights oriented, have all interrogated what it means to be a man, and what it could mean, and what it should mean.

Equally, the rapid decline of the primary and secondary sectors of the economy have negatively impacted men's employment and incomes. This has been due to a host of factors: outsourcing, downsizing, robotization, part-time, and contract work, both to reduce labour costs, and due to declining natural resources from coal to fish. Similarly the rise of the service sector, which is female-dominated, has substantially benefited women.

Men's roles in the family and in society generally, are in flux. Men are no longer the sole providers for the family: women's participation in the labour market has increased dramatically over the last 30 years; and men are often not even the main economic provider. And with women's greater success in tertiary education and in the professions, the balance is likely to shift further and faster in many ways.

If the past belonged to men (a big if), the future may belong to women – or it may be shared; but the present is contested.

Men have had to adapt very rapidly to changing domestic and global circumstances: always a difficult process. As one author phrases this, perhaps with some hyperbole: "Over the past thirty years, the institution of manhood – the experience of being a man, largely unchanged since time immemorial – has been ripped apart, burned, repaired, reinvented, rediscovered and remade, almost beyond recognition" (Brown, 2005:xvi).

Men are a polarizing population in the social sciences: both male and female students of men and masculinities diverge widely in their views and ideologies. Some see men as having all the power: hegemonic. Others see them as in crisis: the majority of the homeless, imprisoned, addicted, suicides, drop-outs and prematurely dead. Some describe men as violent; others note that they are the majority of the victims of violence. Some argue that men commit most of the violence; others point out that most men are not violent, and that violence stems from small minorities of men *and* women. Some define men and masculinity as *being* "a problem." Others say that men *have* problems, many of them the same as those of women. Some consider misogyny a major social problem; others focus more on misandry. Some think that women's rights are not sufficiently respected, and that women's voices are not heard; others think that men's rights are largely ignored and that men's voices are not heard. Some believe that women are victims of male oppression. Others think that, at least in Euro-America, women are particularly privileged by predominantly male legislators in a female-affirmative culture.

Men's rights activists and women's rights activists compete with each other for what they define as justice and equality, and both types of gender activists compete along with activists for many other causes. Yet there is little agreement or consensus on issues, goals, means or justice. The debates continue (e.g. Farrell and Sterba, 2008; Kimmel, 1995).

On these sorts of issues we cannot just sit happily on the fence and watch like it's a game, since the debates affect our own gender identities, and how others define us. We do have to try to see both – all – points of view and to develop a livable, humanist dialectic and synthesis. Clearly the opposed views outlined above are capable of synthesis, if identity politics can be transcended and eyes, ears and hearts opened.

Historically, men have been defined as the superior sex, at least by men. The Graeco-Roman and Judaeo-Christian traditions converged in this ideology of male supremacism (Synnott, 1993). The human rights revolution, accelerating with the Enlightenment and the American and French revolutions was institutionalized by the U.N. Universal Declaration of Human Rights (1948). This challenged the old Platonist concept of human inequality and affirmed: "All human beings are born free and equal in dignity and rights." The Declaration echoed Jean-Jacques Rousseau's famous sentence opening *The Social Contract* (1767): "Man is born free; and everywhere he is in chains" (1963:3). The UN Declaration not only reflected the Enlightenment but also legitimized the liberation movements which are still continuing.

Yet this value capsize, from ancient Greek and Roman assumptions of human inequality to declarations of human equality, required World War II, the Holocaust and the defeat of fascism to be fully recognized.

The consequences of the Enlightenment have been enormous; they include the abolitionist movement, the suffragette movement, the democratic, nationalist and decolonization movements worldwide, the Civil Rights movement in the United States in the 50s, the second wave of the Women's movement, the Gay Rights movement, the Anti-Apartheid struggle, and so on – and recently the Men's movement. The structural changes have been significant transfers of power from slave-owners to slaves, from monarchs to democrats, from capitalists to unions, from imperial and colonial powers back to the national people, from Whites to non-Whites quite often, from men to women. This last is most fascinating because so much power has been transferred in so many countries so peacefully and so quickly.

This value shift coincided with technological and demographic shifts. The invention of the pill in the 50s coincided with an expanding economy, facilitated a sudden fall in the fertility rate in the 60s, and therefore an increase in the numbers and the proportion of women in the labour force, then the second wave of the women's movement, and steadily increasing numbers in the tertiary education system, leading to increased mobility in the occupational system resulting in increased economic power: in sum, massive female empowerment. So much so that earlier feminist demands for parity in society are now matched by men's demands for parity (Farrell, 1993; Hise, 2004; Farrell and Sterba, 2008). And some feminists support them: male-affirmative women have emerged from the scrum to argue for men's rights (hooks, 2004; Bahramitash, 2005; Parker, 2008).

As gender-relations have changed, so have constructions of men and masculinity, both by men and women, but in various directions – which is confusing.

In the last 50 years, the definitions of men have become increasingly negative, both in popular culture and in some domains of feminism. Cartoons often depict men as stupid and idiots, the butt of the jokes, as do many sit-coms, joke books and advertisements. In the academic literature on gender, many feminists, both female and male, have demonized men as misogynists and hating women, as the death sex, as "all rapists," inventors of racism, genocide, and pollution, as planet destroyers, as half dead, half brained, and often as dumb, dense, pigs and jerks, and especially as "hegemonic" and "oppressive of women." The litany of invectives is endless, and indeed "male-bashing," as this contempt and hatred is so cutely described, is now institutionalized in popular culture (Nathanson and Young, 2001; 2006).

The old male sexism, misogyny, which was so effectively challenged by the women's movement, has been replaced in part by egalitarian attitudes but also by a new sexism: misandry. The prevalence of these negative portraits of men is problematic. This misandry has generated, at least in part, the new men's movements, popularized with the publication of Robert Bly's *Iron John* (1990). Where misandry has painted men as villains (which of course some men, and women, are), this is obviously not the whole truth. Indeed these last 50 years have witnessed a capsize of the old value system: from male-affirmative to female-affirmative; but not yet to the moral equality of both men and women. Not that misogyny and misandry are moral equivalents, historically or anthropologically, because they are not (Gilmore, 2001). None the less, recently several male-positive portraits have begun to challenge the prevailing culture. So gender relations are perhaps improving, and the pendulum is beginning to swing to egalitarianism and humanism.

Feminists used to say that what is good for women is good for men. To which we might add that what is good for men is good for women – and one thing that would be good for men is less misandry in popular culture and in some feminist and pro-feminist circles.

That said, the old simplicity of dictionary definitions of masculinity (and femininity) has been clouded by countervailing perspectives. Now, I suggest, three paradigms of men dominate the cultural landscape, which I present as follows. The traditional perspective, and expectation, of men as *heroes*: a reminder of men's roles yesterday and today in building our societies and our worlds. Second, the more recent paradigm of men as *villains*, both in fact, sometimes, but often also in stereotypical misandry. And third, the latest paradigm of men as *victims* echoing, and sensitized by, victim feminism. Heroes, villains and victims persist, all three and in both genders; and we need to compare and contrast all three paradigms.

Two caveats: first, while I try to review the status of men in contemporary western (for want of a better word) societies, the issues they face, and the range of attitudes towards men, much has been omitted. In focussing on these *moral* constructions, I have tended to downplay men's social roles: men as fathers, husbands, workers, lovers, queer theory, etc.; and the roles of love, risk, sports, violence, sex, competition etc. in men's lives. Obviously these are very important, and they are considered, but they are not my primary concern here.

Second, I have framed these three paradigms – all three of which can be read in the newspapers every day, for men and women – within the contexts of more general views about men and masculinities, gender and power.

The goals of this book are threefold. First, to counter the rather unbalanced, jaundiced and misandric view of men which has become so prevalent in so much of the literature on gender and on men. So the goal is to praise men – to recognize their massive and heroic contributions to social life and to civilization. (This point is balanced, however, by the other paradigms of men as also villains and victims.)

Men dominate the commanding heights of politics and economics, but also the depths. Sociological discussions of the "hegemonic male" (Connell, 2000), all-powerful and dominant, have tended to ignore the far more numerous *powerless* males. They have stressed the victimization and suffering of women and ignored the victimization and suffering of men, which persist, usually in different ways and to different degrees. Some men are powerful, certainly, and they dominate the economic, political, religious and social pinnacles of power. Most are not. And many "dominate" the valleys, the depths, the bottom rungs of the ladder (if they are on the ladder): the homeless, the incarcerated, the victims of suicide, homicide, work accidents, executions, premature deaths, addictions, the war-dead – and the victims of the health, education, welfare, justice and cultural value systems. Most men are somewhere in between. Not that most men are victims, or see themselves as victims (though most of us, men and women, are sometimes victims of some things); but nor are they hegemonic, nor obviously are they all deserving of praise as heroes. The status of men, in sum, is bi-polar: dominating both the top and the bottom, the powerful and the powerless.

The third goal is to try to offer a balanced perspective on gender and power relations, one which integrates both masculinist and feminist insight on our worlds. In the current climate of "the battle of the sexes," many authorities fight for one side against the other in what is surely a rather futile exercise in mutual destruction. People can disagree of course, but so often these matters are dialogues of the deaf – and the blind to other points of view. Men have been ill-served in the gender literature, so my focus is primarily on men. This is the other side of the coin to the usual one, and with a positive (albeit complex) spin.

Gender studies these days are minefields, and often they are less about scholarship than about ideologies – particularly in those studies which define men as oppressors and women as victims. But, at the risk of accusations of "backlash," "sexism," and being defined as an AWM (angry white male), I do suggest that gender relations are a bit more complicated than simply oppression of women by men.

* * *

The organization and rationale of this volume is straightforward. In Chapter 1 we discuss men, what it means to be a man – and opinions vary widely – and the plural meanings of masculinities in a new millennium but also the core meanings of masculinity. Some of the old and new ideals of manhood are discussed, from the knight, the gentleman and the self-made man to the "new man," the sensitive new age guy and the metrosexual. Masculinity itself runs along a horizontal continuum, with many options from hunk to sissy, warrior to metrosexual, and is also ranked vertically from positive to negative, princes to pigs; although there may be little agreement on the ideals or the rankings. Some have argued that men are hegemonic in a patriarchal society; others that men are "in crisis" – but that tends to depend upon which men we are discussing; and there is again little

agreement on whether men are "in crisis," and if so, which men and what sort
of crisis. The tendency to generalize and to stereotype men is problematic: men
are heterogeneous, fragmented, diverse, populations, including princes and pigs;
heroes, victims and villains; alphas and omegas. The paradox of masculinity, as
of femininity, is the diversity, and the difficulties of generalization. The effort to
re-think men is necessary, but difficult.

In Chapter 2 we explore this further with a discussion on gender. How we think
about men and women and our relationships with each other is curiously puzzling. We
often describe men and women as *opposite* sexes: Mars and Venus. Why? Both sexes
are members of the same species. Furthermore chromosomally the two sexes are
almost identical: only one chromosome out of 46 separates them. The sex chromosome
is XY for men and XX for women. In percentage terms therefore the chromosomal
difference is only 2.17%. Yet this 2% biological difference is somehow miraculously
converted into a social difference of 100% and opposition – opposite sexes. The way
we conceptualize gender therefore translates a 98% physiological *similarity* into an
100% social difference, and not only difference but *opposition*. This dualistic, binary
and dichotomous categorization of gender, which many people accept as right and
normal and even biological in origin is highly problematic. Indeed there are perhaps
five models of gender currently in circulation, which makes for some muddles in
our thinking, and for further controversy. These are the romantic model of love and
marriage, the old male supremacist model, the female (moral) supremacy model of first
and second wave feminism, the post-modern model since Darwin and Freud and up
to Fausto-Sterling, Butler and BGLTI which blurs the gender boundaries, and finally
the multiple conflict model in which gender is only one of many fault lines in society.
The issues work around dualism (conflict or complementary?) and egalitarianism,
difference theory, continuum theory and performance theory, in a bewildering tangle
of theories, theorists and data – bewildering but also enlightening.

Chapter 3, Heroes, emphasizes a contrast to the familiar portrait of men as villains,
and to the depressing portraits of men as victims; we discuss the massive, and largely
unacknowledged, contributions of men to the building of our civilizations. Women,
too, have contributed of course, and it is interesting to compare the types and degrees
of contribution as assessed by the end of century and the end of millennium lists
of the Top 10 or Top 100 most influential individuals, from various sources. The
dominance of men in these lists indicates not only their contribution but also the
prevalence of the rapidly disappearing traditional sex roles, and the blurring of
gender realities over time.

Chapter 4, Villains, discusses male villains, both real and constructed. The
ideological construction of men as villains is rooted in reality, and relatively well
understood (or misunderstood: it is difficult to tell how much male villainy is a
function of power or gender, since the two cannot be separated). We also discuss
the fiction of male villains in the constructions of the new sexism, misandry. This
teaching of the fear, hatred and contempt for men is a significant component of
popular culture, as well as some streams of feminism and pro-feminism. Despite
the occasional complaints from men about male-bashing, this new sexism has not

received the attention it deserves, nor the condemnation it requires until quite recently (Nathanson and Young, 2001; 2006).

Chapter 5, Victims, discusses the victimization of men, often by other men, both personal and systemic. This is counter-intuitive. We are more accustomed to hearing about the wars against women, wars waged by men. Yet men are also victims, often in similar ways to women; but to different degrees, and their victimization, pain and suffering has been largely ignored (indeed this phrasing may have elicited a startled reaction). It has been almost invisible, yet it is costly in terms of men's lives – and deaths.

There are several wars and several types of wars, with varying casualty rates both literal and metaphorical. The *military* wars killed about 40 million men, mostly young men, in the last century: killed mostly by other young men. Women too are killed in war but not in the same numbers nor usually in combat. By the end of 2008, almost 5,000 American troops have been killed in Iraq and Afghanistan, and under 100 women; and almost 100 Canadian military men have been killed in Afghanistan, and one military woman.

There are the violent *social* wars: the thousands of male deaths every single year by suicide (which are 80% male), homicide (about two-thirds male) and accidents (about two-thirds male), including work fatalities which are over 90% male. Over 100,000 American men and 9,000 Canadian men die by these three types of violent deaths every year: over twice the number of women.

The *cultural* wars are a very different type and include the joke-books, cartoons, T-shirts, TV programs and so much of our entertainment media which trivialize, ridicule and express contempt for men: men as fools. These wars perhaps reflect but surely reinforce the *ideological* wars: the widespread misandry in so much of the feminist and masculinist literature of the last few decades, from such feminist icons as Germaine Greer, Gloria Steinem and Betty Friedan to such pro-feminist authors as R.W. Connell and Michael Kimmel (all this was discussed earlier in Chapter 4).

The *systemic* wars refer to the failures of many of our social systems with respect to men. The education, health, welfare, justice, media, political and economic systems often fail men in ways that we might take for granted as normal and even right and fair – and if not right or fair, then justified by "centuries of male oppression" or as "leveling the playing field." These issues are developed further in Chapter 6 on Power.

But first, some caveats: the wars against men are waged mostly by other men in military wars and homicides, and as self-inflicted by the individuals themselves, in suicide. Similarly the systemic wars against men are also mostly waged by other men, since men largely run the systems. So the wars are complex and largely internecine: men against men (mediated by politics, race, class, and other systemic factors). We therefore may conceptualize men as not only victims, but also as victimizers in a sort of internecine *civil* war – in a sense, architects of their own destruction – while largely protective of women in the same systems.

Second, many of the wars against men are similar to the wars against women, since men and women face many of the same problems in this world. Some are different, both qualitatively and quantitatively, in degree or in kind. We try to understand both the similarities and the differences and to adopt a comparative – as well as a historical – perspective on these gender realities and wars. Men and women are not on different sides of the fence on these issues. Both men and women commit suicide, die by homicide, lose custody of their children – we all face common problems, and need to face them together.

The wars against women have been well-analyzed and understood for years (French, 1992; Faludi, 1992). The wars against men have not – partly because men have been constructed as the hegemonic sex, with all the power, and oppressive of women. The architects of these flawed descriptions have failed to notice that most men are not hegemonic. They have also failed to notice that some women are hegemonic and oppressive of both men and women in an unequal class and race system. And while concentrating on females as victims we have ignored the male victims and men in crisis: the homeless, the beggars, the incarcerated, the executed, the school drop-outs, the prematurely dead, the 5–6 year shorter life span, the confiscation of children, the inequity of the draft, the war dead, and the widespread misandry in popular culture, the media and even in some feminist and masculist literature and scholarship.... Identity politics have resulted in deeply flawed scholarship. The point is that women are not the only victims in this world, and males are not the only victimizers.

These presentations of men as heroes, villains and victims are intended to clarify some of the dynamics and complexities of men's lives. They are not generalizations about men so much as lenses through which to understand facets of men's lives. Clearly any particular individual may be all three at once, or in transition from one or two to others and back in the course of time. And to some extent, heroism or villainy may be in the eye of the beholder. Equally we have to consider gender relations as power relations, as we do in Chapter 6.

So in Chapter 6, Power, we shift from the binary model of gender theory to a post-modern multiple conflict and multiple alliance model, with discussions on economic and political power, cross-cut by complementary discussions on the three paradigms of women as hegemonic, as victims and as villains. This is a more useful, and realistic model than the binary model of so much gender studies.

Finally in Chapter 7, Theorizing Men, we conclude with a discussion of some of the principal theorists of men – sorry, not all – Bly, Farrell, Kimmel, Tiger, Connell and Nathanson and Young. They tend to look at men differently, see different issues and cite different data, which makes the comparison interesting. Some value masculinity, some condemn it as pathological. Some praise men and their achievements and values, some blame them, some sympathize with them in their adversities, some try to understand. Since the 1970s various men's movements have emerged. These include the National Organization of Men against Sexism (*www. nomas.org*), the National Coalition of Free Men (*www.ncfm.org*), the Mythopoetic movement of Robert Bly, the Promise Keepers (*www.promisekeepers.org*) and the

Nation of Islam's March on Washington. The goals vary between pro-feminist and pro-masculinist, religious and secular, political and personal, gay and straight, but readers can review the options for themselves and decide which, if any, deserve their support. Some portray men as villains, others see them as victim of many of the same forces as oppress women. We also consider the Fathers 4 Justice movement, the Men's Health Network and the Innocence Project.

A few final points: the scope of this book is restricted primarily to the U.S., U.K. and Canada for obvious reasons of space and time, but hopefully the research will be developed further in other countries.

Any discussion of gender is likely to paint with a broad brush. The infinite intersectionalities of race, class, faith, region etc. can get lost in the shuffle, as can the individual variations and especially the overlaps and similarities between men and women. We are not dealing with watertight binary biological compartments of male and female here, but rather with social trends which affect both sexes – usually unequally: sometimes favouring or disfavouring one, sometimes the other.

With all these controversial issues, therefore, we have to avoid homogenizing the sexes in an essentialist mode. Since we are generalizing however (as well as particularizing), this is not so easy to do. While much of this work is comparative, we need to avoid the "blame game," especially since so many authorities have blamed men for the oppression of women, and now we seem to be blaming men for the oppression of other men too. But it is more complicated than that. All these wars against men are not matters of gender so much as of power: political, economic, religious, ideological etc. – and of how power is exercised, by whom and for what ends, and how powers change and evolve and conflict.

In all this, we do need a sense of proportion as well as a healthy dose of common sense in an age of identity politics, and a great sense of humour. We need also to remember that most men and women are not sexists, neither misogynists nor misandrists. Despite the much-publicized work on the battle of the sexes, most members of both sexes like and even love each other. This mutual respect and affection is something to celebrate, and offers our best hope for the future. We should celebrate each other, our similarities and differences, our power and glory and creativity, our joys and sorrows and heroism. Certainly there are challenges, both within and between the sexes – the biggest of which are perhaps seeing each other's plural points of view, and differentiating self-interest from equity and justice.

Chapter 1
Men and Masculinities

About 3.3 billion men are living on, and occasionally off, this planet. Each one is unique in terms of DNA, finger-prints, odour-plume, retinal scan etc., but they are not all equal or identical in terms of masculinity, nor in what this manhood may mean to them.

The first paradox of masculinity is this wide but strange gap between being male, a biological phenomenon, and being masculine, which is both a personal and a cultural construct. "He was not man enough for me," a female friend said to me, explaining a recent break-up. And, perhaps surprisingly, 61% of young British men said that they did not feel masculine in a recent survey – compared to only 35% of older men born from the 1920s to the 1940s (The Brylcreem Mandom Report 29 May 2008). The gap between *being* masculine and feeling masculine is therefore wide, and also opening wider.

The second paradox is that sociologists now usually refer to multiple or plural masculinities to foreground different dimensions or ideals of masculinities. But how many are there? And what are the border-lines? This is not so clear.

The third paradox is that increasingly masculinity is not restricted to males. Some women are quite masculine, which is a construct or a characteristic, not a gender, and some men are quite feminine or, in the jargon of the day, more in touch with their feminine side. Some prefer the terms "stereotypically" masculine or feminine. Margaret Thatcher, also known as the Iron Lady, is cited in a recent book entitled *Manliness* as a classic example of a "manly woman" (Mansfield, 2006: ix).

These three issues, then, the gap between male and masculine, the idea of plural masculinities and the processes of masculinization and feminization of what we conventionally regard as the "opposite" sex, are at the heart of this chapter. These are interesting and important topics to explore, and to relate to the men and women whom we know and perhaps love.

What makes men masculine, as opposed to feminine? What is masculinity? What does being male mean, in this day and age? Not just possession of the Y chromosome, passed on from father to son; and it is surely more than the biological fact of possessing a penis. Yet what is meant by describing men (or women, for that matter) as more, or less, masculine (or feminine)? Lady Macbeth asked her husband: "Are you a man?" (Macbeth 3: 4: 57) – implying, of course, that he was not, and challenging him to: "Be a man."[1]

---

1   Men have written endlessly about history, politics, economics, philosophy, the theory of relativity etc. – but only recently about men as men (for an early bibliography see

Three principles we might emphasize are first, that masculinity is plural: masculinities, and includes a range and variety of options and choices, not only between different cultures but even within them. And second, masculinities change over time, reflecting and reinforcing changing societal norms and values. Being male and the ideal(s) of masculinities are not the same as they were 100 years ago, or even 50 years ago. We need to be aware of variations over cultural spaces and changes over time, therefore, in considering the concept, and reality, of masculinities. Both are fluid.

But thirdly, despite the variations and the contested nature of masculinity, certain core themes do seem to be almost universal (Gilmore, 1990; Williams and Best, 1990). It varies and changes but remains much the same. At the same time, we have to consider the degree to which the concepts of masculine and feminine are still useful and relevant in the post-modernity of the new millennium. Are masculine and feminine as "opposite" as they once were? Are we moving towards a postmodern unisex: fe/m/ale?[2]

This raises a fourth issue, that masculinity is not exclusive to males nor are "feminine" traits exclusive to women. Women may be more or less masculine and men more or less feminine. This cross-over effect does rather negate our cultural and fairly universal definitions of male and female as opposite; in practice masculine and feminine do not necessarily apply totally to all. Furthermore C.G. Jung suggests that men become more feminine as they age (partly due to declining levels of testosterone) and that women become more masculine (Jung, 1933/1966: 106–7): a double cross-over. But more of gender in the next chapter, and androgyny.

Here we will restrict ourselves to two principal topics: some of the current thinking about masculinity, and then some of the historical contemporary ideals of masculinity: the knight, the gentleman, the self-made man and the sensitive millennial man.

Franklin, 1991); for more recent discussions see Connell, 2000; 2002; and Michael Flood (http: //mensbiblio.xyonline.net), and a shorter one on line drawn from the above (http: //www. mensstudies.com.content/M65371) – which is keen on Connell and Kimmel, but omits Bly, Farrell, Tiger and Nathanson and Young. See also a more psychologically and spiritually oriented bibliography, which is keen on Bly and Farrell, but not Connell and Kimmel (http: //www.menweb.org). On health (http: //www.menshealth.org). See also the *Encyclopedia of Men and Masculinity* (HQ 1090.3 M436).

2   This question is discussed in more detail in Chapter 2. Some say yes, since gender battle lines are being blurred by various factors including multiple sexualities, gender as a continuum, theorists who see gender as performance, and the medical option of gender change. Others say no, since the above only affect a small number of people and the debate is mostly academic; gender conflict is now being heightened as men increasingly are fighting for what they consider to be their rights, and justice. Some consider the latter, exemplified by Bly, Farrell, the Promise Keepers and others as "backlash" (Connell, 2000; Kimmel, 1996; 2006) – so the issues are complex.

Being a Man

What does being a man mean? What does it mean to you? What does masculinity mean? What do you (male or female) think of men in general? And is male *opposite* to female?

To these questions, many answers can be given, and are, as we shall see. These are not mathematics questions, with the right answers at the back of the book but human questions, and more complicated. Many authors insist that there are "multiple masculinities," and that the definition of masculinity is historically contingent, culturally relative and individually subjective; and that the definition varies from time to time, place to place and person to person. This is surely correct. On the other hand some authors argue that there is a "core" masculinity which is common across time and place, and that all societies demand pretty much the same qualities in their men – and women too, perhaps. So we need to bear in mind both the differences *and* the similarities in our efforts to understand masculinities: in their core and in their variations on that theme.

R.W. Connell popularized the idea of plural masculinities in *Masculinities* (1995) distinguishing between hegemonic masculinity, subordinate masculinity, gentry masculinity, working class masculinity and complicit masculinity – also true masculinity: the belief that there is a natural, fixed masculinity. This is not so, he says (1995: 45). Such a belief is biologism and essentialism. Complicit masculinity refers to the (alleged) fact that men benefit from what Connell calls "the patriarchal dividend": "the advantage men in general gain from the overall subordination of women" (1995: 79).

In a later book he added more masculinities: frontier, gay, military, protest and transnational business masculinities (2000). They begin to proliferate as "types of men," by occupation or socio-economic status, orientation or ideology. In *Gender*, he critiques the usual theory of how we learn to be a man, through imitation and socialization, by emphasizing again that masculinities are multiple: "These result partly from class differences ... and the ethnic pluralism of modern societies" (2002: 77). While he is right that there are variations, and options, and boys may resist particular ideals or demands, it is not always clear that these masculinities are fundamentally different, still less opposed, or mostly just variants on the same themes and core values. Furthermore, gay masculinities are not all the same (Nardi, 2000).

The American sociologist Michael Kimmel, author of *Manhood in America*, argues are that there is a "crisis of masculinity" today, part of the crisis being that "proving manhood – manhood as a relentless test – has been and continues to be a dominant [theme] in American life" (1996: vii). He distinguished between three "archetypes" of masculinity at independence: the Genteel Patriarch, part of the heritage from aristocratic England, the Heroic Artisan, a working-class ideal, and the Self-Made Man who became the iconic American. Numerous themes meander through this fascinating account of manhood changing over the last 250 years: the rise of sports, then body-building, fraternal lodges and the Boy Scouts, capitalism and personal mobility, Muscular Christianity, the Gay Liberation movement, the Women's movement and feminism, and more. This was the first history of men and manhood in the United States.

As the two leading authorities in Men's Studies, and pioneers in the field, Connell and Kimmel deserve our respect and gratitude. Both have self-identified as pro-feminist, and Kimmel is a founder of NOMAS: the National Organization of Men against Sexism – male sexism, that is. Unfortunately both scholars seem to have identified pro-feminist with male-negative, and have therefore reinforced misandry in popular culture and some streams of feminism. Connell, for instance, argues that: "Men's gender practices raise large questions of social justice, given the scale of economic inequality, domestic violence, and institutional barriers to women's equality." Furthermore "masculinities are deeply implicated in organized violence, such as the civil wars ... and in technologies and production systems that threaten environmental destruction and nuclear war" (2000: 200). We might argue the opposite, that men's gender practices over the centuries have been deeply involved in expanding social justice and human rights, in improving the quality of life universally, as evidenced by the United Nations Human Development reports, and so far as possible in restraining aggression, by diplomacy if possible but by force if necessary. Men are surely associated far more with positives than negatives (cf. Chapter 3).

Connell's single-minded focus on power: men's power over other men and women, and relations of domination and subordination, is certainly instructive, useful and heartfelt. But there are other relations and other values: there is the power of love, the enlightenment values of liberty and equality, and not all power relations are dominations – they may also be liberating, enlightening and altruistic. Connell himself uses his intellectual power to try to enlighten, for example. Furthermore, this "patriarchal dividend", whether real or alleged, is complemented by the male *tax*: the costs men pay for being men, it's not just benefits from the oppression of women. Men pay high taxes in so many ways, from early deaths and high suicide rates to loss of children, as we discuss later. Also, in all fairness, Connell might have discussed the *benefits* men have given to men *and* women: the patriarchal *donation*, not domination.

A similar prejudice afflicts some of the work by Kimmel. The first paragraph of *Manhood in America* is a long list of real or alleged male villains: "Clarence Thomas. William Kennedy Smith. Senator Bob Packwood ... Mike Tyson. Woody Allen. O.J. Simpson. Michael Jackson. Tailhook. Spur Posse. The Citadel ... " (1996: vii). And in his third paragraph he cites "humorist" Garrison Keiller approvingly, that manhood now "is a problem to be overcome" (1996: vii). Then, in a later book, *Men's Lives*, he merely adds more male villains to his list and suggests: "Perhaps we should slap a warning label on penises across the land. WARNING: OPERATING THIS INSTRUMENT CAN BE DANGEROUS TO YOUR AND OTHERS' HEALTH" (Kimmel, 2004: 565. His emphasis). This is unconscionable – but does indicate his anti-male bias.

He omits any countervailing list of male heroes, Peace Prize winners, Nobel winners, bravery award winners, or just fine husbands and fathers and sons and workers – this is surely blatant misandry and male-negativism. Happily Kimmel removed this first paragraph from the second edition of *Manhood in America* – but not the core attitudes. Unhappily he added a new chapter to the edition which is an extraordinary caricature of scholarship. One small example: "You see them everywhere. They're the ones who cut you off on the freeway, screaming with road rage if you dare to slow them down. If their kid doesn't make that suburban soccer team or that heartland hockey team, they're the ones who rush out onto the field to hit the coach or strangle the referee. [I was a soccer coach for seven years. They never hit me once!] They seethe with rage at their ex-wives (and their ex-wives' lawyers) in family court. They hiss, sometimes silently [sic] with venomous anger ...." (2006: 217). These are the "angry white males" of his pro-feminist anti-male ideology; yet Kimmel himself is one angry white male – but angry at men – or a caricature of a minority of men.

Connell's emphasis on abuses of male hegemonic power and Kimmel's portraits of male villains are not the whole picture. In presenting the negatives and ignoring the positives they both misrepresent men and also reality; they also misrepresent women as solely the victims of hegemonic and villainous men. Implying that men are only villains, and villains are only male is just silly and wrong – to put this very simply and very obviously. We should be beyond such simplistic moralistic theorizing of men/bad and women/good-but-victimized. Connell and Kimmel are not the only ones standing for social justice and gender equality – most men do. It does not help to demonize men. Nor does it help to ignore men as victims and good guys, nor women as powerful and also, sometimes, villains too. Men and women can be seen from all three perspectives.

We started with Connell and Kimmel partly because they are probably the most well-known writers on men, but also to give some idea of the polarized politics of gender. A very different perspective on men, manhood and masculinity is presented in an encyclopedic review by a Canadian political scientist, Waller Newell (2000). In *What is a Man?* he offers a selection of writings about men: "3,000 Years of Wisdom on the Art of Manly Virtue," from the Greeks (Homer, Plato, Aristotle) to the Romans (Cicero) to India (the Bhagavad-Gita) and China (Confucius) to Chaucer, Castiglione, Capellanus up to the present. Newell distills the essences of manhood. These are the ideals of man as chivalrous, the gentleman, wise, the family man, the statesman, the noble man, and finally the American man and the invisible man – concluding with an interview with Kurt Cobain. The selections are treasures over the millennia on the beauties and wonders of manliness. Not all men live up to these ideals of course, which is partly why Newell produced the book.

Newell followed this up with *The Code of Man*, wise essays on the manly virtues of love, courage, pride, family and country. He does say that "There is a crisis of manliness in America" (2003: xv); almost everyone says there is; so "We also need a positive account of the manly virtues" (2003: xvi). On the one hand we have "Save the male" in "fatherless America"; on the other we have the return of the masculine at 9/11 and in Afghanistan and Iraq. We have the young male (and female) murderers, but we also have the young male (and female) police officers who risk their lives to capture them.

Masculinity is a cost-benefit analysis. Newell's point is that ideal masculinity favours the benefits. The real is a bit more controversial. But he concludes, thinking about his students: "Manhood is coming back" (2003: 257).

In their various perspectives on men, Connell focussed on plural masculinities, male hegemony and male oppression; Kimmel on American history and the three "archetypes" of masculinity, before sliding into abuse, and Newell on the global and complementary ideals of manliness over the millennia and around the globe. Their methods and scope vary as widely as do their values and central ideas.

While these social scientists have offered their ideas about men, an alternative approach is for men themselves to talk about their ideas about, and their experience of, manhood and masculinity. As might be expected, this is diverse, depending on their socio-economic status, age, ethnicity, sexual orientation, and a host of other factors.

One successful effort is the collection of stories about themselves written, in the editor's words, "about what it's like to be a man, a male human" (Brown, 2005: xx). The men talk about everything from erections to being a volunteer firefighter to touch to fidelity and more. The book was probably written more for women than for men, but it is a useful starting point.

I think the first survey on masculinity was done by Carol Tavris (1977) for *Psychology Today*. About 28,000 people responded, equally divided between men and women; and while this too was not a random sample, her findings are most interesting: women admire their men far more than the men themselves do; they also consider their men more masculine than the men do. Even in 1977 both sexes were grappling wih androgyny – some saying that there is no such thing as masculiniy or femininity, only humanity; others were conflicted and confused. Some defined masculinity by their actions and achievements, others by their feelings; and some in relation to men, others in relation to women. Men defined the "ideal man", from a set of 20 traits, with considerable consensus: Able to love (88%), Stands up for beliefs (87%) and Self-confident (86%). Women agreed for the top two – but with a greater consensus: Able to love (96%), Stands up for beliefs (92%) and Warm (89%) – followed by Gentle and Self-confident (86%). There is considerable agreement between men and women, but women were much clearer on the ideal. As to whether these traits were "highly characteristic of themselves" men scored themselves lower on 16 of the 17 traits presented than women scored "their spouse or lover" (and only three traits were above 50%) (1977: 37). There is more, of course, but this is enough to indicate that men's self-concepts were already low.

This survey was followed by *The Hite Report on Male Sexuality* (Hite, 1981) which also interrogated men on masculinity as well as sexuality. She asked: "What is masculinity? What qualities make a man a man? What qualities do you admire in men?" She received 7,000 responses; again, not a random sample, but certainly useful. Indeed she effectively recognized "plural masculinities" long before Connell, though she did not invent the now well-known term. Still, Hite did discuss six different male identities: the traditionals (the majority), the deniers, the egalitarians, the rebels and the SNAGS (sensitive new age guys). No one defined themselves as macho; indeed this option was defined in negative terms by the respondents, and universally rejected.

We can only briefly summarize the responses, but the traditionals affirmed that a man should be confident, self-sufficient, keep his word, have qualities of leadership, work, be honest, be a defender of home, wife, family, honor and territory. Hite added that: "Most men said, in addition to the characteristics already listed, that masculinity was the *opposite* of femininity" (1981: 64. Her emphasis).

The deniers rejected these ideas, one calling masculinity "a biological accident" and another saying: "I have no idea what 'masculinity' is." Egalitarians said that they looked for the same qualities in men and women: honesty, justice, integrity etc. The rebels argued that the traditional ideals were absurd, and rejected them. The most eloquent of them stated that: "[Men] are supposed to be a cross between John Wayne, the Chase Manhattan Bank, and Hugh Hefner. We are only human, for Christsake." A few men, whom I called SNAGS, rejected the traditional definition totally and adopted a stereotypically more feminine version of masculinity: "I'm masculine. Very. Love to cook, can cry, feel deeply, care a lot." And: "warm, kind and tender, sensitive" (1981: 60–83).

The Hite Report was wonderful for giving men their own voices about themselves, including 30 autobiographies at the end of the book. And probably most men can squeeze themselves into one or more of these identities and self-definitions. Certainly they are fascinating glimpses of men's rarely voiced ideas about themselves and compare favourably with some of the more negative judgements of outsiders *telling* them who they are.

Henry Gates (1997) in his *Thirteen Ways of Looking at a Black Man* was upset about what he saw as portraits of Blacks in the media which were both negative, stereotypical and homogeneous, so he offered his own essays on black men whom he knew well or had met or interviewed. These included such diverse characters as James Baldwin, Colin Powell, Harry Belafonte, Louis Farrakhan, O.J. Simpson and others. He could have included other well-known contemporaries from Nelson Mandela and Kofi Annan to Martin Luther King, Mohammed Ali and others.

Similarly the *Washington Post* polled nearly 3,000 Americans across the country in 2006, about half of them Blacks, and interviewed in depth many black men, in their exploration of "Being a Black Man." This was a fascinating analysis of the diversities of black masculinities as well as the similarities, but also the value-differences not only from Whites, but also from black women (Merida, 2007). The range of options, opinions, values and expectations of these men, and their wisdom, in face of an often hostile and racist environment, offer testimony to individualism and conflict, triumph and failure, in a still divided country.

The German sociologist Max Weber was the first to consider masculinities, in the context of economics. Weber noted the *contributions* that men make to the building of society, varying according to the values and ideals of different cultures. The normative male is not quite the universally dominant, oppressive *problem* that Connell implied. He pointed out that warrior cultures valued the warrior, religious cultures valued the ascetics, priests, mullahs, rabbis, monks etc. and trading nations valued smart businessmen. Agricultural societies valued successful farmers. The Chinese esteemed the mandarins, the Japanese valued the samurai and the Hindus recognized the superiority of the Brahmins in the caste system (Weber, 1958: 267–301). Cultural ideals vary, as do the insights of sociologists.

Long before that Plato wrote that: "There are three classes of men: lovers of wisdom, lovers of honour, lovers of gain" (Republic 9: 581) ruled respectively by the head, the heart (the symbol of bravery for the Greeks) and the belly. These he described as men of gold, silver or bronze, and the hierarchical rankings of these men are reflected still in the medals of the Olympic Games. These men are fitted for different roles in society: the rulers (gold) and the ruled, who included the warriors (silver) and the workers (farmers, tradesmen, craftsmen): bronze. This was a clever synthesis of body, politics, values and, analogously, precious metals and was, he thought, the perfect utopian meritocracy. Democratically, he included women in this scheme; but the position of slaves, upon which the glory of Athens was built, was not clear.[3] This was the first typology of Homo sapiens, based on the *inequality* of men and women. This fundamental assumption and belief that people are not only different but also unequal has been a legitimizing ideology for *social* inequality.

Plato's three fold typology of men might be "pretty obvious" to some, but also as immensely controversial. Karl Popper (1966) argued that Plato's assumption that all humans are unequal was the basis for fascism, and by implication for all ideologies of supremacism from racism and anti-Semitism to the sexism propounded later by Aristotle. Yet Plato did not extend his views to *group* inequality, nor did he assert any doctrine of biological determinism.

Plato's embryonic theory of class, linking men, principally, to occupations in the polis, was challenged in three ways relating to gender. First by his student, Aristotle, who propounded a theory of *gender* inequality which became one of the origins of male supremacism (see Chapter 2). Plato was also challenged several centuries later by the Christian doctrine of the *spiritual* equality of all believers, men *and* women (John 14, 15; 1 Cor. 12). This was a paradigm shift in a world founded on the belief in, and practice of, human inequality and slavery. Finally, the premise of inequality was overturned in the Enlightenment, most effectively by Rousseau, and the assertion of human *secular* equality. This belief legitimized

---

3   In practice, as has often been observed, the lovers of gain are the ones who rule, and the lovers of wisdom and truth, the philosophers, researchers and teachers, are at the bottom of the pile: underpaid, overworked and disvalued. It's a free market system not entirely a meritocratic system. Yet any unequal social system, even a meritocracy, is tense with the demand for equality, as Michael Young (1964) demonstrated in a brilliant satire, as insightful as George Orwell's *Animal Farm* and 1984.

the War of Independence, the French Revolution, and the abolition of slavery, and was enshrined in the new U.S. Constitution and summarized in the slogans of the French Revolution: "Liberté. Egalité. Fraternité," and legitimized eventually the emancipation of women and men.

Evidently men are not all the same, but nor are the men and women who write about men. Plato developed a three-fold typology of men by merit and metallic value, Weber another by economic value and Hite yet another by self-identified type of masculinity. Connell defined men as hegemonic and oppressive of women, and Kimmel argues that men are dysfunctional. Brown's work illustrates some of men's feelings and concerns, while Gates' work demonstrates the heterogeneity among black men, Nardi's clarifies the heterogeneity among gay men and Merida's the themes of resistance to, and triumph over, white racism.

And there is more: the anthropologist Matthew Gutmann (1996/2007) has offered a compelling ethnography of complex and contradictory masculinities in Mexico City. Fathering, machismo, sex and alcohol are all there, and often familiar. The anthropologist Rafael Ramirez reflected on masculinity in Puerto Rico, rejecting the stereotype of the Latin American male as macho, insisting that in his own socialization "the emphasis had been on the obligations of masculinity, on the responsibilities involved in being a man, and particularly on being the provider and breadwinner for others" (1999: 2). Echoing Simone de Beauvoir, he suggests that "men are not born, they are made" (1999: 39). For something completely different, on masculinities in Argentina, Eduardo Archetti (1999) discusses football, polo and the tango.

Other recent works employing a variety of lenses, methodologies and interests have discussed masculinities in Uganda (Heald, 1999), the Promise Keepers (Bartkowski, 2004), Muscular Christianity (Putney, 2003), as fathers (Doucet, 2007), in a high school (Pascoe, 2007), after divorce (Braver, 1998), and more. Gay Studies joins Men's Studies in discussing the many ways men "do" masculinity and masculinities. Men and boys are finally becoming a topic of research, rather than an object of ideological misandry, and our theorization of men is developed further in Chapter 7.

Three of the latest books on men indicate some confusion. All express their concern about the current status of men. Two are male negative but the third is male positive: the author believes that society should change. Michael Kimmel's latest book *Guyland* (2008) tackles what he calls guys – code for losers. "In college, they party hard but are soft on studying. They slip through the academic cracks ... they drift aimlessly ... spend more time online playing video games ... "hook up" occasionally with a "friend with benefits," go out with their buddies, drink too much, save too little." Again: "Many post-grads move in a languorous mass, a collection of anomic nomads looking for some place to go." "Welcome to Guyland" (2008: 3–4). he continues: "Many do suspect that there's something rotten in the state of Manhood" (2008: 7) – which is the continuing theme in Kimmel's work. It's too bad that he, or his assistant who did the interviews, did not interview the troops, or the recipients of the bravery awards. It's too bad he focussed primarily on the white middle-class kids, with his jaundiced lens. Young black men would have different stories to tell. And cracks like: "Guys love girls – ... It's women they can't stand" (2008: 13). He admits that not all young men live in Guyland, and gives a few examples – but as exceptions to his generalizations. Young men can be boorish, gross and criminal – no doubt young women can be also, but Kimmel fails to consider them – but to stigmatize a generation of males, and then to offer a few stars of hope, is rotten.

He opens his book with his wish (quoting a feminist poet) for his newborn son at his naming ceremony nine years ago: "If I could have one wish for my own sons, it is that they should have the courage of women" (2008: xvii).

Historian Gary Cross echoes these ideas in *Men to Boys: The Making of Modern Immaturity*. He opens with: "Everywhere I turn today I see men who refuse to grow up." And: "A common query (really a complaint) today, especially from women, is, where have all the men gone?" (2008: 1). The answer, from one guy (not in this book), was "Look under your feet!" They are there with the chewing-gum. Cross himself complains about the failure of these "boy-men" to commit to marriage, family, jobs and community – much as Kimmel does. But Cross focuses more on narcissism and Kimmel on feminism, the former on childish pursuits, the latter on crime. But both are appalled by the younger generation of men.

So are many of my female students. Their phrase this year is "man up" i.e. men should be more manly, self-confident, less SNAG – wimp and metrosexual, less feminine, more masculine and, to my surprise, "hit on" them more. Not quite Kimmel or Cross.

The third book, rather than being the by-now familiar criticism of (young) males is titled *Save the Males* and is a criticism of feminism for creating an anti-male culture and substituting vagina worship. Raised by her father, and a mother of three sons and two stepsons, the journalist Kathleen Parker has written the funniest exploration of men and masculinities, as well as the most understanding. Strange that the negatively critical works of men by Kimmel and Cross are contradicted by the sympathetic and appraising works of women, from Parker back to Doucet, Laframboise and Paglia – though men are there too with Newell and Mansfield.

There are many other analyses and typologies of men, as we shall see: not all so serious. *Cosmopolitan* has offered another typology of the "dating and mating habits of six common guy types" and how to trap and tame them. These were the starving artist, the generic guy, the new age dude, the sporty guy, Mr All Business and the eternal frat guy (Miller, 1999). It's not Gates or Weber or Plato, but the types are well observed, amused and amusing, affectionate and exasperated, as are the tactics to trap these guys.

Masculinities not only vary cross-culturally and change through history – though only marginally, perhaps – but they also evolve as men age. Shakespeare commented on this in his perceptive, if depressing, account in *As You Like It* (Act 2, Sc. 2):

> All the world's a stage,
> And all the men and women merely players:
> They have their exits and their entrances;
> And one man in his time plays many parts,
> His acts being seven ages.

There is first the infant "mewling and puking," then the schoolboy, whining "with his shining morning face," then the lover, "sighing like a furnace," the soldier, "full of strange oaths ... / Seeking the bubble reputation / Even in the cannon's mouth," then the justice – a man in his prime of wisdom – and sixth the retired man, "his big manly voice / Turning again towards childish treble," and finally: "Last scene of all ... / Is second childishness, and mere oblivion / Sans teeth, sans eyes, sans taste, sans everything."[4]

These seven ages of about a decade each still have their relevance; but now men have perhaps more choices in their masculinities – not really as infants, but some as schoolboys; retirement at 60 or 65 is often now a renaissance rather than an early death, and the "last scene of all," – "sans everything" – is probably more the exception than the rule nowadays, alleviated by dentistry, optometry, spices and palliative care. Still, Shakespeare's review of changing masculinities talks to the adolescent, the lover, the husband and father, the worker, the retiree and the grandfather, implicitly, as a chronological sequence for many men. And what *type* of men they will be is largely their own choice: gold, silver, bronze or a base metal: villain.

Despite all the variations in types of men and types of society, however, the norm of masculinity (singular, not plural) in the "western" world is explained in any thesaurus. The new Penguin Thesaurus, for instance, defines masculine as "...manly, virile, macho, (inf), gallant, heroic, strong, muscular, strapping, rugged, mannish, butch. OPPOSITE: feminine." And for feminine: "1. (feminine hands) womanly, girlish, ladylike, pretty, soft, gentle, tender, delicate, graceful. OPPOSITE: masculine. 2. (a feminine young man) effeminate, womanish, unmanly, sissy, effete. OPPOSITE: manly" (Fergusson, Mauser and Pickering, 2004: 367, 227).

Clearly many of us do not fit the norms for either sex, and may not aspire to do so; but those who profess to be confused about what masculinity or femininity is can simply look it up in a thesaurus.

---

4   Shakespeare only described the physical and social aspects of aging. C.G. Jung described the four psychological stages of life in seasonal terms: spring, summer, autumn and winter, but with little autonomy in spring and winter. He focussed therefore on summer and fall, rephrased as morning and afternoon, and described as "individuation," a conflict between the old man and the new, and a cross-over for both sexes to the opposite sex (1933; 1966: 106–7). The same point was noted by Betty Friedan in her research (1981). Other researchers on aging, the life cycle and changing concepts of the self include Gail Sheehy (1977, 1998), Daniel Levinson (1978) and George Vaillant (1995).

Evidently, masculinity means far more than just being male. A penis and a Y chromosome do not constitute "masculinity" in a social sense. Male, yes; masculine, not necessarily.

Indeed to men who are not manly, and not masculine, a long series of epithets apply: wimps, wusses, nerds, geeks, dorks, dweebs, sissies, yellow-bellied, cowards, mama's boys, babies ...

This introduces the matter of *degrees* of masculinity, and masculinity as a continuum. I suggest we use the term "masculinity quotient," (MQ) which may be high or low or in between. So we have the low MQ wimps, sissies, fags, nerds and all those other negative epithets applied to the omega males, especially at high school during the adolescent developmental stage of manhood, the medium MQ average guys, and the high MQ alpha males, the supermen, the hyper-masculine at the other end. This "macho" end tends to be defined first in physical terms and by the male code of honour, bravery, duty, integrity; "to protect and serve" in the police motto, or "fidelity, bravery, integrity" of the FBI. They are symbolized in film by such characters as Rambo, the Terminator, James Bond and the roles played by John Wayne, Clint Eastwood, Arnold Schwarzenegger, Sylvester Stallone, Bruce Willis, Chuck Norris – cool cats with more than nine lives.

Reality is stranger than fiction as we confuse actors with their roles. John Wayne never fought in combat, nor did the others, unlike so many U.S. Presidents – with high MQs by other criteria of power. High MQ occupations include the military, firefighters, police, and when Mother Nature attacks us with storms, floods and power-cuts, then linemen too. As do the recipients of the bravery awards, male and female. All risk their lives for others, just like the fictional heroes of films, novels and comics. Top athletes also have high MQ, but are less altruistic, risking injury for themselves and for cash, rather than for others and their country – but Mohammed Ali is an exception, losing his freedom and cash to protest the Vietnam war. These high risk occupations and individuals exemplify, to different degrees (symbolic or real) and by various criteria this high MQ, as lawyers, accountants, plumbers and professors do not. (This is why there are Firefighter Calendars in North America, but not Accountant Calendars – even though the latter, uninjured, may be laughing all the way to the bank.) Note that MQ shifts over time from physique and looks to other criteria of MQ: power – economic, political, intellectual and so on. The high school heroes may simply vanish in adulthood. Those were, as Bruce Springsteen sings, the "glory days."

At the other end of the spectrum it would be invidious to name names, though Willy Loman (low man) expemplifies the type: failures, losers, castrated somehow, they have given up the fight, they are tired and broken. Some are homeless. Some cannot cope with PTSD or physical injuries. Some medicalize themselves. These are the extremes, overlooked and forgotten, until they commit a crime. Less extreme are the brains and intellectuals in schools especially, who perhaps despise and are despised and bullied by the jocks. Denigrated as wimps, sissies, nerds etc. they just have to survive to wait for the physical criteria of masculinity at school to morph into economic criteria at work. Bill Gates famously talked to this:

"Don't laugh at geeks! Some day one of them will employ you." The point here is that though one prime criterion of masculinity is physical, especially initially at school, the criteria change with time to include other types of the alpha male. The low MQ by one criterion may be or may become high MQ by other criteria. But masculinity is a battle.

We might add that the bullying and teasing of the low MQ but often high IQ boys at schools tends to have negative multiplier effects throughout the society, as education is disvalued in favour of sports or deviance, and much male talent is wasted to the nation. It may also contribute to crime and death in the school shootings which have plagued the United States.

A second perspective on men relates to evaluation. Attitudes towards men vary from the very positive to the extremely negative, princes to pigs with most people probably somewhere in the middle along a vertical axis. Such attitudes are learned from experiences, family and teaching. So women's attitudes to men will likely be influenced by their own personal experiences, especially by their attitudes towards their father and their brothers, as well as by what they have been taught – perhaps about the universal oppression of women in patriarchies. (Chapter 3 expands on the positive and Chapter 4 on the negative.) And if men have been bullied by other men in school they may well be hostile to jocks and the traditional definition of physical masculinities. In any event, my survey research in class shows a range of attitudes towards men from positive to negative, and usually a mixture of both.

The intersection of these horizontal and vertical axes presents four quadrants, integrating the continuum of masculinity (alpha to omega) and the continuum of attitudes (princes to pigs). Such quadrants overstate their distinctiveness: these are not water-tight compartments, but continua; yet they do hopefully clarify the differences.

This four box conceptual framework illustrates the idea of multiple masculinities both along the continuum we recognize from high MQ to low MQ, and also in the evaluation of men in general (whether reality-based or ideological) from "love 'em" to "chauvinist pigs" along horizontal and vertical axes.

This model as a 2×2 table is of course too simple; it should be multi-dimensional given that the criteria along both axes, are themselves multiple and fluid. Again, the subjective elements of men's own definitions of themselves – what masculinity means to them – have to be considered, and these opinions also vary.

It is not enough to be male to be masculine. That is a start, but it is not enough. Men have to *prove* their masculinity. And other men are constantly testing the limits in their different ways: income levels, types of cars, physical prowess, weights bench-pressed, number or quality of lovers, length of penis, bravery, medals ... there are any number of ways; but mostly they hinge around the ideas of achievement and success. Men have to compete to *prove* their masculinity and their worth, or risk being categorized as unmasculine, and they have to be successful, winners, number one, in at least some particular domain, and in their own eyes. Parents initiate the process, and schools try, but often fail, to continue it. They can marginalize too many boys.

Norman Mailer asserted: "Masculinity is not something given to you, something you're born with, but something you gain ....And you gain it by winning small battles with honor" (1966: 201). While it is suggestive that he selected a militaristic metaphor to emphasize the struggle to win battles, none the less, today we could substitute "self-esteem" for masculinity, and his remarks would work as well for women as well as men. The militarism, however, might not work so well if it were seen as a violent struggle instead of as a focussed effort. In his view, in retrospect, masculinity is winning by effort.

Masculinity has been largely invisible in the social sciences until recently. The anthropologist David Gilmore (1990) was the first to attempt a cross-cultural study of why masculinity is an achieved and tested status in so many societies (unlike femininity) and to consider the "continuities" – the almost universal similarities – of masculinities. Ideals of manhood, he argues, are similar because they constitute one of the principal social bonds of society. While the ways different cultures "create" manhood differ, the ideals of manhood which they construct and create are very similar. Only two "virtually androgynous cultures" are discussed – or are known to anthropologists – the Tahitians of Polynesia and the Semai of Malaysia.

Here: "There is little or no social pressure to "act like men" and they both lack a "manhood ideology" (1990: 201–19). Gilmore suggests that this "strongly supports the feminist notion that gender norms are ascribed rather than innate" (1990: 219). This may be true for these two small-scale societies, of course, but they are the exceptions. The bulk of the evidence from every other culture indicates that culture builds on a substratum of biology, and that gender norms are fairly similar, dictated both by biology and by culture. There is, he concludes, "no Universal Male" but a "Ubiquitous Male" – "a quasi global personage something like 'Man-the-Impregnator-Protector-Provider'." These three male imperatives, to father, defend and work "are either highly dangerous or competitive" – against fellow-men, animals and enemies, all in a struggle for scarce resources. Hence the demands on men to both recognize masculine virtues and also to recognize their expendability for the survival of the group. The male psyche and the social need coincide. "So manhood is the defeat of a childish narcissism that is not only different from the adult role but antithetical to it" (1990: 223–4). I would add that it is also different from womanhood.

Gilmore adds an important point which will recur as a theme here, but with a contemporary Western valence:

> One of my findings here is that manhood ideologies always include a criterion of selfless generosity, even to the point of sacrifice. Again and again we find that "real" men are those who give more than they take; they serve others. (1990: 229)

Men are nurturing, but in different ways than women nurture. He was one of the first to point this out, in contrast to the stereotypes offered by such male "liberationists" whom he mentions by name: Pleck (1981) and Brod (1987) who, he says, assert that: "our Western masculinity is a fraud, unnecessary and dispensable" (1990: 230).

The Canadian sociologist Andrea Doucet makes this point very clearly in her book *Do Men Mother?* and she dedicated her book "to three fathers whose impact here is profound" – her husband, her father and her father-in-law. She interviewed 118 primary care-giving fathers in Canada, and 14 partners or wives. Most were stay-at-home dads, but some had sole or joint custody, others were widowers or on parental leave etc. She says she experienced a sense of "vertigo" as she heard the "ethic of care" demonstrated by these fathers – an ethic she had (surely surprisingly) associated solely with women. Doucet has rich and also poignant data – every father should read this – concluding that mothers and fathers often parent in dissimilar but complementary ways. She concludes that while "*men are not mothers and fathers do not mother*, there are times and places where men's caregiving is so impeccably close to what we consider mothering that gender seems to fall completely away, leaving only the image of a loving *parent* and child" (2007: 246. Her emphasis). Fathers are now about 18% of all stay-at-home parents in the United States and about 10% in the U.K. and Canada (2007: 14) – so the issue of fathering is increasingly important. And what a joy to read about loving dads instead of the usual myth of deadbeat dads as the norm (cf. Braver, 1998).

The male ethic begins early with exhortations to "Be a man!" "Don't cry!" "See if you can climb a bit higher – or hold on a big longer – or lift this weight once more – you can do it!" etc. Fathers' advice in the home and the playground tends to differ from the mothers' hugs and advice: "Be careful!" (Doucet, 2007). Stereotypical, but true. Both sets of advice are useful in helping children to develop.

At high school it is the athletic stars who are most admired by the girls, it seems. The quarterback gets the cheerleader, or vice versa. Later, the conspicuous consumption of the rich is evidenced by the size of the diamonds, bank balances, estates and the value of the car collection or portfolio and so on (cf. Veblen, 1899/1953). In academic circles the Nobels are the acme of achievement, but the steps on the ladder are marked by the level of the degree, the discipline, the university, the number and quality of publications. All these variables are factored into estimates of social capital. In media circles, Genies and Emmys and Oscars and Country and Western Awards etc. are all indices of recognition and excellence. On construction sites, knowledge and skill and strength are valued assets. We have soccer and rugby and baseball leagues; every sport and hobby from chess to mountaineering has criteria of excellence, awards and prizes. The Olympic medals mark the pinnacles of athletic achievement, and are also symbols of national status. Physical bravery, moral courage and altruism are also rewarded (cf. Chapter 3).

There are many criteria by which men are evaluated on scales (plural) of masculinities, from low to high; and the multiple criteria may conflict. Bill Gates, for instance, the wealthiest man in the world, scores high in social capital for wealth and altruism: he donates over one billion dollars a year to charities, mostly to his own foundation but also to Third World health and education projects; but he scores low on aesthetics and some of his business ethics. Likewise Bill Clinton was evaluated positively for his many achievements as President, but re-evaluated down after his dalliance with Monica Lewinsky. Similarly former President George W. Bush was the most powerful man in the world: the alpha plus male. Some loved him. Some hated him. For some he was a hero, for others a villain, and his legacy is in dispute.

In recent years there have been criticisms of the competitive nature of masculinity (as if women did not compete); but in a material world, material values still apply. Nonetheless, the masculine ideal is not monolithic.

Here we will consider four historical and contemporary ideals of manhood: the knight, the gentleman, the self-made man and most recently, the New Man, also known as "l'homme rose" or the sensitive new age guy (SNAG).

The Knight

The knight and warrior ideal, or model of masculinity, is as ancient as written history, dating back to the Homeric heroes and up to contemporary warriors. The history of the world is written in blood. Civilizations and empires rise and fall: Assyrian, Egyptian, Persian, Greek, Roman, Islamic, Spanish, Ottoman, German, British, American ... and what next? All this violence, mostly of men against other men, has created the modern world – and the wars persist, as does the peace.

The ancient Greek heroes were the military men of Homer's "Iliad", telling of the Greek attack on Troy, following Paris' abduction of Helen: the beauty whose face launched a thousand ships, and indirectly caused the war. Odysseus (Ulysses) is the first iconic male in the Graeco-Roman genre: a model of masculinity for his bravery but perhaps more for his cunning: planning the Trojan horse, outwitting the Sirens and Cyclops, and eventually returning home to Penelope.

Another Greek hero, Hercules, who is reknowned for finishing his twelve labours, including slaying the Gorgon and generally rescuing humanity from monsters, is still remembered on children's television. Our western mythology of masculinity is founded both in war and in love.

Our history still lives on in the present as the battle of Thermopylae (480 BCE), and the defeat of the Persian army under Xerxes by Leonides and his 300 Spartans is remembered in film: "300" (2007).

The Roman heroes included Aeneas, one of the Trojan survivors, whose epic story of the origins of Rome was recorded by Vergil in "The Aeneid." Virgil began with the line "Arma virumque cano: " I sing of arms and men – as if the two were equated, which in a sense they are and always have been – in the sense that if one sings of arms one sings of men almost exclusively (Yael, Boadicea, and Joan of Arc, being conspicuous exceptions); though if one sings of men, we sing of far more than simply arms. The history of Rome from its founding in 753 BCE to the establishment of the Empire was recorded by Livy. The generals, kings and emperors who built the empire, defeating the Etruscans, the Carthaginians, the Gauls, and the British and others were eventually themselves defeated by the invading Huns, Goths and Visigoths, and internal corruption. Despite the extraordinary achievements of Rome, in architecture, law, government, philosophy, these histories of Vergil and Livy are primarily military – and male. Indeed the military conquests grounded the expansion of Pax Romana and civilization.

The first king of Israel was the redoubtable warrior, Saul, and his successor was David, who slew Goliath. This kingdom too was established by battles, as the state of Israel today has been defended by wars; but spiritual and political leaders may be as valorized as military leaders, as Abraham, Moses and Solomon. This history is still contemporary in the persistence of these men's names thousands of years later.

The Christian life is also a battle. In Revelations it began before Christ with the battle in the heavens between the Archangel Michael and Lucifer, the light-bearer (Rev. 12: 7). The war continued in the Garden of Eden with the fall and the expulsion. It continued after the birth of Christ with Herod's massacre of the infants and the beheading of John the Baptist. Christ himself advised: "I came not to send peace, but a sword" (Mat. 10: 34); and he clarified the consequences of belief. Christ himself was a spiritual rather than a military leader, but the militarism followed with the Crusades and the Wars of Religion.

Paul described the life of the Christian, and his own life, in striking military metaphors:

> Put on the whole armour of God, that ye may be able to stand against the wiles of the devil. For we wrestle not against flesh and blood, but against principalities, against powers, against the rulers of the darkness of this world, against spiritual wickedness in high places. Wherefore take unto you the whole armour of God … (Ephes. 6: 11–3)

The armour includes "the breastplate of righteousness," the feet shod with "the gospel of peace," "the shield of faith" and "the helmet of salvation, and the sword of the spirit, which is the word of God" (Ephes. 6: 14–7). He encouraged Timothy to "fight the good fight" (1 Tim. 6: 12). The fight is not only against external enemies, principalities and powers, but also within the self – between mind and body, the law of God and the law of sin: "I delight in the law of God after the inward man: but I see another law in my members, warring against the law of my mind, and bringing me into captivity to the law of sin which is in my members (Rom. 7: 22–3, cf. Gal. 5: 17).

This central theme of the Christian as warrior and fighter against external and internal foes has persisted through Christian thought up to and including Muscular Christianity (Putney, 2003) and the Promise Keepers (Bartkowski, 2004). War is of course not the only theme; John the evangelist emphasized that "God is love" (1 John 4: 8); but these spiritual battles applied to both men and women, as secular militarism did not, neither in the epics of Beowulf nor of King Arthur nor in today's military.

In the saga of Beowulf, written during the Dark Ages, some time about 800 AD, and now (2007) a film, the warrior again is valorized. Beowulf slays the monster Grendel, and then the mother of the monster who had stirred from her lair deep in the earth. He becomes King, but then has to fight a dragon, and this third contest cost him his life. Yet his values of honour and glory live on, perhaps modified by changing times; here he encourages his lord to join the attack against Grendel's mother.

> Let whoever can
> win glory before death. When a warrior is gone,
> that will be his best and only bulwark.
> (Beowulf 1999: 46)

Before his last battle, Beowulf affirms his duty as King, aware of his imminent death; and he decided to fight alone against "the evil one." The themes of honour and glory and duty persist, and good against evil; for Beowulf was no killer. The last lines of the epic are the lament of his people:

> They said that of all the kings upon the earth
> he was the man most gracious and fair-minded,
> kindest to his people and keenest to win fame.
> (Beowulf, 1999: 99)

Ulysses, Hercules, the Spartans, Aeneas, David, Beowulf – all affirm mutually reinforcing ideas of masculinity: glory, honour, duty, service, kindness, bravery, ingenuity (especially Ulysses and Hercules); and many of these classic themes recur in Chaucer's portrait of the knight in *The Canterbury Tales* (1386). This "verray, parfit gentil knyght" is the first person to be described as Chaucer describes his fellow pilgrims on their way to Canterbury. (Rather than using one of the many prose translations, I have just modernized his spelling and only altered a couple of words whose meanings have changed over the years).

> A knight there was, and that a worthy man
> Who from the time that he first began
> To ride out, he loved chivalry,
> Truth and honour, freedom and courtesy...
> And though he was worthy, he was wise,
> And in his style as meek as is a maid.
> And never any villainy he said
> In all his life to any man
> He was a very perfect gentle knight.

It is the union of the brave warrior who is yet gentle and as meek as a maid which is so appealing; and the ancient values of chivalry, truth, honour, freedom and courtesy – brave, but wise, meek and gentle.

The knight's son, his squire, was also on the pilgrimage: a lusty bachelor with curly hair. He had campaigned in Flanders and Picardy with some success. Chaucer describes him in contrast with his father:

> His clothes were embroidered, like a meadow,
> All full of fresh flowers, white and red.
> Singing he was, or fluting, all the day;
> He was as fresh as is the month of May.

The squire was the knight in embryo, and a younger model of masculinity. The ideal of masculinity changes with age. This knightly ideal was further reinforced by Sir Thomas Malory's *Le Morte d'Arthur*, printed by Thomas Caxton in 1485 and in Edmund Spenser's *The Fairie Queen* (1590). But these were the last of he medieval epics. By this time Shakespeare was wriing, Machiavelli had published *The Prince* (1517), which had nothing to do with virtue and everything to do with power. In France, Rabelais had published his obscenely satirical "Gargantua and Pantagruel" (1532–64) – with the body and society turned upside down. In Spain, Cervantes composed Don Quixote (1605–15), a satire on knights and chivalry, in which Sancho Panza is the realist about war and women, and the Don is quite mad. The modern world was emerging in England with the Civil War and the execution of Charles I (1649). The monarch and the aristocracy were defeated by the Parliamentarians; the church and feudalism were replaced by representative government, the Puritans and the new merchant class and commercial gentry. The peasantry were eaten by sheep and the wool trade, and land became money. The old ideal of the knight and the warrior was becoming, it seemed, irrelevant in the new age of emerging capitalism.

The medieval ideal of the knight is not restricted to Europe, and indeed finds a clear expression in the ancient Japanese ideal of the *samurai*. Since the arrival of Commodore Perry's ships off the coast of Japan in 1853, and particularly since the surrender of Japan in 1945 after Hiroshima and Nagasaki – all this in under 100 years – the conquest imperative was extended from military to economic affairs. Indeed one of the striking aspects of this Samurai ideal was how easily it was converted from war to peace, from the regiment to the corporation, and from military conflict to economic competition. The same values (loyalty, self-sacrifice, hierarchy, discipline, team-work, the endurance of pain) were simply reapplied in different contexts. The fighter for victory became the worker for profit.

The epitome of the samurai ideal was, in the past, the ritual suicide of *seppuku* (also known as *hara-kiri*). Nothing indicated a warrior's disdain for the value of his own life, and his high esteem for his personal honour, his family and his community as his willingness to die – to kill himself – for the good of the whole.

A wrong or a dishonour was thus avenged by his death, and the community was made whole again.

Towards the end of World War II American naval forces sailed into Japanese waters. The Japanese counterattacked with the *kamikaze* pilots (literally, divine wind) who attempted to crash their bomb-laden planes on their targets. All the pilots were volunteers who willingly gave their lives in the defence of their country.

Similarly in Germany, towards the end of that war, Hermann Goering approved Operation Wehrwolf: a mission for volunteer pilots to ram American bombers during their massive daylight raids. The operation was cancelled after two relatively unsuccessful attacks (Price, 2002: 145–52). Both the Japanese and the German initiatives, however, indicate that men may and do volunteer to give up their lives in defense of their country.

The warrior ideals of knighthood and chivalry are not dead. King Arthur lived on in President John F. Kennedy's White House, known as Camelot. The musical "Camelot" revived the ideals in ways King Arthur would never have imagined. And Hollywood still produces films of the Arthurian legends, as did Monty Python. And men are still socialized into bravery ideals in the ever-popular comic book heroes, action movies and westerns, with reminders of the Jedi Knights in *Star Wars* and the recent re-makes of Thermopylae and Beowulf.

Although the warrior ideal of masculinity was challenged by the anti-war movement during the Vietnam War, it has revived again with the widely perceived justice of the Gulf War (1991), the bravery and sacrifice of the 9/11 responders (2001), and the invasion of Afghanistan (2001), and the more controversial attack on Iraq. Yet even the critics of the war admire the courage of the young Coalition fighters and are appalled by the terrorists' attacks on civilians, the suicide bombings and the televised beheadings.

Indeed the 2004 and 2008 U.S. presidential elections were fought in part at least between contending versions of masculinity: President Bush, son of a former president and bomber pilot, who avoided service in the Vietnam War, and apparently did not complete his duties in the Texas Air National Guard – versus John Kerry, a much decorated and wounded officer, who became a vocal anti-war protester. Bush, however, achieved warrior status with the successful attacks on the Taliban in Afghanistan, and the removal of Saddam Hussein in Iraq. As Iraq quagmired, however, he was re-defined as *too* militaristic, *too* aggressive, with other people's sons and daughters being killed. The same themes were re-played in 2008, pitting the old war hero John McCain against the charismatic young black lawyer, Barack Obama. Personal bravery, proven patriotism and sacrifice are still highly valued attributes in a man, and have vote-value in U.S. elections, though both Kerry and McCain lost.

A word of caution: the ideal of the warrior, as exemplified in Homer, Beowulf, Chaucer and King Arthur's Knights has not always been realized on the battlefield. Some deaths and battles and massacres and atrocities are still vividly remembered centuries later, and even commemorated: the crucifixion, the destruction of the temple in 70, the battle of Karbala in 680, the Crusades, Cromwell in Ireland, the battle of the Boyne (1690), the U.S. Civil War, and so on up to Armistice Day and Veterans Day.

The ideals of chivalry in war died in the mud and blood of the Somme (1916), it is often said. But Shakespeare had criticized them earlier in *King Henry IV*: "Can honour set to a leg? : or an arm? no: or take away the grief of a wound? no. Honour hath no skill in surgery, then? no. What is honour? a word. What is in that honour? air" (v: 1: 133–7).

The military and social values of honour, duty, sacrifice and chivalry may not be as highly esteemed as they once were – they are forgotten in peacetime but revive in wartime. And as women volunteer for the armed forces and for combat duty they too adopt the same values. The warrior today may be a man or a woman.

The Gentleman

This is generally thought of as a particularly English ideal of manhood, though it is more universal. Chaucer's knight is described as a gentle man, and the two models are not antithetical – but the gentleman need not be a knight nor a warrior. The prime criteria are gentleness, certainly (not to be confused with weakness), but also civility, integrity, generosity and egalitarian good manners. Anyone can be a gentleman: it is not a class or occupation or religious-based ideal – although it used to be – but it is also today an ideal which some believe to be in decline (Drew, 2008).[5]

The classic statements on being a gentleman are Lord Chesterfield's *Letters to His Son*, from 1738 to 1768 when his son died. The 300 or so letters are subtitled: "On the Fine Art of Becoming a Man of the World and a Gentleman." The letters are wise, often amusing, erudite, even affectionate – but wasted on his son who never even bothered to tell his father that he was married with two children. Chesterfield's emphasized "THE GRACES, THE GRACES" (12 April 1749) – mostly manners, including gracefulness of speech, gestures and dress, the art of pleasing and flattery, and cleanliness. He died in 1773, just before the wars in the now United States and across Europe, and the revival of the warrior ideal.[6]

---

5 An early description of the perfect courtier by Castiglione, at the court of Urbino and written in 1507, presages many of the ideals of the "perfect gentleman" – but it is very much class and education based. Nonetheless, Castiglione emphasizes virtue as the dominant characteristic (1976: 284–5, 320), in contrast to Machiavelli's *The Prince*, published only 10 years later. The prince was not a gentleman nor a gentle man.

6 There is something sad about Chesterfield. His only son pre-deceased him, and only then did he learn that his son had married and had two children. And his advice on laughing is strange to our ears: "I must particularly warn you against [laughing]: and I could heartily wish, that you may often be seen to smile, but never heard to laugh while you live … I am sure that, since I have had the full use of my reason, nobody has ever heard me laugh" (9 March 1748).

The sociologist Philip Mason suggests that the golden age of this ideal was the 100 years from Waterloo to the Somme, with its apex in the Victorian era.[7] Four main types can be identified: the knight/warrior already discussed, the gentleman scholar, the Christian gentleman and the sportsman: the hunting – shooting – fishing type (Mason, 1982: 13, 227). This last type is the portrait of the landed gentry, intermediate between the aristocracy and the peasantry and, increasingly, the urban working class created by the industrial revolution. Henry Fielding satirized them as Squire Western in *Tom Jones*, and C.S. Surtees stereotyped them amusingly in his stories about Jorrocks, which were so popular in the Victorian era.

Waterloo introduced decades of international peace, but also massive internal unrest: the Chartists in Britain and the Communists in Europe. 1848 was the Year of Revolutions in Europe, and Marx and Engels published the Communist Manifesto in that same year. But the developing capitalism brought its benefits as well as its costs – and it certainly changed the gentry. In an essay entitled *Old and New Squires*, Surtees noted how the penny post, the new newspapers and magazines (from *Blackwoods* to *Punch*) were transforming the lives of the rural gentry. But "the grand, the crowning benefit of all, however, were railways." The journey from Edinburgh to London, which used to take 16 noisy jostling days by coach, now took only hours. Furthermore, the railway boom and then the canal boom introduced higher employment, a booming economy and made the Chartists irrelevant (1860: 188).

With the repeal of the protectionist Corn Laws (1846), Adam Smith replaced Marx, and capitalism replaced mercantilism in the U.K. And with the First and Second Reform Acts (1832, 1867) the franchise was extended to include the gentry, and the democratization of the U.K. proceeded slowly. The railways began "unlocking the country," and the gentry too from their land. With the railways came the comfortable hotels, replacing the inns; and with the hotels came the even more comfortable clubs; and with all this came new needs.

> The old squires were rich – rich in the fewness of their wants, but the new squires have found wants that their forefathers were ignorant of. The old home manor won't do, they must have a moor; the row on the river won't do, they

---

7   Siegfried Sassoon, who fought at the Battle of the Somme in 1916, agreed about the Somme: "The chivalry (which I'd seen in epitome at the Army School) had been mown down and blown up in July, August and September, and its remnant had finished the year's 'crusade' in a morass of torment and frustration" (1930/1965: 155). His is probably the finest memoir of the infantry in World War I, and a classic memoir of masculinity. "Rotten business about poor old 'Longneck'" was one obituary. A friend wrote to him in hospital (Sassoon had been wounded): "A lot of our best men have been knocked out recently." (That officer was knocked out later.) And another officer wrote of an abortive attack to describe "What rotten bad luck we had yesterday," with a list of his fellow battalion officers killed and wounded (1965: 116, 131–2).

must have a yacht on the sea; the couple of hunters ... won't do, they must have six, and go upon grass. (1860: 191)

As needs expanded and expenditure increased, so "the new squires have begun to turn their attention to what their fathers had a great aversion to, namely, a little trade, and ... a little speculation" (1860: 191). The railways began the integration of country and town, gentry and business, land and money and, at least in the U.K., the decline of the gentleman as an ideal, and the rise of the self-made man: from giving to taking, from service to accumulation, but also from consumption to production.[8]

While the 1840s saw massive changes in the politics and economics of the U.K., the 1850s introduced important developments in the ideologies and expressions of masculinity: *Tom Brown's Schooldays* (Hughes, 1858), Samuel Smiles' *Self-Help* (1859) and the loss of *H.M.S. Birkenhead* (1852). Slavery had already been abolished in the British Empire (1834) and the Abolition movement was growing in the United States, leading eventually to the Civil War.

Smiles epitomized the emerging new world in writing the best-selling *Self-Help*, translated into at least 11 different languages with nearly a quarter of a million copies sold by the end of the century. Smiles advocated four criteria for self-help and mobility: energy, courage, cheerfulness and perseverance – which contrast totally with Chesterfield's three Graces from 100 years earlier. Smiles writes more about the (supposedly) American self-made man, but also about the (supposedly) English gentleman. Smiles illustrates his eloquent tribute to the gentleman with numerous examples. Also, he introduces the element of power and concludes his book:

> There are many tests by which a gentleman may be known; but there is one that never fails – How does he *exercise power* over those subordinate to him? How does he conduct himself towards women and children? How does the officer treat his men, the employer his servants, the master his pupils, and man in every station those who are weaker than himself? The discretion, forbearance, and kindliness with which power in such cases is used may indeed be regarded as the crucial test of gentlemanly character. (1958: 379)

The exercise of power is certainly a decisive indicator of the gentleman or the bully. Smiles argues that: "Gentleness is the best test of gentlemanliness" (1958: 380). His last line refers to Sir Philip Sydney, dying, "handing his cup of

---

8   Surtees was a much-beloved Victorian novelist of the sporting life. His men loved fox-hunting in particular, and his novels greatly amused Siegfried Sassoon. As well as his *Memoirs of an Infantry Officer*, Sassoon also wrote the *Memoirs of a Fox Hunting Man*, which included his first hunt as a boy of about nine. The fox strolled across the path where he and a friend were waiting. His friend hallooed for the hunt. Sassoon exclaimed: "Don't do that; they'll catch him!" (1929: 49).

water to the private soldier on the field of Zutphen" (1958: 380). Indeed, it is the examples which made Smiles' work so popular, as well as his egalitarianism, so unlike Chesterfield: "The inbred politeness which springs from right-heartedness and kindly feelings is of no exclusive rank or station. The mechanic who works at the bench may possess it, as well as the clergyman or peer" (1958: 369).

These elements of gentleness, kindliness and politeness overlap in meaning and behaviour, and are important. The word politeness stems from the Greek word "polis," the city state, so the characteristic conduct of citizens towards each other demands "politeness" (especially by "politicians," the rulers of the polis). Similarly, civility, from the Latin word "civis," city, is required of the "citizen." Politeness and civility thus become the characteristic of the gentleman, from mechanic to politician.

Certainly the norms of gentleness, as befits a gentleman, and violence, as befits a knight, may seem contradictory; but each norm applies in its proper place, as in the title of the film *An Officer and a Gentleman* (1982). The title indicates obliquely the equation of the two.

The contrast between civilian life and war-time is well-known. Henry V described the conflict between the gentleman and the warrior in his speech before Harfleur. Addressing his troops

> In peace there's nothing so becomes a man
> As modest stillness and humility;
> But when the blast of war blows in our ears,
> Then imitate the action of a tiger:
> Stiffen the sinews, summon up the blood,
> Disguise fair nature with hard-favoured rage.
> (*King Henry V,* 3: 1)

And so on, in one of Shakespeare's most famous patriotic speeches (and a total contradiction to the speech in *King Henry IV*). It is difficult to integrate "humility" and the "tiger"; but Shakespeare asserts it is necessary to "*imitate* the action" and to "*disguise* fair nature." Beneath the tiger and the rage of the warrior is the stillness, humility and fair nature of the peaceful citizen. Indeed most warriors do adapt successfully to peace, eventually. Some do not, and misuse their killing skills, like Timothy McVeigh, the Oklahoma City bomber; others develop post-traumatic stress syndrome; others cannot cope at all and kill themselves. More Vietnam veterans have committed suicide than were killed in Vietnam (Farrell, 1993: 145–7). The real casualty list of Vietnam is therefore at least double the 58,000 official number. And the real casualty list of the wars in Iraq and Afghanistan are not only the deaths, but also the disabled, physically and emotionally, and the suicides – up to 24 in January 2009, the highest monthly total since records were first collected in 1980, up from five in January 2008, and exceeding the number killed in combat in that month (Alvarez, 2009).

The original notion of the (landed) gentry is, like that of the Knight in the feudal era, based on the class system. The post-modern idea has transcended class, recognizing that virtue is not class-based, and that scum, as well as cream, rises to the top and that the elite may be corrupt; and also that gold, which sinks to the bottom, is to be found in the working class. The social hierarchy does not correspond to the moral hierarchy.[9]

The finest description of the gentleman is surely Cardinal Newman's in *The Idea of a University* originally a series of lectures delivered in Dublin in 1852.

> [I]t is almost a definition of a gentleman to say he is one who never inflicts pain. ... The true gentleman ... carefully avoids whatever may cause a jar or a jolt in the minds of those with whom he is cast; – all clashing of opinion, or collision of feeling, all restraint, or suspicion, or gloom, or resentment; his great concern being to make every one at their ease and at home. He has his eyes on all his company; he is tender towards the bashful, gentle towards the distant, and merciful towards the absurd; he can recollect to whom he is speaking; he guards against unseasonable allusions, or topics which may irritate; he is seldom prominent in conversation, and never wearisome. He makes light of favours while he does them, and seems to be receiving when he is conferring. He never speaks of himself except when compelled, never defends himself by a mere retort, he has no ears for slander or gossip, is scrupulous in imputing motives to those who interfere with him, and interprets every thing for the best. (Discourse VIII: 10; 1982: 159–60)

The citation is long but surely these are still the requirements in civil, polite, gentle society, but not necessarily those of the knight nor the self-made man, nor quite the same as the "new man" so admired by some. This famous description also raised the question: what is the difference between the gentleman and the Christian. The Cardinal never discussed that.

The Christian ideal of the saint, as applied to both men and women, is described by Christ. Certainly Christ's admonitions to "Love they neighbour as thyself" (Mat. 19: 19), the Eight Beatitudes (Mat. 5: 3), and the criteria for salvation specified at the last judgement (Mat. 25: 35–40) are clear enough. Paul's list of what have come to be known as the Nine Cardinal Virtues are less worldly-wise than Newman's. Paul explained that: "The fruit of the Spirit is love, joy, peace, long-suffering, gentleness, goodness, faith, meekness, temperance" (Gal. 5: 22); and more famously: "And now abideth faith, hope, charity, these three; but the greatest of these is charity" (1 Cor. 13: 11). These are not the criteria of the knight

---

9   William Hazlitt wrote an essay *On the Look of a Gentleman* (1821), but it was mostly about looks (elegance, style, bearing – the externals) and manners (politeness) rather than ethics and morality; but he has one sentence which I like. "He gives the wall to a beggar: but does not always bow to great men" (1952: 195). To step aside for a beggar is indeed respectful, democratic and gentle.

or the English gentleman, though there is some overlap with both (gentleness), but of the Saint, an ancient Christian ideal.

Newman starts with the definition that the gentleman "is one who never inflicts pain." But even his description is mostly about good manners and social skills, not goodness: a very different ideal. The definition of a Christian could be one who will "Love thy neighbour as thyself" – which sets a far higher standard. And that is quite apart from the counsel of perfection. "If thou wilt be perfect, go and sell that thou hast and give to the poor, and thou shalt have treasure in heaven" (Mat. 19: 21).

A rather different ideal of manhood was composed by Rudyard Kipling (1865–1936), the poet and Nobel Prize Winner for Literature in 1907. His poem *If* expresses a stoic Victorian ideal of masculinity, and no doubt reflects his own experiences living in India.

> If you can keep your head when all about you
> Are losing theirs and blaming it on you,
> If you can trust yourself when all men doubt you,
> But make allowance for their doubting too;

Kipling's vision is bleak. The man can expect to be blamed and doubted, and as the poem continues, to wait, to be lied about and hated, he should be stoic, accustomed to betrayal, a gambler, a democrat, and also emotionally invulnerable – nothing can hurt him – and very busy all the time. If you can be all that, "you'll be a Man, my son!"

But who would want to be all that? Is this an ideal for the new millennium? Was it even a fine Victorian ideal? Probably not, by today's standards; but it was Kipling's ideal, and it probably expressed the ideals of his class at this time: the male as leader, tough, autonomous, clear-sighted, emotionally distant and a moral warrior – but with the common touch. This was important. Yet there is nothing about his love for his wife and children! And Kipling himself was totally destroyed by the loss of his only son, killed on the Western front in World War I. The poem therefore is defective by omission as an accurate portrait of the Victorian ideal, or of the real Kipling; but it was probably accurate, so far as it goes, as a component part of the British imperial mandate.

Many of these themes still persist in these days, as we shall see. The greatest change is surely in the acceptability of the line: "If neither foes nor loving friends can hurt you." What is that man? Stone? Yet the ideal persists as Paul Simon sings: "I am a rock. I am an island" which expresses precisely this same notion of emotional invulnerability and total self-sufficiency and autonomy. Rocks, however, do not swim very well, and shatter rather than bend – nor are they much use in relationships. Flexibility and adaptability are more emphasized today; so is love and fathering.

Kipling's Victorian ideal is certainly far removed from the Christian ideal of the saint, the model of the warrior from Homer to Beowulf, Chaucer, Malory,

Spenser and Tennyson. In the poem *Guinevere*, King Arthur states that he founded the Round Table: "A glorious company, the flower of man / To serve as a model for the mighty world, / And be the fair beginning of a time." His knights were sworn "To ride abroad redressing human wrongs" (1905: 463). Nor is Kipling's model close to Chesterfield's portrait of a gentleman, or Smiles' or Newman's.

Kipling's poem can be debated from another angle also. To the extent that the qualities lauded here are valuable, one can question how unique they are to men. Women too have to cope with lies, betrayal, being doubted, being blamed etc. and still carry on by sheer will-power, long past the point at which they might be expected to break.

James Joyce reflected on some of the related dilemmas of masculinity in his *A Portrait of the Artist as a Young* (1916) in Dublin. "The question of honour here [in school] raised was, like all such questions, trivial to him. [At the same time] he had heard about him the constant voices of his father and of his masters, urging him to be a gentleman above all things and urging him to be a good catholic among all things...When the gymnasium opened he had heard another voice urging him to be strong and manly and healthy and when the movement towards national revival had begun to be felt in the college yet another voice had bidden him to be true to his country...[and] as he foresaw, a worldly voice would bid him raise up his father's fallen state by his labours and meanwhile the voice of his school comrades urged him to be a decent fellow..."etc. (1992: 88). These conflicting demands to value honour, be a gentleman, a good catholic, manly, a nationalist, a hard worker, a decent chap etc left Joyce lonely. After his school years he would face more demands from his wife, two children, work and publishers and especially in his case, the pub. Such conflicts are not unique to men, but Kipling and Joyce articulate them well.

Perhaps this ideal of the gentleman is dead or dying. The concept of *honour* as a prime male value, and duty, might almost be defined as the value of a sucker or a loser today. Is a man's word his bond? Is a handshake enough to seal a deal or a bet? Can a verbal promise be relied upon now? Are the contracts worth the paper they are written on? With the indictments of top corporate officials in major corporations, political corruption relatively widespread (relative to the ideal, not to other countries), politicians and lawyers low on the status hierarchy, and the work ethic in question – some might answer "NO" to all the above. Honesty (from the same Latin root word as honour) and integrity are only valued (an economic term) insofar as they are useful i.e. valuable: make a profit. They are now means to an end, not virtues nor ends in themselves, at least for some men. For many, however, the ideal of the gentleman still stands – perhaps for both sexes.

The Self-made Man

The prime American model of masculinity is surely the self-made man in a self-made country. The man who made it from rags to riches. The immigrant who arrived at Ellis Island with nothing and worked his way up the slippery ladder to the top. The man makes himself, as God made man.[10]

Such rapid social mobility was possible in the expanding states – more so than in class-bound England, which probably accounts for the contrasting ideals. The new land had created a new man, according to a French visitor in 1782, who:

> leaving behind him all his ancient prejudices and manners, receives new ones from the new mode of life he has embraced, the new government he obeys, and the new rank he holds. The American is a new man who acts upon new principles. (In Kimmel, 1996: 20)

The distinctive feature of the new American man was that he was self-made – in contrast to the English and French systems of tradition and inheritance, the relics of feudalism. The term was first coined by Henry Clay in 1832, in a speech in the Senate in which he referred to the wealthy manufacturers of America as "enterprising, self-made men, who have whatever wealth they possess by patient and diligent labour" (Cawelti, 1965: 43). This was a self-serving characterization, since so much of the wealth was built on Indian land, black slave labour and a "diligent" working-class; but the phrase does highlight the self-reliant individualism of the expanding nation, and the confidence that hard work was profitable in an open society. The English system emphasized, as Edmund Burke had affirmed in his prescient *Reflections on the Revolution in France* (1790): order, gradualism, tradition and hierarchy in contrast to the "rage and phrenzy" of mob rule (1986: 279–80). That Burke approved of the American revolution but not the French suggests that he was personally far more aware of the British parliamentary misgovernance, as an M.P., than of French royal misgovernance.

Perhaps the two men who best exemplified this "new man" were Benjamin Franklin (1709–90) and Ralph Waldo Emerson (1803–82) of the 18th and 19th centuries. Ben Franklin was born in poverty and Boston, made his fortune in printing and Philadelphia, and became one of America's leading statesmen, scientists and writers. In his writings he was one of the first apostles of the self-made man, both in terms of the pursuit of wealth and the pursuit of virtue: the two coinciding very neatly. In this, wrote Max Weber (1904/1976), the Protestant Ethic was the spirit of capitalism, indeed Protestantism created capitalism and ideology determined economics. (The theory is disputed. Some argue that capitalism created Protestantism, and others that Catholicism was deeply influential (Tawney, 1964).) Two of his books were particularly important: *The Way of Wealth* and *The Art of Virtue*, with both advocating remarkably similar behaviours. Indeed Weber cites some of Franklin's maxims to exemplify precisely the spirit of capitalism: "*time* is money," "*credit* is money," "[m]oney can beget money," "honesty is

---

10   Cawelti (1965) offers an excellent treatment of this theme, tracking it from Franklin and Jefferson through Alger to Dewey, and in the novels of the times. Kimmel (1996) is also useful for his history rather than his ideology.

the best policy" (1976: 48–9, 151. His emphasis). This last maxim illustrates the coinciding of the acquisition of wealth and virtue simultaneously, for honesty is both profitable and virtuous.

Franklin, of Puritan background, was also deeply concerned with moral self-improvement and developed a system of moral book-keeping (Weber, 1976: 124). He listed 13 virtues: Temperance, Silence, Order, Resolution, Frugality, Industry, Sincerity, Justice, Moderation, Cleanliness, Tranquillity, Chastity and Humility – then kept a daily check-list for progress, or otherwise in each one. The overlap between the twin pursuits is clear in some of these virtues: frugality, industry, temperance; but Franklin intended to pursue them for their own ends, and self-improvement, not for wealth. Fortunately the two coincided, in Franklin's view – though probably not in the minds of many of today's cheats for whom dishonesty is the best policy.

The importance of Franklin's work was not simply his almost revolutionary insistence on self-improvement, both economic and moral, in *this* world (in contrast to the traditional Christian view of salvation in the next), but also his insistence that wealth – gold – is good; not greed: the ideology that "greed is good," exemplified by Midas, was late twentieth century.

Franklin's teachings were complemented by those of John Wesley, the founder of Methodism. This came generally from Wesley's rejection of the doctrine of predestination, and his insistence on good works; but also more specifically from his insistence on "industry and frugality" (echoing Franklin), which will generate riches, but the riches will in turn generate "pride, anger, and love of the world in all its branches." Wesley's solution was both capitalist and Christian: "We must exhort all Christians to gain all they can, and to save all they can, that is, in effect, to grow rich." And then to give away all they can, to save up treasure in heaven: an echo of Christ's teaching (Weber, 1976: 175–6). The essential difference between Franklin's ideas and those of Wesley was that Wesley was solely interested in the after life and salvation.

Complementary to Franklin's advisories was Emerson's insistence on rugged individualism, self-reliance and personal autonomy – a Darwinian ideology in a brave, new, but highly competitive world. Emerson equated manliness with self-reliance, reflecting the original values of the early settlers on the frontier rather than those of the "joint-stock company" of emerging urban capitalism. In his essay on *Self-Reliance* (1841), Emerson insisted:

> Society everywhere is in conspiracy against the manhood of every one of its members. Society is a joint-stock company, in which the members agree, for the better sharing of his bread to each share-holder, to surrender the liberty and culture of the eater. The virtue in most request is conformity. Self-reliance is its aversion. (1997: 25–6)

"Whoso would be a man must be a nonconformist." And on this theme he explored ethical relativism: "Good and bad are but names, very readily transferable to that or this; the only right is what is after my constitution, the only wrong what is against it" (1997: 26). He was not a nihilist, but above all an individualist, concerned with what he saw as the demise of traditional values of masculinity. "Trust thyself: every heart vibrates to that iron string." He adds: "It is easy in the world to live after the world's opinion, … but the great man is he who, in the midst of the crowd keeps with perfect sweetness the independence of solitude" (1997: 26–8). Here he anticipates Kipling, and Thomas Carlyle (Chapter 4) but also Friedrich Nietzsche whose idea of Superman personalized Kipling and Emerson (Nietzsche, 1985: 41, cf. 65). He noted that every great man was misunderstood: Pythagoras, Socrates, Jesus, Copernicus, Galileo and so on; and that every institution is "the lengthened shadow of one man": the Reformation: Luther; the Quakers: Fox; the Methodists: Wesley; Abolition: Clarkson. "Man is timid and apologetic. He is no longer upright" (1997: 30–1, 34). He insists on "a greater self-reliance – a new respect for the divinity in man" (1997: 39). "Nothing can bring you peace but yourself. Nothing can bring you peace but the triumph of principles" (1997: 46).

This insistence of Franklin and Emerson on "the self" was popularized by Samuel Smiles (1812–1904) in the United Kingdom, with his advice books *Self-Help* (1859) and *Thrift* (1875), and by Horatio Alger in the United States (1834–99) in his moralistic tales written particularly for young boys. Smiles has already been mentioned as writing about gentlemen. Smiles' basic principle was the first sentence of his book: "Heaven helps those who help themselves." He expanded on this principle by articulating "energetic individualism" as the key to success:

> … It is energetic individualism which produces the most powerful effects upon the life and action of others, and really constitutes the best practical education. Schools, academies, and colleges, give but the merest beginnings of culture in comparison with it. Far more influential is the life-education daily given in our homes, in the streets, behind the counters, in workshops, at the loom and the plough, in counting-houses and manufactories, and in the busy haunts of men. (1958: 39)

While he did not directly address issues of men and masculinity, his work was aimed at men as what was known as the "head of the family" and the principal wage-earners. Self-control not self-indulgence was the secret – as is work: "Labour is not only a necessity and a duty, but a blessing: only the idler feels it to be a curse" (1958: 58–9).[11]

In *Thrift*, he returned to the theme of work, but emphasized that men must *save* their wages, and he redefined savings as not simply a personal matter, but a national issue: "It is the savings of individuals which compose the wealth – in other

---

11   Smiles perhaps forgot the Genesis story in which God curses Adam: "in the sweat of they face shalt thou eat bread, till thou return unto the ground; for out of it was thou taken: for dust thou art and unto dust shalt thou return" (Genesis 3: 19). Work was intended as a curse; and Smiles probably never worked in a coal mine or on an accelerating conveyor belt.

words, the well-being – of every nation ... every thrifty person may be regarded as a public benefactor, and every thriftless person as a public enemy" (1875: 14).

Smiles' dream was to help men to help themselves, to acquire capital and become capitalists – so different a perspective from his contemporaries Karl Marx and Frederick Engels. Their "Communist Manifesto" damned the bourgeoisie for their exploitation of the working class. Smiles ignored all this. For him the social system was given. A man's purpose was to climb it: by hard work, self-control, energy, battling and even cheerfulness. His whole book was an exploration of these themes in the lives of famous men who conquered adversity: inventors (Arkwright, Watt, Stephenson), potters (Wedgewood and others), explorers, soldiers (Wellington), artists and musicians, abolitionists (Granville, Sharp, Mansfield). The stories are interesting, as well as inspirational; and the advice clear: "All work and no play makes Jack a dull boy; but all play and no work makes him something greatly worse. Nothing can be more hurtful to a youth than to have his world sodden with pleasure" (1875: 318). The word "sodden" indicates the core asceticism – "sparkling" does not have the same effect. Then again a Darwinian theme: "The battle of life is, in most cases, fought uphill; and to win it without a struggle were perhaps to win it without honour ... The school of Difficulty is the best school of moral discipline" (1875: 325). By winning, Smiles did not necessarily mean worldly or financial success (and here he differs from Horatio Alger). He cites Carlyle at the head of *Thrift*: "Not what I have but what I do is my kingdom" (1875: 13). He insisted:

> That is not the most successful life in which a man gets the most pleasure, the most money, the most power or place, honour or fame; but that in which a man gets the most *manhood*, and performs the greatest amount of useful work and of human duty. (1875: 300. Emphasis added).

This is an excellent definition of manhood: doing useful work and your duty. "Hence energy of will may be defined to be the very central power of character in a man – in a word it is the Man himself" (1958: 229). Ultimately, the aim of *Self-help* was to create the gentleman (cf. 1958: 374), and the aim of *Thrift* was to create the capitalist – the self-made man – but the two aims converged.

Similar themes are prevalent in the work of the best-selling American novelist, Horatio Alger; but there are differences: Alger's books sold better: 17 million copies. Also, as novels they presented romantic views of the world compared to Smiles' historical anecdotes; and Alger allows luck as a reward, rather than perseverance, which play key roles in the success of his youths. The key to Alger's message of self-help is in the titles. My only copy, purchased at 30 times its original 50 cents, is titled *Helping Himself*. Others listed are *Bound to Rise*, *Making His Way*, *Brave and Bold* and *Do and Dare*. The Preface to my copy states that the protagonist has "to go out into the world to make his own way."

> He doesn't have an easy time, but by being honest, honorable and truthful, he
> succeeds. He not only is successful in helping his parents out of their poverty
> but becomes a keen, alert business man, loved and honored by his fellow men.
> (Alger, ca 1870, n.p.)

Samuel Smiles and Horatio Alger echoed the ideals and values of Franklin
and Emerson, and popularized them and, judging by their sales, were extremely
popular. But even more popular were the novels of the day with similar messages:
Tom Brown's Schooldays (Hughes, 1857), Mark Twain's classics *The Adventures
of Tom Sawyer* (1876), *Huckleberry Finn* (1885), Stevenson's *Treasure Island*
(1893), Kipling's *Just So Stories* (1894) and *Kim* (1901). While these stories,
written mostly for boys, were more about adventure than social mobility – and
quick thinking rather than virtue were valorized – none the less, they were all
about survival and the triumph of good over evil.[12]

Similarly, a century later, Frodo Baggins, Luke Skywalker and Harry Potter are
the young male heroes fighting evil male villains. The socialization into heroism
persists. And survival is the basis for self-making.[13]

Historically, the archetypes of the self-made men in the United States were the
Robber Barons – known initially for their robbery rather than their virtue. Such men
included Andrew Carnegie (1835–1919), the steel magnate; John D. Rockefeller
(1839–1937), oil; Andrew Mellon (1855–1937), financier and industrialist; Cornelius
Vanderbilt, Paul Getty (1892–1976), also in oil. This worship of money, condemned
by some as greed was epitomized by Carnegie's little book *The Gospel of Wealth*
(1889/1998) – which neatly equated the accumulation of wealth with the Christian
virtues associated with the four gospels, and totally contradicted the Christian
message. The four evangelists would have been horrified. This capitalist ethic was
echoed in the political power structure. President Coolidge famously stated: "The
business of America is business." It was echoed too in the slogan: "What's good
for Ford is good for America." This value system is epitomized in the speech of
Gekko (played by Michael Douglas) in *Wall Street* (1987): "Greed, for lack of a
better word, is good. Greed is right. Greed works ... Greed in all its forms – greed
for life, greed for money, for love, knowledge – has marked the upward surge of

---

12 The importance of sports in men's and increasingly women's lives has surely not
been fully recognized by sociologists. Dr Arnold (and Hughes) evidently found sports highly
beneficial at Rugby. Others have been more ambivalent. One woman critiques sport as "a
repository for dominant ideology in its celebration of ruthless nationalism, racism, militarism,
imperialism and sexism" (in Horrocks, 1995: 147). Five "isms"; but apart from that, it can be
fun! Nicholas Hornby's *Fever Pitch* (1992) is a classic on soccer, Eduardo Archetti (1999)
writes well on football and polo, and Beard (2003) is great on rugby.

13 We cannot go further into the topic of boys literature as socializing agents, but the
20s brought out Henty and Westerman, and after the war William Brown – no relation to Tom,
but another "everyboy" (by Richmal Crompton), the Hardy Boys (the name was probably
intentional), the Biggles books (W.E. Johns) and Eagle comics kept up the "pressure" of high
risk adventure, altruism as the willingness to sacrifice self for others, and bravery.

mankind." In this view, greed is a mechanism of social evolution. Summarized as "greed is good," this philosophy flips greed as a vice to greed as a virtue, legitimizing capitalism.

The apostle of capitalism, Adam Smith, did not view greed as the engine of this "upward surge of mankind," but rather self-interest. As he famously remarked in *The Wealth of Nations* (1776): "It is not from the benevolence of the butcher, the brewer, or the baker, that we expect our dinner, but from their regard to their own interest" (Vol. 1. Bk 1, ii; 1976: 18). He explained further that: "The natural effort of every individual to better his own condition ... is so powerful a principle, that it is alone ... capable of carrying on the society to wealth and prosperity" (Vol. 2. Bk 4, v; 1976: 49–50). Each individual is therefore "led by an invisible hand to promote an end which was no part of his intention" (Vol. 1. Bk 4, ii; 1976: 477). And the "avarice and ambition in the rich" are problematic (Vol. 2. Bk 5, i, 2: 1976: 232).

Indeed Alan Greenspan, Chairman of the Federal Reserve Board, stated in his semi-annual Report to the U.S. Senate in 2002: "An infectious greed seemed to grip much of our business community." This destroys the trust that is essential for "free market capitalism and, more broadly, to the underpinnings of our society." He added: "It is not that humans have become any more greedy than in the past. It is that the avenues to express greed had grown so enormously" (http: //www. federalrserve.com/boarddocs/hh/2002/july/testimony.htm).[14]

Greenspan's words were prescient, and the collapse of Enron, WorldCom etc. and then the meltdown of the U.S. and the global economy in late 2008 testified to his foresight, the failures of capitalism and the danger of the self-made man as an ideal of masculinity. Indeed the proud self-made man often became the self-*unmade* man.

For a completely different but factual account of achieving manhood, consider Frederick Douglass. He was a slave who escaped from slavery, became a famous abolitionist, advisor to President Lincoln and ambassador to Haiti. He recalled in his autobiography how his fight with his foreman in 1834, which he won, made him a man:

> This battle with Mr. Covey ... was the turning-point in my "life as a slave." It re-kindled in my breast the smouldering embers of liberty ... and revived a sense of my own manhood. I was a changed being after that fight. I was nothing before – I was a man now. (1962: 143)

Douglass fought for his manhood, and won. He added that: "A man without force is without the essential dignity of humanity. Human nature is so constituted, that it cannot honor a helpless man, though it can pity him, and even this it cannot do for long if signs of power do not arise" (1962: 143). The reality of "the self-made man" is very different for Frederick Douglass, Ben Franklin, the robber barons

---

14   For a broader discussion of greed, please see Tickle (2004).

or, more recently, Bill Gates. Equally, the self-made men are complemented now by the self-made women from Margaret Thatcher to Condoleezza Rice, Oprah, Angela Merkel, Mother Teresa and Sarah Palin. There are many ways of "making oneself"; and equally, that "self" is variously defined: as freedom, virtue, wealth or power.

Two Vietnam veterans told stories similar to that of Douglas. In 1965, in the opening battle of that war, units of the 7th Cavalry were dropped into the La Drang valley and were immediately surrounded by a superior force of the enemy. Recalling the first attack later one soldier stated: "I think we all became men that day. After that afternoon, I don't remember feeling real fear again." And a sergeant echoed this: "I remember feeling that I had been tested and found to be a man" (Moore and Galloway, 2002: 183, 266). Passing a test, overcoming fear: these are achievements in becoming a man, very similar to Douglass' point.

In sum, despite the assurances of Franklin, Emerson, Smiles, Alger and all those other authors that hard worked and moral virtue would ensure social mobility, critics argued that racism restricted such mobility, that education was more important than hard work, that "rags to riches" stories were mostly mythical and exceptional, and that these authors were largely delusional (Cawalti, 1965).

Survival, not mobility, is the goal. Becoming a man may require violence. Material success may demand utter ruthlessness. And social skills may be as important, or more so, than violence, education, or being a gentleman. Nor is "success" defined solely by material wealth, despite the ethic of the self-made man.

Indeed, ironically, in the last 50 years or so, Americans have turned increasingly to self-help literature to become self-made men and women. This began with Dale Carnegie's (1936) *How to Win Friends and Influence People*, continued with Norman Vincent Peale's (1955) *The Power of Positive Thinking*; Thomas Harris' (1967), *I'm O.K. – You're O.K.*, and M. Scott Peck's (1978), *The Road Less Travelled*. Then came Stephen Covey's (1990) *The 7 Habits of Highly Effective People* and the genre accelerated. So we all began to rely increasingly on the others for emotional survival, material success and, a new phrase, "personal growth." Life coaches, grief therapists, social workers, psychologists, counsellors and gurus of all sorts now abound.

In the new millennium the guru of self-help is "Dr Phil", but the goal is not material, still less money, but the recovery of the self: "to take control of your entire life [by] reconnecting with what I call your *authentic self*" (McGraw, 2001: 9).

The irony of all this is that the self-help movement is the antithesis of the self-reliance that contributes to the self-made man or woman. According to Steve Salerno in *Sham* (2005), the movement is an $8 billion business, with about 4,000 new self-help books published in 2003 alone. Salerno argues that the self-help movement has made America helpless.

The self-made millionaires and now billionaires were not all industrialists or venture capitalists, of course, nor are they all men. Mobility can be achieved, and is achieved to the pinnacles of wealth, fame or power. Avenues include the military (Colin Powell), sports (Tiger Woods, Michael Jordan, David Beckham), entertainment (Oprah, the Beatles, Shania Twain), and politics (Bill Clinton, Margaret Thatcher, Sarah Palin). The rise may be spectacular, but so is the fall. The former bouncer, milkman and motel owner, Bernard Ebbers, built WorldCom into the second-largest phone carrier in the U.S. He has been sentenced to 25 years for his $11 billion fraud which costs thousands of individuals their jobs, pensions and investments. Jeffrey Skilling of Enron was sentenced to 24 years in 2006. Similarly John Rigas, founder of Adelphi Communications, was sentenced to 15 years. James Otis of Dynegy was sentenced to 24 years, and many more. Conrad Black is in jail. Martha Stewart was criminalized. And Dennis Kozlowski, the former CEO of Tyco International, was convicted of fraud, conspiracy and grand larceny. And there are many similar examples every year in business, politics, the church, the university, the media etc. Some self-made men and women have made themselves by illegal means, which are themselves the means of the un-making. The self-made man becomes the self-unmade man.

The phrase itself, the self-made man, is curious as equating self-making and upward social mobility and only males! The phrase valorizes winning, being top dog, top gun, numero uno, top of the heap, the gold medal – as if the silvers and bronzes are not self-made too. In this paradigm, very few men and women are winners: the vast majority of us are losers. Great as have been the benefits of this ideal, the costs have also been high. As they say, the silver is for the first loser.

Two final points: despite the prevalence of the particularly American ideal of the self-made man, the rugged individualist in the land of opportunity, the reality today is very different. Indeed the latest research shows that the United States has much lower social mobility rates than France, Germany, Sweden, Canada, Finland, Noway and Denmark. (Only the U.K. has even lower rates, of the countries surveyed.) Mobility is measured as the correspondence between the incomes of parents and children. In the U.S. the correlation is .46 i.e. almost half of the income inequality is "inherited"; this compares to correlations in Germany (.30), Canada (.20) and Scandinavia (.15). This American relative immobility is due to a number of factors: inequalities of education and, before that, the inequality of school preparedness, the high poverty rates (17% overall, the highest in the G7), and the highest concentration of wealth (69.8% owned by the wealthiest 10% of the population) after Switzerland in the developed world – compared to 56% in the U.K., 53% in Canada and 39.3% in Japan (Esping-Andersen, 2007; Dreier, 2007).

The ultimate in the self-made man genre is surely the California journalist, Norah Vincent, who passed as a man, Ned, for almost a year. She changed her appearance with a new haircut, stubble, a prosthesis and clothes, learned a new walk and a new talk, and then joined a bowling league, became a salesman, went to a monastery, a strip club, a men's consciousness raising group and tried a few dates with women – not successfully, until she allowed as she was really a woman. Like John Howard Griffin's book *Black Like Me* (1961) – a white journalist who coloured his skin to pass as black in the South – but less dangerous, this is an insightful discussion of men by a self-made man (Vincent, 2006).

The Twentieth Century: Changing Men

These three models of masculinity (warrior, gentleman, self-made man, epitomized by three different virtues or graces: bravery, gentleness or gentility and success) have persisted and have tended to reinforce and complement each other, rather than to compete or contradict. Men are still expected to protect their family and their country and, like the vast majority of firefighters and police officers, their communities also. This is still the knight/warrior model of men as brave and strong. Men are also expected to be gentle: politeness is the mark of the man in the polis, and civility is the mark of the citizen; and violence is usually criminal. And men are still expected to work and to make something of themselves, and to climb up the ladder of success.

During the Victorian era, these normative ideas were probably unknown or irrelevant in the sense that they were taken for granted – as they are not today. Most men were farmers, miners, soldiers and sailors, fishermen, lumberjacks, railroad workers, construction workers, canal builders, factory workers, steel workers – tough jobs with high injury and mortality rates, as they still are. White collar workers, whose numbers expanded with literacy levels and capitalism, had more mobility options; but were then a minority.

Yet the norms of masculinity persisted. The persistance of wars, and the escalation of military (and civilian) casualties with "improved" military technology (machine-guns, howitzers, battleships, aircraft, the atom bomb) renewed the knight norm. From 1900 to 1945, much of the world was at war, and the first half of the twentieth century had contradictory impacts on men, and definitions of masculinity. On the one hand the military were valued as heroes and patriots and warriors; on the other hand, they were disposable and victims in a war of attrition.

After World War I, with nine million military deaths in that war, the German economy collapsed, in part due to the stringent terms of the Peace of Versailles, which in turn caused massive social unrest and contributed to the rise of Hitler, Naziism and militarism in the 1930s. Visually this militarism is captured in two of Leni von Riefenstahl's films *Olympia* and *The Will to Power*. Meanwhile the 1929 Crash of the New York Stock market precipitated the Great Depression and mass unemployment in the United States, which in turn led to the New Deal initiated by President Roosevelt in 1933. The rise of fascism in Germany, Italy, Spain and Japan resulted serially in the annexation of Austria, the invasion of the Rhineland, the Spanish Civil War, the Italian invasion of Abyssinia, the Japanese invasion of China, the German invasion of Poland and finally World War II.

The increasingly *important* role of men as warriors was at odds with the increasingly *unimportant* role of men as providers – replaced by the state with the New Deal and, in the U.K., the rise of the Welfare State. The unemployed men of the 1930s and the dead men of the 1940s necessitated the increased role of the state in the hitherto private domain of the family. In sum, the traditional male role, and definition of masculinity, as provider, began to be displaced, and replaced, by the state. These structural changes benefitted both men and women, supplying a safety net to both and equalizing life chances throughout society; but as transfers of power and responsibility from men to the state, they also initiated changes in men's and women's relations to each other. Men were being replaced by the state.

With the invention of the pill in the 50s, males became even more disposable in the family, except as bread-winners. Women now determined the number and timing of children, if any. The pill also inaugurated the sexual revolution of the 60s, a re-definition of sex, and a rapid decline in the fertility rate. This in turn facilitated increased numbers of women in the labour force, and then the rise of the women's movement, which in turn accelerated the rate of change of traditional sex roles, and therefore gender identities and relations. The depression, the war, the pill, the sexual revolution, shifts in gender employment, the women's movement all had their roles to play in successive decades.

The 50s and 60s were prosperous in Europe and North America, and created the Hippy movement on both continents: eulogizing peace and love, drugs, sex and rock 'n' roll, and not working. The work ethic was critiqued. Militarism was critiqued. Leisure and pleasure were valorized. Traditional ideas of masculinity were being examined from within, by men. But they were also being affected by changes in the labour force. In his classic work *The Organization Man* (1956) William Whyte described the rise of a new type of man, believing in individualism and the American Dream, but locked into the security of large organizations. The 1950s men were:

> the business trainee off to join Du Pont ... the seminary student who will end up in the church hierarchy, the doctor headed for the corporate clinic the physics Ph.D. in a government laboratory, the intellectual on the foundation-sponsored team project, the engineering graduate in the huge drafting room at Lockheed, the young apprentice in a Wall Street law factory. (Whyte, 1956: 3–4)

The corporatization of work, he argued, negated individualism as reality, though it persisted as ideology. But Whyte neglected to discuss the *mechanization* of men working on conveyor belts, component parts of Charlie Chaplin's *Hard Times* and Fordism. The objectification, utilization and *disposability* of men on the battlefields by all sides persisted with the Korean War and then the Vietnam War, but also in the mines, on the factory floors and on the dole. I have appropriated the term objectification from feminism, where it has more usually applied to women as "victims" of the male gaze, beauty competitions and advertising. I suggest that it is far more appropriately applied to men than to women. *Beauty competitions do not kill women. Wars kill men.* A difference which feminists have ignored while so vigorously protesting objectification. The competitions were and are a matter of women's autonomous choices and agency – a curious thing for feminists to protest. The draft and conscription are not matters of choice. The former may bring joy, smiles, rewards. The latter may bring injury and death. Furthermore the mechanization of work objectifies men (and women), as anyone who has worked on a conveyor belt is unhappily aware. Such men are "units of production" with neither autonomy nor creativity. The focus on "the male gaze" as problematic for women is fair enough, but needs to be contextualized with the far more problematic objectifications of men as (disposable) units of production and warfare.

In the 60s and 70s, the Women's Liberation Movement, as it was then called, modelled on the earlier Civil Rights Movement, had begun to question what it means to be a woman, and to be a man. The pill had given women control over fertility, the economy was booming, rights and status were clearly unequal, and Friedan, in *The Feminine Mystique* (1963) had described women as oppressed by men, home and family (see ch. 4). In her view, marriage was slavery, work was freedom, and freedom was work (very un-Marxist, but she was of the bourgeoisie). Implicitly she recommended autonomy, divorce, few or no children, a room of one's own (in Virginia Woolf's phrase), a job and an income of one's own. She practiced what she preached, and careers began to replace children as priorities for women. The fertility rate kept falling and, free of children, women began to take jobs in the expanding labour force and to improve their educational qualifications. This gender mobility was epitomized dramatically by the election of Margaret Thatcher as Prime Minister in the U.K. in 1979, and her re-election twice more after that. And this in the Conservative party in the supposedly conservative kingdom.

Simultaneously, the rise of the Peace movement critiqued the traditional role of men as warriors. As criticism of the Vietnam War mounted, in direct relation to the widely televised casualties, the military were widely blamed by the public. Protesters spat at and abused the men on leave. The slogan was "Women say Yes to Men who say No." Draft-dodgers who fled to Canada were redefined as draft-resisters; and refusal to fight was redefined from cowardice to bravery.

Simultaneous with, and subsequent to, the changing balance of power between the sexes, and the critiques of men and masculinity by both the feminist and the peace movements, men were beginning to question their own identities as men. One of the first to articulate this redefinition was Jack Nichols, author of *Men's Liberation* (1975) – a quick response to the Women's Liberation movement with which he was sympathetic. He argued that men are at a crossroads of values, between today's "machine economy," and men as machines, and fresh, new possibilities.

> A saner society will flower when men liberate themselves from contrived, socially fabricated prohibitions, cultural straitjackets, and mental stereotypes that control and inhibit behavior through arbitrary definitions of what it means to be a man. (1975: 317)

Nichols critiqued men's admiration of intellect rather than the body and sensuousness, the idolization of competition, the resort to violence, and says that "it is certain that masculinist values have outlived their usefulness in a nuclear age and are downright dangerous" (1975: 317–20). He recommended pleasure rather than power as "the hallmark of a fulfilling existence" (1975: 323). This was precisely the opposite of advice to the Alger-Smiles-Hughes literature of only 100 years earlier, but in line with the sexual revolution and the new leisure economy.

This "new liberated man" was expected to be in touch with his body and his feelings, to be non-violent and refuse to fight, to be able to cry and to cook and to "emote," as the phrase was. Alan Alda and Troy Donahue were often mentioned as role models. Masculinity had to be redefined, and the new men were expected to replace the dinosaurs like knights, samurai, tycoons, the out-dated gentlemen – and to be a man fit for women to live with as equals: fine husbands and fine fathers, centred not on work or war, but on home and relationships. Ironically, this prescription emerged just as women were leaving the home in large numbers, entering the workforce, volunteering for the military, entering politics, declining large families and replacing husbands and fathers with alimony, child support and government child allowances as well as, if necessary, welfare allowances. There were now three in the bed. Gender roles changed rapidly and drastically after the 1950s, and are still changing. Women's greater success in the education system is now impacting distribution in the professions (law, medicine, dentistry, the university) as well as the corporations, and therefore the distribution of income (see Chs. 6 and 7).

The demise of the family as a private and personal institution continued with C. Henry Kemper's *The Battered Child Syndrome* (1962) which brought family violence against children out of the closet and into government hands. This was followed by Lenore Walker's *The Battered Woman* (1979), which brought violence against women out of the privacy of the home into the legal spotlight. During the 1980s and 1990s a battery of legislation was introduced criminalizing stalking, sexual harassment and marital rape, and recognizing the battered wife syndrome as a valid legal defense for homicide (Weiss and Young, 1996).

Then in 1994 the U.S. Congress passed the Violence Against Women Act, which was re-authorized in 2000 and 2005, establishing zero tolerance for violence against women, with particular emphasis on domestic violence. The U.S. Dept. of Justice, Office on Violence against Women states: "Domestic violence can be physical, sexual, emotional, economic or psychological actions or threats of actions that influence another person. This includes any behaviors that intimidate, manipulate ... etc." (www.usdoj: ovw: About domestic violence). This is an extremely broad definition of violence – far broader than the usual popular understanding of violence or the dictionary definition of violence as physical injury. By this criterion, we have all probably been victims of domestic or intimate violence. That said, Congress has failed to pass legislation offering equal protection of the law for men. Indeed it refused to pass proposed legislation, a Violence against Men Act in 2005.

By the end of the twentieth century, then, feminist ideology and practice were dominant, men were questioning their own identity – critiqued especially by misandric feminists (Chapter 4), and having difficulty coping with new structural and ideological realities. Men's movements were emerging, sometimes criticizing "toxic" masculinities – and what a man was or should be was not always clear. The demands often seemed to be contradictory: a warrior and also a nurturer, a money-maker and a family man, a male and also a female, but not equally protected by legislation.

Millennium Man

In 2001 terrorists attacked the two towers of the World Trade Center, the Pentagon, and attempted to attack either the White House or Camp David, but failed. About 3,000 people were killed, mostly Americans, and the 19 (male) terrorists in the four plane crashes. This opened up a new debate about masculinity.

The bravery of the men who attacked the terrorists on UA 93, and foiled their attack – the bravery of the NYPD and the FDNY who saved so many lives at the World Trade Center, often at the cost of their own – the bravery of the men who invaded Afghanistan in 2001 and Iraq in 2003 – all this has reinforced the value of men as heroes, warriors, altruistic. Men still risk their lives for others, and for their country, and lose them.

Freud asked, famously: "The great question that has never been answered and which I have not been able to answer despite my thirty years of research into the feminine soul, is "What does a woman want?" (in Jones, 1954: 468). Today we know, because we have the personal ads in our daily newspapers. Perusing the "Men Wanted" columns in newspapers suggests that times have changed, again. Women do not want sensitivity so much as, typically, "n/s, n/d, fit and financially solvent" males. And men often stress their solvency in their own self-portraits, their "athletic builds" or fitness – but neither women nor men discuss their emotional sensitivity and the sensitive New Age Guy. Indeed in Quebec the SNAG is dismissed by women as "l'homme rose" – a man who is not happy with his masculinity.

Today some say that there is a crisis of masculinity: a crisis of identity – men who do not know who they are, what they should be, what they want. Some feel guilty about being male – perhaps a direct consequence of the prevalent critiques of masculinity, perhaps also a direct consequence of the changed roles of men since their father's time.

This chimes with Robert Bly's complaint in *Iron John* that today's men are "soft." "They're lovely, valuable people – I like them – they're not interested in harming the earth or starting wars …. But many of these men are not happy. They lack energy, are life-preserving but not life-giving." Bly is almost describing the SNAG as not masculine enough – unlike the women they are often with: "strong women who positively radiate energy" (1990: 2–3) – perhaps the NSSNAW: the not so sensitive new age woman.

There is a spark missing in these nice, mild sensitive young men – or an iron core, to reflect Bly's title. In that old movie, *Zorba the Greek* (1964) there is a wonderful scene in which a Greek peasant, Zorba, played by Anthony Quinn, confronts the quiet and repressed English tourist, played by Anthony Bates. He shows the Englishman how to dance. This is not, you will recall, listed in Kipling's poem as a requirement for being a man. (On the contrary, one suspects.) Zorba insists: "A man needs a touch of madness." And as the Englishman comes alive, one would have to agree. One line does not prove a sociological point, but may exemplify it.

Watching young boys as they play: riding bikes and skateboards so recklessly, so unabashedly physical as they attack passing railings with so much energy and making so much noise, then yell obscenities at totally innocent and horrified passers-by, hurtling through space at top speed – crashing – picking themselves up if they can – a touch of madness, certainly, which should be loved not medicalized, nor even tamed.

The old stereotypes – or ideals – seem to be alive and well, at least in the newspaper advertisements which are nothing if not frank. Men want a younger (and shorter) sex object. Women want an older (and taller) success object. Usually. It's a trade, and a trade-off.

The self-made man (or success object), the gentleman, the knight and the "new" man persist as different male ideals. There are others, of course: the good husband, the fine father, the good provider/worker, which are more personal and individual. They are not the same and may indeed conflict with each other on occasion. A man must juggle them and balance them, keep his wife, his children and his boss happy. Indeed these role conflicts are part of the unrecognized and stressful domain of men and, increasingly, of women.

The Beach Boys sang the question: "Will I grow up to be a man?" Plaintive, really, but the question recognizes that being a man in the social sense is not just a matter of being born male, and then aging, it is a matter of learning, achievement and personal choices over the years, with varying success rates and different values and options.[15]

Conclusion

In sum, five points stand out. First, the (horizontal) *continuum* of masculinity from wimps and sissies to "real men," from omega males to alpha males: what I have

---

15 Changing the sex: "Will I grow up to be a woman?" The answer for a girl would surely be "yes" rather than "it all depends." Whether this is double standards or Mars/Venus lifestyles or both is not so clear. But that men should be concerned about how they will grow up does indicate that masculinity is problematic.

called the Masculinity Quotient. Multiple criteria apply along this continuum, and they are variable over time and space; they include many dimensions of social capital and power: physical, economic, political, intellectual, etc., which probably do not coincide. Today's teased or bullied geek in school is tomorrow's alpha male.

Second, the *evaluations* of men on a continuum from negative to positive, low to high, along a vertical axis: pigs and problems to protectors, providers and heroes. (More on the positive in Chapter 3 and the negative in Chapter 4.)

Third, ideas about masculinity and ideals of masculinity are not monolithic: they vary some from culture to culture as Weber noted, they change with age, and in war and peace, as Shakespeare noted so poetically, and they have evolved historically over time in the west: the warrior, gentleman self-made man to SNAG, metrosexual etc. or, in Kimmel's formulation for the U.S., the patriarch, the artisan and the self-made man. These multiple masculinities or "plural masculinities" in Connell's term imply the social construction of gender and of masculinity. Constructionists emphasize difference, change, fluidity and even contradiction – all of which are likely to cause confusion about male identity or identities in our rapidly changing world. Yet, at the risk of essentialism, there are limits to costructionism in practice.

Plural masculinities can be complemented by "core masculinity." This is indicated in the dictionary definitions of masculinity, in the self-definitions of men in the Hite Report, in the vast domain of anthropology (Gilmore, 1991) and in popular culture: "Be a man!", "Man up!" The common themes of provider and protector are universal, though not exclusive to males. A man must work to provide, and a man must be brave: to protect himself, his family and his country. Overall a man must, as they say, "have balls." We can recognize and integrate both the plural and the core, which embraces both culture and nature, sociology and biology.

Fourth, the two most significant themes in the lives of men have been first, the expansion of options for men in the last 50 years – the idea expressed in plural masculinities – including the options both of relative femininity and the reality of sex-change. The John Wayne/James Bond models are no longer so compelling. The other, and related change is the decline of the old ideal of the brave warrior. Perhaps that was dealt a death-blow, to use a rather unpleasant military metaphor, by the high casualty rate of the Somme (1916) or by the moral critique of the Vietnam War, or perhaps by the changing technology of warfare which, in the North American and Western European model, demands few casualties. This is a massive saving of men's lives (and a totally different concept of warfare from the attrition casualties suffered particularly in World War I); and also requires a re-evaluation of the definition of masculinity. A generation of men has now matured without having had to fight in war; unless they chose to volunteer for the services. This is surely the most remarkable shift in the self-definition of men in the last millennium.

Finally, the increasing feminization of society (Lenz and Myerhoff, 1985) is not only shifting the balance of power between the sexes but has also generated men's movements, with various goals and orientations. These are discussed further in Chapters 6 and 7. Some have argued that men are "in crisis"; others that men are "hegemonic" (Connell) and "in power" (Kimmel), still others that this is a myth (Farrell).

Men's identities as workers, warriors, husbands and fathers are in flux, as are women's identities as workers, wives and mothers. Each dances to each. The only constant here is change and variance: the various definitions, the multiple ideals, the changing roles, the reversal of evaluations, the many options ... We consider gender relations in the next chapter.

Chapter 2
Men and Women:
Models and Muddles

The first paradox of gender is that, although both men and women are of the same species, we define each other as "opposite" sexes. This surely is profoundly strange. We differ from each other by only one chromosome out of 46 pairs – we are 98% chromosomally identical – yet we define each other as socially opposite on a bi-polar scale: not only opposite but even at war. There is, therefore, a massive contradiction between our biological and our social realities.

A second paradox is that gender, which seems so simple, normal, natural, and even visibly obvious, is so controversial. Insects, fish, reptiles and mammals are all gendered; almost all either male or female (some species like flatworms are hermaphrodites, but not many) and seem to have no major ideological problems with this biology. Humans, however, have cultures, and construct their own realities and meanings. In Western nations we have constructed five different models of gender. Unsurprisingly, this profusion of models creates confusion and muddles.

Gender studies are minefields these days, highly sensitive and deeply politicized – both between and also within both genders. Maintaining a balance between conflicting ideological perspectives is probably impossible, and perhaps not even desirable; but trying to appreciate them all, to see the multiple points of view, is surely highly desirable.

The two thorniest questions that seem to bedevil gender relation relate to identity and equality: Are men and women the same? or different? and if different, how different? opposite? and complementary or, as so many feminists have argued, in conflict and at war. And what are the causes of difference: biological or social or both? And what are the societal consequences? These matters are tangled up with the second question: are women equal to men (in the Euro-American orbit)? Equal to which men? That is the question. Men are not equal. Equal to the Presidents and CEOs, or equal to the homeless, the incarcerated, the injured veterans, and the prematurely dead? The equality issue is difficult, and many people quickly respond "No!" And much depends on what indicators are used to measure equality (e.g. longevity, educational attainment etc.), and how variance is theorized (e.g. male discrimination or female agency). Both the World Economic Forum at Davros, Switzerland (*Time* 28.11.07; weforum.org) and the United National Development Program (2006) are researching these issues.

And both these questions are tangled up with arguments about rank: is one sex superior to another? So there are debates about male and female supremacism, misogny and misandry – and also power: who has it? what is it? in whose interests are political and economic power wielded? and so on.

These questions are so old it is a wonder that they are still around, and that there is no consensus, even in a classroom. Plato was egalitarian and his student, Aristotle, was a male supremacist. Today John Gray is the archetypal "difference" or "two worlds" theorist with his Mars/Venus books. And difference theory is widely propagated in magazines like *Time* and *Newsweek* whose cover-page articles tend to stress the *differences*: "The Sexes: How They Differ and Why"; "The New Science of the Brain: Why Men and Women Think Differently"; "Guns and Dolls: Scientists Explore the Differences between Girls and Boys" and "Why are Men and Women Different?" (*Newsweek* 18.5.81; 27.3.95; *Time* 28.5.90; 20.1.92). More recently they have articulated difference theory not so much in direct comparisons as in separate issues on boys: "How to Build a Better Boy" and "The Boy Crisis" and girls: "In Defense of Teen Girls" and "Early Puberty: Why Girls are Growing up Faster." Only one cover issue discusses boys and girls together: "Being 13" (*Newsweek* 11.5.98; (*Time* 30.1.06; *Newsweek* 3.6.02; *Time* 30.10.00; 8.8.05). Many other topics tend to be gendered, and have received front-cover publicity: prostate cancer and breast cancer, women and the military, testosterone, fatherhood, female midlife crisis, and so on. Difference theory is institutionalized equally in these magazines, not so equally in pop culture (Chapter 4).

Similarly, difference theory is taken for granted and documented in the hard sciences, notably biology and evolutionary psychology. We are all equal, but men and women are *not* the same ("let me count the ways," they say), and the differences are *not* due primarily to socialization and upbringing, furthermore the differences can be quantified scientifically (Baron-Cohen, 2003; Buss, 1999; Kimura, 1999; Moir and Jessel, 1991). All these differences may have evolved over the millennia while men were hunters and women were gatherers – and sometimes they still are.

The similarities and differences, then, may be of three types: biological, systemic and personal. The biological refers to hormonal, chromosomal and brain structure and function differences that affect cognitive and behavioural variations. The systemic refers to structural factors related to power, empowerment and (often forgotten) powerlessness: income levels, occupational distribution, political participation rates, education levels, rates of incarceration, addiction, suicide, violence-victimization and homelessness etc. Some of these measures of equality are measured by the U.N. Human Development Index and the World Economic Forum. And personal refers to the uniqueness of men and women who create their own lives and in post-modernity their own gender scripts: quite divorced from conventional dualism.

Researchers have been working for decades to try to determine what, if any, psychological and/or value differences may exist between the sexes, without much success, except in political polling; but also what people *believe* them to be – with more success. One of the more interesting efforts offered the 300 item

Adjective Check List (ACL) to university students in 25 countries asking them to say which applied more to men, or more to women. The results are presented in Table 2.1, indicating a "high degree of pancultural generality" (Williams and Best, 1990:303). They conclude that: "The sex stereotypes in different countries are more similar than they are different," and very different for each gender, as we can see (1990:71). Psychological sexual dimorphism is the norm – supporting the conventional wisdom of the sexes as opposite.

Several points are interesting here. First, the *oppositions* between the descriptors of men and women. The authors summarize the findings from 23 of the 25 countries:

> Men are said to be autocratic and independent, while women are said to be dependent. Men are said to be aggressive and dominant and women are said to be submissive. Men are active, adventurous, daring, and courageous, while women are fearful. Men are strong, robust, and forceful; women are weak. Women are emotional; men are unemotional. Women are sensitive; men are rude. Men are progressive, enterprising, and wise compared to women, who are dreamy and superstitious. Women are affectionate, sentimental, and soft-hearted, while men are stern and severe. (Williams and Best, 1990:78)

They omitted the descriptors (from 19–21 of these countries) that women are kind and gentle, while men are unkind and cruel, and that women are sexy but men are humorous.

Second, the strong cross-cultural agreement about male and female psyches. For instance, in all 25 countries men were described as: adventurous, dominant, forceful, independent, masculine and strong; only three adjectives were female-associated in all 25 countries: sentimental, submissive and superstitious (Williams and Best, 1990: 75–6).

Third, which sex is described in more positive terms? Men do not fare particularly well. They are portrayed as autocratic, boastful, cruel, disorderly, lazy, loud, obnoxious, rude, stern, unkind – but apart from that... . Fortunately there is also a positive portrait. But, on balance, how do women compare? And which would you rather be? And what is *your* portrait of the two sexes. I applied a variation of the ACL in my classes requesting the top five descriptor adjectives for each sex. This elicited a range of evaluations, a different set of adjectives and, when students were asked to check which adjectives apply to them, a considerable cross-over from their gender to the other, i.e. masculinity is not just for men nor femininity for women – which itself negates the simple definition of the two sexes as *opposite*.

Fourth, the semantic overlap is considerable: adventurous, courageous, daring, reckless; meek and mild; anxious and fearful; logical, rational, clear-headed, unemotional; but the contradictions are many and very strange. Men are described as stern and humorous, energetic and lazy, stolid yet disorderly, wise but hard-hearted. It is a little difficult to reconcile these apparent contradictions.

Finally, despite the massive agreement about these "opposite" portraits of men and women, there were some exceptions. Some typically male adjectives were associated with women in Nigeria (arrogant, lazy, robust and rude – three negatives), Malaysia (assertive, humorous and ingenious), Japan (boastful, disorderly and obnoxious) and Pakistan (lazy). And a few female-associated descriptors were applied to men in France and Italy (sympathetic) and Germany (affected). Most of the 300 adjectives were intermediate: associated with both sexes, but not primarily nor exclusively (Williams and Best, 1990:76, 78).

The politics of these descriptors/stereotypes can be imagined: they are true/ not true, the research is flawed/not flawed, the conclusions are unacceptable/ unavoidable, they justify male dominance/female empowerment, and so on. My own research with my patient students suggests that the consensus about men and women tabulated above, and the contradictions within that consensus, reflect their very divergent views. Some are very positive about one sex or the other, some very negative, and some balance the two valences about both sexes. This would at least explain the contradictions. And indeed these contradictions are evident in the five contradictory models of gender.

The romantic model is presented first as the most popular model, also as the most positive since it is egalitarian and stresses complementarity, and is the most romantic and sexy. The other three models follow in chronological sequence: the patriarchal, feminist and post-modern models. This last model negates the binary models of egalitarianism, male supremacy and female supremacy and indeed negates gender – but from various and multiple perspectives. The fifth model is presented in Chapter 7.[1]

Two caveats: these models or paradigms are not like plastic scale replicas of the real thing, toy boats or planes; they are fictions and ideological constructs. They do bear a resemblance to real life, but they cannot capture all the complexities. Each model has some validity, utility and truth, but none is the whole truth. Indeed heterosexual students of gender may start with a romantic rosy view of gender, be disillusioned by divorce and adopt a more negative view of the opposite sex; then

---

1   One caveat on these terms. All labels are controversial and oversimplify, and so are these. The label "patriarchal" is not only negatively loaded as assertive of the oppression and suppression of women, but it is also a vast over-simplification when intended as a description of gender relations over time and across cultures. Some have even described patriarchy as a war against women. This sort of rhetoric is, I suggest, a product of misandry rather than scholarship. Patriarchy has sometimes oppressed women, but has also protected and liberated women: though liberation from patriarchy by patriarchs need not elicit much gratitude but is a matter of historical record. But how to label this third model? As an opposition to patriarchy, the label could be "matriarchy"; but that is too motherly. The "sisterhood" model is too seventies. The "feminist" model might be taken as implying that all feminists are misandrists, or misandristic, (even the words are new, though the phenomenon is not), which they are certainly not. Most feminists are probably pro-equality rather than anti-male; and many male pro-feminists are certainly anti-male. So the most appropriate term seems the "misandric model."

Table 2.1   Five models of gender

1. The Romantic Model
  * Equal but different.
  * Complementary dualism: opposites attract.
  * Plato: two halves theory, yin and yang, couple theory.
  * John Gray: Mars and Venus.
  * Theme: love, and unity in difference: "it's biological."
  * Critics: divorce, violence, hate.

2. Patriarchal Model
  * Contradictory Dualism.
    Male supremacism: patriarchy as oppressive of women:
                               :women as victims of men as villains.
  * Hesiod: Pandora; Genesis: Adam and Eve; Aristotle.
  * Themes: conflict, hierarchy, power, sexism, misogyny.
  * Critics: Patriarchy has also liberated women, and also oppressed men.
    Bipolar status of men: men are also victims.

3. Misandric Model
  * Contradictory Dualism.
  * Reversed values to patriarchy: female moral supremacism.
  * Contemporary gender/radical/feminists:
    Dworkin, French, Solanas, Steinem, Stephenson, etc.
  * Women as morally superior, angelization.
  * Men as villains: pigs, jerks, violent, rapists etc.
  * The new sexism, misandry.
  * NB: Not all feminists misandric; most egalitarian.

4. Postmodern Model: Chaos Theory
  * Humans are biologically bisexual (Darwin) – Biology.
  * Humans are psychologically bisexual (Freud, Jung) – Psychology.
  * Sex roles cultural and variable not biological (Mead) – Anthropology.
  * Gender a performance and a psychic choice (Butler) – Sociology.
  * There are 5 sexes (Fausto-Sterling): intersexuals – Physiology.
  * Gender a personal, elective, medical choice of transexuals – Medicine.
  * Multiple and fluid sexualities: BGLT1 Rights.
  * Differences within genders greater than those between them.
  * Continuum and Bell curve theory.
  * Blurring of dualism: gender a continuum, not binary; doing, not being.

5. Gender/Class/Ethnic Conflict Model
  * 4 + Quadrants: intersectionality theory.
  * Theory of cross-cutting cleavages and multiple identities.
  * Gender, class, race, language, politics, faith etc criss-cross

in later life they may perhaps have a sex change operation or finally recognize their feminine or masculine side. The models are therefore resources, tools or lenses, more or less useful for specific purposes, rather than replicas of society.

Second, whichever model one adopts or prefers is not simply an academic matter, or a question of personal taste; it is also a political choice with social, legal and demographic consequences. Indeed these models deeply influence our intimate relationships, and our relations with other people. The political is extremely personal. But the personal is also highly political, and our own personal experiences tend to be decisive factors in our paradigms: romantic, misogynistic or misandric or humanist. How we construct gender, and which paradigm we select, makes a difference to our lives, as does understanding the differences between them, and the limitations of each model.

The Romantic Model: Love

This is probably the most popular model of gender, and certainly the first. Everyone is born of the physical and probably loving union of a man and a woman – except for the few conceived by rape or turkey-basters or in petri dishes and other forms of the new reproductive technologies. As they grow up, most boys and girls become interested in and attracted to members of the other sex, have sex with them, and most will marry, perhaps more than once and have children. As couples, the two individuals bond and raise their families in their different ways all around the world. The two become one. The fundamental norm is that men and women need each other, desire each other, and are somehow better, and more complete with each other. The two individuals most obviously become one and completely complementary in the act of making love. This is the ultimate unity in duality and unity in difference.

This model is evident in the Christian wedding ceremony when the two become "one flesh." Christ's words are cited, that in marriage "They are no more twain, but one flesh. What therefore God hath joined together, let not man put asunder" (Matthew 19:6).

Wedding invitations mirror this model. One reads: "Two hearts, one love"; and another, adopting a more fiery metaphor, states: "Two flames unite and blend into one". Another asserts: "One love that is shared by two". Certainly the two in one theme of romance is clearly expressed.

This unity is also evident in "the couple syndrome." Individuals lose their identity in the couple: the two individuals become one couple. They become one socially as we invite the couple over for dinner. They are one legally by marriage, and one economically as they share the mortgage, file joint tax returns and share bank accounts (but they revert to two again if they later divorce, and fight over alimony and child support). The couple may even lose some of their individual identities as they share their bodies, beds, house, children, parents and thoughts and perhaps become increasingly emotionally dependent on each other. Emotionally, too, they may become one. In the end they may become one in death, as the one partner dies, and the other sometimes dies very shortly afterwards, of a broken heart, we may surmise; and the couple are buried beside each other.

This romantic model is portrayed with "the happy ending" in countless Hollywood and Walt Disney movies. The top five love stories, in terms of dollars, are *Gone with the Wind* (1939), *Titanic* (1997), *Doctor Zhivago* (1965), *The Graduate* (1967) and *Love Story* (1970). *Brokeback Mountain* was another huge success (Luscombe, 2007). Unfortunately, none of these movies had a happy ending. Sad, but true. The sculpted icon of romance is no doubt Rodin's "The Kiss." Our pop music celebrates this equation of love, sex, marriage perhaps, and happiness "ever after." The Beatles sang interminably: "All you need is love. Love is all you need." Although in fairness we should add that rap is often misogynistic.

The idea of the two sexes as opposite but complementary was first put forward by Plato in the creation myth in the *Symposium*.[2] In the beginning there were three sexes, men, women and mixed, who were descended from the sun, the earth and the moon. They were double what we recognize as humans, with two heads, two sets of genitals, four arms, and four legs and so on. (They must have looked like double-headed spiders or octopi.) They were also ambitious, and they tried "to scale the heights of heaven and set upon the gods." Zeus was extremely angry and sliced them in half. This bisection, according to the story,

> left each half with a desperate yearning for the other, and they ran together and flung their arms around each other's necks, and asked for nothing better than to be rolled into one. (Plato, 190; 1985:543)

It is a charming, as well as brutal, story but it does explain that search for unity which we feel when we are in love and as love deepens, and which we also see all the time in the Arrivals sections at airports. Also it explains both heterosexual love and the homosexual love which was such a conspicuous theme in the life of ancient Athens (Bullough, 1979). Furthermore Plato's ideology is egalitarian: "We are all like pieces of the coins that children break in half for keepsakes . . . and each of us is seeking for the half that will tally with [complete, complement]

---

2   This theory of "the war of opposites" is most ancient, and based on the ancient Greek metaphysics and medicine, Anaximander postulated that the universe consisted of the four elements Water, Air, Earth and Fire, with each at war with their opposites: hot/cold, wet/dry; and as in the universe, so in humanity. Our contemporary terms still reflect these ancient ideas: fiery, earthy, airy, hot-tempered, cold and cold-hearted. The English term for a useless individual, especially a male, is "wet" or "a drip" – but this is not exactly opposed to a dry sense of humour, a dry old stick nor a phlegmatic personality. These metaphysics and psychologies were developed further by Parmenides and especially Pythagoras, who first placed male and female in a 10 point Table of Opposites – which persists today. (See Aristotle, Metaphysics 986; 1984:1559; Guthrie, 1965:77–80; De Crescenzo, 1990:17–22; Synnott, 1993:40–1). Opposites may be complementary, as with Plato's theory, or conflicting, as in humoural theory, and also the patriarchal and misandric ideas about gender.

himself" (Plato, 190; 1985:544) (or herself – a Platonic slip). Some people express this idea of unity by referring to their spouse or partner as "my better half" and referring to themselves as "soul-mates." In this view, the two divisions of humanity are different but equal, and complement each other like yin and yang: which together create the tao, which is the whole, unity and completeness. This in turn is symbolized by the circle of a coin, and the circle of the rings given and exchanged at the wedding ceremony. The ring itself symbolizes eternity, for it has no end. The cynic might add that it just goes round and round in circles; but that demonstrates a failure to appreciate the ideal.

Plato foregrounded the mutuality of desire: the desire "to be rolled into one." Going to bed is one thing, but earning a living and supporting a family is another; and gender complementarity is not only physical and emotional, it is also economic. In Plato's day as quite often today, men and women occupied different domains: domains which were complementary rather than antagonistic. According to this "dual spheres of power" theory, men worked primarily outside the home in the public domain, women primarily inside the home in the private domain. Traditionally men worked to support their wives by paid labour, the wives worked to support their children and their husbands with, largely, unpaid or part-time labour, and together in their different ways each supported the other and their children.

For centuries this has been the typical model of gender relations: mutual interdependence. The man needed the woman for his survival, to enable him to work. The woman needed the man to support her as she supported their children, and him. The children needed both to survive and grow. And the parents needed the children to support them in their old age. This interdependence and reciprocity moved not only horizontally between the genders but also vertically up and down the generations. This *economic* model of gender relations is more prosaic than Plato's *pleasure* model. Love is lovely, but survival is the first imperative in this unromantic view of life. And the secret of survival was role specialization: each sex supreme within its own sphere of power to maximize economic and social advantage in a reciprocal exchange of services.

More recent theorists have tended to argue that the spheres are not equal, that the power is unevenly distributed and that in fact the husband or male is dominant in a patriarchal system of the family. Now, with more women working outside the home the gender rhetoric refers to occupational apartheid, the pink or lace ghetto and, for working mothers, the double load. The interdependence and reciprocity of the romantic model is ignored, and the exploitation and oppression of women by men is asserted – with some truth; but the exploitation and oppression of men is ignored.

Both men and women have always worked. In the past, and still sometimes today, in hunter-gatherer societies, the division of labour was sex-segregated. Even today the division of labour is notable. The ideal wife – "her price is far above rubies" – is described in the Bible with a heavy work load; rising before dawn she shops, cooks, sews, and also buys a field, plants a vineyard and sells linen to local merchants, and "her candle goeth not out by night"; she is also wise, kind, cares for the needy, and is adored by her husband and her children (Proverbs 31:10–31). She must also be exhausted.

The classic description of these specialized sex roles, or segregated sex roles in the more critical term, is Tennyson's poem *The Princess*, which clarifies not only the division of labour but also the traditional hierarchy of patriarchy:

> Man for the field and woman for the hearth:
> Man for the sword and for the needle she:
> Man with the head and woman with the heart:
> Man to command and woman to obey:
> All else confusion.

Much has changed since this nineteenth century male supremacist formulation, not only the command – obey equation, since the second wave of the women's movement, but also the rigidity of these polarized dichotomies. Roles are more fluid now. Yet much remains surprisingly the same. The outside/inside equation still holds up to scrutiny. Even though most men and women work inside, in offices and factories, most of the outside work is done by men: forestry, farming, fisheries, construction, the military, trucking and fire-fighting. The sword/needle equation has some validity, though less than it once did, with more women in the military, and many men in the fashion industry. And the head/heart equation still resonates: women are allowed more emotional latitude, and often decorate their computers, mail-boxes, clothes and necks with hearts everywhere: the symbol of love and the romantic model of gender. Men do not.

Plato was not only a romantic, he was also an egalitarian: possibly the first in history. In *The Republic* Socrates argues that the two sexes "differ only in just this respect that the female bears and the male begets" (454e, 1985:693). He concludes: "Then there is no pursuit of the administrators of a state that belongs to a woman because she is a woman or to a man because he is a man" (455d,e, 1985:694 cf *Laws* 805:1985:1376)

The romantic model is an egalitarian model, and has been from ancient times based on the two legs of the love-pleasure theory of Plato and dual spheres theory epitomized by Tennyson: a union of love and economics. Today, however, the economic model has less utility and validity: women can acquire an education, earn their own livings, do not need men for economic support, raise children alone or with massive state support; and gender relations are closer to Plato's original description of emotional (and physical) need-satisfaction. Anthony Giddens (1999) has referred to the development of "emotional democracy" as the basis of contemporary gender relations.

The most recent and popular theorist of romantic love is John Gray. In his best-selling books, television appearances and his marital therapy franchise, he has argued that men and women are from very different planets – but complementary and mutually attractive planets. His first book in a long series, *Men are from Mars,*

Women are from Venus complements the Platonist "two halves" theory, and the corollaries of yin-yang, public-private, dual spheres theory. Gray echoes Plato's theory of descent from the sun, earth and moon: three cosmic objects, but thought that two planets were sufficient and explained:

> Not only do men and women communicate differently, but they think, feel, perceive, react, respond, love, need and appreciate differently. They almost seem to be from different planets, speaking different languages and needing different nourishment. (1994:5)

Gray's intent is to improve communication between the sexes by holding a mirror up to each gender, and by clarifying the differences so that everyone can see, understand and adjust. He explains that: "Martians value power, competency, efficiency and achievement ... Their sense of self is defined by their ability to achieve results ... They are more interested in 'objects' and 'things' rather than people and feelings." He adds that: "Venusians have different values. They value love, communication, beauty and relationships ... Their sense of self is defined through their feelings and the quality of their relationships" (1994:18). The polarization is everywhere.

While we cannot go into detail summarizing his ideas, anecdotes and suggestions, we can note his dualism: "Men are like rubber bands. When they pull away, they can stretch only so far before they come springing back" (1994:92). "A woman is like a wave. When she feels loved her self-esteem rises and falls in a wave motion" (1994:112). Rubber bands and waves: this is as dualistic as it gets. Mars and Venus; men stretch along the horizontal axis, women rise and fall on a vertical axis; rewards and relationships; power and love; objects and people; fields and hearth; swords and needles; heads and hearts; dualism is everywhere for men and women.

And then, to make it even worse, Martians and Venusians have different methods of resolving their/our problems and feeling good: "To feel better Martians go to their caves to solve problems alone ... to feel better Venusians get together and openly talk about their problems" (Gray, 1994:31).

Gray has been criticized for validating hoary old gender stereotypes, thinking in black and white binary boxes, over-emphasizing gender differences and for attributing all intimacy difficulties in relationships to gender. Responding to these criticisms, Gray notes, following Darwin, Freud and Jung, that we are all Martians *and* Venutians, and that we must honour both; furthermore he suggests that there are Venutian males and Martian females, and thirdly: that women become more Martian as they adopt more provider roles. Yet the success of Gray's books indicate the popularity of the complementary dualistic model of gender.

The validity and utility of this romantic model of gender relations is evidenced in part by its popularity: the yin-yang symbolism, better half and couple theory, the flame of love, the hugs and kisses and sex – and its persistence from Plato to Gray.

Yet this romantic and egalitarian model clearly does not explain everything about gender relations. There is misogyny, misandry, divorce, rape, and there is gender violence. Love can turn to hate. Relations between men and women and the family have changed more in the last 100 years than in the last two millennia; so it is necessary to critique this model and to consider some of the other prevailing views.

First, the rise of the welfare state has contributed to the decline of the traditional family, and to changed gender relations. The compassionate state has assumed many of the burdens of the family formerly assumed by various family members at different stages of the life cycle. This includes the care of children, the sick, the old, the handicapped, the abused, the divorced, etc. The strength of the economic bonds uniting husbands and wives, and parents and children has been weakened, for better or for worse (Tiger, 1999).

Second, the division of labour has changed and women now constitute almost half of the full-time paid labour force in North America and Western Europe. In about 30% of the families in the U.S. the wife earns more than the husband (Tyre and McGinn, 2003). The old structure of reciprocity, interdependence and "dual spheres" has been fractured in the industrialized post-modern world. This has contributed to women's empowerment and broader options in life. The rise of the welfare state and the changed division of labour have contributed to dramatically changed gender roles – indeed almost to their abolition. The balance of power in the family and the state has therefore shifted substantially.

Thirdly, high divorce rates since the 1960s have facilitated the breakdown of the nuclear family, and the increase in the blended families and serial families, with many types of fathers and mothers. Divorce is now more likely to part us than death. Realistically this should be reflected in the marriage vows: "to have and to hold until death or divorce do us part, whichever comes first". Divorce of course evidences the limitations of the romantic model; as does domestic violence. Furthermore many couples are deciding not to get married but to live in common-law unions. Others talk about "starter marriages" (Paul, 2002).[3] The bonds of love unfortunately can and do morph into bondage.

Fourthly, the new reproductive technologies are not very romantic. Test-tube babies conceived in petri dishes, in vitro fertilization, sperm and ovum donors, selected from catalogues with price lists attached, and surrogate mothers…all this has changed the biology and emotion of parenting. A child may now have five parents, three of them anonymous.

Finally, a feminist critique of this love model is that it totally neglects the power differentials between the male and the female. Equality in romantic

---

3   Starter marriages or drive-through marriages are defined as those first marriages lasting for less than five years with no children. Pamela Paul, a journalist whose own marriage lasted for less than a year, interviewed 60 people for this. About 25% of first marriages "fail" within two years. This book is a must for anyone thinking of getting married and it includes a list of risk factors.

relations between unequals is, in this view, impossible: a contradiction in terms. This humorously portrayed in a *New Yorker* cartoon. Two women are chatting as one says to the other: "Sex brought us together, but gender drove us apart."

Despite the problems, however, the model has validity. After the happy couple have "flung their arms around each other's necks, and ... rolled into one," they often do marry, have children, and stay together. And even if they divorce, many men and women marry again, sometimes the very same person from whom they have recently been divorced. So the "romantic" and "conflict" models of gender may follow each other in sequence; or not.

The Patriarchal Model: Male Supremacism

The romantic model of gender relations is based on the assumption of gender equality. The patriarchal model is based on the assumption of male superiority. And the extreme feminist model, which has emerged recently, is based on the assumption of female superiority. All three models persist today, and I suggest that all three are useful in some respects, and flawed in others. The difference between the patriarchal model and the the misandric model which follows lies, not only in the actual gender structure of society but also in the *perception* of that structure. The gender structure of any particular country is what it is; but how it is evaluated may vary considerably. Gender relations may be evaluated as oppressive of women, or as liberative of women; or as even *more* oppressive of men, by some criteria; or as oppressive of both men and women. They may be thought of as making hare-like progress towards gender equality, or as tortoise-slow, or as having passed gender-equality and now oppressing men. And so it goes, depending on the nations under consideration and the ideologies.

Patriarchy is conventionally defined in such terms as the rule of women by men; and in a parody of Lincoln's Gettysburg address: government of men by men and for men; and as ideologically oppressive, suppressive and depressive of women. Marilyn French is more extreme: "I believe patriarchy began and spread as a war against women" (1992:14).

Beliefs are one thing. Reality is another. None the less, male supremacism was foundational in both the Graeco-Roman and the Judaeo-Christian traditions. Both the Pandora myth in Hesiod, and the Adam and Eve myth in Genesis, assert the inferiority of the female to the male. These two creation myths not only allege the chronological priority of the male but also their biological and moral supremacy. So the two myths coincided in their messages and reinforced each other, while at the same time legitimating the contemporary male-dominant (patriarchal) social structures.[4]

---

4   Genesis actually has two creation myths, the familiar one of Adam and Eve: Eve created after Adam and from his rib with the purpose of being his "help," but ultimately betraying him (thereby proving her dominance, according to some); but the other story is

Although Plato was relatively gender-egalitarian in the "Republic," Aristotle was not. In his "Politics" (1254b) he argued that: "The male is by nature superior and the female inferior; and the one rules and the other is ruled; this principle, of necessity, extends to all mankind" (1984:1990). Not only did he rank the two sexes, with males superior to females, but in his "Economics" (1343–4) he explained that they are also opposite in many dimensions. So, he argued: "The woman is as it were an impotent male" and "We must look upon the female character as being a sort of natural deficiency" (Generation of Animals 728, 737; 1984:1130, 1144).

Aristotle's theory of male superiority deeply influenced the Christian Church right through to St Thomas Aquinas and up to the Reformation. The Church itself is widely regarded as highly patriarchal and by some as misogynistic: in its theology with the male godhead of Father and Son; in its hierarchy of the male Papacy, episcopacy and priesthood; in some of its teaching including St Augustine, St Albert the Great, and St Thomas Aquinas (Badinter, 1989; Ranke-Heinemann, 1990). The "Witches Bull" of 1484 and the volume *Malleus Maleficarum* in 1486 which inaugurated the European Witch Hunt was particularly obnoxious (Trevor-Roper, 1969).

Paul famously reminded men and women of the divine hierarchy and the gender hierarchy:

> I want you to understand that Christ is supreme over every man, the husband is supreme over his wife, and God is supreme over Christ … A man has no need to cover his head, because he reflects the image and glory of God. But woman reflects the glory of man; for man was not created from woman, but woman from man. Nor was man created for woman's sake, but woman was created for man's sake. (1 Corinthians 11:3, 7–9 cf. Ephesians 5:22–33)

St Peter reminded women to "be in subjection to your husbands" and abjured husbands to give "honour unto the wife, as unto the weaker vessel, and as being heirs together of the grace of life" (1 Peter 3:1, 7).[5]

Conversely, Paul also reminded his listeners of the unity of all Christians in Christ: "There is neither Jew nor Greek, there is neither bond nor free, there is neither male nor female: for ye are all one in Christ Jesus" (Galatians 3:28). This doctrine of *spiritual equality* was a powerful paradigm shift in the Roman Empire

---

prior: "So God created man in his own image, in the image of God created by him; male and female created he them. And God blessed them … And God saw every thing that he had made, and, behold, it was very good" (Genesis 1:27–8,31). This story asserts gender equality.

5   Feminist theologians who have criticized Christian patriarchal theory and practice include Mary Daly, 1975, 1978; Rosemary Reuther, 1983; Uta Ranke-Heinemann, 1990; and others. Criticism from within the ranks of the church is particularly powerful, though I believe all three have now left the church. Some feminists suggested that if the man was the head of the wife and family, then the woman is the neck that turns the head.

which, like the Greek before it, was based on slavery. Christian fundamentalists however cherry-pick their quotations to support their views, sexist or egalitarian.

These male supremacist attitudes have persisted and reappear in the work of such philosophers as Rousseau, Schopenhauer, Nietzsche and Sartre (Synnott, 1993; O'Faolain and Martines, 1973; Holland, 2006). Indeed in 1998 the Southern Baptist Convention reiterated these views and included in its statement of beliefs the declaration that a woman should "submit herself graciously" to her husband's leadership and that a husband should "provide for, protect and lead his family." (It also states that both have "equal worth" before God). Some women loved this. Some did not (Niebuhr, 1998).

Misogyny is virtually a world-wide phenomenon according to the anthropologist David Gilmore (2001). This might be attributed to the social requirement of an ideology to legitimate dominance. Sexism will do this, as will racism and fascism in their domains. Gilmore argues that misogyny is rooted in Buddhism, Christianity, Hinduism, Islam, and Shinto, and has existed in almost every culture explored by anthropologists. And yet he recognizes that: "Everywhere we look, men are sorely divided in their feelings toward women" (2001:219); and he says in the beginning that the guys he listened to in bars in Spain "tipsily denounced females as deceivers and cheats, valuable only as sex objects." But they would also "vociferously idolize women, especially their own mothers and sisters, praising them as saintly, sacrificing and pure" (2001:xii). Even in Gilmore's terms, therefore, the issue is not so much misogyny as ambivalence – a very different issue. Men have difficulties with women? Of course! Women have difficulties with men? Of course! As the old joke goes: if it has four wheels or a penis, you're gonna have problems with it. That said, both *sexisms* are problematic, once they are recognized. Equally, men's desire for women, and love of women and work for women is probably a more conspicuous feature of all cultures through history than misogyny – a point Gilmore does not discuss.

Certainly there has been and still is much injustice; and worldwide women have protested injustice and demanded their rights. In the "west," feminists have protested against job discrimination and occupational apartheid, political disenfranchisement, wife battering, gynocide, the objectification of women, glass walls and glass ceilings, sexual harassment, rape, income inequality, under-representation in Parliaments and the U.S. Senate and Congress. The list is endless. Feminists have travelled back in time and across space to condemn misogyny: the witch-hunts from the 15th to the 18th century, suttee in India, the lotus in China, female genital mutilation in parts of Africa and the Islamic Middle East. Indeed some believe that there is a *war* against women (French, 1992; Faludi, 1992; Canadian Committee on the Status of Women, 1991).

Most recently some have suggested that not only Christianity but also Islam is misogynistic – for the practice of clitoridectomy, the ease of male divorce, the double standards in the penalties for adultery, and the practice of veiling. The Taliban in Afghanistan were thought to be the epitome of this sexism. Others have argued that the Quran does not condone sexism, and is indeed egalitarian and protective of women. Policies vary from one Muslim country to another, as do interpretations of the Quran (Esposito, 2003:160–76; Bahramitash, 2005). Islamophobia seems to be the latest form of racism, sometimes in tandem with sexism. The Iranian-born Azar Nafisi, author of the best-selling *Reading Lolita in Tehran* manages to insult both Islam and men quoting her friend who parodied Jane Austen: "It is a truth universally acknowledged that a Muslim man, regardless of his fortune, must be in want of nine-year-old virgin wife" (2003:257).

The patriarchal model of gender relations, like the previous romantic model, is already somewhat passé, for three reasons. First, it has been by-passed by the fresh gender issues of postmodernity (see below for Chaos theory). Second it has been critiqued, especially by anthropologists, for essentialism, for homogenizing women and men, for denying agency and autonomy to women, for failing to understand power and powers, for equating separate sex roles as oppression rather than specialization and interdependence, and for privileging politics over scholarship. This is not to deny that political, economic, military and religious power through most of history has been exercised mostly by men, despite the many powerful queens in the past and the many female presidents, prime ministers and chancellors in the recent past and present. But to homogenize republics, democracies, monarchies and dictatorships, capitalist, fascist and communist as simply "patriarchies" is not very helpful for understanding gender relations and the politics of gender. It is too blunt an instrument.

Furthermore, the plays from Aristophanes and Euripides to Shakespeare, and the tales of Chaucer, Boccaccio and Rabelais up to the present, and Lilith, Eve and Judith, do not suggest the quiet, passive, subservient, weak and "oppressed" women of male misogyny and supremacism. Nor do the female heroines and alpha-females throughout history suggest a war against women (Chapters 3 and 7). Actually, I suggest that there are more deadly wars against men, and that this mysterious "patriarchy" – i.e. any sort of rule or social order – both oppresses *and* liberates both men and women.

Elizabeth Badinter, a distinguished French philosopher and feminist, announced two decades ago that: "In most Western democracies, the patriarchal system has received the *coup de grâce* in the last two decades ... The power of the father and husband is becoming extinct. Men's ideological, social and political domination has been seriously eroded." And she announced "the death of patriarchy" (1989:130). But who killed patriarchy? If it ever existed in misogynistic mode, presumably it was the alleged patriarchs, who could not have been quite as oppressive as they have been painted.

Fourth, since the Enlightenment and especially since the Second Wave, these western democracies have not so much oppressed women (to the degree that separate sex roles constituted oppression) as gradually *liberated* women. Government, corporations, and the medical, legal and academic establishments opened their doors at the same time as women, freed from biology by the pill, demanded access. Women were given access, peacefully, in a momentous transfer of power. But it was the hegemonic men who implemented these changes. It was only they who had the power to do it, in response to demand certainly, but nonetheless, credit where credit is due. This was not women as the enemy, as patriarchy theorists imply, but humanism. It is time to set the historical record straight.

And women are still afforded special protection by a battery of recent legislation which institutionalize gender inequality before the law (Weiss and Young, 1996). Some consider this fair. Others, not so much.

The conventional feminist portrait of women as victims and men as patriarchal villains does articulate some truths for some countries at some times, but not the whole truth. Other portraits may be drawn. There are other sides to the coin, and to patriarchy: less publicized, certainly, but no less cogent. The flip side of patriarchy is the valorization and privileging of women, and the victimization of men. Women are often victims of men in various ways, and some men are certainly villains; but women are also privileged in numerous ways, and men are also victims, and women are also villains. Furthermore both men and women may be heroes. A reality check of gender shows a far more complex picture of men and women than the standard ideology of women good, men bad; and woman = victim, man = villain and oppressor.

One of the most remarkable achievements in the last century was the massive, peaceful and rapid transfer of power from men to women, and the expansion of women's rights. This has been accomplished in a generation. It was only 60 years from the granting of the suffrage in the U.K. to the election of Margaret Thatcher in 1979, and her re-election twice more. This was also patriarchy in action: in the U.K., Canada, New Zealand, Ireland, India, Pakistan and dozens of other countries around the world where women have been elected Prime Ministers or Presidents. (See Chapter 6.)

To explore the origins and development of this process we need to go back in time, and consider the context of changing gender relations within the broader historical trends. During the Enlightenment, the concepts of equality, liberty, justice and rights were endlessly debated by philosophers like Jean-Jacques Rousseau, revolutionaries like Thomas Paine and conservatives like Edmund Burke. This was, initially a challenge to the old orders of colony, monarchy, church, slavery and, ultimately, gender. Rousseau asserted in the opening sentence of *The Social Contract* (1762): "Man is born free; and everywhere he is in chains" (1963:3). The doctrine was revolutionary, and in many social dimensions.

The American Revolution overthrew British colonial rule and the monarchy. The new U.S. Constitution declared: "We hold these truths to be self-evident; that all men are created equal." Shortly afterwards the French Revolution overthrew the monarchy and the Catholic Church with the slogans: "Liberté, Egalité, Fraternité." The Constituent Assembly proclaimed the Declaration of the Rights of Man in 1789 and sent Louis XVI and his Queen to the guillotine in 1793; and the Catholic Church was disestablished.

With the overthrow of traditional colonial, royal and religious power systems, it was but a short step to overthrow traditional gender power systems, and to demand gender equality. Olympe des Gouges, a member of the Constituent Assembly, published a Declaration of the Rights of Woman in 1791: "Woman is born free and her rights are the same as those of man." This echo of Rousseau, who had inspired both revolutions, did not suffice to save her life. She was guillotined during the Terror (O'Faolain and Martines, 1973:307).

In England Mary Wollstonecraft was also moved by the double standards by which freedom was expanded for males but not for females. She published *A Vindication of the Rights of Woman* (1792) demanding "JUSTICE for one-half of the human race" (1985:89). Challenging received opinion, she insisted that woman "was not created to be the solace of man," but for perfection, truth, reason and God; she dismissed the notion that women were created for men as a "poetical story" – and she challenged patriarchy: "I love man as my fellow; but his sceptre, real or usurped, extends not to me" (1985:142, 109, 121). She deplored "the tyranny of man" and looked forward to the day when women will be "free in a physical, moral and civil sense" (1985:318–9).

Meanwhile the Anti-Slavery movement was gaining momentum, especially in Haiti which successfully revolted and gained independence from France in 1805, and in the U.K. where slavery was abolished by Act of Parliament in 1834, effective in 1838. The values of equality and liberty, fought for so strenuously in the American, French, Irish (which failed) and Haitian revolutions, as well as numerous slave revolts in the Caribbean, the United States and South America were quickly being realized. Similarly the rights of children, women and workers were also increasingly being realized in protective legislation, in the rhetoric of Karl Marx and Friedrich Engels, in the rise of unions and eventually, in the U.K., the emergence of the Labour Party. The abolitionist, women's and worker's movements all articulated the same persuasive values of the Enlightenment, and still do.

Wollstonecraft's demands for justice and freedom and equality of political, legal, educational, familial, and civil rights were echoed in the United States at the First Women's Rights Convention held at Seneca Falls in 1848. The Declaration of Sentiments echoed the U.S. Declaration of Independence:

> We hold these truths to be self-evident: that all men and women are created equal ... The history of mankind is a history of repeated injuries and usurpations on the part of man towards woman, having in direct object the establishment of absolute tyranny over her.

"Tyranny": the precise word which had been used earlier by Wollstonecraft. Within 75 years from the Seneca Falls Convention the franchise had been extended to include women in the United States (1920), Canada (1918), the United Kingdom (1919), and in some countries much earlier: New Zealand (1893), Australia (1902), Finland (1906), Norway (1913). In other countries the suffrage was granted much later: Japan (1945), Italy (1945), France (1944), Kenya (1963), and Switzerland (1971).

The democratization and liberation of the U.S. from colonial power, of France from monarchical power, and of the slaves from slavery; the expansion of the franchise to men and later to women; the liberation and decolonization movements worldwide, across Africa, the Caribbean, and around the world – and still continuing – this has been an amazing process.

The First Wave of the Women's movement, the Union movement, World War I, the Great Depression and the rise of the Welfare State, World War II, the Holocaust – huge waves of social change were crashing on shores worldwide, both malign and benign, and the malign generating the benign.

Ultimately the Enlightenment was crystallized in the foundation of the United Nations after World War II, in the Universal Declaration of Human Rights (1948). Article 1 states: "All human beings are born free and equal in dignity and human rights." This was an egalitarian and libertarian assertion by the "patriarchy."

The old idea was that patriarchy oppressed women – forgetting that whites (women and men) oppressed non-whites, that the rich (women and men) oppressed the poor, that people of all monotheistic faiths oppress each other, and so on. This is "patriarchy" as myth.

The new idea is that patriarchy and men have liberated women. Camille Paglia was, I believe, the first to make this point: "it is patriarchal society that has freed me as a woman. It is capitalism that has given me the leisure to sit at this desk writing this book" (1991:37–8). But what is transparently obvious to her seems to be anathema to others.

That women have succeeded in "male-dominated" societies and occupations is a tribute to the women, and also to the men – who are not usually misogynistic but love their wives, their mothers, their daughters and possibly other women too. Men in patriarchy have not clung to power, fought to maintain privilege, asserted old doctrines of male supremacism, but have democratically shared power, transferred power, even at some cost to themselves. In this view, patriarchy has perhaps in the past been oppressive of women but it has certainly, especially in the democracies, contributed substantially to women's empowerment and liberation.

Titanic: Men's love for women, chivalry, and privileging of women was poignantly demonstrated in the loss of *R.M.S. Titanic* off the coast of Newfoundland in 1912. This occurred at the height of capitalism and at the apex of patriarchy; women were so "oppressed" that they did not even have the vote in either the U.S. or the U.K. Yet 80% of the male passengers and crew, some of them the richest and most powerful men from two continents, died so that 70% of the women and children could survive. This male self-sacrifice exemplified the motto: "Women and children first" (Kuntz, 1998). This was patriarchy.

9/11: On September 11, 2001, when the two World Trade Center towers were hit by terrorists, 343 NYC firefighters and 60 police officers lost their lives helping to rescue thousands of office workers (*Time* 11.9.02:58). Their heroism in the line of duty was widely recognized, praised and rewarded. This sort of male heroism happens every day – all the firefighters and police officers were male – but this *is* patriarchy. Both the *Titanic* and the World Trade Center disasters indicate the flaw in the patriarchal model of female oppression so popularized by so many feminists.

The draft: women are exempt from compulsory military service virtually everywhere, except in Israel, but even there they are exempt from combat duty. This privileging of women by men is curious, for it is not oppressive of women; indeed it is liberating. Yet it is lethally oppressive of men. In sum, men have their duty to serve, and women have the right not to serve.

War: In World War I over 8 million men were killed in combat and another 21 million men wounded. In World War II about 20 million men were killed in action, and about the same number wounded. Civilian casualties are estimated at about half that number (*Encyclopedia Britannica*, 1997: Vol. 29:1023). If this is patriarchy, it is hardly government "*for*" men: it is remarkably lethal to men and protective of women and children. The same pattern of predominantly male military casualties is typical of other wars with far fewer casualties: the Korean War, the Falklands War, the Gulf War, the Arab-Israeli wars, the four India-Pakistan wars, and so on. In discussing victimization, we should be aware of male as well as female victims.[6] If this is patriarchy, it is extremely expensive in men's lives and deaths and injuries.

The privilege value of being female is almost universal. It underpins the examples which valorize women's lives over men's, and ironically this in a supposedly patriarchal society! Men devalue themselves or sacrifice themselves; and this costs them their lives – not only on the *Titanic* and in the World Trade Center and in war but throughout their shorter lives. Men spend most of their lives working to support their wives and children, *not* to oppress them; and sometimes give their lives to protect them. For a number of reasons sometimes (not always) related to these male roles of work, defence, self-sacrifice and altruism, men live shorter lives than women. This is the other, hidden side of "patriarchy": forgotten for 40 years.

In sum, although much of the male *philosophy* of the female has been relatively negative, much of the male *practice* has been, and still is, relatively positive. Patriarchy has oppressed women; it has also liberated women. It has also oppressed men – so it is not exactly government of men by men and for men. Patriarchy, as traditionally defined or invented, is a myth. Indeed, the three principle fallacies of conventional feminist wisdom on patriarchy are the failure to note 1) how patriarchy has liberated women, 2) how patriarchy has victimized men and 3) how in class and race (and other) ethnic systems, women in the dominant group like

---

6   Some of my resolutely feminist students and colleagues respond: "But it is men who started the wars!" The implication being that a) it is all their fault; and b) that if women were in charge, we would all live at peace. In fact, however, it is whoever is in power who start wars; in the past this was usually men – but Elizabeth I, Isabella of Spain, Boadicea, Joan of Arc and others fought a few wars in their time; more recently so did Margaret Thatcher, Benazir Bhutto, Golda Meir, and others (Fraser, 1989). The critical factor is power rather than gender.

their menfolk, have oppressed women as well as men in the subordinate groups. Indeed this failure to recognize the racism of white and middle-class women, and their oppression of the Other, rankles among many feminists (hooks, 2004; Bahramitash, 2005). Women also victimize women in this so-called patriarchy. The conventional feminist wisdom that societies are patriarchies, and that patriarchy is oppressive of women has some truth-value, but not much.

The Misandric Model: Female Supremacism

Accepting an Emmy for a TV role, Sally Field announced: "Let's face it. If the mothers ruled the world, there would be no god—"(Fox censored the rest, but the audience heard "damn wars in the first place") (*Time* 1 October 2007:13). The moral supremacy of women is widely asserted and believed these days.

That same month *Cosmopolitan* featured an advertisement for Trojan contraceptives: nine pigs are seated in a bar with three women, who are looking either distraught or bored; a smiling man and a smiling woman are spotlighted with the caption: "Evolve. Choose the one who uses a condom every time" (October, 2007:139). The message is clear: nine out of 10 men are pigs.

Hillary Clinton recently argued that the media treated her more harshly because of her gender than they treated Barack Obama because of his race: "It does seem as though the press at least is not bothered by the incredible vitriol that has been engendered by comments and reactions of people who are nothing but misogynists" (Safire, 2008). Men, presumably. Is this misandry?

The Second Wave of the Women's movement originated in part in the Civil Rights movement, beginning with Rosa Parks and Martin Luther King, in part in the Peace movement in opposition to the Vietnam War in the United States and in the Ban the Bomb Peace movement in the United Kingdom. These mass protests over several years set the stage.

At the same time, political emancipation did not create economic equality, and many women began to see themselves as (still) victims of male power and gender inequality. Again, the thesis of male supremacism generated its antithesis of female supremacism; and male sexism generated the reaction of female sexism. Misogny created misandry.

The extension of the suffrage to women was one turning point in gender relations. This first wave demanded equal *rights* and political power and, at least in the case of Wollstonecraft, was explicitly premised on love. The second turning point was the pill which was marketed in the 1950s. This resulted immediately in a rapid decline in fertility rates, an increase of women in the labour force, a dramatic shift in the balance of power in the family and, as new divorce legislation was passed, an equally dramatic rise in the divorce rates.

The third turning point was the Second Wave of the Women's movement: distinct both in ideology and in practice from the first wave. Christina Hoff Sommers (1995) makes the distinction between the "equity feminism" of the first wave and the "gender feminism" of the second wave: characterized by demands for "liberation", power not equity, identity politics, and more by a sense of victimization, entitlement and even hate than by any sense of love (see Chapter 4).

Events moved swiftly. Simone de Beauvoir's *The Second Sex* (1949; 1953 in English) was followed by Betty Friedan's *The Feminine Mystique* (1963), which was hugely popular, then the formation of the National Organization of Women (NOW) in 1965. 1968 saw the mass protest against the Miss World Beauty Pageant in Atlantic City. Protesting the objectification and (alleged) exploitation of the female body for visual and commercial purposes, the women threw articles of make-up and beautification into the "Freedom Trash Can" as symbols of female servitude.

Two distinct processes enlivened these developments: the demonization of men and the angelization of women. The first became evident in the common phrase of the seventies describing men as "male chauvinist pigs" – a theme that persists up to today as we saw in *Cosmopolitan*, and as misogynists, war-mongers and oppressive of women. This was not Wollstonecraft's view: she rejected male protectionism and chivalry; the oppression theme only emerges in the 1848 Seneca Falls Declaration. Nor did Wollstonecraft consider men her inferiors but her equals. This changed too.

An early example of this female supremacism was coined by Maria Montessori, the Italian sociologist and famous educator: "Perhaps ... the reign of women is approaching, when the enigma of her anthropological *superiority* will be deciphered. Woman was always the custodian of human sentiment, morality and honor" (in Gould, 1981:107. Emphasis added).

More recent examples include the rich domain of popular culture. Indeed our first ideas about gender may be learned from nursery rhymes:

> What are little boys made of?
> Slugs and snails and puppy dog's tails.
> What are little girls made of?
> Sugar and spice and all things nice.

Boys are taught early on that they are not nice. How sad. *Newsweek* (28.5.90:62) asserted the superiority of women in a lead article:

> Women, after all, are not a big problem. Our society does not suffer from burdensome amounts of empathy and altruism or a plague of nurturance. The problem is men – or, more accurately, maleness.

In the 1990s the "Battle of the Sexes" became the "War Against Women" – an entirely different concept, and much sharper. The phrase first gained wide currency in Susan Faludi's *Backlash* (1992), which was subtitled *The Undeclared War Against Women*. This was a critique of the media's portrayal of feminism.

Faludi argued that the mainstream media was anti-feminist and was also guilty of misrepresenting feminism, its goals and ideals, and so was waging war against women – but a metaphorical war. Hyperbole sells. The real wars are against men.

Marilyn French's *The War Against Women* (1992) escalated the conflict further. Arguing that the war against women is not just media bias, she catalogues a list of horrors that are inflicted on women: female infanticide, clitoridectomy, foot-binding, suttee, the range of systemic discrimination in money, politics, law and religion, and the ever-present physical violence. This was as powerful an indictment of men as *villains* as her earlier work *The Women's Room* (1978) had been a powerful description of women as victims – but the two portrayals are not merely different sides of the same coin but an escalation of conflict from female victimization to the demonization of the male.[7]

The *U.S. News and World Report*, a journal not noted for its feminism, ran its cover and lead article with the banner headline: "The War against Women: women are falling further behind in country after country – and men like it that way" (28.3.94). The "war against women" was now front page news.

In Canada the brutal massacre of 14 female students by Marc Lépine at a Montreal university in December 1989 – he shouted that he hated feminists – galvanized the nation. The Canadian Committee on the Status of Women submitted a report to the Federal Government entitled *The War Against Women* (1991). The massacre was discussed, and also the 119 women murdered by their husbands or partners in 1989. And a series of recommendations were suggested to the Government which in the following year in turn instituted a zero-tolerance policy against violence against women and established a National Panel on violence against women. There was no discussion of a policy of zero-tolerance for violence against men nor any concern for violence by women – which was, and is, usually assumed to be justified, or is ignored (Walker, 1979; Miles, 1991; Stephenson, 1995; etc.).

This was followed by the federally inaugurated Canadian Panel on Violence against Women. This report also ignored violence by women and also ignored men as the majority of victims of violence. It was a million dollar opportunity lost to

---

7   These feminists have followed Hobbes, Darwin, Spenser and Nietzsche in their conflict paradigms of life. Where Hobbes had stated that: "During the time men live without a common power to keep them in awe, they are in that condition which is called war; and such a war, as is of every man, against every man ... and the life of man, solitary, poor, nasty, brutish and short (Pt. 1, 13; 1960:81–2). Nietzsche declared that: "The free man is a warrior" (1977:271). Furthermore, "Life is essentially appropriation, injury, overpowering of the strange and weaker, suppression, severity, imposition of one's own forms, incorporation and, at the least and mildest, exploitation" (1977:229). Both Hobbes and Nietzsche saw a war of all against all, rather than a war against women or a class war, or a race war, or a holy war, or the wars against poverty or drugs. Fundamental is the Darwinian struggle for the survival of the fittest in the evolutionary species war. There are many wars.

break the stereotypes of women as victims and men as villains. Instead the Report reinforced them.

By now a few activists and the media had created a moral panic which influenced the Violence against Women Acts in both the United States and Canada. The totally laudable effort to end or diminish violence against women was deeply flawed in its apparent assumption that one could do this while ignoring the broader problems of violence *by* women and violence by men against *men*. The Panel also ignored the fact that such violence is committed by a very small sector of the population. It also ignored the fact that deaths by homicide are few compared to deaths by suicide, smoking and accidents. The consequence therefore was an escalated demonization of men and a misrepresentation of reality.

These portraits of women as innocent victims and of men as guilty – the angelization of women and the demonization of men – have created the feminization of the deity and the deification of women. Having infantilized women as victims needing special legislative protection, clearly some counter-balance was necessary. This came both from therapists and theologians.

In her *Goddesses in Every Woman* (1985) Jean Bolen explores the pantheon of Greek goddesses as emblematic of different female personality types today. She adopts the Jungian notion that God is immanent rather than transcendent, i.e. within the self and indeed *is* the self rather than outside the self as "*He*" is so often imagined. The discussion of these goddesses is no doubt enhanced by our appreciation of the sacrosanctity of the time-tested Ancient Wisdom; and Bolen does not labour the obvious point that these creations of the male Greek imagination might not be entirely appropriate for women today – any more than Aristotle.

Feminist theologians have insisted that a male God worshipped in a patriarchal faith which does not accept the biological or spiritual equality of women and forbids women the rights to ordination and to administer the sacraments is not an appropriate vehicle for feminine salvation. The message may be divine but the secular institution is deeply flawed, in this view. Furthermore the principles of Birth, Creativity and Love are universally conceptualized as female in the Western tradition, as are Mother Earth and Mother Nature – now conceptualized as Gaia, the first mother in Hesiod's work, but not a very lovable character. The works of Mary Daly (1975, 1978), Rosemary Reuther (1983) and Susan Badinter (1989) have been particularly important in this regard. Though we are still stuck with the anthropomorphic baggage of gods who have to be either male or female.

So the gods change sex according to the political needs of the decade, and ancient theology is replaced by feminist ecology as the guiding light for life.

The divinization of women and the feminization of divinity is complemented by a third theme of wildness, freedom and action. Theology was complemented by history in Antonia Fraser's *Warrior Queens* (1989). She discussed the lives of famous warriors: Boadicea, Joan of Arc, Cleopatra, Elizabeth I, Catherine the Great of Russia, Isabella of Spain, but also less well known women: Zenobia of Palmyra who fought the Romans, the Rani of Jhansi who fought the British in nineteenth century India, Tamara Queen of Georgia in the twelfth century, and others. In the same vein but on a different continent was Margaret Truman's *Women of Courage* (1976): portraits of American women.

Then psychology followed history. In *The Hero Within*, Carol Pearson (1989) offered six friendly archetypes by which women particularly, but also men, may live their lives. Following and developing C.G. Jung and Joseph Campbell within a feminist framework, she suggests that we all can be heroes, and that the (male) warrior is only one of many heroic types. She discusses six: the Innocent, the Orphan, the Wanderer, the Warrior, the Martyr and the Magician. It is both a very personal and also a spiritual psychology, but a couple of sentences are germane to our topic: "I know women who see men as either potential rescuers or villains, so most of the men they find usually fall into the latter category ... [When they develop] their more masculine side (i.e. self-sufficiency and courage), suddenly they discover men who are neither rescuers nor villains, but people just like themselves, and rather nice people at that!" (1989:135).

Mythology followed psychology with another best-seller. In *Women Who Run with the Wolves* (over a million copies sold, the cover says), Clarissa Pinkola Estes (1992) has offered a selection of stories mostly from European mythology to counterbalance the old Greek myths from Hesiod, Homer, Plato and the rest. The selection is obviously intended to maximize female empowerment and to reinforce the women's movement, which is fair enough: it has to sell and it is not an academic study of women in myth but an ideological work. The title is particularly ironic, for wolves are quintessentially a *male* animal: carnivorous, wild, violent, believed to be very dangerous and in the old days shot on sight with a bounty on their heads, just like the villains in the Wild West. So Estes capsized the old view of women as passive, domestic, mothering, nurturing, loving and so on, and painted a new portrait of women as wolves, indeed as stereotypically *male*! This used to be the vision which they totally rejected. Now it is a vision of choice. Dances can get very tangled. Formerly wolf = male = bad; now wolf = female = good.

Feminists have now begun to appropriate the old myth of men as wolves: aggressive and carnivorous; but also the myths of men as warriors and even as gods. So women are morphing into the warriors and wolves which earlier generations had condemned as the dark side (or typical) of men. And women were demanding that men be Sensitive New Age Guys. So the dance continues as partners switch sides.

It used to be that men were being urged to calm down, grow up, change and generally to be a New Man. Now women are being advised to find the "goddess within" or even the "wild wolf within" – and to admire the female warrior. Prescriptions for happiness seem to change at light speed.

A final theme in the new feminism is that of power. Naomi Wolf was the apostle of victimization in her bestseller *The Beauty Myth* (1990), in which she presented women as victims of Hollywood and the fashion and advertising industries with disastrous consequences for women in terms of low self-esteem, low achievement levels and an epidemic of anorexia. She was, I think, all wrong (see Sommers, 1995 for a brilliant critique), but it was interesting and it sold well. We always want to blame someone else for our sorry state. In *Fire with Fire* (1993), however, a far more aggressive title, Wolf flips her politics, and claims to inaugurate the third wave of the women's movement replacing the old "Victim Feminism" with the new "Power Feminism."

These fresh, new portraits of women and the developments in the women's movement(s) have an immense impact on our personal identities and also on popular culture. And Hollywood and Feminism intersect.

In recent years there has been a spate of movies portraying women as action heroes – or totally empowered, in the movement jargon. This re-construction of women from usually victims to action heroes began perhaps with *Terminator* (1984), and *Aliens* (1986), escalated with the more controversial *Thelma and Louise* (1991) – a reverse role western, except for the suicides. It continued with *To Die For* (1995) in which Nicole Kidman plays a woman who plans the murder of her husband, and *Eye for an Eye* (1995), the ultimate revenge movie as the mother avenges the rape and murder of her daughter by planning the death of the killer, and executing the plan. In *G.I. Jane* (1997) Demi Moore is in the Navy Seals doing one-armed push-ups. And the action heroes continue with Angelina Jolie saving the world in *Lara Croft: Tomb Raider* (2003) in some fetching outfits. Likewise Milla Jovovich in the *Resident Evil* series and Kate Beckinsale in the *Underworld* series.

Meanwhile the men are being feminized in *Forgetting Sarah Marshall* (2008), *Made of Honor* (2008) and *Failure to Launch* (2006). They persist as action heroes of course, and as villains, but the feminization of men and the masculinization of women are new. The real villains, serial killers Aileen Wuornos and Karla Homolka were portrayed in *Monster* (2003), for which Charlize Theron won an Oscar, and *Karla* (2004). The movie presentations of women as evil, which perhaps originated in such cartoonish figure as the wicked witch of the west and the wicked queen in *Snow White*, are more realistic today. *Mr and Mrs Smith* (2005) as assassins (but nice people). *Kill Bill* (2003) with Uma Thurman as an assassin who assassinates her would-be assassins (so she's only half a villain but with double the violence). Other female villains appear often enough, but none with quite the same psychoses as the all-male villains in the Bond-Eastwood-Willis series. The real female villains surpass the celluloid female villains. The latter tend to have some redeeming graces: they assassinate only the bad guys, or women, in vigilante justice, and the Smiths fall in love while Uma gets revenge. They may kill more, but with reason. Indeed the most evil woman on the screen may be Linda Fiorentino in *The Last Seduction* (1994): she is sexy, manipulative and destructive – kills no-one, but destroys them.

The movie presentations of the new action heroines are reflected in the television series *Buffy the Vampire Slayer*, *Xena: the Warrior Princess*, *Charlie's Angels*, *Wonder Woman* and so on. Women no longer need to be rescued by chivalrous white knights in shining (or slightly rusty) armour – they can rescue themselves, slay the dragon, and save the knight. Options for women are much broader than they used to be, in fact and fiction, and violence is no longer a male preserve – not that it ever was, but it is often thought to be.

These portraits of women as *heroes* negate the ideology of women as *victims*, which is surely a more positive self-concept and an ideological advance. The violence in the cause of righteousness reflects the traditional action films directed towards primarily male audiences, notably the westerns, and other action movies as men defend or avenge women or their communities or nations. These reflections of hitherto traditional male values tend to a convergence of gender options and realities – but ironically at the very time that men are reprimanded for their violence and instructed to be "sensitive."

Hollywood is not a location known for its feminist values. But perhaps because the female market demand has changed, or perhaps because more and more women are producers and directors, the movies now portray women in far more active, autonomous, violent, heroic and also criminal roles.

From victims to heroes to villains, both in image and reality. Life is full of ironies, and no sooner do we conceptualize women as morally superior and goddessess and action heroes than we reconfigure them as villains.

Several high profile murder cases captured the public eye in the 1990s: Susan Smith, Karla Homolka, Rosemary West, Aileen Wuornos and others. Similarly female suicide bombers and terrorists in Iraq, Indian, Israel and Russia, which were headlined by *Newsweek* (12.12.05) surprised those who were convinced that women really are all "sugar and spice and all that's nice," and goddesses.

The emerging portraits of women as villains, not necessarily angels or goddesses, both in film and in reality, is now generating the redefinition of men as not necessarily villains, but perhaps heroes. And a new male-positive literature is emerging: Newell (2003), Mansfield (2006), Montefiore (2007), Farrell and Sterba, 2008) and Parker (2008).

9/11 reminded us of the heroism of men: those who rescued so many men and women from the Twin Towers at the cost of 403 of their own police officers and firefighters. The invasion of Afghanistan to defeat the Taliban and the subsequent invasion of Iraq which overthrew a dictator who had initiated two wars and threatened the world with WMD reinforced this heroism – whatever one might think of the politics.

The feminist rhetoric of wars against women must be contextualized in the face of the casualties that Coalition forces face in these wars and others which are not of their choosing. The wars against men persist too.

At the same time, while we reconstruct men from villains to heroes, we also reconstruct them as victims: victims of their heroism in New York, Afghanistan and Iraq, but also – like women – victims of a range of other factors, including suicide, homicide, homelessness, addictions, accidents, incarceration, systemic discrimination and misandry.

In sum, who or what men and women are has been the subject of intense debate over the last 50 years; and their relationship with each other has been in question, and in flux. The old male supremacism has been replaced by a new female supremacism, which is not so much "levelling the playing field," I suggest, as playing the same old war games.

Since the sixties women have been variously and successively portrayed as victims of men in the wars against women, as superior goddesses, warriors, wolves, heroes and then in opposition as villains. Men, originally supremacist, have been recast as villains, but most recently as heroes and also victims. Clearly portraits of men and women are various, zigging and zagging in a complicated dance.

For all these debates about difference, equality, identity, power, biology, culture, misogyny and misandry – in postmodernity, for many people, the emergent issues are less about gender *relations* and more about the *meanings* of gender, if any.

The Post-Modern Model: Chaos

In the new millennium, all these old debates about gender superiority, equality, misogyny and misandry, wars against women, level playing fields – they now often seem irrelevant, out of date, passé to many members of a new generation. Those are old wars.

The romantic, patriarchal and, for want of a better word, misandric (or radical feminist) constructions of gender were, and are, all dualistic – either complementary in the first case, or contradictory in the other two. In postmodernity, however, such dualism is widely regarded as an oversimplification of more complex realities, both as to gender and as to conflict.

Today the debates are more about gender itself. What is it? What are we, as men and women? How many genders are there? and does gender matter? Are we not all mixed up, male and female, anyway? And thanks to surgery, we can change sex, and be a bit of both! Since we are all descended from a hermaphrodite fish, does it matter? What does gender mean?

The new wars are about the realities and rights of gays, bisexuals, transsexuals and intersexuals. Indeed, while many still problematize misogyny, misandry and homophobia, others problematize *heterosexism*. What used to be the norm is now the problem. In post modernity, gender is turned upside down and inside out. It's all a muddle.

There are several converging themes in post-modern theory and the social constructions of gender: bisexuality, performance theory, surgery and sex re-assignment, multiple sexes, and continuum and bell-curve theories. The issues have emerged from several disciplines: biology, psychology, anthropology and sociology, each with sub-themes. And the debate begins with Charles Darwin.

Bisexuality

Darwin not only famously blurred the line between humans and animals in *The Descent of Man*, he also blurred the line between men and women. In a letter to a friend Darwin wrote:

> Our ancestor was an animal who breathed water, had a swim bladder, a great swimming tail, an imperfect skull and undoubtedly was an hermaphrodite! Here is a pleasant genealogy for mankind. (1887: Vol. 2:266)

Bad enough to be related to monkeys; how much worse to be descended from an hermaphrodite fish! Such creatures challenge the Noah's Ark tradition of two by two, and the virtually universal division of all life into sexes. Darwin did not dwell on the implications of the hermaphrodite ancestor; but Freud did.

In the first of his *Three Essays on Sexuality* (1910) he asserted that: "It is popularly believed that a human being is either a man or a woman. Science, however, knows of cases in which the sexual characters are obscured" (PFL Vol. 7. 1977:52). This led him into a discussion of hermaphroditism and then of bisexuality, and his, at the time, scandalous conclusion: "In human beings pure masculinity or femininity is not to be found either in a psychological or a biological sense. Every individual on the contrary displays a mixture of the character-traits belonging to his own and to the opposite sex" (PFL Vol. 7. 1977:142).

Freud pursued this idea further in *Civilization and Its Discontents* (1930):

> Man is an animal organism with (like others) an unmistakably bisexual disposition. The individual corresponds to a fusion of two symmetrical halves ... We are accustomed to say that every human being displays both male and female impulses, needs and attributes ... [and] each individual seeks to satisfy both male and female wishes in his [or her: a Freudian slip!] sexual life. (1985:295–6)

This idea of the "two symmetrical halves" is strikingly reminiscent of Plato's theory of gender, but whereas Plato referred to men and women as opposite halves, complete only with each other, and also recognized same sex attraction, Freud sees the "fusion" of both halves in each individual, rather than in the couple.

This theme of psychological bisexuality was developed further by Freud's former friend, Carl Jung. Jung described men and women at the conscious level as totally opposite: Logos and Eros, and even Sol (Sun) and Luna (Moon) which in turn are associated with fire and air on the one hand, and water and earth on the other: the old Greek opposites. Somewhat stereotypically, Jung explained: "By Logos I meant discrimination, judgement, insight, and by Eros I meant the capacity to relate" (Jung, 1976:85). This equates to the old dichotomy: Man = Reason = Mind = Culture versus Woman = Emotion = Body = Biology. This reflects the ancient 10 point Table of Opposites of Pythagoras, and anticipated the Mars-Venus polarity of John Gray.

Jung also argued that men and women have an archetype of the opposite sex buried deep in the unconscious, born from their mother and father respectively, which also expresses the feminine and masculine sides of themselves: "in the unconscious of every man there is *hidden* a feminine personality, and in that of every woman a masculine personality" (1983:221. Emphasis added). From his own experience as a male, Jung was more familiar with the archetype of the female, which he termed the anima. He explained that "the anima is the female part of a man's psychology" and the animus is the male part of a woman's psychology; these forces are often derived from their images of their mother and father respectively.

The Jungian analyst Robert Johnson (1989) argues, like Jung, that being out of touch with the anima or the feminine side is the "wound" of modern man. He takes the old myth of the wounded Fisher King from the Arthurian legends, suspended between life and death, as the story of modern man.

This "wound" is deep: first, the psychic separation from the *mother*, from whose body the boy has grown, when the two were one. Yet this separation is intrinsic for growth from child to boy; second, or perhaps part of the above, the denial of the feminine in the male self as the boy realizes that he is not female. This is followed by an intense identification with the father as an ultimate role model – yet both father and son love the same woman, so there is conflict there, and competition (Freud's Oedipus complex). This is followed by yet another psychic transition: an intense attraction in adolescence, usually, for the female Other; and then finally the necessary psychic separation from the father as the adolescent transits into adulthood to become autonomous. This it is sometimes said is not a process of "self-discovery" so much as a process of self-creation. Separation from the mother while identifying with the father; separation from the mother while desiring other women; identifying with the father and then separating from the father. These are difficult psychic processes. No wonder it is a difficult time for so many young men, and especially for those boys and young men growing up without their fathers.

The concerns of Freud, Jung and Jungians are far removed from misogyny and misandry and perhaps closer to those of a new generation.

Gender as Performance

> All the world's a stage,
> And all the men and women merely players:
> They have their exits and their entrances;
> And one man in his time plays many parts.

So says Shakespeare in these well-known lines from *As You Like It* (Act ii Scene vii). To which we might add that one woman in her time also plays many parts. Men and women play them in the sequence of seven ages, but also simultaneously, switching from one role to another and back depending on the relationship involved: lover, parent, sibling, judge, retired... We all play many parts depending on whether we are with friends, colleagues, parents, children, team-mates of various sorts, and so on. Our identities are fluid and multiple, contradictory and evolving.

The American sociologist Erving Goffman expanded on Shakespeare's portrait of the self in his very popular book *The Presentation of Self in Everyday Life*. Using the model of social life as a stage, and the self as an actor, Goffman considers the way in which the individual "presents himself and his activity to others, the ways in which he guides and controls the impression they form of him, and the kinds of things he may and may not do while sustaining his performance before them" (1959: xi). While there are problems with the model, notably the reciprocity between actor and audience in real life, for the audiences are also actors, this attention to performance of role and to the art and science of impression management is crucial in the successful enactment of gender, and all the other parts we play on the stage of life.

Women and men have presented themselves as the opposite sex throughout history; not only on the stage but also in real life. The presentation of self may indeed be totally false. Two classic cases of women passing as men were Anne Bonney and Mary Reid, eighteenth century English pirates later hanged for their crimes. A recent case was Billy Tipton, a married jazz musician with three adopted sons, who died in 1989 and was then discovered to be a woman (Garber, 1992:68).

Gender passing has been featured in various films: *La Cage aux Folles* (1979), *Tootsie* (1982) and *Mrs Doubtfire* (1993), with men passing as women. In *Victor/ Victoria* (1982) the plot is more complex, with a woman playing a man playing a woman. All four films were comedies, or comedies of manners, and tended to trivialize the issue of the meaning, significance and power of gendered identity. Cross-dressing was played for laughs.

If cross-dressing was not seriously explored, transsexuality was investigated in the cult film *Orlando* (1992), from the eponymous book by Virginia Woolf (1928). The film treated the gradual sex change from man to woman over 400 years. The climax of the film occurs as Orlando gazes into the mirror and sees, for the first time, a woman gazing back at her. She says: "Same person. No difference at all. Just a different sex." Identity, in this view, is purely personal rather than social. Also, gender is not binary, but a point along a continuum. (We will return to this point later; it does somewhat reflect the views of Freud and Jung, but not popular culture.)

In *The Crying Game* (1992) an IRA volunteer falls in love with a transvestite and both he and the audience are shocked when a penis indicates that the woman is really a man. The issue which the film explores is: What difference does gender make? Is this love for a person, or is this an illusion because the person's gender is not what he thought?

The same theme is explored in *M. Butterfly* (1993), based on a true story of a French diplomat who falls in love with a Chinese actress, played by a man, who spies for his government. The deception is not uncovered until the end, and the Chinese man (who is also in love with the Frenchman, in the movie) tries to reassure his shocked lover that this makes no difference to their love. The diplomat commits suicide.

These stories and these films raise the question of the relation between biological gender and social gender; and which has priority. Traditionally, biology is destiny and determined the social gender. Indeed for a man or woman to masquerade as the other was often a capital offense. It was living a lie, deception, and upsetting of the whole "natural order" of things.

But what if the order is not "natural" but cultural? *Boys Don't Cry* (1999) for which Hilary Swank received an Oscar, was based on the true story of a woman who was murdered for passing as a man. In the film she says she has a "gender identity disorder." Clearly there may be a contradiction between biological gender and social gender. The films are important as reaching a far wider audience than most academic theorists of gender, as being based sometimes on real life, and as raising awareness of the issues involved.

This contradiction can be resolved in various ways depending on the depth of the contradiction: by passing (transvestism), temporarily or permanently ("drag" is playing such a sex-change for performance or amusement); by gender re-allocation surgery; by psycho-therapy, which is based on the idea that such gender "confusion" i.e. a gender identity disorder, can be "remedied"; or by becoming what anthropologists call a "third sex," as with "berdache" in some traditional North American tribes (Callender and Kochens, 1983) and the Hijras of North India (Nanda, 1999). Finally, the contradiction may not be resolved at all.

These films and these people and these issues raise questions about the meaning of gender. One leading theorist is Judith Butler, who has discussed such issues as the range of sexualities, the hierarchy of gender and the clash between the conventional cultural ideals and the real. She questions: "What best way to trouble the gender categories that support gender hierarchy and compulsory heterosexuality?" (1990: viii). Her answers are fairly obvious: to affirm feminist egalitarianism and to valorize any behaviour that is not heterosexual.

Drawing both from social constructionism and from Foucault she is interested in how the concept of gender and especially woman is socially constructed. Reacting against biological determinism, long discredited by race relations theorists as well as gender theorists, Butler attempts "to understand how the category of 'woman' is produced and restrained by ... power" (1990:2). If gender is socially constructed, then who constructs it? how? and why is this construction binary and hierarchical? Butler suggests that we should understand that gender is a choice, a performance, a decision determined by the individual, not by biology. Her work is popular in post-modernity among those who reject gender hierarchies (i.e. stereotypical "patriarchy") and binary heterosexual genders (lesbians, gays, bisexuals, transsexuals and others). It purports to be subversive of traditional gender norms in the name of individual rights and human freedoms.

Backtracking, Simone de Beauvoir argued in *The Second Sex* that "One is not born, but rather becomes a woman." She continues: "It is civilization as a whole that produces this creature, intermediate between male and eunuch, which is described as feminine" (1989:267). Hence her description of women as the *second* sex, and the title of Germaine Greer's later book, *The Female Eunuch* (1970). Beauvoir pioneered the theory of woman as victim – many others had complained about discrimination and unfairness and demanded equal rights; but de Beauvoir changed the debate and the vision. She stated explicitly: "The female is the victim of the species" (1989:20): a victim of biology, of male sexuality and of civilization. So a victim of men. Men are villains who victimize women. And women are the innocents, the morally superior gender in an oppressive structure.

The logical sequelae would be developed over the next decades, but the first step is taken here: the definition of the female as victim by one of the most privileged and white women in the entire world, at the apex of Parisian society.

Whether one accepts her victim theory or not is a personal matter; but I think she is right about the "becoming" as a social process. One must learn how to behave as a woman or a man. The anthropologists Marcel Mauss (1936) and Margaret Mead (1949) had already discussed how men and women learn their bodies differently, and use them differently; but both had avoided the victim trap: women as second, women as Other.

In her Introduction, de Beauvoir asks: "What is a *woman*?" – a question strikingly reminiscent of Freud's related question: "What does a woman want?" Her answers to her question are many and various and relate both to power, biology and gender. She is "victim," living in the "iron grasp" and "the servitude imposed by her female nature"; women have within themselves "a disturbing frailty" and "a hostile element" – they "have infirmity in the abdomen" (1989:30–1). This is her negative view of the female body. Then there is society: "Woman has always been man's dependent, if not his slave; the two sexes have never shared the world in equality." And she formulates the binary comparison to men and women as superior and inferior castes (1989: xxvi–xxvii). The sexual dimorphism of the body physical is translocated to the body politic.

Above all, men and women are different – and here she echoes Marx and Engels in The Communist Manifesto of almost exactly 100 years earlier: "Humanity is divided into two classes of individuals whose clothes, faces, bodies, smiles, gaits, interests and occupations are manifestly different" (1949/1989:xx–xxi). This is where Judith Butler advances de Beauvoir's thesis.

Butler reinterprets de Beauvoir, suggesting that "one is not born a woman, and one may or may not become one – it depends on one's performance." This postulated disjunction between biology and identity is her theoretical empire. In her view, the norm of heterosexuality is the "hidden" power that enforces binary genders (1990:22–3); in her view homosexuality and bisexuality and plural sexualities would destroy the binary system. The combination of only two sexes reinforced by only two sexual orientations is the problem. Then, she continues: "if sex and gender are radically distinct, then it does not follow that to be a given sex is to become a given gender" (1990:112). But that is a big "if"; and most people surely do not believe that sex and gender are "radically distinct." This is not in tune either with contemporary realities, nor historical realities, save in a small percentage of the population who, not surprisingly, deeply admire Butler (e.g. Bornstein, 1995:14). Passports and driver's licenses state: "Sex." For most people sex and gender are synonymous, with few exceptions, rather than "radically distinct."

Butler, as the apostle of psychological determinism may be seen as a reaction to the cultural determinism of Margaret Mead, Franz Boas and the anthropological school of gender, which in turn was a reaction to the biological determinism of racism and of gender (Freud). But transsexuals assert that their psyches do not match their physical bodies, as in "I am not my body." The wheel does not stop rolling, and Butler's determinism has been challenged by the biological determinists of evolutionary psychology. The degree to which gender is determined by biology, psyche or culture is still a matter of hot debate. We all tend to fight our own corners, but with so much evidence in support of each proposition, it seems likely that gender is a complex, and unique, blend of all three determinants.

In any event, for Butler, any relation between sex and gender is purely coincidental – to caricature her position, but only slightly – and due more to the power elite of heterosexuals than to biology, physiology or evolution. Gender is only performance based on a false premise, as she explains in her trade-mark opaque prose:

> acts, gestures, enactments generally constituted as performance are *performative* in the sense that the essence or identity that they otherwise purport to express are *fabrications* manufactured and sustained by corporeal signs and other discursive means. (1990:136)

De Beauvoir said it better referring to the "two classes of individuals." But Butler's point is that "clothes, faces, bodies, smiles, gaits, interests and occupations" can all be changed; so gender can not only be camouflaged, but also be performed on a Shakespearean or Goffmanesque stage.

Butler's theory of gender as performance is certainly useful in explaining the occasional gap between biological and social gender, between physiology and psychology. It is also useful as explaining the role of "clues" and "signals" in gender assignment: physical clues (size, musculature, hair, face, voice), behavioural clues (dress, cosmetics or lack of them, gestures, posture, demeanour) ... all the ways we instantly try to assess whether this is a man or a woman, gay or straight, friend or foe, drunk or sober, their socio-economic status, age, ethnicity and so on. Gender is only one of the many elements in how we present ourselves and how we calculate the identities and intentions of others.

On the other hand, Butler overstates both the hierarchy and the dichotomy of gender: she sees only the victimization of women and ignores the victimization and oppression of men, and she exaggerates the dichotomy by ignoring the continuum of masculinity-femininity and the bell-curve of overlaps between the sexes.[8] Also to ignore the biology of women's and men's bodies is, simply, silly. Gender is not just performance, or "performativity" – we *are* gendered and we *do* gender, and the two may not always be the same; but to prioritize the latter is to ignore biology – always a mistake.

Martha Nussbaum has argued most emphatically that being a woman (or a man, presumably) is far more than mere "performance," and that it is futile to ignore biology. She also insists that Butler's philosophical concerns about performance and subversion totally ignore the real problems of real women in the real world and are therefore a betrayal of feminism; she believes that Butler's "hip quietism" is itself far from being subversive, indeed it "collaborates with *evil*. Feminism demands more and women deserve better" (1999. Emphasis added.).

Surgery

The first sex-change operation was performed on a young Danish artist, Einar Wegener, who was convinced that he was two people, a man and a woman. In 1930 he underwent surgery in Germany. The surgeon removed his male organs and attempted to transplant ovaries. Wegener changed his name to Lili Elbe, and wrote that "It is so lovely to be a woman here among women, to be a female creature exactly like all the others." But she died in the following year – never having painted again (Morris, 1974:45–6).

The failure of this operation and then the Second World War halted this pioneer surgery; and the first successful sex re-assignment surgery was performed on the American George Jorgensen in 1951. Since no American surgeon would consent to do the "sex change" operation, he had it done in Denmark and changed his name to Christine. The case received enormous publicity. It is over 50 years since this operation was performed, yet the debates about the ethics of such surgery continue, and the legal, psychic and social complications of the surgery are still considerable. Here we will simply review what two very well-known but very

---

8   Gender is not just performance. Giving birth is not just performance, nor are lactation, menopause, menstruation, brain structure, physical structure etc. Biology is not sociology. Nor are the higher male mortality and morbidity rates just performance. Male infants have higher mortality rates long before they learn about sex roles. That there are performative aspects to gender does not mean that gender is performance; it is far beyond that.

different transsexuals, Jan Morris and Kate Bornstein, have had to say about their experiences, and their insights into our gender system.[9]

Jan Morris

James Morris was born the youngest of three brothers in Somerset, England. He enjoyed a happy childhood, was brought up "kindly and sensibly" and remembers the sunshine. He was sent to a distinguished English public school, Lancing (all boys), then volunteered for the army towards the end of the war, passed out from Sandhurst, joined a crack cavalry regiment, served in Italy, North Africa, Austria, Palestine and Suez as an Intelligence Officer, and left the army in 1953. He then studied at Oxford University, became a foreign correspondent for various news agencies, travelled widely, wrote books, covered the very successful British 1953 Everest Expedition, and resigned in 1961. Meanwhile he fell in love with and married Elizabeth, and they had five children. By all accounts his was a very successful military, professional and marital career.

Morris was unusual, however. "I was three or perhaps four years old when I realized that I had been born into the wrong body, and should really be a girl" (1974:3). As he grew older, every night he would pray: "And please, God, let me be a girl. Amen" (1974:20).

Morris had sex at school with various admirers, but this merely confirmed him in his idea of his own femaleness. He distinguished clearly between sex and gender:

> To me gender is not physical at all, but is altogether insubstantial. It is soul, perhaps, it is talent, it is taste, it is environment, it is how one feels, it is light and shade, it is inner music, it is a spring in one's step or an exchange of glances, it is more truly life and love than any combination of genitals, ovaries, and hormones. It is the essentialness of oneself, the psyche, the fragment of unity. Male and female are sex, masculine and feminine are gender, and though the conceptions obviously overlap, they are far from synonymous. (1974:25)

He added that this was not "gender confusion," as is often alleged. "I have had no doubt about my gender since that moment of self-realization beneath the piano" (1974:25). He insisted: "I was born with the wrong body, being feminine by gender but male by sex, and I could achieve completeness only when the one was adjusted to the other" (1974:26).

Perhaps surprisingly he loved the army and writes in glowing terms of his regiment and the brave men he knew; but he adds that: "Far from making a man of me, it only made me feel more profoundly feminine at heart" (1974:27). As

---

9   A number of transexuals have told their stories: Jorgenson, 1967; Morris, 1972; Cossey, 1992; Richards, 1993; Bornstein, 1995; McCloskey, 2000. There is also some research literature: Bolin, 1988; Califia, 1997; Garber, 1992.

neither male nor female he felt like a nonperson, or a prisoner, or as "two people in one, two truths," "isolated, neither one thing nor the other, neither seducable nor seducible" (1974:39, 40, 51, 56). This was, of course, a paradox, a conundrum – the title of the memoir of his and her life.

Over time the crisis deepened. He began to loathe himself as a man, and it became apparent to both Elizabeth and James that he could not continue to soldier on. The time had come to change sex. But what is sex? For Morris there are four definitions of sex. There is anatomical sex (the physical primary and secondary characteristics), chromosomal sex (XX or XY), hormonal sex (the balance of testosterone, androgen, estrogen and progesterone) and psychological sex: who people feel they are (1974:103–4). Psychologically, Morris felt that "I had been woman all along." And now it was time for the body to adjust, gradually, first by hormone therapy and later, if all went well, by surgery. So, after 35 years as a man, Morris spent eight years becoming partly a woman and swallowing at least 12,000 female hormone pills, from 1964 to 1972.

Morris described the physical changes to her body, and also the psychological changes: "I felt ... physically freer and more vulnerable. I had no armour" (1974:106). But she kept her sense of humour and described the stereotypical national reactions to her evolutionary process:

> Americans generally assumed me to be a female, and cheered me up with small attentions. Englishmen, I think, ... found the ambiguity in itself beguiling ... enlivened always by that instant flicker of amused attraction which every woman knows and no man can quite imagine. Frenchmen were curious ... Italians, frankly unable to conceive the meaning of such a phenomenon, simply stared boorishly, or nudged each other in piazzas. Greeks were vastly entertained. Arabs asked me to go for walks with them. Scots looked shocked. Germans looked worried. Japanese did not notice. (1974:111–2)

Kate Bornstein

Bornstein describes herself as a "gender outlaw," a "transsexual lesbian whose female lover is becoming a man." She adds: "I'm writing from the point of view of used-to-be-a-man, three husbands, father, first mate on an ocean-going yacht, minister, high-powered IBM sales type, Pierre Cardin three-piece suitor, bar-mitzvah'd, circumcized yuppie from the East Coast. Not too many women write from that point of view." She added: "I identify as neither male nor female"; but as a "third" (1995:3–4; 98). A complicated and multiple, fluid, point of view, and a post-modern identity!

Bornstein says that "I knew from age four on, that something was wrong with me being a guy," and "I would pray each night to wake up and be a girl" (1995:59, 94). Before the "genital reassignment surgery" Bornstein had two years of therapy, and then another therapist had to validate his own therapist's opinion; the hormone treatment can start during this time. Then there is the so-called Life Test: one or two years living as the other sex. Finally there is the surgery: which is not the end of the problem. This "Third" faced numerous humiliations before and after the surgery from ridicule to "urinary segregation" (at IBM she was not allowed to use either the men's or the women's washroom!) to exclusion from women's groups and festivals (because she was not "woman born woman") (1995:82–8).

Bornstein is particularly critical of our gender system, describing it as a "particularly malevolent and divisive construct," a "social disease" and a "system of oppression": "Gender is no different a form of class oppression than the caste system in India or apartheid in South Africa" (1995:12, 78, 105). She adds that for women "It's not men who are the foe so much as it is the bi-polar gender system that keeps men in place as more privileged" (1995:106).

Resistance to the system, and the "gender outlaws" like herself, are to be found in the transsexual, gay and lesbian communities; but she says that even they have a hierarchy: post-operative transsexuals look down on pre-operative transsexuals who look down on transgenders (they live "opposite" but will not have surgery) who look down on drag queens who look down on out-transvestites (1995:67–8). So, the struggle will be long with this hierarchy so prevalent even among the resisters: the gender benders.

She argues: "It's the gender system itself – the idea of gender itself – that needs to be done away with" (1995:113–5). She argues too that gender is not sane: "It's not sane to call a rainbow black and white; and it is not consensual: it is assigned by a doctor, documented by the state, enforced by the legal profession, sanctified by the church, and it's bought and sold in the media." We cannot question it or play with it (1995:123). In sum, it's not fair! And she demands a (non-violent) revolution to blur the lines, cross the lines, and abolish the lines.

She concludes that "After thirty-seven years of trying to be male and over eight years of trying to be female, I've come to the conclusion that neither is worth all the trouble" (1995:234). But when asked: "And if you knew what you know now, would you do it again?" She replied "Big-time yes!" (1995:244). Morris argued that there are two sexes, but one can switch. Bornstein says that there are three, and that she is a third sex. Fausto-Sterling believes that there are five sexes. The muddle continues.

Five Sexes: Intersexuals

In 1993, Anne Fausto-Sterling, a developmental geneticist and professor of Medical Science at Brown University, published an article "The Five Sexes: Why Male and Female are not Enough" in the prestigious journal *The Sciences*. This article provoked the proverbial storm of controversy, since it challenged the core cultural norm of two sexes.

Fausto-Sterling's argument was simple: the two party sexual system, enshrined in state, in law and in popular culture, is "in defiance of nature." Gender is not just a matter of the presence or absence of the Y chromosome, but also of levels of testosterone and estrogen, which fluctuate over time anyway.

> For biologically speaking, there are many gradations running from female to male; and depending on how one calls the shots, one can argue that along that spectrum lie at least five sexes – and perhaps even more. (1993:21)

Hermaphroditism, the possession of both male and female sexual characteristics, has long been recognized. Indeed Ovid wrote a delightful description of its mythological origins. Hermaphroditus, the son of Hermes and Aphrodite, was a handsome boy who found, in his travels, a translucent pool, "clear as glass." In this pool dwelled a water-nymph, a naiad, who "saw the youngster, and wanted what she saw." She begged for a kiss, but he blushed and refused; so Salmacis, for this was her name, trembling, left him alone and departed – so he thought. He dived into the pool. She dived in after him, caught him, held him, and prayed:

> "O grant me this," she cried
> In prayer to the gods, "May no day ever come
> To separate us!" and they heard her prayer,
> And the two bodies seemed to merge together,
> One face, one form ...
> So these two joined in close embrace, no longer
> Two beings, and no longer man and woman,
> But neither, and yet both.
> (Ovid, 1967:93)

"Is it a boy or a girl?" has to be one of our more frequently asked questions; and usually the answer is physically obvious at birth. Genitals-R-Us. But some people have "unruly – even heretical – bodies" with the physical characteristics of both sexes (2000:8). Fausto-Sterling takes the example of such intersexuals to challenge our binary gender system, and indeed the conventional notion of gender. Gender is not simply genital, external and visible, it is also brain function and structure, chemistry (both hormones and chromosomes) and behaviour, which in turn may be both nature and nurture, biology and culture in a tangled knot (2000:235).

In the past, intersexed individuals were likely to be dealt with promptly, soon after birth, after gender assignment consultations (often without parental involvement) by "corrective" surgery. Recently, adults who have had such genital surgery have come forward to testify to their emotional and physical pain: medical complications, absence of sensation and so absence of sexual pleasure, psychic confusion, and they have often argued that such surgery is not necessary (Navarro, 2004).

Fausto-Sterling suggests that the "true" hermaphrodites and the "pseudo" hermaphrodites, either male or female dominant (whom she calls "herms," "merms" and "ferms") should be recognized as three distinct sexes. She cites John Money of Johns Hopkins University as estimating that "intersexuals may constitute as many as 4% of births" (1993:21) – or as few: The rhetoric of statistics is always interesting. Dr Money, considered an expert at the time, argued that gender identity follows socialization into gender roles and that biological sex was largely irrelevant. This position was hugely popular in the sixties. But both he and this position have been largely discredited by John Colapinto's (2000) report on David Reimer's gender re-assignment surgery after a botched circumcision.

The poor boy had his penis virtually destroyed by an inexperienced doctor using an electric current. On Dr Money's advice he was raised as a girl, but not successfully. Dr Money, meanwhile, was allegedly fraudulent in his reports of success. When David Reimer was told the truth, he reverted to being a man, married but committed suicide. Colapinto's book discredited the doctor, a star at Johns Hopkins, and the political theory founded on Margaret Mead's anthropology of gender (also discredited) and feminist identity theorists of universal androgyny.

Fausto-Sterling argues that although the "management" of intersexuality has been benign in intent and largely successful in its outcome, it is nevertheless "a mode of discipline." Hermaphrodites are being "forced" into one or other sex. "Society mandates the control of intersexual bodies because they blur and bridge the great divide." They challenge the basis of our social structure. "But what if things were altogether different?" she asks, and we recognized multiple sexes, not just two. She raises the question: how would we raise an intersexual child? (1993:34). We do not even have the vocabulary for someone who is both him and her, and also neither.

This article elicited a considerable correspondence both for and against the demolition of the binary system, and Fausto-Sterling wrote a follow-up article a few years later. In this she revised the estimate of various types of intersexual births down to 1.7%, while the number of infants who might be eligible for surgery would be much less: one in a thousand or two thousand (2000:20).

Two developments have changed the picture and the pattern. First, the David Reimer case, an example of failed gender reassignment (Colapinto, 2000); and second, intersex activism and the foundation of the Intersex Society of North America (www.isna.org) in 1993 by Cheryl Chase. Consequent to both these developments, members of the medical profession are beginning to recognize that some forms of intersexuality are normal, not disease states; that genital ambiguity is not a medical emergency requiring immediate "corrective" surgery; that therapy not surgery is the preferred technique, at least until the situation has been clarified and more generally that surgery cannot resolve a social problem. Intersexuals, those with chromosomal, hormonal or anatomical differences from the normative gender ideal may be few in number, but they are mighty in their ability to challenge the dimorphic binary norm (Gorman and Cole, 2004).

Similarly transsexuals, who identify themselves as members of the "opposite" sex, also challenge the traditional gender system. While some societies have institutionalized this "third sex" (Nanda, 1999), we have not. And although "true" hermaphrodites are rare – "possibly only one in 100,000" – in Fausto-Sterling's estimate (the rest "are really hidden males or females"), the emerging wisdom is now to upset the gender apple-cart.

Not only intersexuals and transsexuals challenge the tradition, so do performance theorists. Suzanne Kessler, for instance, argues against giving the genitals primary significance in the attribution of gender: "What has primacy in everyday life is the gender that is performed, regardless of the flesh's configuration under the clothes" (Fausto-Sterling, 2000:22). Fausto-Sterling agrees with this, describing it as the "ideal"; and she suggests that a first step is the elimination of the category "gender" from all official documents, arguing that such attributes as height, eye-colour, finger-prints and genetic profiles "would be more expedient." Concerned activists have now drawn up a Bill of Gender Rights, including the rights to define one's own gender, to change it, and to marry whomever one desires. She concludes her article with the statement that "Some of the most feminine people I know happen to be men" (Fausto-Sterling, 2000:23). And, in post-modernity, no doubt the most masculine just happen to be women.

All this raises the question of the relation of biological male and female to social masculine and feminine, but the biological is rarely a continuum, while the social masculine and feminine is always a continuum, evaluated by multiple and overlapping criteria.

So the muddles persist. Freud and Jung say that we are all both sexes; Morris argues that we are one or the other, but we can switch; Bornstein says that there are three sexes – or none at all; and Fausto-Sterling suggests that there are five. We might just agree that there is a continuum of masculine and feminine – but very rarely of male and female.

Continuum and Bell Curve

Fausto-Sterling's point that "There are many gradations running from female to male" (1993:21) is surely worth considering although in social rather than physical terms. There are many gradations running from masculine to feminine – and male does not coincide exactly with masculine nor female with feminine. It is axiomatic that there are masculine women and feminine men.

The gradations run from hyper-masculine to hyper-feminine. The models of the former include Daniel Craig, John Wayne, Clint Eastwood, Bruce Willis, Arnold Schwarzenegger, James Bond etc., in a fine confusion of Hollywood and reality; and the most masculine professions (which ironically do *not* include acting!) are perhaps fireman, cowboy, boxer, lumberjack, soldier, which emphasize the traditional values of bravery, physical strength and, often, outside work. (All of these occupations are now of course open to women – which muddles the models still further.) They might be referred to as "macho" – though this has negative connotations for some. *People* magazine runs its annual competition for "the sexiest man in the world." Matt Damon was the 2007 choice; and Hugh Jackman in 2008.

The hyper-feminine include such icons as Marilyn Monroe, and such entertainment stars and sex symbols as Scarlett Johansson, Paris Hilton, Lindsay Lohan, Britney Spears, Halle Berry, Beyoncé Knowles. The list could be long: beautiful, shapely, seductive, smiling, indoor-types, and the polar opposites of the hyper-masculine.

In between we can locate the regular, normative masculine men and feminine women, without the iconic and celebrity status.

A third gradation along this continuum refers to those who do not meet the norms. They are the opposite of the hyper-types: cross-overs. Boys and men who are thought of as feminine or non-masculine may be called a sissy (after sister), wuss, nerd, geek, dork, or other such epithets. Except for sissy, these terms are not usually applied to girls or women. Similarly girls and women who display stereotypically masculine traits may be described as tom-boys or butch – this latter term (like gays and fairies for boys) tends to have implications of homosexuality.

Homosexuality is itself yet another point along this continuum: seen as a deviation from the gender norm – no longer a mental illness but sometimes a social inconvenience and, for some, a moral transgression. But sexual orientation does not relate to masculinity or femininity directly.

A second angle of sight is provided by some feminists who used to refer to women who had succeeded in traditionally male occupations as "male-identified": a pejorative term. It could be applied to politicians, CEOs or others, but especially to Margaret Thatcher. Thatcher was certainly not butch; indeed her handbags were notorious as fashion statements and fetch huge sums at charity auctions. Her extraordinary achievements as Prime Minister, elected three times, however, were mocked by some of her "sisters" who defined her as a man with a handbag. Conversely, gay men are often presented as feminine (e.g. in *La Cage aux Folles* (1979), *Will and Grace* and to some degree *Queer Eye for the Straight Guy* but not *Queer as Folk*. Whether the stereotypes have positive or negative impacts on homophobic attitudes is not clear; but since homophobia is declining, probably the former.

Times change, of course, and models and ideals of masculine and feminine now permit a far broader range of options than in the 1940s and 1950s, during and after World War II – a global clash of warriors. Nonetheless the continuum still persists, with gender identities largely different and opposite.

The eight-point continuum, of alpha, regular, omega and cross-over types for each sex and sexual orientation is too schematic: there are really no clear "points" on a scale, just subtly shifting colours of the light spectrum (the symbol of gayness) – not just two: black or white.

Clearly there are, and always have been, not only the bi-polar stereotypes but also in practice the far more flexible gender realities which permit a wide range of behaviours for both sexes with no stigma attached. This includes female generals and warriors (Boadicea, Joan of Arc) and gay artists (Michelangelo, da Vinci) and macho gays, and geek billionaires laughing all the way to the bank.

Furthermore we all recognize, following Plato, that the genders overlap like two Bell curves in their capacities and abilities and talents. One or other gender may excel in one or other particular skill, but generally speaking, the differences *within* each gender are probably greater than the differences *between* each gender.

Whether we model genders as a horizontal eight-point continuum or as overlapping Bell curves (with the average men and women at the apex of their respective curves) or with men on a U curve, predominant as alphas and as omegas, does not much matter; but what does matter is the realization that the binary mutually exclusive model is an ideological construct rather than a portrait of reality. And for all the rhetoric of identity politics and the so-called gender wars, this is clearly recognized in practice. This is progress, of a sort. But this is a very different model from the patriarchal and the feminist models, which polarize genders on (reversed) vertical and binary evaluations.

Muddles

All five models of gender co-exist today. All are useful. All are flawed. All these theories explain some aspects of our gendered lives, but fail to explain others. So the models are all a bit of a muddle.

The romantic model explains the partnership of marriage and the loving relationships that engage most men and women "rolled into one"; but the rosy lens does not illuminate gender inequality, the differential victimizations of men and women, and the struggles and competitions for rights and power, i.e. conflict.

The patriarchal and feminist models certainly clarify the dimensions of conflict and oppression from opposite ends of the hierarchy on a vertical axis, or from opposite ends of the spectrum on the horizontal axis. The two models do have opposite valences; but neither explain love, unity and complementarity, and both are flawed by their tunnel vision and polarizing lenses. They are strong on power and conflict, but weak on love and peace.

The postmodern model is the most complex in that: first, it recognizes that we are all both male and female; thus it negates the binary model of gender so typical of the previous three models. The biological determinism of old was negated by the cultural determinism initiated by Mead and anthropologists ("gender is a cultural construct") which in turn was challenged by the psychological determinism of Butler ("gender is a psychic choice") and transsexuals, which in turn was challenged by such feminists as Nussbaum ("gender is real, political and biological, deal with it!") and evolutionary psychologists ("the science of gender cannot be ignored").

Some believe in two God-given genders; others also believe in two, but say you can change. Bornstein suggests either recognizing three, to add on transexuals, or denying it exists at all, because it's such a problem. Some cultures recognize three genders. Fausto-Sterling favours five, recognizing intersexuals. Many say it doesn't matter because, thanks to medical science, people can be neither or both: she-men or he-women.

Conclusion

Gender is not what it was, and gender-relations are not what they were, for better and for worse. All four models discussed here have their utility, and proponents, but the choice of a model is not simply a matter of personal taste, with no consequences. Equal rights, women's rights, men's rights, gay rights, transgendered rights – all these issues are hotly debated. They have wide-ranging implications for legislation, economics, politics and traditional family values.

People have died for their gender models. What is right for some is wrong for others. Both men and women have suffered from discrimination, usually to different degrees: in jobs, salaries, custody disputes, child support payments, prison sentences, and social responsibilities (e.g. the draft), sex changes and gender identities. Such inequities reflect cultural norms about the models, and the muddles about roles, responsibilities, rights and ethics.

So we muddle on, loving the opposite sex, or hating it, or denying it exists, or claiming to belong to a third sex, or to be both sexes in one human being; and then arguing about who is equal to whom, and about our rights as men, women, gays, fathers, mothers, grandparents, transsexuals, intersexuals, same sex couples, and the distribution of power and justice. Our models cause more muddles every year!

Chapter 3

Heroes

Let us now praise men and masculinity. One of the goals of this book is to valorize, or re-valorize, men just as the women's movement has valorized women (but sometimes in the process has de-valorized men). Gender relations are not a see-saw, when one goes up the other goes down, or at least, they should not be. As human beings, we rise and fall together.

In recent years we have begun to re-think men in more positive terms, in recognition of their heroism, bravery, hard work and altruism. This is the resultant of many forces: 9/11 and the bravery of the police officers and fire-fighters in New York; the courage of the Coalition forces in the retaliatory invasion of Afghanistan in 2001 and the subsequent invasion of Iraq in 2003; the issue of war heroes was raised in the 2004 election in the United States with respect to John Kerry, and in the 2008 election with John McCain. John Kerry served with distinction in the Vietnam War, mostly in Swift Boats earning the Silver Star and the Bronze Star, and three Purple Hearts for wounds received in action. McCain is a genuine war hero: a navy aviator who flew 23 missions over Vietnam, was shot down in 1967, broke both arms and a leg, was bayonetted in the groin, was imprisoned and tortured for five and a half years in the Hanoi Hilton, and then made peace with his former enemies. During his 17 years in the Navy he was awarded the Silver Star, Legion of Merit, Distiguished Flying Cross, Bronze Star, and the Navy Commendation Medal.

Physical courage is a valued and expected attribute in a man, and in a presidential candidate in the United States. In a 2007 poll Americans considered military experience the most desirable attribute in a President (*Economist* 5.4.08:36) though clearly this alone is not enough to guarantee election. Since World War II, Presidents Eisenhower, Carter, Nixon, Kennedy and Bush (41) all had military experience, as did de Gaulle in France; but no recent Prime Ministers in Canada or in the U.K. have been elected on the basis of their military experience. There the military tend to keep away from politics.

In contrast, Barack Obama is a peace hero. The broad outlines of his story are well known. His father was from Kenya and his mother from Kansas, black and white, at a time when such a marriage was illegal in 16 states of the Union. Not an advantage. His father left when he was one. Not an advantage. His mother was poor. Not an advantage. But with the encouragement of his mother and his grand-parents, he studied hard, won scholarships and graduated from Harvard. His ascent was meteoric: elected junior Senator in Illinois in 2000 to U.S. Senator in 2004 to President-elect in 2008. His gifts to the American people – and beyond them to the world – are his messages of unity, hope and change. The "skinny kid with the funny name," as he described himself, is trying to move beyond the great divide between the red states and the blue states: "There's the United States of America." Hope "is God's greatest gift to us, the bedrock of the nation; the belief in things not seen, the belief that there are better days ahead." That Americans can change things: "Yes we can!" – and a joy in America, which had been widely reviled under Bush: "In no country on earth is my story even possible."

This hero's hero was his grandmother, Madelyn Dunham, who died the day before he won the presidency: "She was one of those quiet heroes that we have all across America. They're not famous. Their names are not in the newspapers, but each and every day they work hard." This is the testimonial of a self-made man who acknowledges the contribution of others to his creation.

The militarization of the world following the global war on terror has contributed both to the revival of heroism in practice but also to the revival of interest in heroism. The recent best-seller *101 World Heroes* (Montefiore, 2007) includes an inspiring list of heroes. The author writes:

> We live in an unheroic age, and an unheroic age has a desperate need to learn about heroism. The stories of the great heroes bring history to life. They inspire and teach us about values and the nature of responsibility, the bonds that keep societies together. (2007:6)

The 101st hero is the lone Chinese protester standing in front of a tank in Tiananmen Square in 1989: a reminder of the singular importance of each individual hero. The 'Tank Man', as he has come to be known, was broadcast around the world as a symbol of democratic resistance to the tyranny of the government of China. The journalist Jan Wong reported the incident from her hotel room: "So the tank is turning, then the young man jumps in front of the tank, and then the tank turns the other way and the young man jumps down that side. They did this a couple of times. Then the tank turned off its motor." Later that day the army rolled in and opened fire. It is estimated that about 2,600 potesters were killed and 30,000 injured. The fate of this unknown hero is unknown (Montefiore, 2007:316). Most men are not heroes, of course; but most heroes are, or were.

Who and what are heroes? No doubt we all have our own heroes, in fact and fiction, but the origin of the idea is rooted deep in the past. In the original Greek, the word referred to a god or demi-god, or a man with super-human qualities, according to the etymological dictionaries, and was cognate with the later Latin "servare": to save, deliver, preserve, protect. It was not found in English until the 16th century when it meant "illustrious warrior", evolving again in the 17th century to mean a "man admired for his great deeds and noble qualities." Later still the hero became the protagonist in a poem or play: the lead man, if not a villain – and a heroine if female.[1]

---

1   The etymological dictionaries consulted were The Concise Oxford Dictionary of Etymology, and the dictionaries compiled by R.K. Barnhart and E. Klein.

The meanings have evolved over the centuries, but the core meanings persist; and we all grew up with heroes such as Superman, Batman, the Green Hornet, the Hulk, the X Men, Spiderman, as well as the old cowboy comics, and the war comics like Sgt. Rock. They all reinforced the same core male values of bravery, doing good and fighting crime and bad guys everywhere: in the wild west, in the trenches or in the city. As the sex roles changed, so Wonderwoman joined the cast of heroes, and many others.

Heroes still persist on television and in video-games and in cyber –space, now fighting aliens as well as the regular human villains, and usually winning.

But do we need them? And where do they come from? Heroes are ancient, as the etymology suggests. Karen Armstrong (2005) suggests that the old heroes originated in the ancient Paleolithic myths, before the invention of writing, as early humans wondered where we came from, who we were, where we were going, and pondered the meaning of life. The heroes they invented suffered much and achieved much – as did the hunters, the young men initiated physically into adulthood, the mothers giving birth and the children being born. The myths of Herakles (Hercules) and Artemis may stem from the Paleolithic era, and the structure of these hunting myths still survive in the stories of Aeneas and Prometheus. These heroes are role models, teaching survival and conquest skills and values. But Armstrong adds in Nietzschean vein: "Every single one of us has to be a hero at some time in our lives" (2005: 37). In contrast the myths of the Neolithic age (8,000 BCE – 4,000 BCE) refer to the life and death struggles for the harvest, and the changing seasons. These myths from Syria, Egypt and Mesopotamia emphasize life and death and re-birth rather than male and female heroism.

The iconic heroes of the European tradition are the contrasting pair of Achilles and Ulysses/Odysseus: Achilles, the greatest warrior of the Trojan war who was offered to choose glory or a long life by a goddess, and chose glory; and Ulysses, the cunning, tricky warrior, who survived both the war and his odyssey, and returned home to Penelope. These are pre-Christian Nietzschean heroes: they are not saints, not King Arthur, not Christian in John Bunyan's "Pilgrim's Progress", they are not "good", kind, loving and lovable types – and many men do effectively choose glory over longevity, and many do not have much of a choice.

Heroes in mythology have been described as fulfilling five criteria: extraordinary or superhuman achievement, a quest or adventure, a risk to the self, moral fortitude and a gift to humanity (Campbell, 1972; 1988).

Given these stringent qualifications for heroism, popular press labels of heroism are often highly inflated. Champion athletes and rock stars are often considered heroes, particularly in the United States, but that is to confuse fame with heroism: they are not the same. Some regard their parents as heroes, which is wholly admirable, but too local in range and achievement to qualify. Nor is the hero the same as the celebrity (Rojek, 2001) – though the two are often confused. Elvis was a celebrity, not a hero.

Real heroes, however, as distinct from mythological heroes, must be defined as having a national or international impact on humanity for the benefit of humanity

– rather than a local impact on one person or family, or one sector: sport, stage, or screen. Not that we cannot have our own personal heroes: with respect, gratitude, admiration or love for others who have been important to us, but if they are only personal they remain too local to qualify as a capital H hero.

Psychologist Frank Farley has suggested a less mythological account of what makes a hero. His "5–D" model includes five factors: Determinants: the six essential character traits of courge, honesty, kindness, intelligence, risk-taking and charisma; Depth: which distinguished heroes from celebrities; Domain: politics ranks first, in Farley's research, followed by entertainment, family and religion; Database: the source of our information which is principally the media rather than, say, history class or books. Farley objects to our focus on abstract "isms" (racism, sexism, communism) rather than on individuals and their times; finally Distance: heroes may be far away and be, or have been, immensely powerful, or they may be local and well-known and loved, like Mum and Dad (Staff, 1995). Farley's points are that we can all be heroes, but it helps if we think about what makes heroes and what constitutes heroism. In one recent survey, he noted, half the children surveyed had no heroes, which suggests poor history teaching perhaps but also perhaps high narcissism and low altruism. My own research has on occasion elicited the nihilistic response: "Heroes are zeroes."

Lucy Hughes-Hallett has offered insightful analyses of eight western heroes. Two are fictional, Achilles and Ulysses, representing opposite types in some ways, the others range from Alcibiades in ancient Greece, a contemporary of Plato, and Cato (the Roman senator) to El Cid of Spain, Sir Francis Drake of 16th century England, Wallenstein (the Swedish general of the Thirty Years War (1618–48)), and Garibaldi, who is credited with the unification of Italy. This is an idiosyncratic selection, no doubt, and includes no twentieth century heroes and has a militaristic bias. All are white male westerners, as she acknowledges, and the list includes no women because "the vast majority of the people accorded hero status in Western history have been men." Furthermore: "To have chosen a female subject would have been to imply that one-sixth of historical heroes were women. That kind of emollient falsification, in my opinion, does women no service" (2005: 8–9).

A more conventional list would probably not include four of the eight heroes from the Ancient world, nor two mythical men, and might include some of the following: Washington, Lincoln, Churchill and such Nobel Peace Prize winners as Martin Luther King, Nelson Mandela and Mother Teresa, and Mahatma Gandhi, who was never awarded this prize. Abraham, Moses, Siddhartha Gautama, Jesus and Mohammed might also be included. That said, any discussion of male heroes and heroism is welcome in the age of misandry.

A few common themes seem to run through the lives of these men: charisma: the ability to attract and compel others to believe in them, a leadership ability; marginality: many were insubordinate, even rebels, or outsiders (Alcibiades, El Cid); high risk types who do not fear death (notably Achilles and Drake, but also Wallenstein and Garibaldi); and winners and high achievers, uncompromising, strong willed (Hughes-Hallett, 2005).

The hero, the strong man, the Superman, has been eulogized before, notably by Thomas Carlyle (1841/1993) and Friedrich Nietzsche (1885/1985). Carlyle, who invented the "great man" theory of history, argued that "the history of the world is but the biography of great men," and he praised the hero from Odin to Cromwell and Napoleon; and again, his choice of heroes seems to be remarkably idiosyncratic and militaristic: the first is mythical, and the latter two are villains to many people – Cromwell to the Irish and Scots particularly, and Napoleon to the English, Russians, Italians and Spaniards, to name a few. Heroes are notoriously relative: a freedom fighter for one is a terrorist to another, and vice versa; but relativism does not imply moral equivalence.

Were we to see heroes as those who have saved lives, rather than taken lives, we might valorize Florence Nightingale and the great medical explorers whose discoveries have saved, and continue to save, so many lives. This list would include the anatomist, Andreas Vesalius, William Harvey, who discovered the circulation of blood, Edward Jenner (vaccination), Antony Leeuwenhoek (bacteria), Wilhelm Roentgen (x-rays), Louis Pasteur (vaccinations for rabies, anthrax, and saviour of the French wine and silk industries), Alexander Fleming (penicillin and antibiotics), Salk (polio vaccine), and Wilkins, Crick and Watson (DNA, genetics and heredity) … and so the life-saving continues (Friedman and Friedland, 1998).

Nietzsche was not as enthusiastic for militarism as Carlyle and Hughes-Hallett: he is enthusiastic for autonomous life. In "Thus Spoke Zarathustra" (1885), one of the last books he wrote before he went mad, possibly of tertiary syphilis, he instructs his readers to *live*:

> *I teach you the Superman.* Man is something that should be overcome….
> What is the ape to men? A laughing-stock or a painful embarassment. And just so shall man be to the Superman: a laughing-stock or a painful embarrassment. You have made your way from worm to man, and much of you is still worm. Once you were apes, and even now man is more of an ape than any ape … Man is a rope, fastened between animal and Superman – a rope over an abyss.
> (1985):41–3)

Nietzsche preached that "God is dead" (1985:14, 114); there is only man, and most men are too much worm, too much ape. He urged men:

> "live dangerously! Build your cities on the slopes of Vesuvius! Send your ships out into uncharted seas! Live in conflict with your equals and yourselves! Be robbers and ravagers… (1985:18)

This passion to "live dangerously" is precisely what so many of the heroes of myth or history have done, and continue to do. Indeed we all do, to greater or lesser degree, as we face the unknown, and take different types of risks from marriage to childbirth to investments to career-choices. "The free man is a warrior" Nietzsche declared (1977:21) – by this he did not mean a fighter or a killer, but someone who fights to achieve goals. Building companies, raising families, writing books, finishing degrees, competing in sports: these are not goals easy of achievement. But Nietzsche meant much more than that. "You must be on your guard against the good and the just! They would like to crucify those who devise their own virtue – they hate the solitary." This is the voice of the herd, to which the free man, the Superman must be deaf. And he advised that: "You yourself will always be the worst enemy you can encounter; you yourself lie in wait for yourself in caves and forests" (1985:88–90, cf. 230). In all this Nietzsche echoes Franklin on the self-made man: man makes himself, and Emerson on self-reliance. (The "man" is generic, of course.)

Today, in a relatively democratic age, we may be somewhat "ambivalent" towards heroes, as Hughes-Hallett has suggested (2005:5). Hero-worship and personality cults are dangerous to society (as well as to the individual), and the rise (and fall) of fascism and communism in the twentieth century have alerted us to the possibilities of the abuse of power by tyrants and dictators, and the dangers of charismatic leadership. Heroes smack of elitism, and even of militarism and violence, in these contexts of Achilles, Cromwell, Napoleon and the warrior.

Yet the possibility of abuse and negativities must be balanced by the realities of achievements, contributions, altruism, self-sacrifice – the gift to humanity, in Campbell's term, and the model for life, in Armstrong's term. In more prosaic terms, what we have been given and have given.

The idea of men, and humanity in general, as heroes is most ancient. One of the first to praise humans as a species, and perhaps men as a gender, was Sophocles in *Antigone*. The greatest wonder is man, as gender and species, who has sailed the oceans, invented agriculture, tamed wild beasts and birds, developed language, built cities, enacted laws, learned how to think, provided food and shelter for all, and conquered everything but death – and even death has been fended off for many years since his time. His poem is worth citing to remind us of our collective human achievements over time and space, and also of men's heroic contributions here.

> Wonders are many on earth, and the greatest of these
> Is man, who rides the ocean and takes his way
> Through the deeps, through wind-swept valleys of perilous seas
>   That surge and sway.
>
> He is master of ageless Earth, to his own will bending
> The immortal mother of gods by the sweat of his brow,
> As year succeeds to year, with toil unending
>   Of mule and plough.
>
> He is lord of all things living; birds of the air,
> Beasts of the field, all creatures of sea and land
> He taketh, cunning to capture and ensnare
>   With sleight of hand.

Hunting the savage beast from the upland rocks,
Taming the mountain monarch in his lair,
Teaching the wild horse and the roaming ox
    His yoke to bear.

The use of language, the wind-swift motion of brain
He learnt; found out the laws of living together
In cities, building him shelter against the rain
    And wintry weather.

There is nothing beyond his power. His subtlety
Meeteth all chance, all danger conquereth.
For every ill he hath found its remedy,
    Save only death.

The omission of love and family from this list of achievements is unfortunate, perhaps reflecting Sophocles' male bias towards Mars rather than Venus. This enthusiasm for the species and the gender (the ambiguity is unavoidable) is echoed by Shakespeare in Hamlet's soliloquoy:

What a piece of work is man! How noble in reason! how infinite in faculty! in form, in moving, how express and admirable! in action how like an angel! in apprehension how like a god! the beauty of the world! the paragon of animals! *Hamlet* Act 2 Sc. ii

The paragon is also a paradox. Ideas about human nature have fluctuated widely, and wildly, over the millennia, and in his *Essay on Man*, Alexander Pope is rather more conflicted than Shakespeare. He employs multiple dichotomies, and concludes with a trichotomy of man (generic) as "The glory, jest, and riddle of the world."

Know then thyself, presume not God to scan,
The proper study of mankind is man.
Placed on this isthmus of a middle state,
A being darkly wise, and rudely great:
With too much knowledge for the sceptic side,
With too much weakness for the stoic's pride,
He hangs between; in doubt to act or rest;
In doubt to deem himself a god, or beast;
In doubt his mind or body to prefer;
Born but to die, and reas'ning but to err;
Alike in ignorance, his reason such,
Whether he thinks too little or too much;
Chaos of thought and passion, all confused;

Still by himself abused, or disabused;
Created half to rise, and half to fall;
Great lord of all things, yet a prey to all;
Sole judge of truth, in endless error hurled;
The glory, jest, and riddle of the world!

The paradox lies in the multiple contradictions; yet the themes of "glory" and "wonder" are precisely the themes of heroism. But glory is complemented by jest: we do need to keep our sense of humour in all this (although Pope also meant that we are all fools: jests of the world), and riddle: why else has it taken us so long to sort out the gender riddles in our "darkly wise" minds with "wind-swift motion."

The wonders are many, as are the jests and riddles; but here we will honour some of the men (and women, though the prime focus is on men) who are heroes in this day and age in so many different ways.

The two classic examples of masculine bravery are surely the 1912 *Titanic* disaster, and 9/11. Both incidents demonstrate men as the heroic sex.

R.M.S. Titanic: 1912

On her maiden voyage, in August 1912, the *R.M.S. Titanic*, the largest moving object ever built at that time, struck an iceberg at 10:07 p.m. and sank at 2:20 a.m., about 100 miles south of Newfoundland and 1,000 miles east of Boston. The berg sliced open her hull along the starboard side for 250–300 feet along her 882 feet length. Of the 2,223 passengers and crew, 1,517 were lost and only 706 or 32% were saved.

Patterns do emerge, however, in terms of those who were saved and those who were lost. This was not a random distribution. The U.S. Senate Subcommittee investigation into the disaster focussed on rank, noting that 60% of the first-class passengers were saved, 42% of the second-class, 25% of the third-class and 24% of the crew. The higher the class, the higher the survival rate. The class distinctions in survival rates were not apparently due to exclusionism, but to the difficulties of egress from the third-class compartments far below the top-decks where the life-boats hung, and to the fact that all cabins below the gash-line (which was below the water-line) would have been flooded swiftly, adding to the difficulties, and causing some early deaths. As the liner began to dip further and further by the bow, and to list to starboard, the inclines became steeper and steeper in both directions, increasing the difficulties.

Rank was one pattern; gender was another. The total complement of passengers and crew included 1,692 men and 531 women and children. 70% of the women and children were saved, but only 20% of the men (Kuntz, 1998:559). Put another way, more bluntly: up to 80% of the men sacrificed their lives so that about 70% of the women and children could survive. This was not a Darwinian "survival of the fittest" scene, nor a Hobbesian "war of all against all" situation. This was a deliberate heroic act of altruism and self-sacrifice by some of the wealthiest and most powerful men in the world.

This male value of "women and children first" requires interrogation. Why did these men valorize the women and children higher than themselves? So strong were and are these protective and altruistic values that they cost these men their lives – up to 1,360 men, to be precise, since some must have been killed on impact or soon after – with little protest or confusion or violence.

The tragedy was caused, as so often, by a combination of several factors. Both the U.S. Senate and the British Board of Trade investigations of the sinking allocated responsibilities for the tragedy as they saw fit, and convenient. Neither queried the justice, fairness and equity of these cultural values.

The immediate causes of the collision were clear: the unusual drift of ice so far south that year; the high speed of the *Titanic*, the decision of Captain Smith, an experienced captain with the White Star Line, to ignore all the ice warnings in order to arrive in New York on time; the White Star Line requirement that their liners be as punctual as trains, whatever the weather conditions; the failure to provide the look-outs with binoculars (this was before radar); the provision of only one radio officer; the failure to construct the water-tight compartments sufficiently high, and to build a double hull (these architectural errors were later remedied on *Titanic's* sister ship, the *Olympic*, in sum, a range of climactic, personal, navigational, commercial, supply and architectural factors.

The many factors affecting the quite unnecessarily high casualty rate are also clear, in retrospect: the inadequate supply of lifeboats, the failure to practice passenger musters at their boat stations; the failure to practice boat drill; the failure to fill many of the lifeboats when they were launched – partly due to initial concerns that the boats in the davits would not bear the weight of a full complement of passengers, and partly due to the expectations that the boats would remain close by to pick up survivors: they didn't. The cowardice of some of the seamen in command of the lifeboats, who disobeyed Captain Smith's orders to rescue swimmers, and the cowardice of some of the rescued passengers who refused to let other commanders rescue survivors were massive failures of heroism.

The officers of the *Carpathian*, stopped in ice within sight of the *Titanic*, astonishingly failed to come to her aid, although sighting the distress rockets. The ship's radio operator had gone to bed, missing the wireless emergency messages. Then again, many of the passengers, at least at first, believed that she would not sink, and that rescue was at hand. So there were many factors, and types of factors involved in the disaster. But there were enough lifeboats for 53% of the passengers and crew, not simply for the 32% who were saved. One authority argues that "the root cause of the great tragedy was simply bad seamanship" (Marcus, 1969:296–7). But this was not the verdict of the official U.S. and British inquiries.

On the following day, the Prime Minister, H.H. Asquith, rose in the House of Commons and declared:

our sense of admiration that the best traditions of the sea seemed to have been observed in the willing sacrifices which were offered to give the first chance of safety to those who were least able to help themselves ... (in Marcus, 1969:190)

Surely "our sense of admiration" should more properly be directed, not to "the best traditions of the sea" but to the best tradition of men, and to the male values of saving "those who were least able to help themselves."

Certainly many men and women displayed immense heroism: the bandsmen who kept playing as she went down; the 35 engineers who kept the pumps working as long as possible – when they came up on deck they found all the lifeboats gone, and they all died; Edith Evans, who gave up her seat in one of the last lifeboats to a woman with children at home; and the senior officers who worked to save lives until they went down with the ship (Eaton and Haas, 1986: 296; Marcus, 1968: 142–61).

The irony of it all is that if the lookouts had sighted the iceberg a few seconds later, and if the Officer of the Watch had not altered course to port, or had been a bit slower to do so, the *Titanic* would have hit bows-on, and only one, or perhaps two, water-tight compartments would have been flooded, instead of six, and she would have stayed afloat.[2]

9/11: 2001

On September 11, 2001, 19 terrorists hijacked four aircraft. They flew AA 11 to crash into the North Tower of the World Trade Center at 8:45; UA 175 crashed into the South Tower 17 minutes later; half an hour later AA 77 crashed into the Pentagon, and half an hour after that UA 93 crashed into a field in Pennsylvania after the passengers tried to regain control of the aircraft. Its destination is thought to have been the Capitol or the White House: 20 minutes flying time away.

This was the most deadly attack on American soil in its history: 2,973 lives lost – more than Pearl Harbor in 1941. The lives of many more were saved by the bravery of the unarmed passengers on UA 93. This was not the first terrorist

---

2   This section on the *Titanic* is compiled from several sources: the 1912 U.S. Senate Subcommittee Report, edited by Kuntz, 1998; also Marcus, 1969; Eaton and Haas, 1986; and Ballard, 1997. The seamen who testified tended to blame, in the words of one officer, "the extraordinary combination of circumstances that existed at the time, a combination that would not happen again in a hundred years. It is extraordinary that they should all have existed on this particular night; everything was against us, everything" (Marcus, 1969:256). He was referring primarily to the climactic conditions: the absence of moon, wind and swell, rather than to the poor seamanship, the unrealistic White Star Line regulations, the out-dated Board of Trade regulations and the inadequate architectural designs. The reforms initiated after the disaster included the establishment of an International Ice Patrol (still in existence), the requirements of a more southerly route, wirelesses (radios) on board, wirelesses manned 24 hours, adequate lifeboat supply, and new design features including raised bulkheads and double hulls.

attack on Americans, nor the first on American soil, but it was the most deadly, and precipitated the war on terror, the invasion of Afghanistan in 2001, and the subsequent invasion of Iraq in 2003.

Over 2,500 people died at the World Trade Center that morning. Among the dead were 343 from the FDNY, 23 from the NYPD and 37 from the Port Authority PD: 403 police officers and firefighters, all men except two (National Commission, 2004:311).

The heroism of these men was recognized by the National Commission without naming names or giving details. The rescue operation was enormously successful in both Towers, with most of the civilians evacuated from below the impact sites before the towers imploded. Some first responders even refused orders to leave as they were still saving lives; others were too exhausted to move. The report notes, and witnesses testified to, the positive life-saving heroism of these men, but also the high cost they paid.

This bravery, altruism and self-sacrifice demands recognition, not as exceptional, except in the scale of the losses, but as normative for so many men. And not just as part of the job, but as part of a man's life. The Carnegie medals and the Stanhope medals, like the heroism on the Titanic, are component elements of this predominantly masculine heroism: high benefits for others but high costs.

All this death, destruction and heroism was generated by 19 young Arab men who had adopted an extremist form of Islam, and more remotely by the fatwa – a declaration of war in this case – issued by Osama bin Laden in 1998. He declared that it is the "individual duty for every Muslim who can do it [to murder any American] in any country in which it is possible to do it"(2004:47). President Bush has insisted that: "All Americans must recognize that the face of terror is not the true face of Islam. Islam is a faith that brings comfort to a billion people around the world. It's a faith that has made brothers and sisters of every race. It's a faith based upon love, not hate" (2004:54).

There have been many terrorist organizations in the last few decades: Al Qaeda is just the latest and most powerful. These include the IRA (Ireland), the FLQ (Quebec), the KKK (U.S.), the Red Army Faction (Germany), the Red Brigade (Italy), the ETA (Spain) and so on around the world. The face of terror is usually male; and the faces of the police and the military who counter terror are also usually male. Men as villains and men as heroes.

Bravery

Bravery, physical bravery, is a core component of the ideal male. To be a coward is not to be a "true" male, even if he is a biological male.

In the United States, Andrew Carnegie established the Hero Fund in 1904. Its mission: "To recognize persons who perform acts of heroism in civilian life in the United States and Canada, and to provide financial assistance for those disabled, and the dependants of those killed, by their heroic acts." The medals are awarded five times a year. In the latest awards (October 2008), medals were presented to 23 men and two women; three men and one woman died in their efforts to save others, and many were injured (www.carnegiehero.org. Accessed 2.12.08). This heroism is recognized as a component part of male (and, to a lesser extent, female) altruism and nurturing: an ethic of care.

In the United Kingdom the Royal Humane Society first awarded medals for saving lives in 1776; the idea was modelled on ancient Roman practice. Their most prestigious award is the Stanhope Gold Medal, founded in 1873. Only one medal is awarded annually. From 1980 to 2000, 21 Gold Medals have been awarded: 16 to men and five to women, for acts of exceptional bravery and courage. The Stanhope Gold Medals for 2004–8 were also awarded to men (medals for 2001 – 3 were not accessible). The society also awards Silver and Bronze Medals. The eight Silver Medals awarded from 2000–7 were all awarded to men, except one, including a Special Lifetime Achievement award presented to a lifeboatman who had rescued more than 1,500 people from the river Clyde over his career. The 45 Bronze Medal recipients listed from 2002–7 included only three women (www.royalhumane.org. Accessed 2.12.08).

Clearly men do not have a monopoly on bravery, courage and altruism. Equally clearly, from this evidence, the vast majority of these bravery awards go to men.

Newsweek offered a cover story "Hero M.D." on Navy doctor Richard Jadick who saved 30 lives in one battle in Fallujah over 11 days – quite apart from patching up so many others (Wingert and Thomas, 2006). His story is interesting also because the doctor, though trained as a marine, never fired a shot, and is therefore a different type of warrior from the other men, wounded, profiled in the article. The switch from the old warrior heroes who took enemy lives to the new heroes who save lives is instructive of new values about life and war. Following this article, ironically, was the obituary of former Serbian president, Slobodan Milosevic. He declared four wars killing 250,000 people, causing 2.5 million more to be homeless, destroyed the once prosperous Yugoslavia and died in custody on trial for genocide and crimes against humanity (Nordland, 2006).

The war veterans are the epitomes of heroism: risking their lives to defend their countries, whether volunteers or conscripts. So many lost their lives in the last century – about 40 million men, mostly young men, in combat (Clodfetter, 2002). And the wars continue. And millions of others were wounded and suffered psychic injuries. Whether the wars were just, or initiated by aggressive war-mongers like Hitler and Milosevic, is less the issue here than the heroism of the men doing their duty to their country – and occasionally the bravery of the men resisting a monstrous dictator, as exemplified by the 1944 resistance against Hitler. The relativity of heroism is a vexing issue discussed below.

War heroes are the archetypal heroes. Sgt. Alvin York in World War I was given a ticker-tape parade when he came back to the States in World War I. Audie Murphy was the most highly decorated American soldier in World War II, toured the country, and made 44 Hollywood movies. Pilot Richard Bong shot down 40 enemy aircraft and was sent home to sell war bonds. Heroes were recognized and rewarded. Similarly in Canada, World War II war hero Georges Vanier became Governor-General of Canada, and Billy Bishop is still remembered as Canada's leading air ace in World War I. In the U.K. old war heroes from Alfred the Great to Henry V to Nelson and Wellington and Douglas Bader and Montgomery are still recalled in plays, films and history books. Their stories were told, written, filmed, glorified, glamorized – and still are, decades and even centuries after the actions.

The current wars in Afghanistan and Iraq have not generated the same hero-worship, however, partly because the wars are unpopular, and partly because casualties would have to be mentioned; perhaps also because such individualism might seem to cheapen or devalorize the group effort, or maybe because people prefer victims to heroes. For whatever reason, heroism is hardly discussed in the context of these wars – just the casualties. The numbers and names are given in the *New York Times* almost every day, and the cars and trucks and debris of suicide bombers are on the television. The heroes are strangely ignored, except in the occasional memoirs of the fighters and journalists' investigations. They are not household words.

The Medal of Honor website lists the 3,465 medals awarded; only one has been awarded to a woman, a Civil War surgeon. 246 were awarded in the Vietnam War, two in the Mogadishu conflict (1993), one in Afghanistan and four in Iraq. The citations for the most recent awards can be accessed at www.history.army.mil/moh.html (Accessed 3.12.08).

Work

In times of war knights are honoured for their valour. The Congressional Medal of Honor and the Victoria Cross are the highest awards in the United States and the United Kingdom respectively. Peace, however, is valued as much as victory, and the Nobel Peace Prize is the world's supreme accolade. Six Nobel Prizes are awarded every year for significant achievements in physics, chemistry, physiology or medicine, literature, and economics. The most prestigious is the Nobel Prize for Peace.

These prizes are an excellent record of the finest human achievements in these areas over the years. We might take the last few years as examples, and as typical. In 2000 the five disciplinary prizes were awarded to 10 people, all men, with the Peace Prize awarded to South Korean President Kim Dae Jung. In 2001 the disciplinary prizes were awarded to 13 men, 10 of them Americans; the Peace Prize was awarded to the United Nations and to Kofi Annan, Secretary General of the U.N. In 2002, 2003 and 2004, 31 of the 34 disciplinary prizes were won by men – but three were won by women, which suggests that as women move further into the full-time labour force, more and more prizes will be won by women. Furthermore, while the 2002 Peace Prize was won by former U.S. President Jimmy Carter, in 2003 it was won by Shiran Ebadi, a lawyer, and the first Iranian and the first Muslim woman to win the prize. In 2004 it was won by Wangari Maathai of Kenya, a forestry conservationist, and nine of the 11 disciplinary prizes were awarded to men. The Peace Prize in 2005 was awarded to Mohamed ElBaradei and the International Atomic Energy Agency, of which he was the Director-General, for their efforts to resolve conflicts by diplomacy rather than war. In 2006 it was awarded to Muhammad Yunus, the economist who developed micro-financing in Bangladesh so successfully. The 2007 Nobel Peace Prize was awarded to the IPCC (Intergovernmental Panel on Climate Change) and to Al Gore. And in 2008 it was awarded to the former Prime Minister of Finland and diplomat, Martti Ahtisaari, for his many peace initiatives around the world.

In sum, since 2000 the nine Peace Prizes this millennium have been awarded to seven men and to two women – emblematic of the changed sex roles, the new equity and the new balance of power and the changing division of labour. In the preceding 50 years, the Peace Prize had been awarded to women only four times, to five women.

The disciplinary prizes continue to be won almost entirely by men to reward the immense amount of work which benefits humanity. It is surely unfortunate that the prizes are not awarded for the Social Sciences, which would no doubt witness a different gender balance.

This is a proud record of male achievements, and of increasing female achievements; but two other points are interesting. The most famous Nobel Prize winner was probably Madame Curie, the only person who has ever won two Nobels in two different fields. And second is the passionate argument of the American feminist Elizabeth Cady Stanton back in 1860:

> If in marriage either party claim the right to stand supreme, to woman, the mother of the race, belongs the scepter and the crown. Her life is one long sacrifice for man. You tell us that among womankind there is no Moses, Christ or Paul – no Michael Angelo, Beethoven, Shakespeare – no Columbus or Galileo – no Locke or Bacon. Behold those mighty minds so grand, so comprehensive – they themselves are *our* great works! Into you, O sons of earth, goes all of us that is immortal. In you center our very life, our hopes, our intensest love. For you we gladly pour out our heart's blood and die, knowing that from our suffering comes forth a new and more glorious resurrection of thought and life. (Montagu, 1968:154)

Stanton's point is well taken. The women create the men who create the world: to woman "belongs the scepter and the crown." Today, of course, her list would include a number of women, as the *Time* and *IWW* lists do. The achievements of so many men and women have historically been magnificent – but largely in different arenas. At the risk of flogging a dead horse, my point is that, despite the culture of misandry, these records of human achievement are mostly records of male achievement. Amazingly, all men are not misogynists, sexists, violent, criminals, rapists, testosterone poisoned and so on. Some are good people, useful to have around.

Some heroes have their lives taken from them, others give them up for others. Captain Oates R.N., on Scott's last expedition to the South Pole, found his hand infected with gangrene at a time when the expedition's resources were running low. Believing that he would not survive, and hoping that the food saved might assist his comrades, he walked out of his tent into the blizzard to die, saying "I may be some time." His heroism was in vain in that his comrades died nonetheless, but it was not in vain as an inspiration of heroism.

Emile Durkheim, the great French sociologist, described such acts as "altruistic suicide." More political examples, and therefore relative to whose "side" you are on, include the Japanese kami-kaze pilots, the 10 IRA hunger strikers in 1981, and suicide bombers. Bravery is one element here, or misplaced fanaticism, and sacrifice is another. Many people give for others in a sacrifice of their lives: Albert Schweitzer, Florence Nightingale and Mother Teresa. The beneficiaries of such dedication may not even be human: Diane Fossey and Jane Goodall have both dedicated their lives to the great apes, and Diane Fossey lost her life.

Raoul Wallenberg, the Swedish diplomat who saved 20,000 Jews from the Nazis, is one such hero whose status is not in dispute and is unlikely to change. Such heroism is rare, and may have cost him his life at the hands of the Soviets. Indeed the State of Israel officially recognizes the Righteous Gentiles as heroes, who risked their own lives to save the lives of Jews at risk during the Holocaust.

In more mundane and microcosmic fashion, parents sacrifice much for their children, athletes for their sports, students for their degrees, idealogues for their causes (political, economic, libertarian etc.), and so on. Such sacrifices may be seen as investments in the future, or as worthwhile in some way; but the degree of altruism varies from quantities of time, money or energy, to life itself.

Moral Courage

Physical courage is one thing; moral courage is often another. Sometimes the two coincide. In China the dissident Wei Jingsheng was condemned to 15 years in prison in 1979 for criticizing the regime. He was released in 1993 after serving 14½ years; six months later when he persisted in criticizing the regime, he was arrested and later sentenced in a mockery of a trial to another 14 years in prison. He was later released but exiled, and now lives in the United States. Another Chinese dissident, Wang Dan, a student leader at Tiananmen Square, was put on China's most wanted list after the 1989 protest and jailed for four years. After his release he continued to protest and again was arrested and jailed, this time for 11 years in 1996. He too was released and exiled to the United States.

Every undemocratic, tyrannical system generates its opposition, its protesters, its heroes and its victims. In Burma, the journalist Win Tin, long an associate of Aung San Suu Kyi, was sentenced to twenty years in prison, where he was frequently tortured. He was finally released in 2008 in very poor health at the age of 76 after serving 19 years.

In the Soviet Union, Andrei Sakharov was a leading nuclear phycisist, worked on the Soviet atomic bomb and then the hydrogen bomb, but later questioned the morality of his work and protested Soviet armaments policies. He also criticized the 1979 Soviet invasion of Afghanistan and was sent into internal exile. He was awarded the Nobel Peace Prize in 1975. His contemporary Alexandr Solzhenitsyn, served in the Red Army during World War II but was sentenced to eight years in a labour camp for criticizing Stalin. After his release he wrote a number of novels, the most famous of which were "One Day in the Life of Ivan Denisovitch", and "The Gulag Archipelago" – exposés of the horrific Russian prison system. He was awarded the Nobel Prize in Literature in 1970. Later he was expelled from the Soviet Union, worked at Stanford University for some years, and then returned to Russia where he died in 2008. Condemned initially as a dissident he was later lionized as a hero of human rights.

In India, Gandhi led the opposition to British imperialism. In South Africa, Nelson Mandela epitomized the opposition to apartheid. In the U.S., the U.K. and Canada, numerous women protested the exclusion of women from the franchise, Stanton and Anthony, the Pankhursts, McClung and others. In Germany, Von Stauffenberg led the 1944 plot against Hitler code-named Valkyrie – now another movie celebrating heroism. Every country and every tribe have their heroes – and villains.[3]

Many authors, eloquent on the topic of male villainy, have been conspicuously silent about male heroism – even when such heroism has brought peace, challenged tyranny or saved women's lives.

The heroes are not all male. Heroines abound in Western history, and they include military leaders, mothers, spiritual leaders, political activists, intellectuals, travellers ... consider the following: Mother Teresa, Harriet (Moses) Tubman, Joan of Arc, Florence Nightingale, Boadicea who led the English against the Roman invaders, Amelia Earhard, the first woman to make a solo flight across the Atlantic who was lost in the Pacific in her attempt to fly around the world. The Suffragettes and contemporary feminists have helped to create a new world. Leading environmentalists include Rachel Carson, whom many credit with initiating the Green movement, to Jane Goodall. Stars would include actresses like Marilyn Monroe and Elizabeth Taylor, artists like Margot Fonteyn in dance and Maria Callas in music. Icons include Rosa Parks, Emmeline Pankhurst, Anne Frank, Helen Suzman, Coretta King and Helen Keller. Plus there is a long list of Queens, Prime Ministers and Presidents at the pinnacles of power. Furthermore many icons of ancient Jewish history are female: Yael, Judith and Ruth in very different ways. And in the Christian tradition many of the saints are female, and again there are many different paths to sanctity: Mary Magdalen, penitent; Theresa of Avila (1515–82), a Spanish nun and mystic who founded the reformed Carmelite order and was influential in the Counter-reformation; Theresa of Lisieux (1873–97), a French nun known as the "Little

---

3   The Black List celebrates Blacks in the U.S. both in their own words and in photographs (Greenfield-Sanders and Mitchell, 2008); and Jessie Carney Smith has published extensively on this.

Flower" who pioneered the "little ways" of holiness, and so on. Indeed the cult of female heroes, particularly female *warriors* is now a growth industry (Fraser, 1989; Jones, 2006).[4]

Winners of the Nobel Peace Prize include Betty Williams and Mairead Corrigan from Northern Ireland in 1976, Mother Teresa in 1979, Aung San Suu Kyi, leader of the opposition in Myanmar/Burma in 1991, Jody Williams of the United States and the International Committee to Ban Landmines in 1997 and, as mentioned earlier, Shirin Ebadi of Iran in 2003 and Wangari Maathai of Kenya in 2004.

But most of our national heroes have been men – as are most of our national villains and victims, but that is another story (see below). Men are trained to be heroes, and to risk their lives not only for their loved ones, but even for perfect strangers, for their country, for the preservation of law and order, . . . and especially for women. We would do well to give credit where credit is due rather than to continually carp and whine about male villains. Certainly there are male villains and indeed female villains too; as there are also male heroes and female heroes. It is time to recognize this, to try to understand it and to encourage it and basically to negate the moral polarization of the two sexes by both misogynists and also misandrists.

The First and the Best

We also valorize those who are the first to achieve goals which are defined as worthwhile, and who do certain tasks best.

We applaud the gold medal winning Olympic athletes, as the Greeks did over 2000 years ago. Competition is intrinsic to much of our lives: sports, grades in university, politics, business, dating – even beauty is competitive with Miss World, Miss Universe and other competitions; and prizes are awarded. Such "glory" may be temporary, but it is nonetheless sweet while it lasts, and it can sometimes be parlayed into more substantial gains.

Similarly those who are first achieve a certain celebrity status: Jesse Owens, the first person to win four Olympic golds, in the 1936 Games; Edmund Hillary and Sherpa Tensing, the first people to climb Everest in 1953; Roger Bannister, the first person to break the four minute mile in 1954; Yuri Gagarin, the first person in space in 1961; Neil Armstrong, the first person to walk on the moon in 1969.

There are many other firsts: Ferdinand Magellan, credited with the first circumnavigation of the globe (1519–22), though he was killed during the voyage. Sir Francis Drake was the first English mariner to do so (1577–80). Joshua Slocum was the first person to sail alone around the world, between 1895 and 1898. The first to fly with an engine were the Wright brothers in 1903. The first solo transatlantic flight: Charles Lindbergh, 1927. The first to reach the North Pole: Robert Peary, 1909; the first to reach the South Pole: Roald Amundsen, 1911. More recently, in

---

4   Canadians are now discovering their female heroines – perhaps in reaction to the poor showing of women in the Maclean's millennium list (Duncan, 2004; Foster, 2004).

2005, Ellen MacArthur a British sailor was not the first, but she was the fastest to sail solo and non-stop around the world, in 71 days. And the late Steve Fossett was the first to fly solo non-stop around the world: 36,000 km in 67 hours, and was the holder of several aviation and sailing records.

The "firsts" escalate from the first person to the first man or woman, the oldest, the youngest, the fastest, the first double amputee to climb Everest, the first to summit the highest seven peaks, and so on. It never stops. The records are all documented in the press for our admiration, and then in the *Guinness Book of Records* and often, eventually, in the obituary columns.

It should be stated again, for the record, that if women have not excelled in some of these achievements, this is not due to any metaphysical inferiority to men on their part, obviously, but rather to their differential allocation in public and private life, imposed or self-imposed, which has itself been a function of differential nature and nurture, biology and sociology – fast-changing though this differentiation is in many parts of the world.

Conquest

A constant theme in the mythology of heroism is that of conquest: the triumph of good over evil, of heroes over villains, and of the self over handicaps, disadvantages and fears. Sometimes the disadvantage is that of having to fight evil while at the same time remaining within the letter and the spirit of the law: a constant theme in the media today.

Conquests might be moral, military, physical or spiritual, or some combination of all four. The conquest of one's fear, addictions, pride or enemies may be as heroic as David's slaughter of Goliath, or Ulysses' destruction of the lazy, leech-like squanderers of his inheritance and the suitors of his wife, Penelope, whom he found in his palace on his return from the Trojan Wars.

All the great heroes must conquer temptation. Christ was tempted in the desert by the devil. The first temptation was of Christ's physical appetite, for after 40 days fasting in the wilderness, Christ was hungry. "If you are the Son of God, tell this stone to turn into a loaf." Jesus replied that "Man does not live on bread alone." The second temptation was for power. "Worship me," said the devil, and promised Christ all the kingdoms of the world and their glory. The third temptation was to pride, as the devil appealed to Christ to prove his divinity by casting himself to the ground from the roof of the temple, for God would surely save him. Christ replied "You must not put the Lord your God to the test." So Christ survived these temptations (Luke 4:1–13). But then he faced others: fear and despair. At Gethsemane before his arrest, he told three of his disciples: "My soul is sorrowful to the point of death." And he prayed: "My father, if it is possible, let this cup pass me by. Nevertheless, let it be as you, not I, would have it" (Matthew 26:37, 39). And later, as he was dying on the cross, he cried out in a loud voice: "My God, my God, why have you deserted me?" (Matthew 27:46).

Conquest of the other and conquest of the self – often the same process in different guises – is intrinsic to heroism. Indeed the Buddha faced similar trials (Campbell, 1988:141).

For some, temptation is just a really good excuse to fail ("I can resist everything except temptation" explained one of Oscar Wilde's characters.) For heroes it is the opportunity to excel. For some of us, a handicap or a difficulty is also a good excuse to fail. For heroes even a physical handicap is the opportunity to excel.

Perhaps most famous of all is Helen Keller (1880–1968) who, though blind and deaf from the age of two, nonetheless learned to read, write and speak, graduated from Radcliffe and devoted her life to the handicapped, and wrote a moving autobiography (1974/1902). Likewise Terry Fox, who had lost a leg to cancer, ran half-way across Canada in 1980 to raise money for cancer research, but his cancer returned and he died soon afterwards. Steve Fonyo, who had also lost a leg to cancer, succeeded in his run across Canada. Rick Hansen, who was paralyzed in a car accident when he was 15, wheeled his chair around the world, competed in marathos, raised millions and supports spinal cord injury research (www.rickhansen.com).

In similar conquests over injuries Monica Seles recovered physically and psychologically after being stabbed in the back on the tennis court in April 1993 to win the Canadian Open in August 1995. And Silken Laumann whose leg was so badly injured in a rowing accident that it was widely assumed she would be out of the Olympics recovered so rapidly that she won a silver in the Barcelona Games in 1992. Similarly Chantal Petitclerc, a Canadian wheelchair athlete, won five gold medals at the Athens Paralympics in 2004. And in 2005, the Texan Lance Armstrong, who had beaten testicular cancer before his first win, has won the Tour de France seven consecutive times.

Stephen Hawking, the internationally reknowned astrophysicist, was diagnosed with ALS when he was 21 in 1963 and given two years to live. Five year later he was in a wheelchair, and since then he has written the best-selling *A Brief History of Time* (1992) and *The Universe in a Nutshell* (2001). He is the father of three children.

All have not only overcome horrendous difficulties which most people have never faced, nor ever will; but they have also *given* a fantastic example to others, handicapped or not, and beyond that some of these have raised money to also *conquer* the problem which incapacitated them. Not only no self-pity, but a successful counter-attack! That is heroism.

The gift of self is perhaps the central theme of heroism. Creativity, originality and the gift of one's work and imagination are part of these gifts to humanity. Following Stanton, one might think of men and women of heroic stature in literature: Shakespeare, Cervantes, Tolstoy, Homer, Euripides, Chaucer; or art: Michelangelo, Da Vinci, Goya, the Impressionists, Picasso; or philosophy: Plato, Aristotle, Aquinas, Descartes, Nietzsche, Sartre, Russell; or the sciences: Newton, Galileo, Darwin, Freud, Curie, Einstein; or business: Henry Ford, Bill Gates; the composers, the inventors, the care-givers from Nightingale to Mother Teresa, the advocates of peace... .

Such individuals and others stand head and shoulders above the crowd in their contributions to the quality of human life. Exemplifying Carlyle's "great man theory of history" – and modifying it to clarify the roles of women – the "great man and woman theory," these exceptional individuals have done so much in so many various ways to transform our lives and create our civilizations.

The End of the Century and the Millennium

1999 was an excellent opportunity to review the most important and influential men and women of history. American, British and Canadian organizations initiated the process, using various criteria. Some included villains in their lists of influential people, some did not. Some even included non-existent fictional characters, which evoked some amusement. But in the end we have a much better appreciation of the extraordinary men and women who have shaped and created our contemporary societies. These, as we shall see, are mostly men.

They are also, as we discuss below, increasingly women, as women migrate out of private and domestic life into public life.

Several groups have listed the Top Ten or the Top 100 people of the last century. These include the rather different lists of *Time* in the United States and the International Who's Who in the United Kingdom. Collectively, the *contributions*, the gifts, of these men and women to the world have been immense.

Time Magazine

The *Time* list of the "100 Most Influential People of the Century" is divided into five equal categories: leaders and revolutionaries, artists and entertainers, builders and titans, scientists and thinkers, and heroes and icons. The five categories include such luminaries as Gandhi, Martin Luther King and the "Tank Man" in China; as Builders: Ford, Mayer, Walton and Gates; as artists: Picasso, James Joyce, Charlie Chaplin and the Beatles; as scientists: Freud, the Wright Brothers and Einstein; as Heroes and Icons: Muhammad Ali, the American G.I., Edmund Hillary and Tenzing Norgay. These are just a few of the men on this wonderful and inspirational list (*Time* 31.12.99).

The list was hotly debated, as expected. Some protested the inclusion of a fair number of villains: including Hitler and Stalin – influential, certainly, but not inspirational; others protested the exclusion of their favourites, notably Elvis, and the inclusion of Bart Simpson who is not even real. Yet the list reflects what Americans believe heroes to be.

Our concern is primarily gender, however, and only 18 of this 100 are female. This speaks to the continuing male dominance of the public sphere in the twentieth century. These 18 women nonetheless did play important roles in a number of disparate spheres of life: politics (Thatcher), civil rights (Parks), entertainment (Ball, Monroe, Graham, Franklin, Oprah), women's rights (Pankhurst, Sanger), fashion and cosmetics (Chanel, Lauder), the environment (Carson), human rights and welfare (Eleanor Roosevelt, Ann Frank, Princess Diana), the disabled (Helen Keller), science (Mary Leakey) and the poor and the dying (Mother Teresa). All these women testify to the contribution women have made in this century to how we live our lives. But the list testifies even more to the massive male contribution: some negative – but mostly positive.

The old gender dualism from Aristotle to Lord Tennyson to John Gray is no more, or so it may seem, save in our stereotypes and caricatures. Yet a further examination of the gender-distribution in these five categories is interesting: only one "builder" out of 20 is female, and only two scientists and three leaders, rising to four artists and seven of the 20 heroes and icons (7½ if we include Jackie Kennedy as half "the Kennedy dynasty"). So this uneven distribution indicates the parallels: both the relative numerical (quantitative) contributions of men and women, and also the degrees of specialization (the qualitative factor) in the five sectors – not too many builders, scientists, leaders and artists, but more heroes and icons.

Also none of these women can be called villains, unlike many of the men. So if we eliminate the villains from the male list, the ratio of women to men in terms of *positive* contribution during this century is substantially higher. Of course this depends upon whom we consider to be villains, which is as personal a matter as deciding who is a hero. I think we can agree on Hitler, Lenin and Lucky Luciano (who surely shouldn't be in the *Time* list anyway); I would include Che Guevara as a villain, whom I used to think was a high-minded idealist but seems to have been more of a cold-blooded killer. Mao Zedong is ambiguous: he was responsible for bringing China into the twentieth century and partly responsible for China being the economic power which it now is; but he was also responsible for over 70 million deaths in peacetime, many deliberately engineered, and he is demonized by his political successors (Chang and Halliday, 2005:3). Ayatollah Khomeini and Ho Chi Minh are obviously culturally relative choices: old enemies of the west. I would wait for history's verdict, especially from their people.

If we eliminate the villains, then, the ratio of women to men rises from 1:5 to 1:4 – a respectable contribution to public life, particularly given the segregated sex roles at the beginning of the century. Numbers are not really the point, however. The point of the *Time* list is that it clarifies the massive and positive and diverse contribution of *men* to our civilization in this century. They are honoured for this. This is not hegemonic *dominance* but *contribution*: *giving*: *donation*.

Time later decided, after some debate, that the Person of the Century was Albert Einstein. In an essay explaining this choice, Stephen Hawking wrote "The world has changed far more in the past hundred years than in any other century in history. The reason is not political or economic, but technological – technologies that flowed directly from advances in basic science. Clearly, no scientist better represents those advances than Albert Einstein." He published his special theory of relativity in 1905, his general theory in 1916, and was awarded the Nobel Prize in Physics in 1921. The runners-up were also both men: Franklin Delano Roosevelt and Mahatma Gandhi (*Time* 31.12.99).

Certainly: "The world has changed far more in the past hundred years than in any other century in history." But I suggest the reason is principally sociological, rather than technological; these include the rapid population growth from 1.7 billion to 6.3 billion, the massive devolution of power from men to women, and from the white European-based empires back to the original populations, and the expansion of democracy and human rights. Technology certainly has reached vast tracts of our world, and contributed to improvements in the quality of life and longevity worldwide; but both Roosevelt and Gandhi are best known for their social achievements and their sociological impact. Einstein's theories have had little impact on most of us. It is ideas about gender, power, colour, freedom, equality and human rights that have had the most impact around the world and have changed the world the most.

Time also selected "a person of each century": "The most important people of the millennium." The nine others, apart from Einstein, were William the Conqueror, Saladin, Genghis Khan, Giotto, Johann Gutenberg, Queen Elizabeth I, Isaac Newton, Thomas Jefferson and Thomas Edison (*Time* 31.12.1999). Nine of this top 10 of the millennium are men.

As a postscript to the *Time* top 100 people of the century, and its selection of Albert Einstein as the Person of the Century, we should note the choice of Rudy Guliani, Mayor of New York for the Person of the Year 2001. In 2002 the Persons of the Year were three women: Cynthia Cooper of WorldCom, Coleen Rowley of the FBI and Sherron Watkins of Enron. Called "The Whistleblowers," they demonstrate that heroism and moral courage come in both sexes. The person of the year in 2003 was "The American Soldier." In 2004 it was George W. Bush, re-elected as President. And in 2005 Bill and Melinda Gates and Bono were awarded the honour for their altruism and generosity. In 2006 it was "You" – for the producers and consumers of the new internet, and free websites such as YouTube, Wikipedia and Facebook. Vladimir Putin was named Person of the Year for 2007, and Barack Obama for 2008. The changed gender balance of power is exemplified and symbolized by the replacement of "Man of the Year" by "Person of the Year."

Time Magazine is rather fond of these "most infuential people" issues, and produced another Top 100 list in May 2008. As always the list is controversial and American-biased (which is fair enough in an American publication); but what is important is the increased ratio of women to men. Using the same categories as in the end of millennium list, *Time* reported that 24 of "The Most Influential People in the World" were women: a 1:3 ratio of women to men, up from 1:5 in 1999 (*Time* 12.5.08).

With women as 24% of the most influential people in the world, and with many women deliberately avoiding the national and international stage, we are certainly beyond tokenism. The age of patriarchy is over.

International Who's Who (IWW)

The International Who's Who also assessed the most important people of the last century, but employed a different methodology. Rather than selecting 20 people in five different sectors, the IWW simply selected its 100 most influential people, in alphabetical order. For purposes of comparison I have allocated them into different categories which approximate, more or less, to those of *Time* magazine. The numerical distribution is rather different, however; 34 politicians and leaders, only three athletes, 16 writers and poets, 10 musicians (singers, composers, conductors, players), 12 in film and theatre, six in the arts (dance, photography, sculpture and paint) and 19 in a catch-all category of innovators, inventors and thinkers. While some of these allocations are surely disputable, in part because the categories overlap, and some people overlap categories, the difference in emphasis between *Time* and *IWW* is clear. *Time* has emphasized business and money more heavily, and *IWW* has included more politicians (34) and more cultural figures, 44 in total (artists, entertainers and writers): (International Who's Who, 1999; *Gazette* 10.6.99).

There is some overlap between the two lists: about 37 people or families are on both lists. This gives a consensus on the Top 37. But 63 are *not* in common, so the dissent outweighs the consensus.

Secondly, the *Time* list has about 58 Americans in the Top 100 (depending on how you count some of these individuals) and only 14 from the U.K. The IWW list has 18 from the U.K., plus four from Ireland, but only 31 from the U.S.A. – a very different balance. *Time* has more than half its most influential people from the U.S.A., while the *IWW* has under one-third from the U.S.A., and more than half from outside the U.K. and the U.S.A. combined. Readers may wish to count their own lists and decide for themselves which is the more credible authority. My suspicion is that it will depend largely on where they reside: in the U.S.A., the U.K., Albania or Zimbabwe.

Finally, the gender ratio is very similar to that of *Time*, which is surprising, since both the sector ratio and the national ratio are so different. Only 10 of the *IWW* list are female, with a distribution that is very similar to that of *Time*: 4 out of 34 politicians and leaders, if we can include Princess Diana in this category, no athletes (3), nor poets and writers (16), but 5 out of 28 in "entertainment" (music, film, theatre, arts) and only one out of 19 for innovators, inventors and thinkers, and that is the wonderful Mother Teresa. Even in this categorization by gender, the sex roles are clearly differentiated.

Again, however, whatever the balance between the sectors, or by national origin (and national prejudice), the consensus of both *Time* and *IWW* is the tremendous male contribution to the twentieth century and to the world. From another perspective, however, this imbalance may also exemplify the relative exclusion of women, or self-selection by women, from the worlds of politics, economics, science and technology.

On the other hand, both these lists cover the entire century; had they considered the last 50 years, or especially the last decade of the century, the gender-balance would no doubt have been more equal in every single sector and in total. The speed of change has been very rapid.

U.K.

The top Britons for the last two millennia, according to an expert panel and readers of *Heritage Magazine*, and published in the *Daily Mail* (20.11.99) are as follows:

> William Shakespeare
> Sir Isaac Newton
> Sir Winston Churchill
> William Caxton
> Charles Darwin
> The Duke of Wellington
> Queen Elizabeth I
> William the Conqueror
> Alfred the Great
> Captain James Cook

Scientists, politicians, leaders, explorers, a printer, a playwright, two kings, a queen, a duke and a couple of knights – but just the one woman.

The degree of overlap with the American *Time* list is again interesting. Since only one person in the British list, Alfred the Great, came from the first millennium, it would be possible for nine of the top 10 to be the same (although the methods were different: *Time* selected one per century, the *Daily Mail* selected regardless of century; *Time* was worldwide, but the *Daily Mail* was "English only need apply"). Nonetheless, three people were on both lists: William the Conqueror, Elizabeth I and Isaac Newton.

Canada

The Canadian weekly magazine *Maclean's* developed a similar list of The 100 Most Important Canadians in History. *Maclean's* assembled a panel of experts, mostly historians – and also mostly males (eight women on the panel of 27) – to select these 100 Canadians in 10 categories: Heroes, Thinkers and Writers, Nation Builders, Discoverers and Innovators, Artists, Scientists, Activists, Characters, Stars and Entrepreneurs. Of the 100 selected, which included one group (the Group of Seven artists) and a couple of pairs, 88 were men. This is not surprising, given the historical dominance of men in public life. Their hard work, creativity, imagination and love: of truth, the game, adventure and exploration, even money, art, writing, and their fellow human beings, has changed the way we live, the way we are, and what we can be.

What is strange in the list, however, is the women. Of the 12 cited, two are fictitious: Evangeline, the subject of a poem by Longfellow after the tragic deportation of the Acadians in 1755; and Anne of Green Gables, a character in a novel and later a television series. *Maclean's* was castigated by the public for its political correctness, its double standards, for confusing the real and the unreal – and also for not finding more women: Karen Kain, the dancer, and Margaret Atwood were suggested by many.

The Top 10 were the top individuals selected in each category:

1. Georges Vanier: soldier, Governor-General.
2. Northrop Frye: literary scholar and author.
3. William Lyon MacKenzie King: three times elected Prime Minister.
4. Samuel de Champlain: explorer and founder of Quebec City.
5. Glenn Gould: musician.
6. Sir William Logan: geologist.
7. Nellie McLung: feminist and author. Champion of women's rights.
8. Joey Smallwood: charismatic Premier of Newfoundland.
9. Tom Longboat: famous Mohawk athlete.
10. K.C. Irving: industrialist.

Vanier (1888–67) served with great distinction in the army in World War I but was seriously wounded and lost a leg. He was appointed Governor-General in 1959 and died in office.

Maclean's was lyrical in praise of Vanier, indeed inspirational: "Heroism is not a word or a concept that comes naturally to Canadian minds. The very idea goes against the Canadian grain, for we are a small country with a colonial past." The editors described him as "the exemplar of service and duty and courage – the great military virtues that he embodied and honoured." They continued: "Duty, obligation, service – those are words that, like heroism, Canadians are inclined to avoid. But Vanier epitomized all these noble ideas . . . and service to a higher ideal than self." Both Georges and Pauline are candidates for sainthood in the Catholic Church. *Maclean's* concluded: "Canadians who think they have no heroes should think again" (*Maclean's* 1.7.98). His wife and son seem equally heroic.

A second survey, however, came up with different results. A National Survey of Canadians conducted by the Dominion Institute and the Council for Canadian Unity sponsored by the National Post found Terry Fox to be Canada's greatest hero. The survey was restricted to those no longer living, which avoids the super-star syndrome; but then, nine of the 10 *Maclean's* Top 10 were all dead; only K.C. Irving was still living. The Top Ten, according to public opinion rather than academic opinion, is as follows:

1. *Terry Fox.* After suffering bone cancer, which resulted in his right leg being amputated above the knee, Terry Fox vowed to run across Canada to raise money for cancer research. He ran 5,373 kilometres for 143 consecutive days, 42 kilometres a day, until he had to stop two-thirds of the way home. The cancer had returned. By February 1981 he had reached his goal of $1 for every Canadian: $24 million. He died in June 1981. The Terry Fox run is now an annual event in Canada and many other parts of the world and more than $400 million has been raised in his name for cancer research (www.terryfoxrun.org. Accessed 3.12.08).
2. *Dr Frederick Banting.* Discoverer of insulin and Nobel Prize winner.
3. *Lester B. Pearson.* Prime Minister and Nobel Peace Prize winner.
4. *Sir John A. Macdonald.* Canada's first Prime Minister.
5. *Louis Riel.* A leader of the Red River Rising in 1870 and fighter for French language rights. Later hanged for treason.
6. *Sir Isaac Brock.* General who defeated American forces in the War of 1812.
7. *T.C. "Tommy" Douglas.* Socialist politician who pioneered universal medical care.
8. *Laura Secord.* During the war of 1812 she walked 22 miles to warn the British of an imminent American attack, which was defeated.
9. *William "Billy" Bishop.* Canada's leading air ace of World War I.
10. *Nellie McClung.* Feminist, political activist and author.

A couple of points about this list are particularly interesting. The first is political, in that no one from Quebec is listed in this Canadian Top Ten; a fact which organizers blame on the refusal of the French language media to publicize the Internet contest. Second, only one person on this list chosen by the general public is also on the *Maclean's* list selected by an expert panel. That person is Nellie McClung. This reminds us of the subjectivity and relativity of heroes.

A third point averts again to this matter of gender. Only one woman made the *Maclean's* Top Ten and only two made the public's Top Ten. Whether we valorize Governor General Georges Vanier or Terry Fox more highly is less important than that we recognize the immense contribution of all these individuals in their different ways to the building of the nation.

The *National Post* researched another question later in the year: "Which Canadians made the most lasting contributions during the past 100 years?" This list was compiled by experts who selected 20 individuals in seven categories: a rather unusual top 140. Again, women were under-represented throughout, and unequally in the different spheres: none in politics, business and the military, three in the arts, and three in science and technology, six in sports and nine in literature, for an overall average of 15% (*National Post* 2.10.99). Again, no doubt this low proportion will be higher in the next century, for almost all the women were named for achievement in the second half of the century. As always, the discrepancies are curious: Nellie McClung and "Billy" Bishop V.C. who made the *Maclean's* list of the Top 10, did not make the National Post Top 140.

In sum, considering American, British and Canadian discussions of the most important and useful people of the last millennium, men (not surprisingly, given the divisions of labour) have performed heroically. Where many misandric authors have stressed the *downside* of men, we can emphasize the positives of both men and women – and redress the balance.

Learning Heroism

Joseph Campbell, the late great student of mythology has described the hero as follows: "A hero is someone who has given his or her life to something bigger than oneself" (1988:123). Normally this requires the hero to leave his or her world (separation); to penetrate some source of power (initiation); and to return with some special gift for the community (donation). Prometheus ascended to the heavens, stole fire from the gods, and descended. Jason sailed through the Clashing Rocks into a sea of marvels, circumvented the dragon that guarded the Golden Fleece, and returned with the fleece and the power to wrest his rightful throne from a usurper. Aeneas went down into the underworld, crossed the dreadful river of the dead, threw a sop to the three-headed watchdog Cerberus, and conversed, at last, with the shade of his dead father. All things were unfolded to him: the destiny of souls, the destiny of Rome, which he was about to found, "and in what wise he might avoid or endure every burden." He returned through the ivory gate to his work in the world (1972:30–1).

Heroic deeds (physical or spiritual), dangerous adventures, temptations (often sexual), and pain and suffering, are all part of the journey, the initiation into power, and the return. Sometimes the heroes lose their lives in the process.

Prometheus, Jason and Aeneas were classical heroes. So too were Odysseus (more familiar in his Latin name of Ulysses), and Hercules who performed the twelve labours, Theseus, who slew the Minotaur, and Perseus who saved Andromeda, and many others. They are also fictional characters, despite the truths they tell us. Later emerged St George, King Arthur and the Knights of the Round Table and Don Quixote, the last hero of the Renaissance, but he was a comic figure, a counterpoint to the earthy peasant, Sancho Panza. This satire was the first critique of the knight ideal and the ethic of courtly love.

The heroes are however also real historical figures, inscribed in our faiths: Moses and Abraham, Christ, the Buddha, and Mohammed – as well as many of those listed by *Time*, the International Who's Who and *Maclean's*.

People have their own heroes: they may be people whom they know, love and admire, or perhaps people whom they have never met. Christopher Reeve, who has probably thought more about this topic of heroism than most of us, is well known as the actor who played Superman in four films. In 1995 he was paralyzed from the neck down in a riding accident. In his autobiography *Still Me*, he has discussed the development of his thinking as he tried to cope with his disability:

> When I was a kid my great heroes were Harry Houdini and Charles Lindbergh because he did something against overwhelming odds: On a couple of tuna sandwiches and sheer determination, he flew for thirty-three hours across the ocean. Imagine staying awake and flying an airplane nonstop for thirty-three hours ... I'd always thought: God, there's a hero, there's somebody who can do it. He beat the limitations of the body, the vagaries of the weather. He got out of a difficult situation, he pulled it off.
> And Harry Houdini. You put him in a straitjacket and he could contort his shoulders and get out of it. (Reeve, 1999:46)

He recalled how he had often been asked "What is a hero?" He would give the usual response, the courageous soldier, and so on, the larger than life individuals like Lindbergh, Houdini, John Wayne and J.F.K., and sports heroes like Babe Ruth and Joe DiMaggio. But all this changed after his accident.

> Now my definition is completely different. I think a hero is an ordinary individual who finds the strength to persevere and endure in spite of overwhelming obstacles. The fifteen-year-old boy down the hall at Kessler who had landed on his head while wrestling with his brother, leaving him paralyzed and barely able to swallow or speak. Travis Roy, paralyzed in the first eleven seconds of a hockey game in his freshman year at college. Henry Steifel, paralyzed from the chest down in a car accident at seventeen, completing his education and working on Wall Street at age thirty-two, but having missed so much of what life has to offer. These are real heroes, and so are the families and friends who have stood by them. (Reeve, 1999:267)

Such "ordinary" individuals are also larger than life, not on the national stage but on the everyday stage. Reeve has described his own efforts to deal with paralysis in a poignant and inspiring memoir. He worked hard to raise resources for medical research and to support the American Paralysis Association; he also founded the Christopher Reeve Foundation to help those who have been paralyzed and to fund research. He also directed a television film and played the lead role in a remake of the Hitchcock classic, *Rear Window*. Christopher Reeve died in 2004.

Harrison Ford, who has played so many heroes, offered a complementary definition. He was interviewed by *Reader's Digest* recently: "Who do you look at in the real world and say, 'That's a hero'"? He replied: "The people who devote themselves to serving humanity at the cost of being less comfortable and less protected than the rest of us. They are policemen, firemen, and those who bring to the attention of the world things that are critical to its health and well-being." He himself has been involved in the Green movement for 15 years (Hockman, 2008:134).

How did they learn? The disability and paralysis literature is full of first-hand accounts of how men and women have coped: the particular circumstances and individuals, the turning-points, the attitudes and philosophy, even the humour. But the socialization of boys and young men at least partially accounts for men's physical bravery, and altruism, and perhaps also for their moral courage.

Boys are socialized into bravery from their earliest days, and by numerous reinforcing sources. Parents instruct their sons: "Don't cry!", "Be brave!" "Don't be a baby!" And later the instructions are more oblique, inspiring stoicism and immunity to pain and fear: "No pain, no gain!" and the marine slogan, "When the going gets tough, the tough get going."

The comics, television shows and children's films are full of superheroes: Superman, Batman, Spiderman, the Hulk, the Six Million Dollar Man, and before them Sgt. Rock, Hopalong Cassidy, Roy Rogers, Dan Dare and of course G.I. Joe – the male equivalent of the polar opposite Barbie. Despite Wonderwoman and Charlie's Angels, boys and girls are socialized in very traditional and opposite directions – and girls are taught to expect their boys to be heroic. Peter Pan, Luke Skywalker and more recently Harry Potter and Frodo Baggins, all create the same brave and stoic models of masculinity for both boys *and* girls.

In adulthood the same binary socialization persists: action movies, where good defeats evil, are usually "a guy thing" (now known as dick flicks), versus the "chick flicks," which deal with relationships. John Wayne in the 60s was followed by Clint Eastwood as Dirty Harry and in spaghetti westerns, James Bond, Harrison Ford, Arnold Schwarzenegger, Sylvester Stallone, to Mel Gibson with *Lethal Weapon* and *Braveheart*, Bruce Willis and now Brad Pitt.

The action movies are reinforced by the action novels of Ian Fleming, Tom Clancy, Robert Ludlum, Clive Cussler, Louis L'Amour, Bernard Cornwell, Patrick O'Brian etc.[5]

Men learn very early what masculinity is, and who they are supposed to be. They learn it on the sports field: to use their bodies as weapons, to be physical, not to be a coward, to be stoic and not to whine or complain, to play on through their injuries, to work as a team and maybe even to be good sportsmen.

Nothing is that simple, however, and men are widely presented in popular culture as complete idiots: in *The Flintstones*, *The Simpsons*, *Beavis and Butthead*, *Boys Behaving Badly*, and now *Trailer Park Boys* (as we discuss in more detail in the next chapter). The humour may be ironic: hegemonic males don't do this! so when they do, it's funny! Or such programs may socialize boys into "behaving badly." Clearly the socialization of boys into bravery, heroism and chivalry does not work

---

5   These are now being counterbalanced by such crime novelists as Janet Evanovich, P.D. James, Minette Walters, Patricia Cornwell and Kathy Reichs (following in the footsteps of Agatha Christie and Dorothy Sayers) rivalling Robert Parker, Elmore Leonard, Ian Rankin, Reginald Hill and others. The gender divide is not as clean and clear as it once was, except that the romance novels, epitomized by Harlequin, are mostly by and for women; and Danielle Steel is unrivalled.

very effectively, or we would have no villains. Alternatively these "civility" values are outweighed by others: cash, or power or sexual gratification. Presumably such films as *The Godfather* and such programs as *The Sopranos* might socialize boys into villainy. These are the anti-heroes. Similarly films like "Jackass" might socialize them into idiocy and injury.[6]

But men's options are not simply the traditional action/warrior model vs. the new idiot model or the pig/villain model. These are the false dichotomies of popular culture. Men have many options, role-models and heroic types to emulate, or not, and these days (as in the past) they are not all male.

Today men are perpetually being urged to "find your feminine side" – as if nurturing or loving is a female monopoly. A man may be a hero to his wife or lover and his family, or within his community or recognized by his country, for quite different qualities. We need to recognize and appreciate the varieties of male altruism, and love, rather than insisting that female culture is, or should be, the yardstick for both sexes, and that only women have "an ethic of care."

Men are now so widely demonized on so many fronts that it sometimes is difficult to see the male caring ethic. Even male-affirmative writers are worried: "in the late twentieth century, we face a crisis in masculine identity of great proportions" (Moore and Gillette, 1991:xx). This is not helped by Maureen Dowd, a Pulitzer wining journalist, whose new book is entitled *Are Men Necessary?* (2005) – implying that they are not. This reverse sexism is now institutionalized and acceptable.

It is difficult to calculate the socialization impact of the mass media and popular culture (video games are often particularly violent) on boys, particularly given that the media construct or portray men in such different ways: heroes, idiots, and villains, fools, – as well as totally lovable in some films of course; usually with Hugh or Cary Grant.

Heroism is, of its very nature, exceptional: it is above and beyond the call of duty. It is rare. We need heroes, both mythological, historical and contemporary. We need them to show us the way, or the ways, to assert our fundamental values and to inspire us. And we have our heroes, men and women both, in similar and also different sorts of ways. The hero lives in all of us. The adventure of the hero, says Campbell is "the adventure of being alive" (1988:163).

Meanwhile, although the giants stand tall, it is the men and women in the crowd, on the ground, who help to make the whole civil system work (or not), as I suggest in my list of the admirable, but not necessarily Heroic.

---

6   *The Sopranos* was perhaps the first TV show to glamourize villains. In the 60s, films like *Butch Cassidy and the Sundance Kid* and *Bonnie and Clyde* did the same; as, later, did the Godfather series. Similarly *No Country for Old Men* socializes viewers into the triumph over evil over good. Realistic sometimes, no doubt, but not a message with a happy ending. This shift in values in the industry is more likely to escalate and legitimize violence than the reverse and is grounds for concern.

Admirable Types

* **Parents**: who hold our futures in trust.

* **Volunteers**: who keep the social system working.

* **Peacemakers**: the UN – though some aspects are less than admirable – diplomats, mediators, Peace Prize winners.

* **Environmentalists and Naturalists**: Rachel Carson to Jane Goodall, to Al Gore, Greenpeace to WWF to the Forestry Stewardship Council – who fight to preserve our world.

* **Human Rights Activists**: the Red Cross and Red Crescent, Amnesty International, Human Rights Watch, Doctors without Borders, the Anti-Slavery Society, feminists (but not misandrists) and masculinists (but not misogynists), and all who promote peace, justice, freedom and equality. King, Mandela, the Tiananmen Square protester, Gandhi, Aung San Suu Kyi, Mother Teresa.

* **Adventurers and Explorers**: who show us what we can do – Scott, Earhardt, Hillary, Gagarin, Armstrong, Fossett.

* **War Veterans**: who have risked and often lost their lives to save ours.

* **Workers**: especially those in the caring, healing and teaching professions, underpaid and overworked; and those in the primary sector, unappreciated, who lay the foundations of our civilization. The Nobel disciplinary Prize winners.

* **Social Scientists**: who have helped us to understand our selves and our societies and to improve the quality of our lives.

* **The Unknown Donor**: who gives time, energy, body organs, blood, thought, a helping hand, cash, a smile, a seat on the bus, encouragement … there's someone every day.

* **The Heroes**: recognized by medals and fame, or unrecognized, and those in the saving professions, who risk and sometimes give their lives for others.

A story of heroism crystallizes many of the points made earlier. While Campbell was living in Hawaii in the early nineteen eighties, a young man climbed over the railing at a mountain ledge to commit suicide. Two policemen on patrol saw him, and one jumped out, grabbed the man as he jumped, and was himself falling when the second policeman held him and hauled them both back. A journalist asked the officer: "Why didn't you let go? You could have been killed." He replied: "I couldn't let go. If I had let that young man go, I couldn't have lived another day of my life" (1988:110).

What happened there? What about the officer's duties to his family, perhaps his wife and children, and to himself to save his own life? Campbell suggests, following Schopenhauer, that in times of crisis, you realize that "you and that other are one, that you are two aspects of the one life, and that your apparent separateness is but an effect of the way we experience forms under the conditions of space and time. Our true reality is in our identity and unity with all life" (1988:110).

This might seem a bit too mystical for most of us. On the other hand, how else do you explain such a reflex action to save life but as instinctive. Perhaps it is the same instinct for life that some, but not all, women experience in wishing to have a child, despite the pain, inconvenience and duration – and sometimes even more than one!

Bill Moyers added a perceptive comment to Campbell's story: "So when Jesus says, "Love thy neighbour as thyself," he is saying in effect, "Love thy neighbour because he *is* yourself" (1988:111).

Campbell notes that we do selfless things all the time – you can see it every day (1988:111). We do look after our neighbours, even if we do not even know them, in a hundred ways of civility: holding doors, picking up dropped items, slowing to let other drivers into our lanes, waving acknowledgements, trying to cheer people up in hospital waiting rooms, and so on. These microscopic altruisms are the building blocks of grand heroism for they express the recognition of the reality and the value of the other. The little things are great in importance.

The Feminization of Heroism

The heroes are not all male, though in occidental tradition they usually were because, so Campbell suggests: "The male usually has the more conspicuous role, just because of the conditions of life. He is out there in the world, and the woman is in the home" (1988:125). This of course is changing now, indeed has already changed, so more female heroes are emerging.

Campbell notes that motherhood is heroic: the Aztecs recognized this in assigning the same heaven to warriors killed in battle as to mothers who died in childbirth. Such heroism is not well recognized in our culture. As he puts it: "Giving birth is definitely a heroic deed, in that it is the giving over of oneself to the life of another" (1988:125). The idea of the mother as hero is indeed classic: there is the journey from the known to the unknown, the transformation from maiden to mother, the suffering, pain and endurance intrinsic to any great quest, the creation of new life, the gift to the world – and that's just the beginning! (1988:126). Campbell's point echoes that of Elizabeth Cady Stanton over 100 years earlier and cited above.

To summarize: heroism is multi-dimensional, exceptional, presumably constituted by both biology and culture, predominantly male and generally reflective of roles in public rather than private life. As these roles have changed and the gender balance (or imbalance) of roles has shifted, so has the gender balance of heroism.

In the bravery awards, a solid percentage go to women. A recent example of conspicuous bravery is Benazir Bhutto, returning to Pakistan aware that she was facing almost certain death – and then she was assassinated. An increasing proportion of the awards can be expected in the future as the lifestyle and occupations of men and women continue to converge.

In the air, Amelia Earhardt triumphed; at sea, Ellen MacArthur; and in space many female astronauts. In 2008 Danica Patrick became the first woman to finish first in an Indy race in the Indy Japan 300. Janet Guthrie was the first woman to qualify, in 1977; but it had been only recently that women had been allowed in the garage area, the press box or the pits – even if she owned the car. The speed of gender-achievement change is so fast that it seems to far outpace our ability to adjust our stereotypes, generalizations and expectations.

Many women are still inspirational: not only the saints of old, but more modern figures from Helen Keller, Ann Frank to Mother Teresa and Oprah, in their different ways. Women's success in politics is discussed in the next chapter, but Thatcher, Rice, Merkel, and Sarah Palin are obvious recent examples. More women than in the past are recipients of the Nobel Peace Prizes and the disciplinary prize, though none of either sex has equalled Mme. Curie. Many of these women, and those listed in the *Time* and *IWW* lists are self-made women, including Monroe, Oprah, Thatcher, Rice and Merkel, who lived in a squat during her student days. But the background of other individuals, including judges of the Supreme Court in both the U.S.A. and Canada, novelists, corporate CEOs etc. is often more private.

Given the extent and range of these achievements and such heroism, it is unfortunate that victim feminism has for too long socialized many women into victimism, with long lists of alleged obstacles to success: glass ceilings, unequal pay etc. (discussed earlier). There are of course many *real* obstacles to success – which apply to both men *and* women; both need to be examined without political bias. Yet many students at university have been taught, usually subliminally, not only to lower their expectations in face of misogyny (or that they have to work *so* much harder), but also to loathe their male oppressors. In sum, *victim feminism victimizes women as well as men.*

Feminisms are advertised as struggles for social justice – and they have indeed expanded social justice, at some cost to both sexes and even though the expansions have been mostly enacted by men: legislators, corporate executives, university administrators, and so on. Yet victim feminism, as exclusionist and as identity politics has also been counter-productive and self-defeating.

Susan Pinker (2008) and others (Chapter 7) have argued that the "problem" – as defined by so many – is not male discrimination, nor testosterone, but differential values. Men and women, despite overlapping and converging roles, structures and values, tend to have different aspirations with respect to work-life balance, and different definitions of happiness and success. As a result, career paths diverge. Quality of life is not defined the same way. Pinker's challenge to the conventional wisdom deserves an award for bravery.

The accelerating feminization of heroism is certainly a more useful world view for both women and men, and more realistic, than the conventional victimism. Not that we should be blind to the oppression of any one, but nor should we be so obsessed by it as to perceive *only* victims, men or women, and to ignore heroism and heroic achievements. This is a more positive philosophy than the third wave "empowerment" ideology – i.e. power feminism, to call a spade a spade. For heroism is not about power, but love: of others, of challenges, of the planet. This could be the fourth wave – but not necessarily feminism, also masculinism.

Relative Heroes

Heroes are controversial. By now that must be apparent. General Custer was a hero to some but he is certainly also a villain to others. Similarly Chief Sitting Bull was a villain to some, but he still is a hero to others. The Duke of Wellington was a hero to the British after the battle of Waterloo, but not to the French, nor was Admiral Lord Nelson, who lost first an arm, then an eye and finally his life in the service of his country. George Washington was not a hero to the British, Abraham Lincoln was not a hero to the white Southerners; nor was Martin Luther King.

The heroes of one side are the villains of the other side in conflict situations. And the winning side has an important role in the writing and re-writing of history. Examples could be multiplied from the history of every nation, and of every group in the nation (Campbell, 1988:127).

The relativity of heroism is not just confined to the protagonists in military, class, religious, political or even gender conflict. Heroes are also relative to time. With the 20–20 hindsight of history sometimes the heroes and villains of the past blur a little. Some of the "great victories" can now be seen as awful massacres, unjustified and evil.

Nonetheless, even though good and evil are sometimes redefined, the great evils and the great goods still stand: slavery and the abolitionists; Nazism and the Allies; racism and sexism and the humanists; apartheid and Nelson Mandela and many others.

The list of names of men and women who have fought evil in its various forms is long and honourable. The "Righteous Gentiles" who fought the Holocaust are recognized by the State of Israel. The status of some heroes is in dispute, as always; and with the passage of time and changing values and judgements, the status of others will change.

Ultimately, however, heroes are also highly individual. We all have, or had, our own heroes. Joseph Campbell has discussed the heroes of his youth; but in his old age he said he had none (1988:132). This is a little sad. Perhaps he realized that so many heroes had feet of clay, for no-one is perfect; or perhaps the human heroes did not match up to the mythical ones. If it is true that we are known by our deeds, as it surely is, then it is also true that we are known by our heroes: they crystallize our values, our ideals and our aspirations, and inspire our deeds and lives. Sincerity is not enough. There is no shortage of perfectly sincere fools and villains. Good judgement is also necessary. Heroes have to be *right*, or they are merely misguided and deluded.

Geniuses are born, not made. Heroes are made, not born. We make them ourselves: male and female.

Conclusion

In recent years we have begun to re-think men, and to revalorize them for their heroism, bravery, hard work and altruism. This is the resultant of many forces: 9/11 and the bravery of the police officers and fire-fighters in New York, the courage of the soldiers in the retaliatory invasion of Afghanistan, and in the subsequent invasion of Iraq, also the emergence of evolutionary psychology as a "difference" theory, in contrast to the "bisexual" theories of Freud, and Jung, and the cultural determinism of Margaret Mead and many feminists; also the rise of the men's movements (see below) and a male-affirmative literature.

Men are the heroic sex. In the next chapter, however, we shall see that men are also the anti-heroes: the villainous sex, both in reality (as with heroes) but also in popular culture and some misandric work by feminists and masculinists alike.

Chapter 4
Villains:
Misandry and the New Sexism

Pigs, jerks, fools, dogs, animals, rapists, criminals, violent, the enemy, sexists, misogynists, testosterone-poisoned, oppressors, the problem, THEM. . . . Men have been widely demonized and vilified over the last 50 years. This is the new anti-male sexism: misandry.

In this chapter we will first explore the depth, extent and dimensions of this new sexism in popular culture and in some feminist and pro-feminist writings; second, we will discuss the origins, functions, roles and consequences of this new social problem; finally we consider policies and recommendations for the resolution or amelioration of the new sexism, like the old. At the start we need to note an important caveat. No doubt most feminists (male as well as female) are not anti-male; but many are, and have been for decades – the label radical feminists is sometimes applied, but there is nothing "radical" about sexism, either misogyny or misandry. Like racism and anti-semitism, which also ranks some people as intrinsically superior to others, sexism is merely a form of fascism.

The theme of misandry in the work of such feminist icons as Friedan, Greer and Steinem and contemporary novelists does need to be addressed. These are not fringe feminists, but the mainstream founders of the women's movement, best-selling authors, contributors to "Ms" magazine and invited speakers at NOW conventions. To be pro-feminist does not necessarily mean to be anti-male; in practice, however, it sometimes does. This misandry is particularly intriguing in the work of such pro-feminist men as Stoltenberg, Brod and Kimmel. It is disappointing to explore misandry in the work of so many who profess egalitarianism and to work for social justice; yet it is not entirely surprising that the old misogyny should generate a new misandry.

Misandry may be defined as the anger towards, and the hatred, fear and contempt of men (cf. Nathanson and Young, 2001:5, 229–33). This is similar or identical to the usual definitions of misogyny, but with reversed genders. Indeed the widespread misandry is in part a response to misogyny, just as female supremacism is a response to male supremacism. The angelicization of women is correlative to the demonization of men.

Misandry in Popular Culture

Misandry today is virtually institutionalized in popular culture: in joke books, cartoons, television programs, on T-shirts, fridge magnets, advertisements, coffee mugs – everywhere. Indeed it is so pervasive that we may not see it: we take it for granted at face value as humour – rather than as contempt, or advocating violence, or defining men as fools. We are sensitive to misognynistic humour, yet relatively insensitive to misandric humour. Why? Some of the bumper sticker "jokes" advocate violence:

> "Dead Men Don't Rape."
> "So Many Men. So Little Ammunition."
> "The Quickest Way to a Man's Heart is Through his Ribcage."

We can imagine the outcry if bumper stickers were sold with the motto "Dead Women Don't Nag" or "So Many Women. So Little Ammo" or "The Quickest Way to a Woman's Heart etc." Yet the fact is that the former are acceptable, and the latter anathema.

T-shirts are sometimes similarly contemptuous: "PMS: Putting up with Men's Shit." In my local mall, a T-shirt on display states: "PMS allows women for one day to do what men do all year." Other T-shirts offer 10 reasons why a Banana or a Beer are better than a man.

Jokes at the expense of women were once commonplace. Now we consider them sexist, insulting and rude. But jokes at the expense of men are now commonplace, and many people must find them amusing, since these books are published and sold. These include such titles as *101 Reasons Why a Cat is Better than a Man*" (Zobel, 1994); *Why Can't a Man be More Like a Cat?* (Kenner and Van der Meer, 1995), *How to Make Your Man Behave in 21 Days or Less, using the secrets of professional dog training* (Salmansohn, 1994), *Women are from Venus, Men are from Hell* (Newman, 1999) – and many more (Garner, 1994 etc.).

And fridge magnets: "No woman ever shot a man who was doing the dishes." And coffee mugs: "All men are animals. Some just make better pets." And the latest T-shirt, which did at least raise a fuss: "Boys are smelly, throw rocks at them"; "Boys are stupid, throw rocks at them" (*Time* 1.3.04). The latter is the eponymous title of a new book of abuse of men – no doubt amusing to some, but unacceptable were the T-shirts to read "Girls are stupid, throw rocks at them" (Goldman, 2005). Misandric humour is institutionalized in all these joke books – almost all by women – and on all of these bumper stickers and T-shirts.

In one gift-shop in Maine, wall plaques announced: "Husband and Dog Missing. Reward for Dog." "Cats are Smarter than Men." "I got a dog for my husband. It was a fair swap." "If we can put a man on the moon, why can't we put them all there?" And there were numerous plaques in praise of daughters, mothers, sisters and grandmas. The other sex was conspicuous by its absence. The only male-positive item was a candle holder which read: "If at first you don't succeed, ask Dad to help you."

The joke-books include such male-negative humour as:

Q: What do you call a man with half a brain?
A: Gifted.

Q: What is the difference between a man and a fish?
A: One is a bottom-feeding scum-sucker, the other is a fish.

Q: Why did God create man?
A: Because a vibrator can't mow the lawn.

The test of hate-humour is to reverse the process: "What do you call a woman with half a brain?" "Gifted." and so on. Or a more violent gender-reversed joke: "How many women does it take to wallpaper a room?" "That depends on how thin you slice them."

It is disappointing that so many in the women's movement protested misogynistic elements in male humour, as instruments in the oppression of women; but they do not protest the sexist misandric elements in female humour.

These "jokes" are constructions of men as villains: to be shot or sliced, or trained like dogs, as beneath contempt, inferior to cats, beer and bananas, half-brained and scum-suckers. The joke-books and T-shirts go on and on. Cumulatively this constitutes a retail culture of misandry.

Newspaper cartoons reinforce the message of misandry as humour. Men are widely portrayed as fools, lazy and/or violent in such cartoons as Hagar the Horrible, Blondie, Drabble, Beetle Bailey, the old Andy Capp – and also victims of violence from their bosses and their wives. Ironically, these portraits of men as pathetic are usually drawn by male cartoonists. You cannot mock women or minorities, but males are fair game.

Television is part of the problem. *The Simpsons*, *Beavis and Butthead* are two of the more popular television programs for the young, but they are not exactly role models for young men. Instead, they establish an anti-intellectual subculture, and not coincidentally while the males are funny but jerks, the females are generally steady and sensible. The latest of these males as jerks TV programs is *Trailer Park Boys*, with viewer discretion advised for the usual list of boys behaving badly behaviours: stupidity, nudity, violence, bad language, sex etc. The films *Jackass* (2002) and *Jackass 2* (2006) are even more ridiculous, dangerous, stupid and popular. Indeed they are hard to explain except as men-as-idiots but making money at the same time.

Fathers used to be portrayed positively in the 50s – as were men in general. Today the fathers are criminal and disturbed (*The Sopranos*), stupid (*Malcolm in the Middle*), lovable but stupid, and often overweight and married to attractive and sensible women (as in *Everybody Loves Raymond*, *Home Improvement*, *The*

King of Queens, Still Standing, Listen Up and *According to Jim*). Apparently these opposites attract each other – but it is not clear why. The message that these sitcoms are sending about men and women is so clear, so continuous, so unrealistic, so male-negative that men might be forgiven for acting-out these stereotypes. The impact on men and women of these ubiquitous reflections of gender is unclear.

There were always bumbling fathers like Dagwood Bumstead and Fred Flintstone, but these were balanced by cartoon characters like Batman and Superman; and there were also bumbling housewives like Lucy and Edith Bunker. But one study by the National Fatherhood Initiative found that fathers on television are "eight times more likely than mothers to be portrayed as incompetent and irresponsible parents" (NFI 5.12.00. www.fatherhood.org).

In England a television program in prime time was entitled *Bring Your Husband to Heel* (2005). Canine behaviourist (i.e. dog trainer) Annie Clayton teaches dog-training skills to wives as husband-training skills. This is the portrait of men as dogs, or fools: surely as unacceptable for men as it would be for women.

Why these male-negative portraits are so pervasive is unclear. Perhaps because the sitcom audiences are mostly female and want to watch gender-polarized shows to boost their self-esteem. But that would apply only to sitcoms, not to the male-negative culture, and to the culture wars. Advocates of this humour perhaps consider it to be resistance to male hegemony: laugh at the oppressors and they are castrated. The purpose of misogynistic jokes was perhaps to maintain the gender hierarchy, and the purpose of misandric jokes is to topple it. Perhaps.

The consequences of such intra-species hostilities are unfortunate. Boys and men may internalize these negative attitudes, and learn to be ashamed of themselves, or perhaps learn to act up to these expectations. "I'm a pig? So be it." The negative stereotypes may become self-fulfilling prophecies and may create a spiral of further adversities from crime and homicide to suicide to failure (cf. Nathanson and Young, 2001:248).

In the United States nearly four in 10 children do not live with their biological father, and three in 10 live in homes with no father figure; by the time they are six they will have spent more time watching TV than they will spend talking to their fathers, on average, over their entire lifetime (NFI 5.12.00 www.fatherhood.org). And then men in general and fathers in particular are portrayed as deadbeats, useless, unnecessary.

Fathers do matter. In a 1996 Gallup Poll, 79.1% of Americans thought that he most significant family or social problem facing America is the physical absence of the father from the home." This is up nearly 10 percentage points from four years earlier (NFI 4.1.00).

This is not apparent from the television, the cartoons, the joke-books, and so on. Not only are there no equivalent shows about doofus moms, or monstrous moms (except *Absolutely Fabulous*) but TV could never get away with such negative portraits of Blacks or Jews or other populations – still less women.

Hollywood is not known for its feminist sympathies; yet a number of films have been anti-male, from *The Burning Bed* (1984) and *Thelma and Louise* (1991) to

Waiting to Exhale (1995) and *The First Wives Club* (1996) (Nathanson and Young, 2001). "Monster" (2003) was curious, depicting Aileen Wuornos, a serial killer of men, as herself a victim. Similarly *Karla* (2006) portrays Karla Homolka, who murdered three women including her own sister with her husband in Canada in 1991, is also portrayed as a victim. Such real or alleged victimization is presented as justifying homicide, but it also socializes women into violence. The latest is *The Brave One* (2007) with Jodi Foster as a righteous revenge killer.

What can we make of all these multi-dimensional aspects of misandry, in all these popular domains of press cartoons, television cartoons, jokes and joke books, T-shirts and bumper stickers, films and TV programs? This mass of diverse data does indicate that there is a problem. Given that, what is the etiology? and what are the solutions?

Several factors seem to converge here. Clearly misandric feminists have been responsible for the original male-bashing – a jovial term for the hate literature, which is what this material would be called if the jokes were gender-reversed. But the current culture in films, television programs, and cartoons, often written and produced by men, suggests a more complex dynamic than just blaming misandric feminists.

And, on the internet the misandry is blatant, even proud, on such web sites as www.ihatemen.com and www.manhaters.com. There is also a misogynistic website: www.ihatewomen.com – although when accessed the misandric sites had far more results than the misogynistic one.

The overall picture is complex, therefore, with misandry institutionalized in many domains and at many levels in popular culture: a cultural norm. There is no need to argue a media conspiracy theory, but perhaps a convergence of many factors including: feminist misandry, male guilt, male self-deprecating humour, and certainly the profit motive in some of the films and T-shirts, coffee mugs, fridge magnets, TV shows and films. Misandry pays.

Real Villains

Part of the matter is the degree to which the popular culture reflects the political reality. Some men really are villains. Indeed the greatest villains of the 20th century are all male. The top ten are, in my opinion: Adolf Hitler and his satellites, responsible for World War II and the Holocaust: at least 50 million deaths and massive global destruction; Mao Tse-Tung, who contributed to the economic development of China at the cost of 70 million civilian deaths in peacetime (Chang and Halliday, 2005:3); Stalin, who created the Ukrainian famine, the gulags, the police state, and remains a hero to some for saving Russia in the war; Pol Pot: responsible for two million deaths in Cambodia; Daniel Malan, the architect of apartheid in South Africa. We might add Nicolai Ceaucescu of Romania, Idi Amin of Uganda, Mobutu Sese Soko of Congo, Slobodan Milosevic of the former Yugoslavia, Jean Bokassa of the Central African Republic, Saddam Hussein of Iraq, Charles Taylor of Nigeria, and Osama bin Laden. That is more than 10 to allow for subjective bias and for the fact that not all will agree with this listing.

Many of those who hold power, abuse it: whether it be military, political, economic, intellectual or spiritual. These include the Turkish authors of the Armenian genocide and the Hutu authors of the Rwandan genocide in 1994. Some of the old dictators have been deposed (Idi Amin of Uganda) or shot (Nicolae Ceausescu of Romania) or tried and executed (Saddam Hussein of Iraq) or died of natural causes (Slobodan Milosovic, while being tried at the Hague). Some would add the Europeans and North Americans – the whites – for slavery, the brutality of their conquests and wars and killings around the world, and their colonialism, racism and imperialism. Benefits have flowed, but at high costs.

Most of the murderers, serial killers and mass murderers are male,(as are most of their victims), and at the time of writing, the Top 10 on the FBI's Most Wanted List were all men (Dec. 2008).

At the risk of spoiling the congratulatory mood of the previous chapter: since we have made a list of heroes, we should also make a list of present-day villains. This list of the 10 worst dictators in the world has been compiled from international human rights organizations including Amnesty International, Freedom House, Human Rights Watch and Reporters without Borders. David Wallechinsky (2006) publishes this list occasionally.

The World's 10 Worst Dictators
1. Omar al-Bashir, Sudan.
2. Kim Jong-il, North Korea.
3. Than Shwe, Burma/Myanma
4. Robert Mugabe, Zimbabwe.
5. Islam Karimov, Uzbekistan.
6. Hu Jintao, China.
7. King Abdullah, Saudi Arabia.
8. Saparmurat Niyazov, Turkmenistan.
9. Seyed Ali Khamane'I, Iran.
10. Teodoro Obiang Nguema, Equatorial Guinea.

These are the top 10. The next 10 include, in rank order, Muammar al-Qaddifi of Libya, King Mswati III of Swaziland, Isayas Afewerki of Eritrea, Aleksandr Lukashenko of Belarus, Fidel Castro of Cuba (since resigned), Bashar al-Assad of Syria, Pervez Musharraf of Pakistan (since resigned), Meles Zenawi of Ethiopia, Boungnang Vorachith of Laos, and Tran Duc Luong of Vietnam. All 20 of these dictators are men, which feeds into the stereotype of men as villains.

Closer to home, the Mafia and organized crime, the terrorists – not only al Qaeda, but also the IRA, FLQ, ETA, 17 November, Red Army Faction, the KKK – the environmental polluters, child abusers, drug dealers – all remain problematic, male and female.

No doubt all these 20 dictators have their supporters and admirers, perhaps because they are beneficiaries of their largesse. And their are issues of relativism between nations in conflict. The International Criminal Court however offers the legal criteria for genocide and crimes against humanity. Nothing relative about that.

This is a long and depressing list which complements, unfortunately, the *Time* and the IWW lists of so many wonderful people, and the poems of Sophocles, Shakespeare and Pope. It is noteworthy that most of the people on the lists of both heroes and villains are male, a function of power rather than gender, as we noted earlier and as the discussion of female villains below will clarify. As more and more women assume positions of public power, no doubt more and more will appear on both lists in this millennium.

The fact that most major villains are male, however, does not mean that most men are villains: the logic of this escapes many of the authors discussed above and below. That all pigs are animals, to take a common metaphor for men, does not mean that all animals are pigs. Indeed most animals (and men) are not pigs; they might be dogs, of course, or even pussycats. Many writers on "the battle of the sexes" have tended to focus on male villainy and piggery rather than male heroism, and achievements. They have also tended to ignore female villainy.

Misandry and the Second Wave

The Second Wave of the Women's Movement was ushered in with Simone de Beauvoir's *The Second Sex* (1953) and Betty Friedan's best-selling *The Feminine Mystique* in 1963, the formation of the National Organization of Women in 1965 and the famous protest against the Miss America Beauty Pageant in Atlantic City in 1968.

The Feminine Mystique ignited the women's movement in the United States and re-evaluated the status of women but also initiated the new sexism. This was perhaps predictable: if women are defined as oppressed, then the oppressors, men, will predictably be hated. This simple analysis was extremely popular, but in hindsight, deeply flawed, ideologically inaccurate and, while the women's movement has brought enormous benefits to women and to society generally, there have been high costs, largely unacknowledged and invisible – notably misandry.

Certainly, Friedan struck a nerve. She declared in her first sentence that "something is very wrong with the way that American women are trying to live their lives today" (1970:7). This understanding began with her interviews in 1957 with 200 women who graduated from Smith with her in 1942, and found "a strange discrepancy between the reality of our lives as women and the image to which we were trying to conform, the image that I came to call the feminine mystique" (1970:7). She referred to this discrepancy as a "schizophrenic split." Friedan describes the suburban situation of women:

Each suburban wife struggled with it alone. As she made the beds, shopped for groceries, matched slipcover material, ate peanut butter sandwiches with her children, chauffeured Boy Scouts and Brownies, lay beside her husband at night – she was afraid to ask even of herself the silent question – "Is this all?" (1970:11).

Friedan was also perhaps projecting her own existential anxieties onto others, as the mother of three children. (Don't husbands ever wonder: "Is this all?" How might this consideration have affected Friedan's work?) She pointed to "the problem that has no name," the "trap" of the suburban life, and to "that voice within women that says: "I want something more than my husband and my children and my home" (1970:15, 26, 27).

So, what do women want? she asked, echoing Freud's question: "more." Not – a room of one's own, as Virginia Woolf had modestly desired; not "to be loved and cherished," as John Gray has suggested, and the Harlequin romances assert; not just better and better sex, as *Cosmopolitan* promotes; – but a job, cash, which equates with freedom, Friedan suggested.

Friedan analyzed the situation of white middle-class American women, probably the most privileged population on earth, and saw the problem (men) and the solution (paid work). The analysis is intriguing: it proceeds by questions and anecdotes. The cover of my paperback suggests that women are in a trap: "Why all the tranquillizers? The liquor? The adulteries? The problem children? The suicides in the suburbs?" Such rhetorical questions suggest that men are the problem, but they do have real answers. The suicides were then and are now 80% male. The alcohol consumption is 80–90% male. The adulteries: probably for much the same reasons men engage in them. But here we have the portrait of women as victims: "They have been sold into virtual slavery by a lie invented and marketed by men."

This is the beginning of the new sexism: men as liars, and virtual slave-owners; and not some, but all men. And all women's problems from suicide to alcohol can be blamed on men! This is the Big Lie, derived from Plato (Republic 382c), and it worked: her work sold well.

In her most famous, or infamous chapter, Friedan described suburban married domestic life as a "comfortable concentration camp" (1970:271). The husbands, of course, are the SS guards. In 1963 Friedan knew about the camps: a comfortable concentration camp is an oxymoron and a gross insult to the victims of the Holocaust – and to men, of course.

Friedan's demonization of men as liars, virtual slave-owners and Nazi SS guards was not condemned at the time as hate literature, or even as silly or plain wrong; although it is doubtful that similar remarks about any other American population would have been so ignored: blacks, Jews, native Americans, or, of course, women.

This was just the beginning. And whatever the very considerable achievements of Betty Friedan in particular and the women's movement in general, they have been achieved at a high cost in terms of gender relations, a pervasive climate of a new sexism, the destruction of family and a bleaker future for children so often deprived of a father. Fathers, once defined primarily as providers for, and protectors of, their families, were now redefined as Nazi concentration camp guards and slave-owners!

While the struggle for women's rights had begun over a century before, with Mary Wollstonecraft's, *A Vindication of the Rights of Women* (1792), the Seneca Falls Conference (1848) and later the Suffragette movement, in the 1960s the struggle had started again with renewed vigour, with the *moral* polarization of men and women.

Valerie Solanas: The SCUM Manifesto

Valerie Solanas was surely the most anti-male of the Second Wave. She is most well known as the woman who shot Andy Warhol and as the author of *The SCUM Manifesto* (1968). SCUM is the acronym for the Society for Cutting Up Men. While she is certainly *not* typical of American feminism, a selection of her work was given wide exposure in Robin Morgan's bestseller *Sisterhood is Powerful* (1970:514–9), with no disclaimer or critique from Morgan. Morgan is clearly responsible for the legitimation and spread of misandry, following Friedan. Solanas states:

> The male is a biological accident: the y (male) gene is an incomplete x (female) gene, that is, has an incomplete set of chromosomes. In other words, *the male is an incomplete female, a walking abortion, aborted at the gene stage*. To be male is to be deficient, emotionally limited; maleness is a deficiency disease and males are emotional cripples.
>
> The male is completely egocentric, trapped inside himself, incapable of empathizing or identifying with others, of love, friendship, affection or tenderness. He is a completely isolated unit, incapable of rapport with anyone. His responses are entirely visceral not cerebral; his intelligence is a mere tool in the service of his drives and needs; he is incapable of mental passion, mental interaction; he can't relate to anything other than his own physical sensations. He is a half-dead, unresponsive lump... .(Solanas, 1971:3–4)

The goals of SCUM were "to overthrow the government ... and destroy the male sex." Solanas goes on to say that: "To call a man an animal is to flatter him; he's a machine, a walking dildo" (1971:5); and her priceless dictum: "Every man, deep down, knows he's a worthless piece of shit" (1971:7). And more: "The male is by his very nature, a leech, an emotional parasite and, therefore, not ethically entitled to live" (1971:37). On the other hand, she says: "A woman ... knows instinctively that the only wrong is to hurt others, and that the meaning of life is love" (1971:23).

Solanas may not have been in the best mental health, but she became a cult figure, a film was made about her, her book has been through three editions and was publicized by Robin Morgan. What otherwise might have been ignored, or condemned as trash, was highlighted. But this raises several issues. Obviously it is inconsistent to recommend mass murder while insisting that "the only wrong is to hurt others." And where did all this hatred come from? We do not know. And why did Morgan publish such hate literature? This is a publication advocating violence against men. A similar publication advocating violence against women would have raised a furious outcry – with Robin Morgan in the forefront. Indeed both the United States and Canada have advocated policies of "zero tolerance for violence against women." Yet some feminists advocate violence against men! While other feminists publicize this advocacy. And there is no policy for zero tolerance for violence against men.

Men have been defined by Friedan and Solanas as liars, virtual slave-owners, SS guards, incomplete, deficient, emotionally limited and crippled, egocentric, incapable of love, half-dead, machines, walking dildos, worthless pieces of shit, leaches, emotional parasites and not entitled to live....

Pigs, jerks and fools are mild invectives in comparison to Friedan and Solanas and publicized again by Morgan. The litany of invectives has become longer as the women's movement developed.

The Normalization of Sexism

In the modern era, democratic movements have challenged the power of monarchy (the executions of Charles I, Louis XVI, Nicholas II), colonialism (the American War of Independence), slavery (the Haïtian Revolution, the slave revolts, and abolitionism), elitism (the Reform Acts in the U.K.), imperialism (the nationalist movements after World War II), capitalism (union movements and socialist parties), white power (abolitionist movements, nationalist, civil rights and anti-apartheid movements, Black Power and Red Power movements) and male power (Seneca Falls Conference, 1848, the Suffragette and the women's movements after 1968). The steady expansion of human and civil rights has continued with concern for Children's Rights, Gay Rights, Disability Rights, and BGLT Rights (Bisexual, Gay, Lesbian and Transsexuals' Rights). The struggles continue over rights to live and rights to die.

Efforts to achieve equality, civil rights and/or independence require first an identification of "the enemy" and "the oppressor," the raising of consciousness, then the unification of the subordinate population, polarization, conflict (physical, legal, moral, verbal etc.) and ultimately a resolution or revolution. The blue-print of resistance was "The Communist Manifesto" by Marx and Engels in 1848, later adapted from class relations to race relations and gender relations, and nationalist movements.

These processes can be illustrated in the development of the women's movement, and this chapter is hopefully a contribution to resolution: to the understanding of the new sexism as a stage in a process, but a stage which has not been recognized; indeed it has been denied.

Perhaps the supreme achievement of the women's movement has been to critique the traditional gender hierarchy of Adam, and men in general, as the first sex – a theme epitomized by Simone de Beauvoir's description of women as *The Second Sex* (1949/1953) – up to Helen Fisher's book, 50 years after de Beauvoir and on the eve of the new millennium which describes women as *The First Sex* (1999). The supreme failure has been the failure to critique this new reversed gender hierarchy and this new sexism. So many pro-feminist activists have preached the contradictory doctrines of gender equality *and* misandry. It is time to cease the competition for first sex, and to consider both the commonalities *between* the two sexes, as well as the variations *within* each sex.

If it was sexist for Hesiod, Aristotle, Paul, Aquinas or Milton to refer to the primacy of the male, by chronological, physical, philosophical or theological criteria, it is equally sexist for Fisher to refer to the primacy of the female and for Friedan, Solanas, Morgan and others to promulgate misandry.

From Friedan to Fisher, in textbooks and joke-books, the new sexism has been normalized. It is so ubiquitous it is not even noticed. Indeed to comment on any of this is widely regarded as being anti-female, anti-feminist and backlash.

This re-definition of men from positive to negative has been, and still is, a *public* process. We must now consider some of the organizations, authors, themes and sites of this process. The treatment necessarily must be brief, and the commentary minimal; but perhaps sufficient to make the point. (For a fuller treatment see Nathanson and Young, 2001; 2006.)

Redstockings, a New York feminist group, published their Manifesto in 1970 which, while passionate and sincere, exemplifies the simplest binary values: women are oppressed victims, vulnerable and virtuous; men are vicious, villains and victimizers. This is Solanas rewritten in pseudo-academic objective terminology:

> Women are an oppressed class. Our oppression is total, affecting every facet of our lives. We are exploited as sex objects, breeders, domestic servants and cheap labour. We are considered inferior beings whose only purpose is to enhance men's lives. Our humanity is denied. Our prescribed behaviour is enforced by the threat of physical violence... .
>
> We identify the agents of our oppression as men ... *All men* receive economic, sexual, and psychological benefits from male supremacy. *All men* have oppressed women. (Morgan, 1970:533–4. Her emphasis).

The Manifesto is long and eloquent and an interesting perversion of Marx. The identification of the enemy, the discussion of exploitation and oppression, the definition as inferior, the denial of humanity, the threat of violence, and the demonization of "all men" – are classic elements of extreme feminism and feminist extremism. There is no awareness that men too might be oppressed, even *more* oppressed perhaps than Friedan or the Redstockings group – condemned to low pay dangerous jobs, the Vietnam draft, death in action, an early death anyway ... while middle-class mostly white women berate them as oppressors. Black men still die 11.5 years younger than white women, on average (U.S. Census Bureau, 2007:80). Who is oppressed more?

Similarly Shulamith Firestone echoed this victimism:

> Women were the slave class that maintained the species in order to free the other half for the business of the world – admittedly often its drudge aspects, but certainly all of its creative aspects as well. (1970:192)

American women as a "slave class" staying home with the children "to free the other half" – men – to work for the money to support the "slaves" and their children is so classic as to be absurd – particularly since then as now men constitute 92–96% of the work fatalities. The work world is hardly freedom. This *false feminism* is the world turned upside down: an unintentional satire.

Germaine Greer's *The Female Eunuch* was one of the first to define the enemy:

> Women have very little idea of how much men hate them ... Men do not themselves know the depth of their hatred. (1971:249, 251)

Perhaps Greer has very little idea of how much men love women. While one might have ignored this as merely political rhetoric, or as Greer's projection of her own problems with her absentee father, or just as a "slip," Freudian or otherwise, she returned to this misandry in another essay: "Men don't really like women and that is really why they don't employ them ... Men are the enemy" (1986:26, 28). She seems convinced and concluded the millennium with more of the same: "The most consistently misquoted sentence from *The Female Eunuch* is 'Women have very little idea of how much men hate them.' " How it is misquoted, she does not explain. But rather than retracting the remark, she adds:

> Some men hate all women all of the time; all men hate some women some of the time. I reckon that in the year 2000 more men hate more women more bitterly than in 1970. Our culture is far more masculinist than it was thirty years ago. (1999:14)

I reckon that Greer was and still is quite wrong, and that most men love most women most of the time, adore some, and that in the new century quite possibly more women hate men more bitterly than in 1970 – thanks in part to Greer herself. Furthermore, it is transparently clear that our culture is more feminist and more egalitarian than it was in 1970; and most people would agree that this is a good thing too. Nonetheless, Greer advocates gender segregation for women, if "the alternative is humiliation" (1999:328). The presumption is that men do humiliate women: all humiliation all the time. The misandry persists, unashamed, unchallenged.

Certainly Friedan's "problem that has no name" in 1963 now has a name given to it by Solanas, Redstockings and Greer. The name of that problem is men – all men – and their alleged hatred and oppression of women.

Andrea Dworkin has long been one of the most misandric of feminists. The rhetoric escalated as she described gynocide as "the systematic crippling, raping, and/or killing of women by men ... the relentless violence perpetrated by the gender class men on the gender class women." Furthermore "under patriarchy, gynocide is the ongoing reality of life lived by women" (1976:16, 19).

These same myths have been repeated by so many others so often that they are taken as truth: never mind that 1) women also kill, or that 2) men are killed so much more often than women, or that 3) most men neither cripple, rape, nor kill, or that 4) most men spend their lives working to support their wives and children, often risk their lives to do so, and even lose their lives in heroic rescues of their families and total strangers. A decade later, Dworkin continues, echoing Greer, on how men hate women:

> Men too make choices. When will they choose not to hate us?
> Being female in this world is having been robbed of the potential for human choice by men who love to hate us. (1987:139)

Her definition of being female is bizarre, but in an even more virulent sexist vein she then goes on to make the now routine comparison of this (alleged) male hatred of women with the very real Nazi hatred of Jews (1987:174–6). One might imagine that such obvious loathing for half of humanity would disqualify Dworkin from an audience, or confine her to the lunatic fringe; but there is an audience for such virulent sexism as there once was for virulent racism. She adds that the evidence for misogyny is about nine million women who were slaughtered in the witchcraft trials (1987:65; cf. 1974:130, 141,149). Perhaps she was trying to outdo the Holocaust numbers for reasons best known to herself, but her wildly inflated figures can only serve to incite female hatred and fear of men. The true figures are about 60,000 total between 1450 and 1750 – and about 25% of these were men (Gow and Apps, 2002; Cawthorne, 2004; Trevor-Roper, 1984). Awful, but not even close to a quarter million, still less one million, let alone nine million. In such absurd feminist "scholarship" lies the genesis of the new sexism.

Rosalind Miles, a leading British feminist, equates males with violence and violence with males, whom she calls "the death sex":

> To explain violence is to explain the male. The reverse is also true ... What remedy for men, maleness, masculinity, manhood? (1991:12, 234)

The word "remedy" does imply that men are a disease and that there might be a "final solution." Andrea Dworkin seems to agree:

> *Men love death*. In everything they make, they hollow out a central place for death, let its rancid smell contaminate every dimension of what still survives. *Men especially love murder*. In art they celebrate it, and in life they commit it. (1988:214. Emphasis added).

Dworkin does admit to being "very hostile" to men, as if this were not obvious; this she attributes to the appalling brutality which she says she suffered from her then husband (1988:58, 100–6). He denied it. Nonetheless, there is undue extrapolation here from one man to all men, from the exception to the rule. And actually, most men do *not* love murder – which is why most men (and women) do *not* commit murder; and those who do, both men and women, are liable to prison sentences and even capital punishment.

Similarly John Stoltenberg argues that "The male sex is socially constructed. It is a political entity that flourishes through acts of force and sexual terrorism" (1989:30). And Adrienne Rich, a well-known American feminist and poet asserts that the "characteristics of male power" are rape, violence against women, incest etc. (1996:36). The litany is constantly echoed, repeated and recycled and eventually comes to be believed; the dynamics of this new sexism are very similar to those of racism and the old sexism – and equally nauseating and hateful – but largely unchallenged.

Men are now a social problem, according to a lead story in *Newsweek* (28.5.90):

> Women, after all, are not a big problem. Our society does not suffer from burdensome amounts of empathy and altruism, or a plague of nurturance. The problem is men – or, more accurately, maleness.

The rhetoric escalated in 1992 from "problem" to "war" with the publication of the best-selling *The War against Women* by Marilyn French. French believes that there is a "global war" against women, and that "patriarchy began and spread as a war against women" (1992:13–14); and that all societies are patriarchal. She adds that "In all patriarchal cultures, woman-hatred is common currency" (1992:25).

Men might be surprised to hear, yet again, that they hate women, and that they are at war against women; but man-hatred "common currency" in the second wave. In the U.K. Jill Radford and Diana Russell edited *Femicide* in that same year. And in Canada the Committee on the Status of Women in Canada submitted a brief to the Federal Government in 1991 entitled *The War against Women*. Furthermore Susan Faludi's 1992 book, *Backlash*, was subtitled "The Undeclared War against American Woman." The notion of a *war* against women is now institutionalized.

Not only are men "villainous" in many dimensions, so are the societies "they" create. Mary O'Brien, a leading Canadian feminist, states:

> Patriarchy is not healthy. It legitimates violent solutions to historical problems in ways which casually destroy whole species, the natural environment and the well-being of individuals; it is pre-occupied with death and infatuated with power; it claims to transcend contingent nature while it invents sexism, racism and genocide. (1989:299, cf. 25)

Gloria Steinem spoke in similar terms: indeed the echo effect in misandric feminist politics is amazing. We have understood that repetition is essential to learning, but this is ridiculous: "Patriarchy requires violence or the subliminal threat of violence in order to maintain itself.... The most dangerous situation for a woman is not an unknown man in the street, or even the enemy in wartime, but a husband or lover in the isolation of their own home" (1992:259–61). This is nonsense, of course, as Steinem must know. The most dangerous enemy of a woman is herself, and death by suicide is more frequent than death by male violence, and both are extremely unusual. Steinem is not so much alerting women to a miniscule danger, but trying to create hatred and fear of men. Smoking, obesity, accidents and heart disease are far more dangerous than "a husband or a lover," and kill far more women – as do the women killing themselves. But Steinem is not concerned with saving women's lives by warning against the real dangers of suicide, smoking, obesity, cancer and lack of exercise; she is more inclined to create fear and hatred of "a husband or a lover in the isolation of their own home." A curious agenda for someone allegedly committed to equity.

The construction of men by many distinguished feminists is very clear, therefore, and very negative. Men are misogynists and murderers, sexists and racists and rapists, the death sex, full of shit, destroyers, violent, genocidal, femicidal, infatuated with power, scum suckers.... The litany of invectives goes on and on.

Not just some men some time, it is clear, but all men all the time. This constitutes what we must recognize as a new sexism.

The villainy of men is evident in the by now familiar list of atrocities allegedly perpetrated by men against women. Steinem has offered some of her own statistics on female victimization and male villainy. "One in four women is sexually assaulted in her lifetime..." (Hagan, 1992:v). To most readers this means that 25% of women are raped – a fearful thought. But sexual assault is very rarely rape: an unwanted caress, pushing and shoving, threatening, swearing – all constitute sexual assault. But they are not rape (Sommers, 1994:209–26).

Steinem says, again: "Domestic violence is the single largest cause of injury in the United States. The most dangerous place for a woman is not in the street but in her own home..." (Hagan, 1992:v). Thus Steinem teaches women to fear their lovers, their husbands and their homes. Yet domestic violence is *not* "the single largest cause of injury in the United States." Accidents are by far – sometimes in motor vehicles, often at home with falls in the bath or downstairs (see Chapter 6; also Sommers, 1994:188–208).

And the person who is most likely to kill a woman is *not*, as Steinem says, so famously "a husband or lover in the isolation of their own home" – it is the person who looks at her in the mirror: herself. But these feminists prefer to blame men! The latest statistics indicate that in the United States in 2005, 6,730 women committed suicide, compared to 3,850 in total who were victims of homicide – mostly NOT by their husbands or ex-partners.[1]

The related tragedy is not only that such feminists are blind to the reality of women, but that they are blind to the reality of men also. Women are not the only victims in this world. The data for men is even more horrific: 25,907 men committed suicide in 2005 in the U.S., and 13,882 more were victims of homicide (National Vital Statistics Reports, 2006:54:13). Victim feminists should expand their horizons to include male victims, at least.

The definitions of men as violent still persist. In a study of violent women as a stereotype-breaking portrait of violent women in Hollywood films, Hilary Neroni asserts that: "It [violence] is nothing less than the foundation of our concept of masculinity" (2005:58). Yet her own analysis indicates that the violence is *protective* of the women in the movies, and is actually indicative of men's search for *justice* i.e. justice is the foundational concept, not violence. Her book was published in the SUNY (State University of New York) series in Feminist Criticism and Theory – which may explain her amazingly anti-male conclusions. Most men have not killed anyone! Violence is *not* at the core of masculinity; protection of women and children is – unless one is publishing in a feminist arena. And when she argues that violence is the foundation of "our concept of masculinity," who is the "our"? Not mine, nor that of most men I know; but it is clearly her feminist stereotype.

Steinem goes on that "about half of women in the paid labour force had experienced some form of sexual harassment" (Hagan, 1992:vi); which may well be so. No data is presented for men, but men would probably not report this so often anyway. She omits to state that although women constitute almost 50% of the paid labour force, about 92% of all labour force fatalities in the U.S. occur to men (Wong, 1997:47). Women are harassed, men die: in mine explosions, logging, at sea, in tractor rolls, on duty in the police or the military (U.S. Bureau of the Census, 2003:429–30; Farrell, 1993). The costs of being in the labour force can be lethal for men, and do not include the long term costs of cancers due to environmental pollution.

Furthermore harassment is penalized very severely. In one recent case, a woman was awarded U.S. $11.6 million in punitive damages from Madison Square Gardens and James L. Dolan, Chairman of the company that owns the NY Knicks and the Gardens because a coach made unwanted sexual advances and subjected this 35 year old to verbal insults (Schmidt and Newman, 2007). Not a bad deal for early retirement: well worth pursuing, considering that a military

---

1   For a brilliant critique of these statistics – and of the failures of radical feminist scholarship generally – see Sommers, 1994; also Patai and Koertge, 1994; Roiphe, 1994; Laframboise, 1996; Friday, 1996; and Paglia of course.

death in Iraq, fighting for your country, is worth about $5,000, and loss of an arm or leg even less. There is some considerable disparity of justice between the jury awards for some nuisance, which she could presumably handle, and the federal awards for death and injury in the line of duty. This exemplifies a double standard of massive economic and social proportions. A fatal accident to a worker is ... just an unfortunate accident.

Steinem dishonours herself and her cause by conflating rape and sexual assault (surely, by this legal definition, we have all been sexually assaulted), by poisoning gender relations and contaminating the cause of human liberation. Her faulty scholarship on rape, on spousal homicide, on the labour force, on domestic violence suggests that her cause is not equity but misandry.

Similarly Susan Faludi, a Pulitzer Prize winner, asserted dogmatically: "By any objective measure – pay, representation in boardrooms, status – men are still ahead" (Halpern, 1999:37). But this is a remarkably subjective selection. Faludi is obviously aware that there are other objective measures: longevity, mortality rates, suicide, homicide, education, health, incarceration, the homeless... . By any of these measures, women are ahead; but Faludi either missed or dismissed these realities. Unfortunate; but that is politics – little to do with reality or personal integrity.

A close reading of *Stiffed: The Betrayal of the American Man* indicates that while he may have been betrayed by American capitalism – a betrayal clarified by the Wall Street meltdown and the failure of the Detroit 3 in 2008 – he has also been betrayed by American feminism. The promise of equity and a brave new world is negated by Faludi's continuing critique of men – some deserved, no doubt, but she asked: "Why do our male brethren so often and so vociferously resist women's struggles toward independence and a fuller life?" (1999:594). Answer: they don't. They have opened up the entire public domain to women rapidly: universities, business, politics, the health system etc. They might resist misandry, such as Faludi's who insists on ubiquitous "fathers' desertion", "fathers' failures", "My father never taught me how to be a man." She added: "For centuries, of course, fathers have disappointed, neglected, abused, abandoned their sons" (1999:596). This is all fathers all the time? Some? A few? No mothers? Blaming the dads is the new feminism? Now men working is abandonment? But women working, says Friedan, is freedom.

She concludes with an ace that "their [men's] task is not, in the end, to figure out how to be masculine – rather their masculinity lies in figuring out how to be human" (1999:607). The hatred is amazing. This is men as *sub-human*. The female (like her – who hates half of humanity) is the human?

Kimmel seems to endorse Faludi's idea that men are not human. Towards the end of his latest book *Guyland* (2008) in which he once again demonizes guys, he asks: "How can we, as a society, make it clear that choosing between one's masculinity and one's humanity is a false choice – that one's humanity ought to be the highest expression of masculinity[?]" (2008:270). Again the assumption that guys are somehow not human. Valerie Solanas would have approved of this pair.

In a poignant memoir, the novelist Mary Gordon described her coming of age, but also the dark side of feminism:

> I was in my early twenties in the first years of the women's movement: I came of age as a feminist. It would be pleasant if one could become a feminist without a consciousness of the injustices and abuses perpetrated on women by men. But it didn't happen to me. For those of us feminists who are heterosexual, it has been a struggle to reconcile our rage against male culture with our feelings for the men with whom we enter into what is perhaps the most intimate of human relations. (1993:46)

We could be more sympathetic to Gordon were it not that she, and other feminists of her time, totally ignored and still ignore "the injustices and abuses perpetrated on" men as well as women, by the powers that be (often male). And to choose to feel only "rage against male culture" reflects precisely the ignoring of male achievements and altruism which has been so characteristic of so many feminists. Hence the absence of empathy, sympathy and even gratitude. People see what they want to see, or are taught to see. This *dark side* of feminism has been largely ignored until recently – and not the least of the "injustices and abuses" perpetrated on men has been misandry. This misandry has in turn been partly based on tunnel vision and exclusionary identity politics. It has also been partly based on reality, and real "injustices and abuses" suffered by women. Gordon sadly failed to realize not only that men also suffer, but also that men love, work, contribute and give generously.

Heading to the 1995 U.N. World Conference on Women in Beijing, Betty Friedan commented that: "The basis of women's empowerment ... can't be saved by countering the hatred of women with the hatred of men" (*Newsweek* 4 Sept. 95:31). This is surely true – though it flatly contradicts the message of "The Feminine Mystique," and was too little too late. By now the hatred of men has been institutionalized.

In academia hatred might be too strong a word. Feminist writers are more likely to simply ignore men, or problematize men. Consider some examples:

- A recent text in the U.K. entitled *Gender in Modern Britain* features two women on the cover, evidently very friendly, but no men; symbolically, "gender" equates with women and perhaps lesbians; and the index includes 76 page references (many of them overlapping) to femininity, feminism, maternal, motherhood, women etc. compared to only 54 for fatherhood, masculinity and paternal. One chapter is headed: "Schooling – It's a Girls World"; the next is headed "Young Men and the Crisis of Masculinity" – with no apparent awareness of any possible relation. This chapter includes a section "Boys as social problem – delinquency" (Charles, 2003). We can recognize that juvenile delinquency is primarily male, but might note also that most young men are *not* juvenile delinquents – and some young women are. It is clear that these political lenses are not only distorting perceptions of reality – delinquents are the social problem, not boys! Also they are likely to have stereotypical binary consequences for readers: girls good and successful, boys problematic and in crisis.

- Another feminist author apologizes for referring to Derrida and Foucault explaining: "At the risk of a further taint of male discourse…" (Whelehan, 1995:251). Males taint? The "taint" is elsewhere, in this feminist discourse.

- Gender studies are now effectively normalized as Women's Studies – which does a considerable disservice to men. R.W. Connell's book, Gender (2002), has one reference to "father," four to "mother," plus 59 to masculinity, men, men's studies, boys compared to 86 to women, feminism, women's studies, girls, housewife. And while Charles (2003) makes complimentary references to Connell, neither even mention Robert Bly (1990) or Warren Farrell (1993) who have been most important in presenting masculinist rather than feminist perspectives on gender, and listening to men's voices. The homeless, the suicides, the victims of homicide, divorce and work fatalities, the imprisoned, the Carnegie medals – they have no place in these discussions of gender. Men are the ignored sex.

- The University of Toronto sustains the Institute of Women and Gender Studies – as if only one gender is worth mentioning. That the administrators of this famous university do not see anything absurd (let alone sexist) in this title is surely alarming.

- CROME, a research network for Critical Research On Men in Europe declares that its current project is "The Social Problem of Men." Nice! Certainly men have problems and create social problems; so do women – often in complementary terms. Equally men create our civilizations. Yet there is no comparative (male/female) perspective on problematization, nor any cost/benefit analysis of progress vs. problems in their discussion (www.cromenet.org). This is the new academic sexism: the definition of men as a social problem.

- Avoiding the men-as-villains trap, for once, and the female-as-victim trap, some fall into the women-as-angels trap. In their book *The Feminization of America. How Women's Values are Changing our Public and Private Lives*, the two female authors list what they say are women's values:

a strong nurturing impulse that extends to all living things; a highly developed capacity for intimacy …; a tendency to integrate rather than separate; an ability to empathize; a predilection for egalitarian relationships together with a resistance to hierarchy; an attachment to the day-to-day process of sustaining life; a spirituality that transcends dogma and sectarianism; a scale of values that places individual growth and fulfilment above abstractions; and a preference for negotiation as a means of problem solving which springs from her antipathy to violence. (Lenz and Myerhoff, 1985:4–5)

Perhaps this list of values is true for some women, but the implication that these values are exclusive to women does indicate that the authors' supposed "strong nurturing impulse" and their "ability to empathize" etc. do not extend to men. Indeed they specifically condemn "a set of values and strategies identified with a specific masculine perception that is bringing us all to the brink of extinction." Again, in case you missed their point: "The male principle ... has conducted the affairs of the world primarily on the basis of competition, confrontation and conflict." And again: "The world we live in can no longer operate on the traditional value system of masculine culture; the ruthless competitiveness, the unchecked individualism, and the exercise of power through violence have brought us to the edge of self-destruction" (Lenz and Myerhoff, 1985:6, 230, 248).

Not only do they loathe men for their values, strategies, perception, principle and culture – all listed above – but they are not too fond of WASPs either. They say that the Blacks have "soul", "the Latinos *corazón*, or heart; the Jews *menschlichkeit*, or humaneness – all terms that suggest a robust vitality missing from the bloodless, goal-dominated narrow pursuits of WASP middle-class mainstream society" (1985:7–8). The authors are not overflowing with nurturance and empathy but are deeply sexist.

Another particularly bizarre "scholarly" feminist work is the book *Men are Not Cost-Effective: Male Crime in America*" (2nd edition. 1995) by California psychologist June Stephenson. The cover asks the question: "Why is crime essentially a male pursuit? It's not drugs, unemployment, housing, single mothers or male hormones. Discover why?" Her method was simple: she clipped all the stories and commentaries about male crimes, sorted them into the usual categories, added the FBI statistics and then argued that men are not cost-effective and that all men filing tax returns should pay $100 each to cover the cost of their crimes and the criminal justice system. She was serious, and the first edition sold out.

But it is bizarre, and seriously flawed "scholarship" for several reasons. She ignored female crimes which, while the rates are lower, should at least result in a percentage-appropriate tax on women to pay for their crime costs. That would be only logical. Second, male criminals are the exception, not the rule (as are female criminals) for the gender, so to jump from male criminals to all males is just absurd. *Criminals* are not cost-effective: male and female – so, logically, they should be taxed – which they are, sometimes by fines, sometimes by prison, sometimes by death. Third, to judge all men solely by their crimes is also silly. They could also be judged by their work and their heroism and by their constructive contributions to American society and to the world – as we have already discussed.

Finally, her explanation for all this crime lies in "*the way* boys are raised" (1995:331. Her emphasis). But, as we know, most boys and men do not become criminals; so the way they are raised, in general, seems satisfactory. The problem is "the way" *criminal* men *and* women are raised. Given her flawed vision, she recommends that boys should be raised more like girls, and that we must raise boys to recognize the feminine in themselves. This is ironic given that women have long recognized the so-called masculine in themselves, as their achievements in politics, business, income, competitive contact sports and education make clear. It is also in defiance of the science of gender by psychologists (Pinker, 2008), evolutionary psychologists (Buss, 1999; Baron-Cohen, 2003), anthropologists (Gilmore, 1990) which affirms that men and women are different: as does popular culture in the assertion of the sexes as "opposite."

More important, perhaps, Stephenson fails to recognize that crime rates vary enormously from state to state in the United States, especially homicide rates, and also between the United States and the United Kingdom, by a factor of about 300%. Yet she would hardly recommend that American boys and girls should be raised like little Brits. This anti-male bias is as pervasive as it is invisible.[2]

Feminist lenses have their value, and have illuminated and clarified our worlds in many ways, and improved our worlds also. They can also be sexist lenses and distorting mirrors, as is so clear from the work of Solanas, Steinem, Dworkin, Faludi, Gordon, Lenz, Whelehan, Stephenson and others. What is required is a binocular humanist lens through which we can see the lives and status of both men and women. This listing of sexism is necessary because the rhetoric of equity has too often camouflaged the reality of feminist sexism.

To her credit, bell hooks was an early critic of second wave feminism. Particularly sensitive to the criss-crossing of gender, race and class she criticized harshly white middle-class feminists for a "virulent" anti-male stance, for "reactionary separatism", and she advocated a "revolutionary struggle" with male comrades. But then, as if to reassure readers of her feminist credentials she insists that: "All men support and perpetuate sexism and sexist oppression in one form or another." And again: "Men *do* oppress women" (1984:67–73). There is, admittedly, some slight recognition that men are victims of rigid sex roles and/or capitalism, but not of (female) sexism nor even of men's early, and violent deaths etc. Too bad.

The origins of this new sexism as an ideology lie partly, therefore, in some of the feminist thinkers from the 60s to the present, and have been institutionalized in popular culture. The remoter origins of misandry lie in the dialectic with the earlier misogyny, which has been a theme in Judaeo-Christian and Graeco-Roman

---

2   Stephenson asserts that the two fundamental causes of male anger are first, male circumcision and second, the first haircut (1995:336–7). And she is a psychologist. But the first of these theories should be easy to verify, at least in principle. Simply check the incarceration rates and crime rates for the circumcized and uncircumcized and compare them with the rest of the population. However, grants might not be available, though her proposal would be amusing. Also, simply asking men would not be sufficient. According to one survey in Buffalo, New York, about one-third of the men who said they were circumcized, in fact were not; and about one-third of the men who said they were not circumcized, were (Smith, 1976:91). Surprise! Alternatively she could compare crime rates and circumcision rates internationally and note the correlations if any. While correlation is not causality, the study could be interesting particularly since Muslim countries and the United States, which both have high circumcision rates, have respectively very low and very high crime rates. Furthermore, differences in homicide rates between states could be attributed to differential circumcision rates. This is a whole new theory of crime which has made it into feminist theory, though not yet into criminology texts.

culture, and embodied in the social and gender structures of society. Explanations for any "isms," from sexism to racism, fascism and anti-semitism, only explain – they do not justify.

Novelists

Novelists like best-selling authors Marilyn French, Terry McMillan and Alice Walker are some of the fiercest and most articulate exponents of misandry. As writers they are also educators, yet they are educating their readers into precisely that gender hatred that feminists complained about, quite rightly, when it was directe at them – and have been conspicuously silent about when it is directed at men.

We cannot study all the misandric passages from each and every book, but we can certainly review some of the more salient issues raised here. Marilyn French is the best-selling author of *The Women's Room* (1977) as well as a number of scholarly works and also some feminist works. This sold over three million copies: a block-buster. The initial premise is women as victims: "Women were victims by nature" (34) and, in case you missed that: "Women were indeed victims by nature" (44). And the book lists sad tales of divorce, women's suffering and pain, injustice, rape, suicide and attempted suicide, breakdowns, insanity and death – all because of men – and their joy and comfort in the company of women. The second premise is the hatred of men: "My hatred is learned from experience: that is not prejudice. I wish it were prejudice. Then perhaps I could unlearn it" (291). Like Friedan and Dworkin she compares men to Nazi prison guards – a standard theme, like the comparison with apartheid. The third theme is the inferiority of men: "Tin gods." "Men were just dense." "I think men are dead you know, they have no life" (170, 195, 263). She defines men: "What is a man anyway? Everything I see around me in popular culture tells me a man is he who screws and kills" (288). Her most famous, or infamous, line: "All men are rapists and that's all they are." This was the character with whom French said she identified most, i.e. she is her personal oracle (*People* 20.2.78). She adds: "They rape us with their eyes, their law and their codes ... *All men are the enemy*" (630–1) (Emphasis added).

The fourth theme is the angelization of women: "He was a bastard, like all men. I've given over hating him, any of them. They can't help it: they're trained to be bastards. We're trained to be angels so they can be bastards" (357).

Bastards and angels, dead and alive, rapists and raped, enemies and friends, oppressors and victims, bad and good – these are the simple binaries of hate literature and propaganda through the ages.

French has a Ph.D. from Harvard. So it is disappointing to read such hatred from such a source. Certainly such a spewing could not be published about women or indeed any population without an outcry, ostracism, scandal and legal action. It is probably the most damning condemnation of one gender since Malleus Maleficarum of 1484, which initiated the witch-hunts. So the modern Harvard

Ph.D. echoes the medieval Dominican monks of the Inquisition. We have not moved forward, or learned much, it seems, since then.

French, Lenz, Myerhoff and Stephenson are not the only ones to savage men so brutally. Anti-black male misandry is the prevailing theme, in counterpoint to black female beauty, strength, courage and virtue, in Ntozake Shange's *For Colored Girls Who Have Considered Suicide* (1977), Gloria Naylor's *The Women of Brewster Place* (1982), and Michele Wallace's *Black Macho and the Myth of Superwoman* (1978).

This misandry was virtually sanctified by the award of the 1983 Pulitzer Prize to Alice Walker's *The Color Purple* (1982). Walker was the first black woman to receive this honour. Many black men protested the award, but Steven Spielberg filmed it nonetheless. *The Color Purple* opens with a 14-year-old black girl's letters to God. The first says that she was just raped by her father. The second that her mother has died and her father has killed the baby. The third that he has sold her second baby, and is eyeing her younger sister. The next that the wife of her sister's boyfriend was murdered by her lover while returning from church. And it is all downhill for men from there. This too sounds like a satire: incest and rape, murder, slavery, potential incest, more murder … all in twentieth century rural America. Furthermore there is racism: the white male police and the local mayor are equally brutal. It transpires that it was not her father who raped her, since her father had been lynched by whites, and so her mother went mad. Despite what seems to be widespread sexism and racism, the book has its points: poignant, intriguing, wise, sad, funny, social commentary, and so on. Should Walker have won the Pulitzer? Was it despite or because of her sexism, racism and anti-Americanism?

Terry McMillan's (1992) *Waiting to Exhale* is far less violent, and was the basis for a film which was particularly popular among black women – as was the book. It concerns the bonding between four almost flawless black women with each other, and their relationships with deeply flawed black men. The book touches all the emotions, is totally stereotypical, and sold well. The list of atrocities committed by these men is long, and so is the list of insults the women apply to them, "all but five, maybe ten per cent." But the rest, 90–95%, are: ugly, stupid, in prison, unemployed, crackheads, short, liars, unreliable, irresponsible, too possessive, dogs, shallow, boring, stuck in the sixties, arrogant, childish, wimps, too goddam old and set in their ways, can't fuck (1992:332 cf. 12). But apart from that … the book ends happily as one of the women wins almost a million dollars from her ex in a divorce settlement, a couple of "decent" men are on the horizon, and the winner is left thinking of how much good she can do with the money.

McMillan's later book, *A Day Late and a Dollar Short* (2001) is her epitaph on men, specifically black men. The gender wars sell well, in fiction and on the screen – with women as the triumphant victims of men.

Again, most female novelists and playwrights are not anti-male, but some are, and there is a market out there for these books, plays and films. Such artistic works may reflect individual experiences and philosophies, but both reflect and reinforce the culture of misandry. There are no male novelists who portray women in misogynistic terms, with similar sales and market potential.

The problem is not so much the portraits of men as villains of one sort or another, as that they are *only* portrayed as villains. All men are villains, and all women are angels. In this literature, to paraphrase Mae West, a good man is hard to find.

The attack on misandry and misandric feminism (or misandry in feminisms) – not to be confused with egalitarian feminism – has already begun. Some have critiqued misandry directly, both in terms of scholarship and values (Nathanson and Young, 2001; 2006). Others, and this is counter-intuitive, challenge the stereotype of women as "sugar and spice and all that's nice", and nurturing, empathetic and angelic. They insist on recognizing the realities of female villains as well as male, monstrous mums as well as deadbeat dads, female murderers as well as male, and removing the curtains of romanticism and victimism (the next chapter).

Hegemonic women, victim women and villain women persist, all three – as with men. Recognition of this trichotomy in both sexes is the first step in the fracturing of moral binaries of misogyny and misandry.

Pro-Feminist Men

One interesting aspect of the new sexism is the degree to which it has been accepted and internalized by so many men. Commitment to ideals of gender equality and the rejection of male sexism is one thing: virtually all of us agree with this, and feminists have no monopoly on egalitarianism. Acceptance and promulgation of misandry is quite another. It is surprising, therefore, that so many men have turned to misandry in their support for feminism. Rather than being intermediaries or peace-keepers, some feminist-identified academics have become extremely male-negative – and then confused the issue by calling themselves masculinists!

In one early text on men, Clyde Franklin, who identifies himself as "a profeminist man," opens with four presumably recent crimes, all horrible, committed by men against women. These he thinks are typical of "traditional men" and *normal*, rather than "social anomalies or pathologies" (Franklin, 1991:vii, 1–2). So he morphs the exceptional male criminal into the norm – as Stephenson did 4 years later. There is no mention of male positivities, nor indeed of women except as victims. This was an early anti-male textbook on men.

John Stoltenberg defines himself as a "radical feminist" (which we might now interpret as really, really anti-male); and in his *Refusing to be a Man* (1990) he suggests that "the ethics of male sexual identity are essentially rapist"; and he describes North American society as "a rape culture." Here he echoes such feminist icons as Robin Morgan, Andrea Dworkin and Susan Brownmiller, whom he cites with approval (1990: 1, 19, 78–9). No proof is necessary: a consensus of misandrists will do. Their disgust and contempt for men is echoed by his own; and not surprisingly feminists laud his work. Few seem to have noted that such vilification is neither accurate nor humanistic; the vilification of no other population would be tolerated in this way; and the competitive demonization of men is part of the problem.

The Sage series of publications on Research on Men and Masculinities is published "in cooperation with Men's Studies Association. A Task Group of the National Organization for Men against Sexism." But we are all against sexism! The implicit assumptions that all sexism is male, that men are all sexists, is grossly insulting to men. It also indicates that a feminist lens will be the characteristic orientation of the series. And indeed it is – which would be fine if the series were also against female sexism, and if the lens were not flawed.

Harry Brod and Michael Kaufman, who have written extensively on gender issues, state their goals quite explicitly: to search for "new feminist understandings of masculinities" and "to further a feminist agenda for change" (1994:1). Is it me, or is this totally bizarre? Not only are these men seeking women to define their own masculinity – can't they do it for themselves? – but they are also seeking feminists, many of whom as we have seen are virulently anti-male! Furthermore (as we will see), most women reject feminism – so whose side are they on? And can one imagine a feminist volume in which the authors search for men to understand femininity and/or feminism? This is a Monty Python satire.

Michael Kimmel, a sociologist, who is the editor of this series, defines himself as a pro-feminist male. He is also the author of *Manhood in America: A Cultural History* – but a history with a bias. He starts his book with a long list of male villains, in typical pro-feminist (and also anti-male) style:

> Clarence Thomas, William Kennedy Smith, Senator Bob Packwood. The names fairly leap off the front pages of recent newspapers. Mike Tyson, Woody Allen, O.J. Simpson, Michael Jackson. Overnight heroes become villains, accused of rape, murder, sexual abuse. Tailhook. Spur Posse. The Citadel. (1966:vii)

And in the sixth edition of his book, *Men's Lives*, co-edited with Michael Messner, he returns to his attack on men – equating them with violence – adding "President Clinton, Columbine, Eminem, Gary, the Roman Catholic Church, Hootie, the Air Force Academy … and us." He continues in this vein: "Not a week seems to go by without another in the seemingly endless parade of 'men behaving badly,' men who embody the seamier side of male sexuality – entitlement, predation, violence" (2004:565).

Equally, of course, not a week goes by without another in the seemingly endless parade of male heroism, altruism, achievement and wonder: men behaving beautifully – from fathers and husbands to workers, from Nobel Prize winners to the firefighters and police officers (how soon they forget), to the troops in Afghanistan, Iraq and who have served with the U.N. in peace-keeping operations around the world, risking and often losing their lives, to the winners of the Carnegie Medals for Bravery, to the men who farm the land, catch the fish, mine the minerals, fix the plumbing etc.

And, of course, to level the playing field, Kimmel could have, in all equity, listed a parade of "women behaving badly." They too are in the paper every week. But this tunnel vision of Kimmel and others, this misandry, is part of the problem.

Kimmel paints a caricature of men and manhood. He defines men as a problem before he starts, and has no respect for men's achievements and contributions to family, society and civilization. This is the new sexism in sociology.

If we can maintain a sense of humour Kimmel can be amusing: "Many still equate a secure sense of themselves as men with the size of their bulges – from bulging wallets to bulging muscles to bulging crotches" (1996:331). He argues that American manhood is, and historically always has been, based on "obsessive self-control, defensive exclusion, or frightened escape" (1996:333) – all of course delusional. His solution that "feminism will make it possible for the first time for men to be free" is ludicrous if the attitudes of these misandric feminists are any guide. Gender equality was argued long ago by Plato, and indeed by others up to and including Karl Marx. Of all the ideologies that promise to make men free – and don't they all promise that? socialism, feminism, fascism, Christianity … one that starts and ends by demonizing men, seems the least likely to do so.

One of the more interesting aspects of some feminist and pro-feminist constructions of men is the conflation of gender and power in both the public and private domains. Says Kimmel: "One central issue that all books about men must address is power. Everywhere we look – politics, corporate life, academic life – men are *in power*" (His emphasis 1992:162). Well, first, that is not "everywhere": he could also look down, instead of up, on the streets and see the homeless, in the hospitals and see the victims of violence and work-accidents and exposure to carcinogens at work, in the prisons where men are brutalized, raped, not taught new skills and are often innocent, on the factory floors working conveyor belts, on the high seas catching the fish for his family, and in the cemetaries and the war cemetaries, where they lie, prematurely dead. They are NOT in power.

And second he could look for women in power: in politics, corporations, the military, and academic life: there are many women *in power*, and increasing in numbers and power annually. The shift in the "balance of power" since 1900 or 1950 has been massive. In my academic life, the Chair of my department, the Dean of my faculty and the President of my university are all female.

Kimmel and others have made useful contributions to these debates about justice, freedom, and equality; but in his struggles against misogyny, he has ignored misandry; in only seeing male oppressions he has ignored men's contributions to the liberation of women; in defining men as villains, he has ignored the victimization of men as well as their "heroism" and their contributions; and in focussing on power he has ignored love. Furthermore, he insists on "embracing [lovely word] the feminist critique of masculinity as a starting point" (1992:163). We don't know which critique that may be – we have seen a few in this chapter – but if he means embracing misandry, that would be unfortunate surely, just as misogyny is an unfortunate critique of femininity!

Hopefully the pendulum will swing in the future towards more balanced, less male-negative, more egalitarian and humanist perspectives.

Origins, Uses and Abuses

Clearly the new sexism has been a powerful component of much feminist thought and scholarship. Some of its characteristic themes and exponents have been discussed. It is also clear that it is problematic – as problematic as the old male sexism was, and occasionally still is: an instrument of alienation, oppression and suppression.

What is also problematic is the failure of non-sexist feminists and anti-sexist interested parties to denounce this new sexism, to report it, analyse it, dissect it and to negate this sexism with the same vigour, enthusiasm and success with which they/we have denounced the old sexism ... and racism, and other such negative anti-human ideologies.

This misandry has sometimes been justified as "payback time" or "levelling the playing field" after thousands of years of male oppression of women. My own suggestion is that patriarchy has two faces: one oppressive and the other which has been liberative of women. Second, women are not the only ones who are oppressed – so are men as we shall see in the next chapter. And third, and most important, this is a *moral* question about the portrait of half of humanity as *evil*. To justify misandry is to justify hate, and also to avoid reconciliation. Revenge for perceived injustices, real or fictitious (and often fictitious, as with Dworkin's witchcraft discussion and Steinem's statistics) is not a useful basis for justice – and should certainly not be confused with equity. Misandry, like misogyny, is not about justice or equity, only hatred.

There have been the occasional warnings and protests against "male-bashing" (e.g. Wolf, 1993: vii) – a phrase which trivializes the virulent hatred and contempt for men which we have just studied. But there has been little systematic discussion of this new social problem. Feminists have perhaps avoided a confrontation out of sisterly loyalty; and men and masculists perhaps out of a sense of chivalry or in the hope that it will run its course and go away.

The question arises, nonetheless, why this new sexism? And the swiftest response is that the new feminist sexism does the same as the old male sexism and also racism (Levin and Levin, 1982).

- It unites the in-group against the other, and thereby increases in-group solidarity and power.
- It simplifies and clarifies the issues: nuances of the criss-cross of gender, class and race are ignored.
- It boosts the self-esteem of the in-group. The angelization of the women and the demonization of men is not only political but moral.

- It legitimizes discrimination, of any and every sort, against the real or alleged oppressing population. The claim of victimization legitimizes counter-victimization as "a levelling of the playing-field."
- It acts as self-defense against the old patriarchal sexism. As violence tends to generate counter-violence and racism to generate counter-racism, so patriarchal sexism has created the new feminist sexism. In Newtonian physics every action generates an equal and opposite reaction. In social physics the reactions are more complex: diffuse, spongy, deflected, sublimated, repressed ... but eventually resistance will out.
- Finally the new sexism has created its own antithesis in the form of a massive rejection by most women of the feminist movement which underpins this sexism, despite widespread acclaim for its egalitarian goals.

The new sexism may be understood as a normal and natural reaction to an oppressive situation. This may be partly why there has been so little reaction to this new sexism. Perhaps it is just seen as an opportunity to vent. This too will pass. On the other hand, however understandable it may be, and however compassionate one may feel, it is a negative ideology, it has had destructive consequences on families and relationships, and it should be challenged as firmly as the old sexism was.

Having written about the old misogynies myself in the past (1993, 1996), I find it ironic to have to write about the new misandries now. Have we not learned anything from the past?

Beyond Misandry

The new sexism is alive and well in different modalities both in popular culture and in some feminist ideology, female and male. There are however signs of change: first an increasing rejection of feminism by the majority of women, in part because of misandry; and second, the counter-attack by new feminists, post-feminists or, as some say, womanists, or better still humanists.

In 1998 *Time* ran a cover story with the provocative question "Is Feminism Dead?" and an equally provocative cover picture featuring from left to right and past to present Susan B. Anthony, Betty Friedan, Gloria Steinem and then Ally McBeal. The answers to the question varied enormously, as one might expect. The most striking aspect of the article were the results of a TIME/CNN poll of women. The pollsters asked: "Do you consider yourself a feminist?" 65% of the women surveyed said "No" and only 26% said "Yes." Furthermore the "No" figures are up from 58% in 1989 and the "Yes" figures are down from 32%.

The pollsters also asked "What is your impression of feminists?" The plurality, 43% of the women surveyed replied "Unfavorable" compared to only 32% who replied "Favorable." The 1998 survey indicates a reversal of attitudes from the 1989 poll which was the plurality 44% favorable and 29% unfavorable.

There may be many reasons for this widespread and increasing rejection of feminism. Faludi argued a media backlash. Steinem suggested that the rejecters "haven't experienced the world yet." (A bit condescending.) Others pointed out that NOW paid little attention to daycare. Of those who self-identified as non-feminists, 50% said that feminists "Don't respect married stay-at-home moms"; and 44% believed that feminists "Don't like most men." The women polled overwhelmingly recognized that feminists work for equal rights (85%), and equal pay (85%) and against sexual harassment (81%) (what about that other 15–19%?) Nonetheless, the negatives outweighed the positives as two-thirds of the respondents do not consider themselves feminists (Bellafante, 1998). Feminist misandry evidently accounts for some, but not all, of most women's refusal to identity as feminists (65%), and the plurality's unfavourable opinion of feminism (43%). The new misandry has therefore generated its own backlash among women. This does provide grounds for hope and for the future, and for more positive definitions of men, as well as more harmonious and egalitarian relations.

The counterattack to the old feminism and its new sexism began with Camille Paglia. She praised patriarchy, she praised men and she viciously attacked what she called "infirmary feminism." She made good copy partly because she was so eloquent and outspoken, both in print and in the media, but also because of the irony that she was, and is, a lesbian glorying in the defence of men. She attacked feminism's central theme: the condemnation of patriarchal society, and even praised it:

> One of feminism's irritating reflexes is its fashionable disdain for "patriarchal society," to which nothing good is ever attributed. But it is patriarchal society that has freed me as a woman. It is capitalism that has given me the leisure to sit at this desk writing this book. Let us stop being small-minded about men and freely acknowledge what treasures their obsessiveness has poured into culture.
>
> We could make an epic catalog of male achievements, from paved roads, indoor plumbing, and washing machines to eyeglasses, antibiotics, and disposable diapers. We enjoy fresh, safe milk and meat, and vegetables and tropical fruits heaped in snowbound cities. When I cross the George Washington Bridge or any of America's great bridges, I think: men have done this. (1991:37–8)

This is so much more male-positive than Michael Kimmel, and evidently more in line with the later 1998 TIME/CNN poll. Then she added the sentence which so infuriated feminists: "If civilization had been left in female hands, we would all be living in grass huts" (1991:38).

She returned to the fray with her second book in an even more combative mood, this time condemning

> ...infirmary Feminism with its bedlam of bellyachers, anorexics, bulimics, depressives, rape victims, and incest survivors. Feminism has become a catch-

all vegetable drawer where bunches of clingy sob sisters can store their moldy
neuroses. (1994:111).

She even included an amusing and interesting television script on the penis. It is
fascinating that an organ of the human body with such creative power and a donor
not only of life but also of pleasure should arouse such politics. Indeed French's
"all men are rapists" slur leads directly to Lorena Bobbitt, and to the widespread
feminist applause for her castration of her husband in 1993 and for the jury verdict
of not guilty of malicious wounding – an applause which caused many men and
women to wonder if the equality rhetoric is merely a camouflage for an entirely
different political agenda. A movement which celebrates castration and lionizes
Ms Bobbitt is hardly one which is committed to equality!

Paglia herself espouses what she calls "equal opportunity feminism," as opposed
to dependency ("infirmary") feminism, which she describes as "infantilizing and
anti-democratic," "tough-cookie feminism" as opposed to "yuppie feminism" and
"street-wise feminism" as opposed to "bourgeois feminism" (1994:ix-xiii). Others
of course described her as anti-feminist. But her importance lies, not so much in
the debates about labels as in the fact that she dared to criticize the established
Women's Movement, by redefining men in positive terms.

Naomi Wolf's best-selling *Fire with Fire* perpetuated the violent military
metaphor of gender wars in her chosen title; but she is generally pro-male as well as
pro-female and, unusually for feminists, dedicated her volume to "David." Indeed,
in a heterosexist mode, so different mode from Paglia, she is proudly pro-male:
"I want men, male care, male sexual attention … Male sexual attention is the sun
in which I bloom" (1993:200–1). And she confesses that: "I fall in love with men
who feed me" (1993:201). She adds, in a point that talks to my thesis: "It is the job
of a feminist, male or female, to fight sexism, female or male" (1993:204); and: "It
is offensive that in 1993 one should have to spell out the ABCs of male humanity
to clear the name of feminism" (1993:205). Offensive, but very necessary still;
and that was about the extent of her fight. Yet her inflammatory and militaristic
title negates her pacific and amicable message. More appropriate is Cathy Young's
title: Ceasefire (1999).

Wolf distinguished between victim feminism (passé) and power feminism
of which she claims to be the first, inaugurating the third wave of the Women's
Movement. While she is critical of victim feminism, she is reluctant to name
names and examine the problems. And although she insists that feminism "must
establish that feminism is anti-sexist and not anti-male," her failure to indict the
new sexists is unfortunate. She blames the decline of the feminist constituency
80% on the media, for omissions and distortions, and only 20% on the movement
(1993:66). In my view however the enormous success of the women's movement
over the decades has been due to widespread media support, and to massive male
support also; the decline of the constituency is surely the responsibility of the
movement, and to its change of direction and emphasis.

Both Paglia and Wolf have enjoyed broad media exposure; but perhaps even more important in the development of critical feminism (critical of itself that is), has been the quiet steady work of such as Christina Hoff Sommers. Sommers distinguishes between "equity feminism," characteristic of the Seneca Falls Conference, and "gender feminism," characterized by conflict ideology rather than the liberal and enlightenment values, and marked by gynocentrism and identity politics rather than universalism and humanism. It is these new "gender feminists" who have created the new sexism. Sommers' reports as an observer of the new feminism are often amusing, sad and utterly amazing but always enlightening; but it is her investigation of how feminist politics has skewed feminist scholarship which is most fascinating, and disappointing. In the university, this includes much rape research, violence research, the American Association of University Women's self-esteem study, the Wellesley Report on how schools (allegedly) shortchange girls, and, as they say, much, much more. While Paglia and Wolf were important in different ways, Sommers launched the first serious academic critique of feminist scholarship, scholars and values.

Indeed the nineties have witnessed a vivid pyrotechnic explosion of work on women, feminism and gender issues. In *The Morning After* (1993) Katie Roiphe has challenged the feminist establishment data on rape statistics and realities. Patricia Pearson (1997) has exposed the unexpectedly wide range of violent female criminality, including serial killers, spousal murderers and child killers – and also the extreme difficulty of the justice system in conceiving of such possibilities due in part to chivalric attitudes and double standards. Michael Weiss and Cathy Young (1996) have critiqued feminist jurisprudence and legal theory which, despite addressing real wrongs in many areas, is also in their view, political, sexist, gynocentric and inegalitarian. Nancy Friday's *The Power of Beauty* (1996) rejects the official feminist line that beauty is a trap for women (Baker, 1984) or a myth, as Wolf (1991) believes – a line that has held since Simone de Beauvoir articulated it in *The Second Sex*; and she suggests that it is an important asset for a woman. In *Lip Service* (1996) the journalist Kate Fillion exposes "women's darker side in love, sex and friendship" and effectively negates the bi-polar dichotomy of woman/good versus man/evil so characteristic of old-style gender feminists. Donna Laframboise, who describes herself as a dissident feminist, in *The Princess at the Window* (1996), insists that the massive changes that have occurred in recent years to expand the opportunities for women are "a testament to the good faith and goodwill of men" – had they really been "oppressors," the "enemy," "pigs" etc. this would not have happened. She accuses contemporary feminism bluntly and broadly of "anger, self-obsession, extremism and arrogance"; and notes that if men's lives were "a lot better" than women's, as Catherine MacKinnon and others insist, then "they wouldn't be killing themselves at four times the rate of women overall, and dying seven years younger than their wives, on average. They wouldn't be the majority of the homeless, the majority of those in prison nor the majority of murder victims." Laframboise is one of the few feminists who have acknowledged men, suggested that the women's movement has made mistakes and that we do not replace one sexist dogma with another (1996:316, 319–20).

Cathy Young has called for a ceasefire, but has also demolished central feminist claims; "Girls are *not* silenced or ignored in the classroom. Medicine has *not* neglected women's health. Abuse by men is *not* the leading cause of injury to American women; the courts do *not* treat violence towards women more leniently than violence towards men. Gender disparities in pay and job status are *not* merely a consequence of sex discrimination…. The climate in our society is not one of "cultural misogyny" … but is far more saturated with negative attitudes toward men (1999:10). She adds that "the greatest impediment" to gender equity "is what passes for feminism today" (1999:11).

The most effective critique of misandry in popular culture and in legislative decisions has come from two well researched volumes by Paul Nathanson and Katherine Young (2001, 2006). Their detailed analysis of film and television programs in *Spreading Misandry*, and of recent legal decisions in *Teaching Misandry* are the first serious efforts to counter-attack misandry.

Some blame men, some blame women, some attack the old sexism, some the new; some spurn feminists, others spurn masculists of varying political stripes and colours. It is a free for all out there; and the struggles continue on a wide range of issues.

There are solutions to this new problem, but the first solution is to recognize and admit that there is a problem, misandry, rather than to miss it or to dismiss it as trivial. Beyond that one might protest this hate literature, the inaccurate data which supports it, the inequitable policies which result from both, and the monocular lens which demonizes men and masculinizes demons.

Conclusion

There are many feminisms (Siegal, 2007:116), and it is fascinating to see how feminisms have changed over the years. It is over 200 years since Mary Wollstonecraft's argument for human rights, justice, and equality, 160 years since Seneca Falls, about 100 since the Suffragettes mobilized with specific demands for the franchise, and 50–60 since de Beauvoir and Friedan. The former introduced victim feminism, and the latter reinforced it with misandry, although both Cady Stanton and Montessori had introduced female supremacism to the debate long before. The Second Wave advocated women's liberation; the Third Wave was announced by Wolf (1993) and described as power feminism: equality and liberation took a back seat to power and *parity with men* – but parity with *which* men? Men are not all the same, nor equal with each other. This facile slogan appeals only to those who parrot it, with no thought behind the parrot brain. The alpha males or the omega males? 50% of members of Parliament or Congress? And 50% of those in prison. 50% of the F500 CEOs? and 50% of the homeless.

50% of the Nobel Prizes? and 50% of the suicides. 50% of the top, and 50% of the bottom, and 50% in the middle. That would be parity.

The transitions from equal rights to victim feminism, female supremacism and misandry to power feminism have transformed our worlds: greater gender equality and also greater gender polarization.

The increased social mobility of women, starting with higher tertiary education graduation rates in the 80s has resulted in increased representation in the professions, business and politics, shifts in income ratios and in the balance of power. Over time this may contribute to a reduction in misandry.

Indeed the "truths" of the Old Guard are now widely regarded as "myths" by the new wave – as we have seen. Similarly the construct of women as "superior", as "sugar and spice" who have an "ethic of care" has been challenged from two directions: a spate of books on female villains – a new discovery, apparently; and a flood of memoirs by women who negate all such notions of victims or sugar; and both contribute to redefinitions of the concept of power. This we discuss next.

Chapter 5
Victims:
The Wars Against Men

Men and women are victims of a wide range of adversities, many of them common to both sexes, but usually to different degrees. Both men and women are victims of the military wars and civil wars that splatter the planet, the societal wars of preventable deaths by accidents, suicides and homicides, the cultural wars from advertising to television to cartoons which can objectify and demean both men and women, the ideological wars of misogyny and misandry and the systemic wars: the failures of our education, health, welfare, political or justice systems which may penalize both men and women. We are all beneficiaries of these same systems, and also of these wars. The so-called "battle of the sexes" has winners and losers – and that there is a battle has been the foundation, the core, of victim feminism and the theory of patriarchy.

We are accustomed to the phrases "the battle of the sexes", "the gender wars" and "the war against women." The idea of a war against men may seem novel to some, or hyperbole to others. But the wars are real and bloody, as well as political, symbolic and metaphorical. We can appropriate victim feminism as a lens to understand victim masculinism.[1]

---

1   The United Nations itself ignores the status and problems of men. The U.N. publications are divided into catalogues on various topics, including Social Sciences. This in turn has lists of publications on Aging, Children and Development through to Satistics and Women. Not only is there no list of publications on men, but I could not find in my own search one single publication on men. The catalog for women is 12 pages long, with 222 volumes in many languages (and some duplication). This includes the "Convention for the Elimination of All Forms of Discrimination Against Women" – but there is no mention of discrimination against men, from the draft to custody to misandry to double standards in the justice/incarceration system. Exemplifying these double standards is another publication: "Trafficking in Human Beings, Especially Women and Children, in Africa" – some people are more "human beings" than others, it would seem. Another is on "Violence Against Women in Couples" – but what about violence against men? They are the victims of between 18 and 24% of intimate homicides in the U.S. and Canada; but they don't count. "Women, Peace and Security at a Glance" (2003) discusses the impact of war on, again, women and children, but not men (www.un.org/publications). UNICEF has not done justice to men. "The State of the World's Children: 2001" sets out to protect the rights and meet the needs of young children; and its cover shows a laughing mother and a child – no sign of the father. The assumption is that the "caregivers" are all female. Their report on "The State of World Population 2000: Lives Together, Worlds Apart – Men and Women in a Time of Change"

Neither men nor women can be totally defined by victimology – nor by potential hero or villain status either; but these three paradigms, or perspectives, clarify the multiple realities of gender. The victimization of women both nationally and globally has been well researched and reported, and still is – it has also been steadily reduced but not eliminated. The victimization of men is often either missed, dismissed or minimized. It is necessary, then, to consider this perspective on men's lives – and deaths – not to "out-victimize" women but to recognize our unique and shared adversities.

These wars are complex not only in their ubiquity and multiplicity but also because gender intersects with so many other variables, notably race and class and other dimensions of inequality; and so much depends on which countries we are discussing.

Over 100,000 American men and about 9,000 Canadian men die violent deaths every year. This is over twice the number of women, with an even higher Potential Years of Life Lost (PYLL) (since men die younger), a differential etiology, particularly with war deaths over the last century, and much higher economic costs. These violent deaths are a massive human tragedy and carry high socio-economic costs. In addition these deaths have implications for classical feminist theories of patriarchy, which traditionally have foregrounded the victimization of women by men while ignoring the victimizations of men by various agents. In this chapter we will explore the multiple etiologies of these deaths and other adversities.

There are two caveats: first, the scope of this chapter is restricted to deaths. Many have argued that the discrimination, prejudice, misandry and wars against men are systemic (Farrell and Sterba, 2008), and include the health system (www. menshealthnetwork.org), the education system (Sommers, 2000), the legal system (Weiss and Young, 1996; Nathanson and Young, 2006), the entertainment media (Nathanson and Young, 2001), while even Susan Faludi (1999) notes that men have been "stiffed" by shifts in national and international capitalism: the economic system. Cumulatively, the focus on women in health, education, law, entertainment, and the ignoring of the needs and rights of men – a privileging of women which flows from the assumptions that women are victims, men hold all the power and that men are villains – has caused immense damage to many men.

Second, the title of the chapter, Victims, is not intended to suggest that all men are all victims all of the time, but merely that some men are victims of some social forces – values and structures – some of the time; and that while alert to the victimization of women, we must be equally alert to the victimization of men. We have heard about "the wars against women" which in the 90s conferred victim status on women and villain status on men, but there are also wars against men, literally as well as metaphorically. Victim feminists (male and female) have foregrounded the victimization, oppression and exploitation of women and often,

---

examines gender inequality i.e. the victimization of women or women's inequality; but not men's inequality. This myopic tunnel vision and biased values at the highest levels of scholarship is part of the problem, not part of the solution.

since Friedan, blamed women's "problems" on men. To discuss this is not so much to engage in *competitive* victimization, as it is to note that women do not have a monopoly on victim status and to engage in *comparative* gender studies. We all have a tough time, but often in different ways. Warren Farrell suggests that "Our anger towards men as victimizers blinds us to men as victims" (1993:221); and this is surely part of the problem of the invisibility of male sufferings, failures and costs. The benefits to men are known, as are the costs to women, but not so well known are the benefits and relative advantages to women, and the costs to men. R.W. Connell (2002, 2000), for instance, discusses the "patriarchal dividend" from which, allegedly, all men benefit – but he has not discussed the patriarchal *tax*, from which all men suffer, and die, from which all women benefit, nor the "matriarchal dividend" nor the male donation.

Kimmel notes that the pain that men suffer should not blind us to the pain men cause (1992:170) – but nor should that blind us to the good that men do. Yet many authors on gender are blind both to the pains of men and to the good that they do. We need to juggle all three perspectives.

The annual violent death toll in the United States – which is almost double the total U.S. combat deaths in the six year Vietnam War every year – is curiously invisible, even taken for granted as part of the male life style. The general trend of research has been to examine specific etiologies: war, homicide, suicide, and accidents, rather than to examine the totality, although exceptions include Farrell (2008, 1999, 1993), Thomas (1993), and Courtenay (2000).

For over a decade some feminist authors have used the term "gynocide" or "femicide" to foreground the violent deaths and injuries to women by men (Gartner and McCarthy, 1991). A more inclusive term "gendercide" was coined by Mary Anne Warren in her book *Gendercide: The Implications of Sex Selection* (1985). Unfortunately she limited her work only to "anti-female gendercide" i.e. gynocide – including a wide range of practices: female infanticide, the witch-hunts, *suttee* in India, female genital mutilation and so on. Similar points were made by Marilyn French in her book *The War against Women* (1992).[2] Though they say they are committed to gender equality, these authors, while highlighting violence against women, have failed to recognize the violence against men, and violent male deaths, from a variety of causes. *"Androcide", to coin a word, is far more common than gynocide and femicide.*

---

2 French blames all atrocities on men, assuming that women have no power and are never autonomous. The reality is more complex. On suttee (banned by the "patriarchal" British in 1829, and again by the government of India), Choi notes that there have been 40 cases of suttee style death since 1947, the most famous in 1987 (Choi, 2004). On female circumcision, Leonard reports that many women in southern Chad, both Christian and Muslim, have been circumcized (not mutilated, in their values), desire it for their daughters, and comment on it favourably (Leonard, 2004). We do not have to approve of women's agency, or men's, but we do have to recognize it.

The numbers of violent male deaths every year in every nation are appalling. And add the nations together, and the situation is almost incomprehensible. The deaths of so many men, mostly young men, in so many horrific ways, and still continuing every day, deserve our acknowledgement, compassion, sympathy and our best efforts to understand them, and to ameliorate these situations – rather than to ignore them or to generally demonize men and blame the victims.

All these deaths are linked, not only in the cemeteries and mortuaries and crematoria around the world, but also more fundamentally in our cultures, and the norms by which we live. We not only tolerate the waste and endure the pain, and the high economic costs too, but we even ignore both, and take them for granted as part of the natural order of things. Misandric feminists tend to see only women's problems and to define men as women's first and greatest problem. Perhaps we can try to see things differently.

We will therefore review violent deaths in war, by homicide and suicide, and in accidents, and conclude with a discussion of masculinity and male values, including the core altruistic value of "women and children first." But first we will contextualize such deaths in the broader international patterns of men's lives and death.

Life and Death

Men pay a high price for being men. The life expectancy data published by the United Nations indicate that in almost every country in the world men die earlier than women. The most striking aspect of Table 5.1, where this data is presented, is the appallingly low life expectancies in the poorest countries in the world. But it is gender not nation which is our concern here, and in the developed world the gender longevity gap is wide: ranging from three years to over seven in France and 13.5 in Russia. The variations are considerable, for reasons that are not entirely clear.

The age-adjusted male mortality rate in the U.S. in 2003 (latest available data) was 9.9 per 100,000 for men and 7.1 per 1,000,000 for women i.e. the male death rate was 39% higher for men. Similarly the age-adjusted mortality rate for blacks was 30% higher than that for whites. But even more spectacular than these life differentials: the mortality rate for black males was 87% higher than that for white females. So while life expectancy in the States in 2003 was 77.5 years at birth, for females it was 80.1 and for males it was only 74.8: a 5.3 year difference; but white females could expect to live to 80.5, while for the black males the expectancy was 69.0: a massive 11.5 year difference (U.S. Census Bureau, 2007:76–7; 80). The costs or benefits of gender and race are clearly indicated by these mortality rates and life expectancies. Equally clearly in these statistics – male to female is as black to white.

Men's violent deaths provide clear evidence not only of "difference" or "two worlds" theory, but especially of the costs of masculinity. Accidents are the third leading cause of death for men after heart disease and cancer (but they are the sixth leading cause for women). Suicide is the number eight cause (after strokes, lung disease, pneumonia and influenza, HIV infection) and homicide is number 10 (after diabetes). Neither suicide nor homicide nor HIV feature in the top 10 leading causes of death for women (Simon, 1999:110).

Some of these violent deaths are mediated by the male ethic of altruism i.e. a combination of what a man *has* to do, as required by law, and what men do, as required by custom. This is exemplified variously by the draft, the "women and

Table 5.1   Life expectancy at birth, selected countries, 2005

	F	M	Gap
Iceland (1)	83.1	79.9	3.2
Norway (2)	82.2	77.3	4.9
Australia (3)	83.3	78.5	4.8
Canada (4)	82.6	77.9	4.7
Japan (8)	85.7	78.7	7.0
France (10)	83.7	76.6	7.1
United States (12)	80.4	75.2	5.2
United Kingdom (16)	81.2	76.7	4.5
Italy (20)	83.2	77.2	6.0
Germany (22)	81.8	76.2	5.6
Russian Federation (67)	72.1	58.6	13.5
Brazil (70)	75.5	68.1	7.4
China (81)	74.3	71.0	3.3
India (128)	65.3	62.3	3.0
Sierra Leone (177)	43.4	40.2	3.2

Source: United Nations Development Report 2007: 326–9.

N.B. Numbers in brackets indicate the Human Development Index rank. Criteria for selection are the top three HDI nations, the G8, Brazil, India, China and the lowest ranked nation by HDI rank.*

---

*   All 15 of the 15 countries with the lowest life expectancy are in Africa. The reasons are many, ranging from AIDS, bad governance and war to the trading policies of developed countries. These issues have been discussed in depth elsewhere. Tony Blair placed Africa at the top of the G8 summit agenda in Edinburgh in 2005, economist Jeffrey Sachs led the U.N. Millennium Project which focussed on tropical Africa, and there are success stories in Ghana and South Africa to counter the failed and failing states.

children first" double standard (the "Titanic" syndrome being the classic example of this), the altruism of the saving professions such as police, firefighters, the military (9/11, war, and the occupational deaths are the classic example). This is the reverse of the familiar portrait of patriarchy as the oppression of women: this is patriarchy as protective and liberating of women and oppressive of men. Certainly this portrait demonstrates, not so much the "primacy of the hegemonic male": men as villains and women as victims; but men as victims of many of the same phenomena as women, although usually to different degrees, with some of these lethal phenomena virtually unique to men.

In trying to explain the higher male mortality rate, some suggest that men are self-destructive and blame the victim, arguing that men are often "complicit" in their own deaths (New, 1991; Courtenay, 2000) – though this perspective has been singularly absent from research on female victims. Caroline New, for instance, does not refer to "The Titanic" or to war (and 9/11 came later – too late for her to change her views) or to the bravery medal winners or even to the homicide victims in the wrong place at the wrong time. Most men are not "complicit" in their own deaths, I suggest; and to the extent that they are (suicide for instance), so are women, though she does not say so. But certainly many nations and people are complicit in male-destruction, in everything from war and work to system failures and academic misandry.

War

Wars are fought between states and societies, and primarily by young men. Men are the first victims of war: they are the fighters, the heroes, the cannon fodder, volunteers or conscripts, so often killed or wounded fighting for their countries. The degree of male self-sacrifice is enormous. Male military sacrifice is a significant component of the total scale of intentional human suffering in the last century, whether as volunteers or conscripts.

Estimates vary of the military deaths in the last century. One author calculates 30 million deaths in about 170 international wars, and another 6 million in civil wars for a total of 36 million – mostly young men. Civilian deaths were not included (Clodfelter, 2002:6). A later estimate is 42 million military deaths, 19 million civilian deaths, 83 million deaths due to genocide and tyranny and 44 million due to human-made famine – for a grand total of 188 million violent, unnecessary and preventable deaths. The "fog of war" makes all such casualties estimates at best, and the costs of war are high for both sexes, but especially high for men, now as then.

The good news is that the casualty cost of war was lower in the second half of the century than in the first. The bad news is that the wars today in Afghanistan and Iraq, the rise of Islamist terrorism, the continuing conflicts in the Middle East, and the militarization of China do not offer much hope for a very peaceful future.

History may be conceptualized as wars with occasional peace, or peace with occasional wars. The perspective adopted will largely depend on one's own particular experience of war, genocide, tyranny and death. The Russian perspective, after Napoleon and Hitler, is likely to be more militaristic than the Canadian, given their historical backgrounds. Similarly men's attitudes are likely to be quite different from women's, given their duties in times of war.

The military and civilian casualties of the various wars of the last century are presented in the appropriate national encyclopedias and the many books on the causes, battles, casualties and consequences of the wars.[3]

The numbers do indicate the horrors of war, however. World War I, from 1914–18, caused over eight million military deaths, mostly young men, including four million Russian men and two million Germans, with another 21 million men wounded. It has been calculated that about one-third of all men aged 19–24 in 1914, from Britain, France and Germany, were killed. About 13 million civilians also died, mostly from disease and starvation (Keegan, 1998).

World War II (1939–45) caused about 50 million deaths all told:[4] 20 million military deaths, over half in the Soviet Union, both in battle and also as POWs (prisoners of war). The war was notorious for the Holocaust, and the genocide of almost six million Jews, the dropping of atomic bombs on Hiroshima and Nagasaki in 1945, as well as the failure of appeasement to prevent war.

More wars followed: communist guerilla wars in Malaya and Greece; nationalist-decolonization wars world wide from India to Kenya to Zimbabwe to Vietnam, Algeria and across Africa; and the Arab-Israeli wars following the establishment of the State of Israel in 1948, and still continuing with the Israeli invasion of Lebanon in 2006 and Gaza in 2008; the India-Pakistan wars following the independence of both countries in 1948.

Some of the principal wars of the last century are presented in Table 5.2. A rough accounting of some of these vast numbers in some of these wars follows, with two caveats. First, the prime focus is on North America and Europe for reasons of space and readership. Second, the various genocides of the last century were indiscriminate: the Armenian genocide (1915–6), the (artificial) Ukrainian famine (the Holodomor, 1932–3), the Holocaust (1936–45), the Pol Pot regime in Cambodia (1975–8), and the Rwandan genocide (1994). They all killed and maimed women as well as men. The twentieth century has been described as "the nuclear age", with reference primarily to the harnessing of nuclear energy; but it has also been referred to as "the genocide age."

---

3   For a depressing overview of military casualties from 1500 to 2000, see Clodfelter, 2002. Veterans Affairs, Canada, present different data from the Canadian Encyclopedia. The website includes details of many of the battles as well as memoirs. http://www.vac-acc. gc.ca.

4   Encyclopedia Britannica reports Soviet losses of 15–20 million men of battle age in World War II (1997:29:1023). Indeed different sources present different data.

In Eastern and Western Europe the Cold War broke out as Stalin refused to permit free elections in the Soviet Union's newly acquired territories and, as Churchill put it in 1946, the "Iron Curtain" had descended. The Cold War did have military implications, both in the Korean War and later (on the domino principle) in the Vietnam War, but also in the Soviet invasions of Hungary (1956) and Czechoslovakia (1968), then Afghanistan and later the two Chechnyan wars, and in Cuban backing for revolutions or civil wars in South America and parts of Africa. Only in 1989 with the fall of the Berlin Wall, and the collapse of the Soviet Union into its component entities did peace seem possible. But the Balkan Wars were the result, with the decomposition of Yugoslavia and then Serbia into component ethnic parts, with conflicts still persisting over borders.

To sum up, about 636,537 Americans sacrificed their lives on active duty military service in the last century according to the U.S. Department of Defense. These include about 117,000 in World War I, 405,000 in World War II, 54,000 in Korea (34,000 in combat), 58,209 in Vietnam (including eight women), 42 in Grenada, 25 in Panama, 382 in the Persian Gulf War.

In the War on Terror, total U.S. deaths in Afghanistan and Iraq since 2001 number about 5,000 by the end of 2008 – which is less than half the number of male homicide victims in any one year (www.defenselink.mil/news/casualty. pdf). The gender breakdown is interesting. In Iraq women constitute about 15% of active duty service members, but only 2% of the total military death toll. This is far higher than the toll in Vietnam. In the six year Vietnam War, eight U.S. service women were killed, and over 58,000 men. This does indicate that women have a privileged status in war – whether they want it or not. Though women are barred from offensive combat, in 1994 the Pentagon permitted "supporting" combat, including piloting helicopters, accompanying house to house searches, military police, medics, and searching female Iraqi suspects; while many are clerks, nurses, cooks and prison guards, all are targets, and some are casualties.

Not all these men and women were killed in action: some died of their wounds or of disease or in captivity, some were killed in accidents, or by homicide or suicide – but all were military in-theater deaths (U.S. Department of Defence, 2005. See Table 5:3). Relatively few American civilians have been killed, but perhaps over 100,000 civilian Iraqis have been killed, mostly by fellow-Iraqis in what now amounts to a sectarian civil war.

Canadians, with about one-tenth the American population, have lost proportionately more men: over 100,000: 267 in the South African War, nearly 69,000 in World War I, over 47,000 in World War II, 516 in the Korean War, more in the first Gulf War and then Afghanistan, and 114 in U.N. peacekeeping operations around the world: including Egypt, Cyprus, Syria, Rwanda, Kosovo and Croatia. These U.N. losses compare to India (127), Ghana (114), the U.K. and France (98) and the U.S.A. (63). Total U.N. Peacekeeping losses have been 2,474 since 1948 (as of May 31, 2008) (www.un.org/Depts/dpko/fatalities).

The U.K. has suffered over one million military deaths since 1900: about 17,000 in the Boer War, 740,000 in World War I, 150 in the battles for Irish independence,

Table 5.2   Principal wars in the 20th century

1899–1902	Boer War
1904–5	Russia-Japan War
1914–8	World War I
1915–6	Armenian Genocide
1935–6	Italian Invasion of Ethiopia
1936–9	Spanish Civil War
1931–45	Japan-China War
1939–45	World War II
1945–9	Chinese Civil War
1948	1st Arab-Israeli War: the War of Independence
1948–9	1st India-Pakistan War: the War of Independence
54–54	1st Vietnam War
54–55	Chinese Invasion of Tibet
1950–3	Korean War
62–62	Algerian War
1956	2nd Arab-Israeli War: the Sinai Campaign
1956	Hungarian Revolution
1959	Tibetan Revolt
1962	India-China War
1965	2nd India-Pakistan War
1967	3rd Arab-Israeli War: the Six Day War
1967	Biafran War
1968	Invasion of Czechoslovakia
1968–75	2nd Vietnam War
1971	3rd India-Pakistan War
1972	4th Arab-Israeli War: the Yom Kippur War
1975–8	Cambodian Genocide
1975–90	Lebanese Civil War (Syrian Invasion)
1978	Cambodia-Vietnam War begins
89–89	Afghanistan War (Soviet invasion)
1980–08	Iran-Iraq War
1982	Falklands War
1984	Sudan Civil War begins
1989	Invasion of Panama
1990–1	Gulf War
1994	Rwanda Genocide
1994–6	1st Chechnyan War
1999–2000	2nd Chechnyan War
2001	Kosovo
2001	Afghanistan: Coalition invasion
2003–	Iraq: Coalition invasion
2006	Israeli invasion of Lebanon
2007	Darfur genocide persists (Sudan)
2008	Russian invasion of Georgia
2008	Israeli invasion of Gaza

Source: Sivard, 1989; Goldstein, 2001.

Table 5.3   War deaths: U.S., U.K. and Canada (20th century to present)

		United States	U.K.	Canada
1899–1902	Boer War	-	16,895	244
1914(1917)–18	World War I	116,516	743,702	60,661
1918–21	Irish War	-	150	-
1939(1941)–45	World War II	405,399	270,687	42,042
1950–53	Korean War	54,246	710	412
	Cyprus	-	104	-
1953–May 08	UN Operations	63	98	114
1956	Suez War	-	22	-
1964–73	Vietnam War	58,209	-	103
1982	Falklands	-	215	-
1983	Grenada	42	-	-
1990	Panama	25	-	-
1990–1	Gulf War	382	24	-
1969–99	Northern Ireland	-	957	-
2001––	Afghanistan	628	134	103
2003––	Iraq	4,209	178	0

For Afghanistan and Iraq, see The Iraq Coalition Casualty Count: www.icasualties.org. Accessed 19.12.08. Also: www.defenselink.mil/news/casualty.pdf.

Sources: Clodfetter, 2002. U.S.A.: Dept. of Defence, 2007. http://web1.whs.osd. mil/mmid/casualty/castop.htm. See also Department of Veterans Affairs: http://www. va.gov/pressrel/amwars01.htm. U.K.: Hicks and Allen, 1999. Civilian deaths are given in this source, notably 64,000 in World War II and over 2,000 in Northern Ireland. Canada: Canadian Encyclopedia.

another 270,000 in World War II, 700 in Korea, 100 in Cyprus, 22 in the Suez campaign, 215 in the Falklands, 24 in the Persian Gulf War, and almost 1,000 in the troubles in Northern Ireland since 1969. In the twenty-first century more lives were lost in Afghanistan and in the still continuing conflict in Iraq. This is equivalent to one military death – i.e. one (young) male death – every 48 minutes for the entire twentieth century. In addition to the 1,105,553 military deaths in the twentieth century, 75,383 civilians were also killed (Hicks and Allen, 1999).

These heavy losses by the U.S., Canada and the U.K. over the last century are miniscule compared to the total losses in World War II alone. The death-toll in the Soviet Union was about 27 million, civilian and military alike – perhaps 10 million military and 17 million civilian deaths. This was more than the sum total of all the other combatant nations combined. Poland lost about 6.5 million in total and Germany about 5.1 million, including 3.3 million military deaths. Both these last figures include many of the roughly 6 million Jews, gypsies, homosexuals, mentally and physically disabled and others killed in the Holocaust. Japan lost about 1.8 million people, including about 150,000 civilians at Hiroshima and Nagasaki. The sum total of death in the Second World War was probably over 50 million.

While emphasizing here the enormous and largely ignored costs of masculinity, we should not forget the various roles played by women in war: but usually not to the same degree as men, and not in the same ways. Some are now front-line combatants in army, navy or air force as the services have been integrated. Some may be spies, like famously Mata Hari, others guerrillas or in resistance movements or suicide bombers. Some play support roles, as Pvts Jessica Lynch and the infamous prison guard at Abu Ghraib, Lynndie England.

Certainly women have been, and still are, massively victimized by war, but usually as civilians rather than as combatants. While there have been relatively few female American and Canadian civilian casualties, the same has not been true in Europe, the Soviet Union, Asia and Africa. Women have also suffered: the rape of Nanking, the Japanese comfort women, Unit 731, the concentration camps, the blitz, the carpet bombings of Coventry, Dresden and Tokyo, the atomic bombs on Hiroshima and Nagasaki, ethnic cleansing in Bosnia, genocide in Rwanda, rape as a deliberate instrument of war (e.g. in Bosnia), and terrorism around the globe.

On a personal note, of my six aunts, one was an ambulance driver in World War I, three were in the army in World War II (one in Special Forces) and one was in the WRNS. Only one stayed out of the services. All but one of their husbands were in the army (he was a doctor), as were all three of my uncles. My mother, formerly a secretary in Montreal, became a long-distance truck driver from Edinburgh to London and back, having previously in the 1930s spied for the Chinese against the invading Japanese. My father was in the Royal Navy. All of them survived their wars, not unscathed, but two male cousins in the RAF and the Fleet Air Arm were killed.

All these men and women are heroes, no doubt, having sacrificed so much for so many. But the glorification of wars which demand such sacrifices is deadly sad, and will no doubt persist, for without the glory such altruism may fade. Yet the gravestones are lined up in cemeteries like regiments on parade. Furthermore, to add insult to so many injuries, the treatment of war veterans after wars is often inadequate. The heroes become victims of politics and bureaucrats in flat contradiction to the rhetoric. The after-effects of war live long after the peace in illness, divorce, post-traumatic stress disorder (PTSD), alcoholism, suicide and homicide. And veterans must continue to fight (political) wars to defend their rights.

This massive male military casualty rate is recognized in war memorials across the various nations honouring their war dead. Inscriptions often quote the words of Christ: "Greater love hath no man than this, that a man lay down his life for his friends" (John: 15:13).

The wars do not end with the peace. More Vietnam veterans have committed suicide than were killed in that war (Farrell, 1993: 145–7). One U.S. report noted that 121 veterans of Afghanistan and Iraq have committed a killing, or been charged with one, since their return from the war. Another report stated that 120 U.S. Iraq war veterans are killing themselves – every week – more than are killed in that war weekly. The suicide rate for veterans aged 20–24 is almost four times the national average for that age group (Montreal *Gazette* 15.11.07). Another report states that about 20% of U.S. combat veterans are returning with PTSD, with minimal counselling available – or even wanted. Often to seek it is to lose your job, or be transferred, or lose out on a promotion (*Time* 14.7.08:13). The lead article in *Time* recently discussed the prescribing of antidepressants like Prozac to the troops to deal with battlefield stress (Thompson, 2008). The return home is another war with PTSD, rehab, divorce, suicide and homicide. The survivors have to keep fighting.

Reactions to these primarily male deaths are many and various. Denial is one common reaction: "Who started all these wars?" caustically remarked one student of mine. The implication is that men did, so it serves them right if they get killed. (A more useful response might be to list the nations which started the wars, usually by invading someone else's territory: Germany, North Korea, Argentina, Iraq etc.) The further implication is that women are yet again, victims of, and oppressed by, men. A complicating factor in this fairly typical male-blaming response is that while men may vote for other men to fight and possibly die, women also vote – but they vote for *men* only to fight and perhaps die. It is invidious but necessary to note in this regard that while "male-dominated" governments granted women the right to vote, they also granted them the right to decide men's fates, but without the responsibility or the duty of the draft or of combat. Women were exempted by men in classic altruistic mode. (Israel and Ethiopia are two exceptions.)

Empathy is another: "All those beautiful young men" one friend said, and wept as he read an earlier draft of this chapter.

Fury is another: "What does it take to make men kill? to storm the beaches at Normandy and be killed." Citing the Tom Hanks movie *Saving Private Ryan*, as an example of the transformation of men, and adding that he had friends who were killed in Vietnam, this man implied that these victims of war were dupes of corporate interests, that the war was futile, that they died in vain. These victims of war, in his view, were not so much heroes as suckers. The heroes were those who refused to fight and fled or protested or managed deferments – perhaps like him or Vice-President Cheney (5 times deferred).

Gratitude and respect, the emotions expressed on the war memorials, are perhaps the attitudes of previous generations with clearer memories of Nazism and Communism, and personal experiences of war, invasion and holocausts. Perhaps these emotional attitudes are reviving in the current war against terror after 9/11 and male warriors are defined positively in their fight against the so-called "axis of evil." To describe entire countries as "evil" is absurd.

The quick answer to the original question as to "Who started all these wars?" is that politicians declare wars (acting on the advice of their military experts and respecting public opinion polls) including female politicians such as Golda Meir (1973) with the 4th Arab-Israeli War, Indira Gandhi and the 3rd India-Pakistan War (1971), and Margaret Thatcher with the 1982 Falklands War. Female politicians may not be so different from male politicians. And female voters may well support such wars. The public opinion polls are consulted precisely to determine popular levels of support.

How these military deaths are constructed depends not only on the specific war, but also on the ideologies of the respondents, their experiences, socialization and philosophy of life. In a pacific and narcissistic age, in which nothing and no one, is worth risking one's life for, nor even injury, military casualties are perhaps more likely to be regarded as waste than as the heroism which has defeated tyranny and made peace possible.

Political deaths are as incomprehensible as military deaths in an apolitical and apathetic age. Yet if military deaths are seen as "martyrs," so may many political deaths. Here we might include Abraham Lincoln (1865), Dietrich Boenhoffer (1944), Mahatma Gandhi (1948), John F. Kennedy (1963), Martin Luther King (1968), Anwar Sadat (1981), Yitzhak Rabin (1995), Ken Saro-Wiwa and eight other minority rights activists hanged in Nigeria (1995), and countless others. Certainly not all political assassinations are martyrdoms; some were richly deserved, no doubt. But among the male war heroes for human rights we might also include the plotters against Hitler, and against other tyrants, from Stalin, to Pol Pot, Bokassa, Idi Amin, Ceaucescu, Milosevic, Saddam Hussein, and so many others.

Von Clausewitz stated that "War is the continuation of policy by other means." Many men have lost their lives in war, and therefore also in politics. Their immense sacrifices deserve to be respected and remembered.

1995: Srebenica and Androcide

The massacre of up to 8,000 Muslim men and boys by Bosnian Serb forces in July 1995 was the worst single massacre in Europe since the end of World War II. The massacre was ordered by the former Bosnian Serb leader, Radovan Karadzic and executed by General Mladic, both of whom have been indicted for war crimes.

The town was captured in July, despite the U.N. affirmation that this was a "safe" town, defended nominally, but not militarily, by 600 Dutch troops. After the fall of Srebenica, the Bosnian Serb troops separated the men from the women, sent the women to other Muslim areas, and sent the men to detention areas where they were killed over three days, and buried in mass graves by the fourth; they filmed the executions. The attackers argued that this was in retaliation for several Muslim attacks into Serbian villages, killing hundreds over previous years. The bureaucratic military efficiency of this specific *androcide* was unique to the second half of the century.

The horror generated by the massacres enabled President Clinton to garner support for the NATO "bombing for peace" that led to an end to the fighting. The lesson of the Rwanda genocide that peace-keeping is not possible under current rules of engagement had not been learned: peace *enforcement* requires a more active role.

Yet this particular androcide is only a small fraction of the other male deaths that occur so regularly in homicides, suicides and accidents.

Homicide

Homicide is a feature of all modern societies; but how significant a feature it is varies widely from the high homicide rate of 62.7 per 100,000 in Colombia, 47.5 in South Africa and 34.4 in Jamaica, to 5.6 in the U.S.A., 2.1 in the U.K., 1.9 in Canada, 0.6 in Hong Kong and the United Arab Emirates and 0.5 in Singapore (United Nations Development Program, 2007:322–5). The range is therefore enormous, from Colombia to Singapore, but both the killers and the killed are usually male.

In the United States in 2005, 18,124 individuals were murdered: 79% of them male. This constitutes a double strike by men against men – in quick succession 14,376 men were removed from life and 3,748 women, and the villains, perhaps 10,000 or so, mostly men, were removed from freedom and their families and, if they received the death penalty, eventually from life itself (Table 5.4).

The breakdown of the U.S. data for 2005 by gender and race is startling. The homicide victimization rate for white females is 1.9 per 100,000, for white males it is 5.3, for black females it rises to 6.1 and for black males it is an astonishing 37.3 per 100,000: 20 times higher than that for white females. Men overall are almost four times more victimized by homicide (9.4/00,000) than women (2.8/00,000), and black men are six times more so than the national average (Kung *et al.*, 2008: Tables 12, 16). Not surprisingly, the victim feminism of so many middle class white women alienated many black women and black feminists, furious at the failure to consider violence against black males as a problem, only the relatively minimal, violence against white women. Among black males in the 20–24 demographic, the homicide victimization rate is an astonishing 155.5 per 100,000, and constitutes the leading cause of death (U.S. Census Bureau, 2007:195).

The data are particularly bleak when looked at over time. In the last 30 over half a million men and women have been murdered. That is more male deaths than American losses in World Wars I and II combined; or, to bring us closer to the present, more than American losses in World War II, Korea, Vietnam, and the Gulf War and Iraq combined. This constitutes a veritable war against men – mostly by men.

Ironically, the heroes who risk their lives to protect the victims and arrest the villains are often forgotten; but sworn law-enforcement officers are 86% male. (Media presentations of the police at work in such programs as CSI show an unrepresentative number of female officers.)

Intimate homicides are a particularly tragic example of one type of homicide, but relatively rare. In 2004, 579 wives were killed by their husbands and 149 husbands were killed by their wives. (The term intimates includes the legally married, former spouses and common-law relationships.) So, while 80% of these homicides were committed by the man, 20% were committed by the woman – rather more than most people think. They are, however, only a very small fraction of the total homicides (4%) and an even smaller total of those married and in common-law relationships. While it is "well-known" that women are more likely to be killed by a "husband" than anyone else, this is simply not true. Wives were only 579 of the total of 3,099 female victims. Another 445 girlfriends were murdered by boyfriends, and 147 boyfriends were murdered by girlfriends: a 75% to 25% ratio, but this still constitutes only a third of the total of women victims.

More worrisome is the grand total of 1,804 homicides which occur within the family, including infanticide, matricide, patricide and fraternal and sororal homicides. This constitutes 13% of the victims – exactly the same proportion as homicides by a stranger.

The good news is that these homicide rates have fallen from 15.0/00,000 and 4.0/00,000 for men and women respectively in 1990 down to 8.7 and 2.4 respectively. Similarly from 1976 to 2002 the number of intimate homicides has declined dramatically: black males killed by intimates dropped 81%, white males 56%, black females 49% and white females 9% (U.S. Dept. of Justice, 2005).

In Canada the homicide situation was similar in some, but not all, respects. 594 homicides were reported in 2007, with a homicide rate of 1.8 victims per 100,000: under one-third that of the U.S. An intensive study of the 2005 data found that, in the United States, about one-third were committed in the family; also 16% were gang related and about two-thirds of the adult accused and half of the adult victims had a criminal record in Canada. About 90% of the offenders and 75% of the

Table 5.4   Homicide victims (the United States and Canada)

	U.S. (2005)	Canada (2007)
Men	14,376	432
Women	3,748	162
Total	18,124	594
Rate/100,000	6.1	1.80
% Men	79	73

Source: U.S.: National Vital Statistics Reports, 2008. Vol. 56, No. 10. Canada: Li, 2008.

victims were male. As in the United States, the "spousal" homicide rate continued its general decline since 1975. The 74 spousal homicides (including divorced, separated and common-law relationships) constituted only 11% the total number of homicides: a small fraction – and only about 0.5 per 100,000 spouses. Two points are particularly interesting here in terms of de-bunking misandric myths. The first is that 16% of the spousal homicides (12 of the 74) were committed by the female (legal or common-law, separated or divorced) – not nearly as many as the husbands committed, but not a negligible number either. Second of the 33 child victims (i.e. under 12 years of age) of homicide, 13 (39%) were killed by their parents: one by the father, seven by the mother (the others by step-parents) – and this has been the similar (but socially invisible) pattern for the last three years: 17 children murdered by their fathers, 32 by their mothers (only two by their step-mothers) (Dauvergne and Li, 2006).

The bad press that men get for all this violence is deserved – insofar as it is applied to the guilty parties; but not as it is transferred to *all* men, most of whom are not guilty, and not as it ignores the homicides committed by women. We might paraphrase Gloria Steinem's misandric and inaccurate remark about men with a more accurate, but distasteful, observation about mothers: *the family member who is most likely to kill children is their own mother*.

Both in Canada and the United States, women are the primary victims of intimate and spousal homicide. It is this fact which has triggered a spate of legislation against violence against women. Unfortunately, equity being what it is, often inequitable, the (predominantly male) legislators failed to recognize that the vast majority of homicides are committed against men, not women, and that men need the protection of the law also. They also failed to notice that women do commit homicide: including the 20% (U.S. in 2005) and 20% (Canada in 2007) of intimate homicides, the plurality of child homicides committed by mothers (Canada), and the roughly 10% of total homicides every year. Men are not only the invisible reality of victims, but also the inaudible reality.

The tragic irony here is that so much public attention and legal action has been directed towards ending violence against women, only, while neglecting the far more serious problem of violence against men – by men and women – and failing to recognize that the "two" problems of violence are in fact one: that to end or reduce violence against women it will be necessary also to end or reduce violence against men, by both men and women.

The 1994 Violence against Women Act In the United States, which was reauthorized in 2000 and 2005, and similar legislation in Canada, is useful in some of its goals of inhibiting the effects of violence; but it also infantilizes women, who are deemed in need of special protection; it ignores men, who suffer far more violence; it ignores the real problem, which is the relatively few individuals, men and women, who are violent; and it institutionalizes the double standards which valorize women (and children) as intrinsically more valuable than men. Indeed the enthusiasm with which this legislation has been passed by predominantly male legislators indicates not only the dominance of the feminist lobby (i.e. government of men, by men, *for* women), but also the degree to which primarily male legislators in what has been called an oppressive patriarchy are indeed protective rather than oppressive of women – and, by omission, oppressive of men. Such legislation is both sexist and ultimately counter-productive.

Most obviously there is no policy of zero tolerance for violence against black males – yet this is the population most in need of such legislation. Democratic legislation should protect *all* citizens; and the target should be violent people, men and women, not violence *against* either men or women. Meanwhile, in default of such legislation, and the attitudes conducive to passage of such legislation, men continue to die violent deaths by homicide about three times more frequently than women in the U.S. and in Canada.

Meanwhile it is ironic, not to say pathetic, that there are no Violence against Men Acts in the United States or in Canada, even though 79% of the homicide victims in the U.S. were male, and 73% of them in Canada (Table 5.4). The VAW Act in the U.S., as re-authorized in 2005, now does include the provision that it is gender neutral – after 11 years – which men's rights activities hailed as a victory of sorts. Given its history, its failure to address prison rape, the widespread feminist definition of men as "the violent sex" (Holliday, 1978), or "the death sex" (Miles, 1991) and the other epithets about men discussed in Chapter 4, it seems to me improbable that men can expect major change or resources any time soon. Neither the chivalrous male legislators nor the feminists in North America demonstrate much understanding of men as the (homicide) victim sex, nor the heroic, life-saving sex.

As with homicide, so with suicide; but here the war against men is not military, nor waged by other men (both the murderers by commission and the legislators by omission); it is a civil war: men killing themselves in huge numbers: far more than are killed by homicide.

Suicide

About one million people commit suicide every year, according to the World Health Organization: 2,700 every day, 114 every hour. This amounts to more deaths annually than the total of all deaths by war and homicide combined. Worldwide the suicide rate has climbed 60% over the last 45 years and now stands at 16 per 100,000 (www.who.int/mental_health). And the vast majority of these suicides are committed by men.

The suicide rates vary widely from country to country, from highs of 38.6 in Lithuania and 35.1 in Belarus to lows of 0.76 in Barbados (latest available years, 2001–5). 97 countries were surveyed by the WHO; but the data for the others, mainly in Africa and the Middle East, were missing. Some countries reported zero suicides, but for earlier dates: Antigua and Barbuda (1995), Honduras (1978), Jordan (1979) and St Kitts and Nevis (1995).

Evidently suicide, much as it is a highly personal decision, is also a cultural matter. The point is clearer upon consideration of the male suicide rates: 68.1 in Lithuania, 63.3 in Belarus, 58.1 in Russia, with rates of over 40 per 100,000 in Hungary, Slovenia, Sri Lanka and Ukraine, and over 30 in another six countries. The gender rates vary as widely as the national rates. The male/female ratios range from about 10:1 in Bahrain and the Seychelles to about 4:1 in the U.S.A., and 3:1 in Canada and the U.K.

Male suicide numbers are higher than female in all 97 countries except perhaps for China, where the female suicide is slightly higher, but the data is incomplete.

Women, it is well-known, attempt suicide more often than men – perhaps 10 times more often; and attempters often do themselves immense damage, and are at risk for trying again. But there is no equivalence between men and women in terms of dead bodies on the ground, nor in the culture of death.

The WHO presents a map with the frequency distributions of suicide around the world: high, medium, low and unknown – colour-coded either red, yellow, blue or white. The red zone includes the old Soviet Union, China, Japan and France; the yellow covers India, the United States, Canada and most of Western Europe. South America and Mexico are blue. Africa and much of the Middle East is white. This indicates graphically the importance of national cultures as determinants of suicide. But we will explore the importance of gender cultures.

The WHO defines suicide as follows:

> Suicide is the act of deliberately killing oneself. Risk factors for suicide include mental disorder (such as depression, personality disorder, alcohol dependence or schizophrenia) and some physical illnesses, such as neurological disorders, cancer and HIV infection.

Table 5.5   Suicides (United States, U.K. and Canada)

	U.S. (2005)	U.K. (2004)	Canada (2003)
Men	25,907	4,086	2,902
Women	6,730	1,468	862
Total	32,637	5,554	3,764
Rate/100,000	11.0	9	11.3
Male rate	17.7	14	17.8
Female rate	4.5	5	5.1
M:F ratio	3.8:1	2.8:1	3.4:1
% male	79	74	77

Sources: U.S.: www.suicidology.org; www.cdc.gov/ncipc/factsheets/suifacts.htm; www. nimh.nih.gov; National Vital Statistics Reports, 2008. Vol. 56. No. 10. Canada: www. suicideinfo.ca. U.K.: www.samaritans.org.

Notably missing from this list is the greatest risk factor of them all: masculinity, and the second greatest, country of location. The definition is informed by medical and psychological orientations (or biases) and omits these two risk factors: a suicidogenic culture: a point of which WHO is obviously very conscious, but neglects in favour of an individualistic perspective. Suicide, as Durkheim noted over 100 years ago is "a social fact", as well as an individual one; and some countries are more suicidogenic than others – and one gender more than the other also.

With this background establishing both the global and the predominantly male problem, we can interrogate the roughly 33,000 suicides in the U.S., 6,000 in the U.K. and 4,000 in Canada – every year. First, however, suicide is a complex phenomenon. We recognize many types, including mass suicides, protest suicides (e.g. the 10 IRA hunger strikers in 1981), impulse suicides (perhaps after a break-up or a disappointment), mimic suicides (e.g. after Kurt Cobain died), rational choice suicides, assisted suicides, suicide bombers, as well as depressive suicides (Synnott, 1996).

Furthermore, Emile Durkheim (1966/1897), the father of suicidology, suggested three main types of suicide: egoistic, altruistic and anomic: a structural theory relating to the types of bonds integrating the individual with the society. Freud argued that suicide is "probably" displaced homicide: "the unconscious of all human beings is full enough of such death-wishes, even against those they love" (PFL Vol. 9; 1979:389). Karl Menninger expanded on Freud's idea of the self-destructive death wish in his book *Man Against Himself* (1938) on the war within the self. He distinguished between four different types of suicidality: the immediate completed suicide; chronic suicide: the attenuated suicide of self-destructive habits and addictions; focal suicide: often focusing on specific body parts as in self-mutilation and unconsciously purposive accidents; and organic suicides: the vexed question of the psychic etiology of illness, disease and death – what Freud had called "the flight into illness" (PFL Vol. 9; 1979:79).

In this view, suicide is not so much either/or, but a continuum not only between completed – attempted – and suicide ideation, but also between three types of parasuicide. The psychologist Jack Douglas (1967) further complexified but also clarified this theorizing by attacking Durkheim's threefold typology as too simplistic and too structural. He emphasized that the meanings people impute to suicide are all different, and that every suicide is unique; then he offered 12 types of suicide, depending on the point of the action: to atone for evil, out of shame or guilt or remorse, to re-unite with a loved one, for revenge and so on; and he offered examples to prove his point.

Edwin Shneidman (1987) known as the Dean of American suicidology, has pointed out that one common problem among suicidal people is bi-polar thinking: all or nothing, black or white, death is the only option. His therapeutic policy is to explore options and to seek a middle ground.

While all these theorists have advanced our understanding of suicide, and its facets and complexity, all of them, and all are men, have ignored the masculinity of suicide. This is strange. Only in the 1990s do some people begin to worry about the high male suicide rates, and to think about how women protect themselves so successfully. David Thomas asked: "Aren't all these suicides telling us something about men's lives?" (1993:14). And Warren Farrell described men as "the suicide sex" (1993:164).

The American Association of Suicidology (AAS) suggests on its webside that Major Depressive Disorder (MDD) is "the psychiatric diagnosis most commonly associated with completed suicide" (www.suicidology.org). And it's true, no one says: "Oh! I'm so happy I could kill myself." While it offers lists of "risk factors" and "warning signs" – useful though they are – it does not address the *social* factor most commonly associated with completed suicide, namely maleness. Nor does it address the question of why three to 10 times more men might have MDD. This is men as the *ignored* sex.

Similarly two Canadian Task Force reports on suicide specify high-risk groups in the population: prisoners, alcoholics, First Nations, the clinically depressed, those with AIDS, the circle of survivors of a suicide – but the authors ignored the elephant in the room: the men who constitute about 80% of the suicides (Health Canada, 1987; 1995). It is difficult to deal with a problem that is not recognized.

The numerous *types* of suicide create one problem in theorizing male suicide, the failure of so many psychologists and suicidologists to notice the problem is another, but a third is intersectionality: the relation of other factors such as age, race and ethnicity as well as nationality with men and women.

The AAS Fact Sheet for 2005 (the latest available data) notes that the white male suicide rate (19.7) is more than double the black male suicide rate (8.7), which is almost double the white female suicide rate (5.0) which is more than double the black female rate (1.8). If suicide is a reliable indicator of ability to cope with the adversities of life – an important type of power – than women cope better than men, blacks better than whites, and black women best of all and white men worst of all. This is an interesting reversal of our usual picture of the white racist and male sexist hegemonic patriarchy.

The white/black pattern in the United States is not reflected in the aboriginal populations of North America, though the gender patterns are. In the United States the suicide rate for the American Indian population was 19.3/00,000: about 1.5 times that of the total population (1998–9 data. The latest available). In Canada the First Nations suicide in 2000 was 24/00,000: double the national average of 12/00,000 – though this is down substantially from about 38/00,000 in 1979–81. The male suicide rate was about 18.7, 3½ times higher than the female rate of 5.2. However, the situation in the Inuit regions of the north is catastrophic: over 10 times the national average. In Nunavut the male suicide rate is 136, nearly five times the female rate; and in Nunavik it is 173/00,000, almost six times higher than the female rate and *14* times higher than the Canadian average (latest available data, 1997, which indicates some lack of concern with this issue) (Kirmayer *et al.*: 2007:13–17). The causes of such high rates, and prevention methods, have been discussed extensively over the years, and implemented with some success among the status Indians, less so among the Innu. But the masculinity of these suicides has been ignored, even by the Aboriginal Health Foundation (Kirmayer *et al.*, 2007).

Age is also an intervening variable. While it is the 11th leading cause of death overall in the States, it is the third for youths aged 15–24 – which is where the sexes diverge. The male to female ratio soars from 3.6 to one aged 15–19 to 5.8 to one aged 20–24. And in old age the rates *and* the gender differences were even higher. The suicide rate for women aged 65+ typically declines slightly, but hovers around four. For men aged 65–9 the rate is 20 i.e. five times the rate for women in that age cohort, rising to 46 in the 85+ age bracket i.e. 21 times the rate for women.

The only good news in these scenarios is that the overall suicide rate has declined from 11.9 in 1994 to 11.0 in 2005: an 8% decline; and the youth suicide rate has dropped 29% over the same period (AAS, 2005).

Finally, the fourth confounding factor in all this is the *invisibility* of suicides. Our media foreground homicide both for our information and for our entertainment; so the general public might be forgiven for concluding that homicide is more frequent and fearful than suicide. In reality the reverse is the case. Suicides outnumber homicides by about 4:1 in the U.S. and 6 or 7:1 in Canada and the U.K. *We have much more to fear from our own selves than from our enemies or our intimates or strangers.* This distortion of reality by our media has consequences for our recognition of suicide as a social problem, still more as a primarily male social problem.

The demographics of suicide are similar in Canada (Health Canada, 1987; 1995) and in the U.K. (www.samaritans.org).

Unfortunately, the actual number of suicides in all these countries is probably higher than reported, for two principal reasons. First, many suicides are camouflaged. Single-car, boating, swimming, flying or hunting incidents described as accidents may not have been such. Second, some coroners refuse to return a verdict of suicide unless the issue is beyond a shadow of a doubt, especially in Catholic countries. This is in the interests of accuracy and of the family.

The most recent theory of suicide relates to humans as chemical beings. The tragic case of Matt Miller, 13, who spent a week on Zoloft, an anti-depressant, and then hung himself illustrated this. Lawsuits against Pfizer followed, and concerns escalated from parents, clinical researchers and medical activists to lawyers, then U.S. Senators and finally a caution from the FDA against the use of all SSRIs (selective serotonin reuptake inhibitors) for children and adolescents under 18.

None the less, for all our data and theories we have as yet no compelling theory of male suicide. Durkheim's integration theory, Freud's displaced aggression theory, Menninger's self-destruction theory, Douglas' meaning theory and Shneidman's binary thinking theory all purport to explain suicide – but none address the suicide sex.

My own theory of masculine values and culture is discussed below, and perhaps integrates all these deaths by war, homicide, suicide and accidents, though it is not restricted solely to men.

Accidents

Accidents will happen, of course; and we may define them as statistical probabilities, chance, bad luck or the workings of divine providence. But many, perhaps most, accidents are the result of human errors of one sort or another: excessive speed, high risk behaviour, carelessness, alcohol or drugs or sleep-deprivation, or sheer stupidity. They are only "accidents" in the sense that the results (death or injury) were not intended; but they are not accidents, in the sense that they were usually preventable or avoidable and involve calculated (or miscalculated) risks. Indeed "accidents" may be systemic, i.e. they may be built into our economic and cultural systems.

Accidents may be consequences of corporate policy to ignore safety legislation and to assume death and injury as "the cost of doing business" or "collateral damage," and calculated precisely as in the infamous Ford Pinto case. They may also be consequential to government policy: inadequate safety legislation inadequately enforced and poorly penalized. These deaths then, especially in the dangerous professions, may reflect cultural attitudes which consider men as "disposable," in Farrell's (1993) term, in peace as in war.

117,809 Americans died "accidentally" in 2005, accounting for 4.5% of all deaths, with an age-adjusted death rate of 39.1 per 100,000. This is 3.6 times the number of suicides and 6.5 times the number of homicides (Kung et al., 2008. Tables 12, 16). Curiously, we fear homicides more than we fear accidents. Yet accidents are the fifth leading cause of death in the United States. Indeed accidents kill more people than suicide and homicide combined. Indeed this total is double the total U.S. military deaths in the six-year Vietnam War – every single year. Men constituted 65% of these deaths: 76,375 in 2005.

The good news is that the accidental death rate (ADR) has fallen over the last decades, not so much because people are more careful as due to improved medical care, more rapid emergency service delivery, new legislation on seat-belt use, helmet-use, and drunk driving, as well as improved industrial safety legislation and enforcement.

The total monetary costs of accidental deaths and disabling injuries in the U.S. has been calculated at $586.3 billion in 2003. This total includes wage and productivity losses, medical expenses, administrative expenses, motor-vehicle damage, employer costs and fire loss (U.S. Census Bureau 2004: Table 176, p. 119).

Gender, age and race all factor into this data – especially the first two. Men are 86% more likely to die accidentally than women – which is why they constitute two-thirds of the victims; but the two sexes not only are killed at different rates, but also often by different causes, as both the U.S. and Canadian data indicate (cf. Tables 5.6 and 5.7).

The casualty list is long and sad. Indeed Will Courtenay, probably the leading authority on injury, disease, and early deaths among men, has avoided the term "accidents" in such discussions "to emphasize the fact that these events are preventable" (2000:87). The litany of these preventable "accidental" deaths is long in the United States: men constitute 68% of all pedestrian deaths, five-sixths of all drowning deaths, 85% to 90% of all bicycle deaths, and about 66% of all motor vehicle fatalities. They are also more likely to have their licenses suspended or revoked, to exceed the speed limit, to drive recklessly, not to use their safety belts, and in one study, to be at fault in almost 8 out of 10 fatal crashes i.e. not accidents – male error. And apart from the deaths, about four million injuries are sustained by men and women in sports and recreational activities (Courtenay, 2000).

Canadian data, using the same standard international classification system (ICD-10) clarifies some of the gender differentials. Most of them illustrate the higher male mortality rates, and by a wide variety of causes. For instance, 61% of the pedestrians killed were men, 85% of the cyclists, 85% of the bikers, 94% of those on farm vehicles, 88% of those on ATVs (all-terrain vehicles); and on the water in sailboats, canoes, kayaks and fishing-boats: 91% male. And in the air, in helicopters, ultra-lights, balloons, hang-gliders, gliders, parachutes: 84% male. Falls constituted about one-third of the accidental deaths (34%) (1,978), but while men constituted just over half of these deaths (52%), the etiologies of death were distinct. Men were more likely to die from falls from scaffolding, ladders, buildings, trees, cliffs, jumping etc. – while women were more likely to die from falls from beds, wheelchairs, slipping and falls down stairs. These were different types of accidents usually at different ages, though both were deaths by falls. Similarly, men were much more likely to die from "exposure to inanimate mechanical forces" – a polite way of saying having things dropped on you, and other such catastrophes (200 out of 220). Men were much more likely to die by drowning: 214 of 266:80%; electrocution and extreme temperatures: (27 of 27: 100%); fire: 120 out of 196: 61% – this would include firefighters as well as those unable to escape wildfires or domestic fires; avalanches do not kill many people every year, but 16 of the 19 killed in 2003 were men: 84%). Of the six killed by "legal intervention", all were male (Statistics Canada Cat. No. 84-208-XIE).

These accidents are surely no accident. This death-toll is systemic, and related to male lifestyles and values, and also to cultural values, political legislation and corporate policies (or lack thereof) towards men, and also to a lesser extent women. These so-called accidents are killing men at a horrific rate.

Our cultural norms are more lethal than our germs and our guns. The guns relate to homicide, suicide and war particularly, but the norms also relate to accidents, suicide, homicide, work and heroism. Life-styles determine death-styles, and so do corporate policies (Ford Pinto, the Sago mine disaster) and political legislators (Katrina in New Orleans).

Self-protection and self-care are not traditional male cultural attributes. They are not mutually exclusive to adventure and altruism; but they are opposed to traditional definitions of masculinity, and normative expectations of male toughness and stoicism. Some authorities seem to blame men for their carelessness and their failure to nurture themselves and their health as well as women do. Courtenay concludes his encyclopedic discussion:

> If men are to live as long as women do, and the evidence presented here suggests that they can, they will need to change their unhealthy behavior. However, they are unlikely to do so until the underlying motivation for their behavior is identified. Only then will men reclaim the nearly seven years that their own behavior has stolen from them. (2000:111)

In sum, it's their own fault: blame the male and blame the victim. This conclusion is unworthy of his text. Courtenay fails to recognize the cultural contexts of these "preventable" deaths. Men recognize that other men, including themselves, and women, do not value men's lives. They are sacrificed in huge numbers in war – and are even willing sometimes to sacrifice themselves for their country and their cause. And then they are blamed for their own deaths, injuries and PTSD. They are largely invisible as victims of violence: there is no zero-tolerance for violence against men as there is for violence against women in both the U.S.A. and Canada – nor is there any demand for it from equity theorists. They are largely invisible in the suicide research – despite the roughly 25,000 deaths *every year* in the U.S. alone. Politicians have been remiss in their failure to legislate enforcement of safety legislation (which is inadequate at best) and courts have frequently failed to penalize those responsible for these supposedly "accidental" deaths (e.g. Ford Pinto, Chernobyl, Bhopal, Westray and Sago mines). Furthermore health authorities demonstrate little attention to men's health, despite the much higher death rates for men for all 10 leading causes of death. Thousands of men are imprisoned every year with little concern for the effects of their incarceration, the effectiveness of the punishment, and the consequences for their families and friends. Courtenay's scrupulous statistical and analytical scholarship is marred by a failure of judgement: an inability to contextualize these deaths within contemporary cultures in which male deaths are devalued, and in which the victims, if male, are often blamed and the failures of the corporate, political, legislative, health and justice systems with respect to men are simply ignored.

Again, the invisibility of male deaths is indicated by the U.S. Census Bureau (2003) which presents deaths by type, but not by gender. Similarly in their book *Risk* by Harvard scholars Ropeik and Gray (2002), there is a discussion of Motor Vehical Accidents (MVAs), which kill almost 42,000 Americans p.a. and injure another three million – but gender is hardly mentioned. Similarly, again, in a discussion of road deaths, the British statistician Simon Briscoe does not present the number of deaths by gender, but does say that in 2002, "men committed 97% of dangerous driving offences, 94% of offences causing death or bodily harm,

89% of drink or drug driving offences ..." etc. (Briscoe, 2002:181). This is another portrait of men as criminals and villains – but evidence-based, not ideological – except that he did not include the data on men and women as victims: two-thirds of them men.

In the U.K., the Office for National Statistics (ONS) regularly publishes a series on different sectors of the U.K. population. First was "Children" (1994), second was "Women" (1995), – but if we expected "Men" as third, we would be disappointed. Women and Children were followed by "Ethnic Minorities," "Families," "Unemployed," "Women and Men," "Older People," "Young People" and finally, at number nine, "Men" in 2002. This gives us some idea of their priorities. Men constitute about 50% of the population, dominate the bottom rungs as well as the top, but are very low as a social priority – perhaps due to this widespread stereotyping of men as hegemonic and dominant. Furthermore, following this invisibility, the analysis is seriously flawed. Purporting to be "A wide-ranging examination of the lives of men in the United Kingdom," the report offers three sentences of change in its summary, then states:

> Nevertheless, differences in circumstances between the genders remain: men have higher incomes; they outnumber women in management and professional occupations; and traditional roles in the home may still exist with women undertaking the bulk of domestic chores.

Yet this is misleading both by omission and commission. Men have higher incomes because they work more hours/week and more weeks/year – not because of gender discrimination. They outnumber women in professional occupations in part because in the past many women have preferred part-time work and child-care to full-time professional work. Indeed men have made enormous efforts with affirmative action legislation, flex time, part-time work, maternity leaves to accommodate and encourage women's participation in the labour force, at all levels. Traditional roles may persist in part because men work longer hours, travel more – both at work and to work – but also because domestic labour often *excludes* much of men's work at home (drains, plumbing, painting, glazing, lawn care, cars, carpentry etc.). There is no mention that gender differences include that men work longer hours, have fewer options as to full-time or part-time work, outnumber women among the homeless, the incarcerated, and constitute the majority of victims of accidents and/or work fatalities, suicide and homicide and early deaths – and also poor research! The so-called "Focus on Men" is clearly *out* of focus.

One aspect of our particularly dangerous culture is extreme sports, which are predominantly but not exclusively practiced by men. Parasailing, mountaineering, sky-diving, hang-gliding, ice-climbing, bungee-jumping – all these are high risk activities. High risk, compared to, for instance, collecting stamps, knitting, aerobics or growing tomatoes. Some might consider such "leisure" or "play" activities as parasuicidal, akin to smoking, unsafe sex, heavy drinking, drug use etc. Others regard it as "living".

Yet even these extreme sports are virtually passé among the young and the reckless. Thrill seekers now engage in BASE jumping – an acronym for leaping from tall Buildings, Antennas, Spans (bridges) and Earth (cliffs and mountains); canyoning –-well-padded adventurers swim, drift, fall, jump, rappel or whatever down mountain gorges, waterfalls, torrents, and occasionally are killed; zorbing, a New Zealand invention, like bungee-jumping, requires T-type personalities to curl up inside a giant plastic ball, to be sloshed with water for lubrication, then to be zipped in and pushed off a mountain, bouncing to the bottom (Zorpette, 1999). Then there's tombstoning: jumping off a cliff into the sea which, since it is tidal, sometimes results in paralysis.

Mountain climbing is also hazardous. As of the end of 2007, 2,436 climbers had summitted Everest, some of them more than once, at a cost of 210 lives. Jon Krakauer (1997) recounted his experiences on a fatal climb in 1996, when a freak storm claimed the lives of eight people. And that was just one climb on one mountain.

The Vendée Globe race around the three capes at the bottom of the world epitomizes extreme sailing: 27,000 miles, single-handed, non-stop and no assistance. Five men have died since 1968. 15 men died in the tragic Fastnet race in 1979; and six more in the 630 mile Sydney-Hobart race in 1998, a tragedy written up by Rob Mundle, in his best-seller, *Fatal Storm* (2005).

Three American astronauts were killed when Apollo I exploded on the launch pad in 1967; a Russian astronaut in 1967 also; three more Russian astronauts in 1972; and another seven Americans when Challenger exploded in flight in 1986. Seven more astronauts were killed when Columbia broke up on re-entry in 2003. The total losses were 18 men and three women.

"Speed is of the essence," it is often said. Speed also kills. The F1 and the NASCAR races still kill. Dale Earnhardt most recently in 2001; but there have been 26 other racing-related deaths at Daytona since the track opened in 1959 so far. All of whom were men.

Speedboats: Donald Campbell, holder of world land and water speed records, like his father, killed on Coniston water in 1967 setting another record.

Flying: Amelia Earhart, the first woman to fly solo across the Atlantic, lost in the Pacific in 1937 in her attempt to fly around the world. Charles Kingford Smith was the first to cross the Pacific in 1928, the year after Charles Lindbergh's solo flight across the Atlantic, and was perhaps the greatest aviator ever with numerous firsts and records; he crashed and died in 1935. Alcock and Brown were the first to fly the Atlantic, eight years before Lindbergh; Brown was killed in a plane crash nine months later. These aviators pioneered the mail flights and the passenger flights we now take for granted. These men, and a few women, had "the right stuff"; and died with it. Chuck Yaegar, who first broke the sound barrier in the Bell X-7 in 1949, survived.

Explorers: the first to reach the North or South Poles, the first women, the first of any particular country, the oldest, the youngest, the first to do it solo … and the first and last to die. Sir John Franklin led a British expedition of two ships *HMS*

Erebus and *HMS Terror* to search for the Northwest Passage in 1845. All were lost, 138 officers and men. Captain Scott reached the South Pole only 38 days after Roald Amundsen in 1912; but he and his four companions died on the return. And so it continues, and will continue. Tremendous efforts, tremendous achievements and tremendous costs.

Rock Stars and Rap Stars: Stardom is a difficult and high risk space. Many stars live fast, die young, but live on in the popular imagination – and set a poor example for their young fans. Some examples: Jimi Hendrix, died aged 27 after choking on his own vomit; Janis Joplin overdosed on heroin while drunk; Jim Morrison of The Doors died in his bath in Paris, probably of a drug overdose; Elvis Presley died of heart failure after years of drug abuse; Sid Vicious overdosed on heroin aged 21; Dennis Wilson of the Beach Boys drowned; Kurt Cobain shot himself aged 27. John Lennon, Notorious BIG, Tupac Shakur and Scott LaRock were all shot dead.

Men and women pay a high price for their amusements, hobbies and extreme lifestyles. Yet it is not accurate to call them victims since their decisions are autonomous and their lifestyle chosen. The risks are high but so are the rewards. Nor is it quite fair to call such daring and brave types para-suicidal; they may get killed, but this is not their intent.

Why do so many men engage in such dangerous and extreme activities: climb Everest, climb the highest 14 peaks, explore deserts, race anything that moves, try to go further, higher, deeper, faster and first? Mallory, trying to explain why he wanted to climb Everest, tersely snapped "Because it's there!" Others explain: "To see if I can"; "better to burn out than rust out"; "Why not?" and opaquely "if you have to ask, you don't understand!"

T-shirt philosophies explain the T-type (Thrill-type) personalities: "If you're not living on the edge, you're taking up too much space." "Just do it!" – The Nike slogan. "No Fear!" And of course the marine slogan, "When the going gets tough, the tough get going" – and Jane Fonda's very similar slogan for very different goals: "No Pain, No Gain." Such attitudes can be productive of immense benefits, but also they are achieved at immense costs of human life, often male. Living on the edge, without fear, sooner or later one falls off, and dies. Another accident.

These extreme endeavours are primarily "a guy thing." The Guinness Book of World Records 2000 opens with a section entitled "Courage"; almost all the records listed were established by men. Records for women are listed separately. Needless to say the women's records exceed anything and everything most male readers can do. The extreme records include: most swords swallowed: nine 27 inch swords, and then rotated 180°; the longest free-fall: 4 miles 1,232 yards; the longest "no hands" motorcycle jump: 17 semi-trucks by Robbie Knievel – like his father an iconic daredevil; most rattlesnakes in bathtub: 35 western diamondbacks; most boards broken on head: 29 in 30 seconds; blown up the most times: in a box, more than 1,100 times (2000:497–9). One or possibly two of these record-holders are women: such dangerous antics are not exclusively "a guy thing"; though perhaps "Courage" is not an appropriate title.

Few men and women are killed in these extreme endeavours in any given year. Yet they generate enormous attention. Scott, Campbell, Lindbergh, Earhart, Yaegar, Earnhardt, Hillary, Gagarin, Armstrong, Fossett are or were heroes to their generations. They were and still are role models in the new millennium, and they set the bar high. All but four of the above died in their attempts. But although few men and women die in these endeavours, from space flights to cave exploration, cumulatively – the numbers add up; and the potential years of life lost also add up; but also they tell us something about male values and culture.

Work Fatalities

Men are killed by war, suicide, homicide and accidents in ways and numbers that women are not. They are also victims of work (Tables 5.6 and 5.7).

The U.S. Department of Labor reported 5,488 work fatalities in 2007 (preliminary data), down 6% from 2006, but down 21% from the high of 1994. Indeed this is the lowest number and the lowest rate (3.7/00,000) since the first fatality census was conducted in 1992. That's the good news. Transportation accounted for almost half of these fatalities. In terms of occupations, the highest number of fatalities occurred among, in order, drivers, farmers and ranchers, and the police; but the highest fatality rates were in fishing, logging and to pilots. Steel-workers, miners (coal, gas, oil), roofers and line workers (electricity) also had high fatality rates. All these occupations are overwhelmingly male. In terms of gender, women constituted 46% of the labour force, but only 8% of the work fatalities. 5,071 men were killed and 417 women (U.S. Department of Labor, 2008. www.bcs.gov).

To put this into clearer perspective:

- 12 times more men than women were killed at work.
- 14 men are killed at work every day, and one woman.
- More men are killed at work every year than women are murdered.

Yet these mostly "accidental" deaths are virtually invisible to men, to feminists and to government – compared to, say, violence against women.

This raises some interesting questions about perspectives on reality. Some have argued that men dominate the work world. They point to sexual harassment, the 75 cent dollar, the glass ceilings and glass walls which restrict women's occupational and economic mobility, the lace and pink collar "ghettoes," the occupational "apartheid," women's double loads, chilly climates, gender discrimination, male dominated occupations, and so on. These claims contain some truth and feminists have done well to clarify injustice and to seek redress, reform and equity. But it is not the whole truth; and much is omitted. Women are not the only victims of work and at work.

Many feminists have done ill in ignoring the appalling death-toll of men at work, in portraying women as the only victims of work, and only as victims and in misrepresenting reality by omission and selection for decades.

Feminists have asserted that there is a war against women (Faludi, 1991; French, 1992; Canadian Committee on the Status of Women, 1991). Yet the data indicate that there is a far more lethal war against men. While the safety of women is of enormous concern to legislators, the safety of men – at work and elsewhere – is largely ignored; such deaths are considered just "accidents."

In general, the more dangerous the profession, the higher the proportion of men in the profession. Many of these accidents and fatalities affect only one or two individuals at a time: a tractor rollover, a tree falling badly, a long-haul truck crash. Others involve dozens or hundreds of men at a time.

Oil rigs are dangerous sites, as the sinkings of the rigs "Ocean Ranger" in 1982, with the loss of 84 men, and "Piper Alpha" in 1988, with the loss of 167 men, both indicate.

Deep-sea fishing has been memorialized in Sebastian Junger's account of the sinking of the 72 foot, 600 ton, longliner "Andrea Gail" with the loss of all hands, six men, in October 1991. *The Perfect Storm*, the title of this account, created record waves of over 100 feet, towering over the craft, with winds gusting to over 120 m.p.h. The author estimates that 10,000 Gloucestermen have perished at sea since 1650. He recalled Sir Walter Scott's poignant dictum: "It's no fish ye're buying it's men's lives."

The intrepid explorer Redmond O'Hanlon spent two weeks on a Scottish deep-sea trawler in the North Atlantic. He describes his seasickness with every pitch, yaw, roll, dip, surge and corkscrew of the boat, the Force 12 gale, the appalling working conditions from 12–20 hours a day for up to six weeks at a stretch, the death-rate of 10 fishermen a month in British waters, the 26 fishing vessels lost in 1998 (the latest available year), the domestic travails of the trawlermen, the effect of sleep-deprivation on the brain (a little madness), even the humour in the danger. His account about why men do dangerous things – in this case because fishing is all they know, like their fathers before them, but do not necessarily love. One crewman, Robbie, assaulted two police officers and was sentenced to six months. He loved the food, the football, the warmth, working in the kitchen until, horrors! "The bastards ... They threw me out for good behaviour. Jeesus!" (2004:104)

Robbie's hope – the hope of all the crew – was that Redmond would write the book and tell the truth. His language deteriorated as his passion increased:

> So we can give this book, if you ever do it, whatever, to our women, you know, the one we really fancy, OK, fuck it, the one we *love*! ... and she'll take it all in ... Can you get our women, *the ones we fucking love*, to understand what happens out here? Can you? (2004:262–3)

It's not just fish that cost men's lives: it is also gold, diamonds, farming, lumber, oil, coal, transport of all sorts, fires, military training, construction and law enforcement

Law enforcement is an altruistic and dangerous occupation. As of March 2008, according to the national website, 18,274 law enforcement officers have been killed in the line of duty since 1792, including 223 female officers. And in 2008 there are more than 900,000 sworn law enforcement officers at federal, state and local levels, about 12% of whom are women. The latest casualty figues indicate that 181 officers were killed in 2007, including 6 women i.e. 3% – well under their level of representation in the force (which suggests that some, at least, are placed out of harm's way, if possible) (www.nleomf.com. Accessed 17.6.08). There is no equality of representation here, perhaps in part due to lack of female interest in the profession; and there is certainly no equality of casualties.

Fire-fighting is another primarily male occupation which is both highly altruistic and also dangerous. According to the U.S. Fire Administration, 118 firefighters died in the line of duty in 2007. Most of these men were volunteer fire-fighters, and many of these deaths were due to heart attacks. Burns, eloctrocutions, smoke inhalation, falls, head injuries, helicopter crashes, airtanker crashes, vehicle crashes were some of the other causes of death (www.usfa.fema.gov; Accessed 18.6.08). Men pay a high price in their efforts to save the lives of other people, and other people's property – just as police officers pay a high price to maintain law and order.

Work-related stress may also cause disease and death and contribute to men's high mortality rates. Work itself can be addictive, and workaholics abound. The precise impact of workaholism on men's health is not known; but the Japanese have a word for it: "karoshi" – death from overwork. The Japanese government recognized this as a cause of death in the 1980s, and applications for this designation, which are recognized by the government, are entitled to compensation. About 4% of applications were successful in 1988, but this has risen by 2005 to about 40%. Family members surviving a *Karoshi* death may receive compensation of about $20,000 p.a. from the government and even more from the corporation in damages. In a recent case Kenichi Uchino, a third-generation worker with Toyota, collapsed and died at work, having put in more than 80 hours of overtime each month for the previous six months. He left two children. The government office denied his wife's claim, ruling that long hours were part of his job. His wife sued and won. (The overtime is regarded as "free" i.e. required but not paid.) The compensation has not yet been decided. While self-sacrifice, which puts the interests of the group above that of the individual, is an important value in Japanese culture, Ms. Uchino argued that: "It is because so many people work free overtime that Toyota makes profits." Toyota has promised to prevent "karoshi" in future (*Economist* 22.12.07:68–9).

Conditions of work may be as lethal as the number of hours worked. Other studies in Sweden, Denmark and Italy have found that heavy responsibility, low autonomy, low social support levels and low physical exercise levels compound the risks of heart disease and heart attacks. The combination of multiples of these factors is likely to have compound geometrical rather than arithmetical consequences. Anger is also a consequence of job stress; and the greater the anger the greater the risk of both heart disease and strokes (Simon, 1999:44–6). Some jobs are more stressful than others; but the full and fatal impact of job stress on men's and women's lives and deaths is as yet largely unresearched.

Wars, homicides, suicides, accidents and work all kill and injure men at much higher rates than they do women. Men often die young, and violently – earning a living, raising a family, saving the lives of strangers, defending their country or by their own hand or just because they are men and potential combatants. Yet many of these deaths are ignored, and the cost of such societal blindness is high.

2006: The Sago Mine Disaster

An explosion ripped through the Sago coal mine in West Virginia on January 2, 2006. 12 miners died. Four other miners were killed within a month in three other "accidents" in West Virginia. These are simply the latest in a long series of disasters in a dangerous profession. Since the 1960s, 78 miners were killed in West Virginia in 1968, another 125 in the same state in 1972, 26 in Kentucky in 1976, 26 at the Westray mine in Nova Scotia in 1992, 13 in Alabama in 2001 and now 16 more in a month in West Virginia. The worst mining disasters in North America occurred in Monongah, West Virginia, which killed 362 men in 1907 and at Hillcrest, Alberta, which killed 189 more men in 1914.

Roof collapses, flash floods, methane gas explosions, coal dust explosions, carbon monoxide poisonings were all causes of these hundreds, perhaps thousands of deaths over the decades.

And this is just the United States. In the Ukraine, more than 3,700 miners have been killed from 1991, when Ukraine declared independence from Russia, to 2002. This is a death rate 50 times higher than the U.S. per ton of coal extracted (Lafrenière, 2002). In China about 5–6,000 miners are killed every year, according to official figures, though independent estimates say the true figure is closer to 20,000. The worst mining disaster occurred in 1942 when 1,549 miners were killed (Elegant, 2007).

We need coal, as we need meat, fish, wood, gold, silver, oil, diamonds – but there is a forgotten cost in men's lives.

Not all miners die: some are injured. Homer Hickam, a former miner now author, delivered the requiem at the Sago miners funeral: "My grandfather lost both his legs in the Coalwood mine and lived in pain until the day he died. My father lost the sight in an eye while trying to rescue trapped miners. After that he worked in the mine for fifteen more years. He died of black lung."

The investigations into the Sago mine tragedy started immediately. The Mine Safety and Health Administration (MSHA) of the U.S. Department of Labour has posted "Questions and Answers" on its website (www.msha.gov), noting that the number of citations issued have increased and the fines have also increased. David

Table 5.6   Male fatalities (from 1980)

1982	Grand Banks. 84 men lost in the sinking of the oil rig Ocean Ranger.
1983	October. Beirut, Lebanon. Suicide bombers killed 241 U.S. marines and a second bomb killed 58 French paratroopers.
1985	December. Gander, Newfoundland. 256 American soldiers returning home for the holidays killed in crash of DC-8 on take-off.
1986	January. Challenger Space Shuttle exploded on take-off. 5 men and 2 women astronauts killed.
	September. South Africa. 177 killed in gold mine.
1988	North Sea. 167 men lost in the sinking of the oil rig Piper Alpha.
1989	USS Iowa. 47 killed in an explosion. Filmed as: "A Glimpse of Hell."
1991	October. Atlantic. "Andrea Gail" lost with all hands, six men.
1993	Westray coal mine explosion killed 26 men. More than 2,600 men and boys died in coal mines in Nova Scotia between Confederation (1867) and the Westray mine explosion.
1994	July. Colorado. 14 firefighters killed in forest fire.
1995	Bosnia. About 8,000 Muslim men and boys killed at Srebenaica: the worst European atrocity since WW2.
1995	November. Nigeria. Minority Rights activist Ken Saro-Wiwa and eight other men hanged.
1996	June. Saudi Arabia. 19 U.S. servicemen killed at Khobar Towers in suicide bombing.
1999	January. China. 35 dead in a coal mine explosion.
	May. Ukraine. 50+ dead in a coal mine explosion.
	July. South Africa. 19 dead in a gold mine explosion.
	August. China. ca 55 dead in a coal mine explosion.
2000	August. Barents Sea. 118 men lost in the Russian submarine "Kursk."
2000	October. Yemen. 17 sailors killed in USS Cole, including two women.
2000	October. China. 155 miners killed in coal mine. The world's worst mining disaster killed 1,540+ miners in China in 1942 (*Time* 16.10.00).
2001	February. East Timor. 50+ East Timorese men massacred by Indonesian troops.
2001	March. U.S. The crash of a National Guard C-23 Sherpa killed all 21 men on board.
2001	March. Kashmir. 35 Sikh men lined up and killed in the insurgency for an independent Muslim state.
2001	March. Ukraine. 80 miners killed in a coal mine explosion: the worst since 1991.
2001	March. Canada. 200 Mounties have been killed since the force was founded in 1873.
2001	April. Bering Sea. "Arctic Rose" longliner lost with all hands: 15 men.

Table 5.6   continued

2001	April. Nepal. 70 policemen killed in raid by Maoist rebels.
2001	May. Turkey. 34 soldiers killed in plane crash.
2002	July. Ukraine. 33 miners killed in coal mine. This makes a total of 116 that year, compared to 290 the previous year. Since 1991, when the Ukraine declared independence from the Soviet Union, more than 3,700 miners have been killed: about four times higher than it was then, and 50 times higher than the U.S. per ton of coal extracted (Lafreniere, 2002).
2003	February. Columbia Space Shuttle broke up on re-entry. 5 men and 2 women astronauts killed.
2003	February. Iran. 276 Iranian soldiers killed in aircraft crash. Iran's worst air disaster.
2004	October. China. 150 miners killed in coal mine explosion. More than 6,700 coal miners were killed in China in 2003, and more than 4,000 so far this year. Coal production, still the principal source of electricity generation, was estimated at about 17 billion tons in 2003, and expected to be about 1.9 billion tons in 2004. About 5,000 factories and mines have been closed this year for safety violations (Cody, 2004, *Economist*, 4.12.04:43).
2005	February. China. 214 miners killed in a coal mine explosion. More than 6,000 were killed the previous year in floods, explosions and fires. The deadliest disaster occurred in 1942 when 1,549 miners were killed in an explosion (*NYT* 15.2.05).
2005	July. Spain. 11 firefighters killed. 10 men and 1 woman.
2006	January. West Virginia. 12 men killed in a coal mine explosion in Sago. Two more men killed later that month in another mine.
	The worst mine disaster in the U.S. occurred in the same state killing 362 miners in 1907.
2006	February. Mexico. 65 killed in coal mine explosion.
2006	May. China. 57 miners killed by flooding.
2007	March. Siberia. 106 miners killed.
2007	October. Ukraine. 100+ miners killed.
2008	October. Mexico. 21+ died in prison riot.
2008	November. Russia.20+ killed in submarine.

Dye, Acting Assistant Secretary of Labor, testifying before a subcommittee of the U.S. Senate in late January, noted that overall mining fatalities had dropped 33% and injuries 25% between 2000 and 2005, while coal mining fatalities had fallen 42% and injuries 22% over the same period. He insisted that enforcement had increased even though the number of coal mines had decreased (from 2,124 to 1,982). Coal mining fatalities have declined steadily since 1978, with highs of 140+ in 1979 and 1981, and 100+ from 1978–1984 (except 1983) down to below 40 from 1996 to the present (except for 2001).

Investigations by many agencies drew attention to the injury rate at the Sago mine (reportedly nearly three times the national average, and about 12 times higher than another nearby mine), the number and seriousness of safety violations, the adequacy of the MSHA in investigation and enforcement, the budget of the MSHA, the use of foam rather than concrete blocks to seal a Sago mine entrance (the former might have permitted lightning strikes in the area to ignite methane gas in the mine), and also the appalling miscommunication when family members were initially told that 12 miners were saved (later announced on CNN), only to be told later that they had all died. Criticism of the media has complemented media criticism of the MSHA and the Bush administration, notably by the *New York Times* (5, 6, Jan.; 5 Feb.; 2006).

After the "accident" the government of West Virginia enacted legislation requiring that miners have better oxygen supplies, wireless communication and location devices (already available) and refuge stations. As the enquiries deepened, reporters revealed that the Bush administration had decreased major fines for safety violations (fines over $10,000 fell from one in 5 in 2003 to one in 10 in 2004), and had failed to collect them in nearly half the cases; plus the median major fines have fallen 13% since 2001. The Sago mine had been cited 273 times since 2004 – no fines exceeded $460 (about one thousandth of one per cent of the $110 million net profit of the International Coal Group, the mine's owner). Many fines are never paid. When one miner was killed in 2002, and a fellow miner seriously injured, the mine was fined $165,000; it has still not been paid. The Sago mine "accident" has clarified that the health and safety legislation is inadequate, and is not enforced. In effect, the industry is lawless. In this sense, the "accident" was not so much an act of God but a failure of corporate and government policy, an act of omission, an act of neglect of men's lives (*NYT* 5 Feb. 06; 2/3 March 06).

Mine foreman Martin Toler Jr. (51) left this note: "Tell all I see them on the other side. It wasn't bad. I just went to sleep. I love you." He and the others died of carbon monoxide poisoning for lack of oxygen supplies stored in "safe rooms": a corporate policy decision.[5]

---

5   Sources used for this include Googling the Sago Mine, the U.S. Department of Labor, the Mine Safety and Health Administration (www.mhsa.gov), Wikipedia and the *New York Times*.

The Male Ethic

To be male or to be female involves certain role expectations. Men are expected to work hard and to provide for their families; to do their duty to defend their countries and, if necessary, to die for their countries; and to put women and children first: that is what they are defending, to the death, if necessary.

This male ethic of self-sacrifice, altruism and bravery is a bedrock of male identity.

- The classic example of this ethic is the loss of the RMS Titanic off the coast of Newfoundland in 1912 (see Chapter 3). The men gave their lives voluntarily for the women and children – *not vice versa. Male "nurturance" takes a different form from female.*
- In a similar, but less well-known incident in 1852, the troopship *H.M.S. Birkenhead*, en route to South Africa carrying both troops and families, struck a rock and began to sink. The men mustered on deck on parade. The military band played. The women and children were placed safely in the lifeboats and pushed off. As the ship was sinking, the captain called for those who could swim to jump and swim for the boats. Capt. Wright of the 91st Highlanders shouted "No! If you do that, the boats with the women must be swamped." So the band played on, the ship sank, the men were lost – but Capt. Wright survived (Smiles, 1958:378–9).
- Again, on September 11, 2001, 343 New York City firefighters and 60 police officers, almost all men, lost their lives saving hundreds or thousands of total strangers. They too were victims, of their work ethic and altruism. This has already been discussed as heroism; but the heroes were also victims of their heroism; and the death-toll of 9/11 continues to rise as many first responders have since developed cancer and respiratory illnesses from the hours and days spent searching for survivors.
- Approximately 40 million men were killed in wars and civil wars in the last century. 40 million men: one-sixth the population of the United States; less than the current population of the United Kingdom, but more than the total population of Canada. The killings continue, as do the male-negative attitudes that "accept" such casualties as the norm or, more simply, ignore them.
- In Colombia a press report stated "Paramilitary group kills 25 civilian hostages" (*Globe and Mail* 5.6.98). The civilians were not genderless, nor gender-free; 24 were men. Had 24 of the 25 been women, is it conceivable that this incident would have been reported this way? No. This would have been reported as a gendered crime: gynocide, like the Lepine killings in Montreal in 1989 – which is still commemorated. But men are the invisible gender in hostage-taking incidents and elsewhere.
- During Montreal's ice storm in January 1998, which knocked out the power in most of the city, a (male) Quebec minister insisted: "No government

wants to see women and children freezing. Money is not an issue" (*Globe and Mail* 12.1.98). And men, presumably, can freeze in the dark. But it was men who restored the power.

• In Algeria in 1994, four Muslim Algerian terrorists hijacked an Air France aircraft demanding the release of two allies under house arrest. An Algerian minister negotiated: "Start by freeing the women, the elderly and the children if you want us to start talking," i.e. keep the men, except the old men! The terrorists eventually released 63 of the 227 passengers, flew to Marseilles for refuelling and were stormed by French (male) commandoes who killed the four terrorists, and released the passengers. Nine of the commandos were injured in rescuing complete strangers (*Time* 9.7.95).

These seven examples out of countless more, from different cultures, exemplify the values by which men (naval officers, firefighters, politicians, terrorists or government ministers) view other men as expendable – and which men hold themselves; and the way men valorize women and children over themselves, and over other men.

In this sense men are the victims of their double standards – which both men and women take for granted – namely that women and children are intrinsically more valuable than men. The U.N. Declaration of Human Rights affirms that: "All human beings are born free and equal in dignity and rights." But, as George Orwell added in *Animal Farm* – some are more equal than others, not only the wealthy, but also women and children, at least in these examples.

This is a complex phenomenon blending oppression by others and voluntary self-sacrifice: a mutuality of values common to the male victimizers and the male victims in the acceptance of male disposability. Men are the *throwaway sex*, and know it, and accept it. The "Titanic" model of gender relations, or the World Trade Center model, are perhaps more valid than the misogynistic model of patriarchy portrayed by so many feminists over the last 50 years. Yet it is the misogynistic model which prevails in so much of the literature and popular culture.

Dead Ends

Death is easy to measure, as injury, disease and ill-health are not. We all die, of course; but when we die, where, how and why are very much gendered realities.

I tried to count my relations and friends who have died violent deaths: two cousins were killed in World War II, two friends committed suicide, four colleagues and friends in Zimbabwe were murdered by terrorists or freedom fighters, four colleagues at my university in Montreal were murdered by a disgruntled faculty member, and one of my students was murdered in a robbery. All 13 were male. Two friends, one man and one woman, died violently in traffic accidents and another, male, in a climbing accident. I have also met five murderers socially (that I know of), all men. My experience is not fully typical since the statistics indicate a different reality. Readers may wish to consider the reality of violent deaths in their own experience, and what this says about men, values, and violence.

The U.S. Census Bureau reports that in 2002, 1.2 million men died for a total of 21.1 million life years lost, an average of 17.6 years each. The total mortality cost was about $340 *billion*, averaging out at $284 thousand dollars each in terms of lifetime earnings lost in premature deaths. All these early deaths (i.e. based on life expectancy at the time of death) are due to a wide range of factors, from genetic to personal to social, the domains of biology, psychology and then sociology. Clearly, however, some of this $340 billion would be well invested in improving men's health, as well as accident, suicide and homicide prevention policies. And women's early deaths (on average 15.3 years early) cost another $134 billion, averaging out at $108,000 each in terms of lifetime earnings lost (U.S. Census Bureau, 2006:91).

Particularly worrying are the deaths by violence: war, accidents, suicide and homicide, which are in principle preventable and reducable. (Other causes of death are also preventable e.g. deaths by lung cancer, AIDS and cirrhosis, many of which are caused by unhealthy behaviours.) These account for only about 6% of the annual mortality in the U.S.: 8% for men and 4% for women. *But*, because of the relative youth of so many of these individuals, men account for a higher proportion of Potential Years of Life Lost (PYLL) and an even higher proportion of Potential Dollars Lost (PDL) to the national economy. This includes the economic investment in each individual as well as lost productivity and tax revenue. Accidents alone cost the U.S. economy an estimated $78 billion in lifetime earnings lost in 2002: about $730,000 per accidental death. The mortality costs were two times higher for men than for women, partly because twice as many men died accidentally than women, they died on average five years younger, their labour force participation rates were higher etc. (U.S. Census Bureau, 2006:91).

The potential dollars lost by suicide and homicide could be added to those lost to accidents. Dollars invested in men's health and safety, unpopular though this may be, would save money. Lives saved are dollars saved.

The data from Canada is equally instructive. In 2003 the age-standardized death rate for men was 733.4 per 100,000 and for women was 475.4 per 100,000. The male death rate was therefore 54% higher than the female death rate (Statistics Canada, 2006: CANSIM, Table 102-0552). Men's deaths are not only a human problem, and a massive social problem, they are also a tremendous economic problem in terms of dollars lost and cost. This is a materialistic culture – as we save lives, so we save money.

Statistics Canada states that "deaths prior to age 70 are considered 'early' or potential years of life that have been lost." In 1996 there were over one million potential years of life lost (PYLL). The most important causes of PYLL were cancer (30%), accidents (19%), and heart disease (13%). Yet despite their roughly equal numbers in the population, males accounted for 65% of PYLL, due to different death rates for all the major causes of death. Overall the total PYLL rate was 85% higher for men than for women (Statistics Canada, 1999:319, 321).

The longevity costs of these early deaths have been calculated in Canada, but (unlike the U.S. Census Bureau) not the economic costs of these violent deaths. This waste of men's lives does require further research, if not for compassionate reasons then for economic reasons.

What Is to be Done?

Men in western societies live bi-polar lives. On the one hand they dominate the commanding heights of political and economic life, (this is what some refer to as the "hegemonic male") commanding "the patriarchal bastions of male power." On the other hand, men also cluster at the bottom of our societal ladders: the homeless, the imprisoned, the drug addicts; and those in ill-health, doomed to an early death; and the men who have died by violence: the victims of war, homicide, suicide and "accidents."

In contrast to the male bipolarity, women are more on a bell curve: there are relatively few women at the very top, and relatively few at the very bottom: a higher proportion are in the middle. Feminists have demanded equity with men; but which men? They are not all the same. They demand equality with the top dogs, the alpha males, the rich, famous, wealthy and powerful. Men aspire to that too. Yet equity would surely demand equality with the omega males too, or, more realistically, at least recognition of their existence. Simply presenting the data on CEOs, MPs and Senators and university presidents and crying "Unfair! Sexism! Discrimination!" if women do not constitute 50% of these populations is itself unfair, sexist and discriminatory.

Clearly the first thing to be done is to recognize that these violent male deaths constitute a social problem of immense magnitude: a massive waste of life – and money. This recognition is no easy task for various reasons. First these deaths are so often invisible. They are often not reported in the official statistics nor analyzed by social scientists; second, if they are reported, they are usually separated out in a reductionist mode (separated by type of death) which conceals the totality of male casualties. Third, they are taken for granted as part of the "male life-styles." We accept that men are regularly killed "in the line of duty," "in a tragic accident at work," or "while doing what he loved," as the obituaries state, or "by his own hand." Fourth, though it may seem contentious to say it, men's deaths have been camouflaged by women's deaths, which have been foregrounded by feminists in identity politics. We have been so pre-occupied with women as victims that we have ignored *men* as victims. *It is difficult for the champions of women as victims to see men, also, as victims.*

Fifth, and this is more controversial, while we have heard for years about misogyny, we have heard little about the equally prevalent phenomenon of misandry. The negative impact of patriarchy as oppressive and suppressive of women is well known, and has been for over 40 years. The positive impact of patriarchy (and men) as protective and liberating of women – and oppressive of

Table 5.7   Life years lost and mortality costs by gender (U.S.A., 2002)

	Number of Deaths (1,000)	Life Years Lost (1)		Mortality Cost (2)	
		Total (1,000)	Per death	Total ($mil)	Per Death ($)
Overall Totals					
Male	1,199	21,137	17.6	340,827	284,264
Female	1,244	19,080	15.3	134,274	107,933
Total	2,443	40,216	16.5	475,101	194,472

(1) Number of years person would have lived in absence of death, based on life expectancy at the time of death.

(2) Value of lifetime earnings lost by persons who die prematurely, discounted at 6%, including value of homemaking services and allowing for inflation.

Source: U.S. Census Bureau, 2006:91.

men – has been ignored, despite the large numbers of violent male deaths and the reduced life expectancy. Men have been demonized as pigs, violent and rapists by many feminists, both male and female, while women have been angelized. Hence the widespread concern and implementation of legislation concerning violence against women – despite the far more serious and widespread problem of violence against men. We need to equalize our attitudes and policies.

Neither legislators, sociologists and feminists nor the general public have grasped the extent, and the social and economic costs of this problem. Indeed violence against men is institutionalized in North American culture for fun and profit: in extreme sports (boxing and hockey in particular), the entertainment industry, the military draft, and the double standard by which men are expected to sacrifice their lives for women and children and also for the nation.

The conflation of the four principal and immediate causes of these violent deaths – war, homicide, suicide, accidents – tends to obscure both the differences within each etiology, and the underpinning values and cultural norms which sustain these deaths. The causes of war, homicide, suicide and accidents are not only many and various but deeply embedded within cultures. And the common denominator in all these death styles is the high proportion of men, and their lifestyles.

Meanings are many and elusive in such a wide landscape of death, and responsibilities are diffuse. Men, and to a lesser extent women, are or may be victims of government policies and national interests, inadequate work safety legislation and enforcement, dangerous jobs, and war, their lifestyles, other people's homicidal actions, their own actions (suicide), the easy access to guns, addictions, double standards, the altruistic ethic, patriotism, unemployment, and changing capitalism (Faludi, 1999), the boy's code (Pollack, 1998), absent fathers (Bly, 1990; Blankenhorn, 1996; Popenoe, 1996; Faludi, 1999), inequitable divorce and custody legislation (Braver, 1998), job stress (Simon, 1999) and, arguably, systemic discrimination in the health, education and justice systems (Chapter 7), and certainly some misandric feminist portraits of men (Chapter 4).

Increasingly post-feminists have drawn attention to misandry, as an ideological victimization and demonization of men, with very practical legal, political, psychic and economic consequences. While misandry mitigates against finding solutions, its recent rise postdates most of the male violent deaths of the last century. It cannot be blamed for all these high death rates, nor the victimization of males. Misandry is a problem, but only a part of the problem, and by no means restricted to some hard-line feminists, but also to male-negative men.

Solutions can be found: the violent death rates for men and for women can be reduced. They are cultural artefacts susceptible to cultural and policy change. In the United States and Canada, homicide rates and accident rates have fallen over the last 30 years, partly due perhaps to demographic changes, partly to policy initiatives and partly to improved medical care. But both rates are culturally determined. Homicide rates are about three times higher in the United States than in Canada, and about three times higher in Canada than in most of Europe, though they all fluctuate. Nonetheless, clearly the North American homicide rates could be reduced further.

There is good news, however. The number of North American and European combat deaths plummetted in the last century. Over half a million Americans were killed in combat in the first half of the century compared to about 112,000 in the second half. Similarly over 100,000 Canadians were killed in combat in three wars in the first half of the twentieth century, compared to just over 500 in the second half. The same is true particularly for the Soviet Union, Germany, France and Europe generally. This comparative peace may be less true for some African and Asian nations, caught up in the independence wars and post-independence civil wars and struggles (e.g. China, Cambodia, Vietnam, Zimbabwe).

Women have often been labelled the altruistic sex: giving life, nurturing the young and the old and caring for others. Nobel Prize winning author, Gabriel Garcia Marquez echoed Ashley Montagu and Montessori writing in his memoirs that women "are the ones who maintain the world while we men throw it into disarray with our historic brutality" (2004:77). Yet men too "maintain the world." And we are back to the hierarchical binary of women as "sugar and spice" and superior to men as "snails". Men too are altruistic, however, even though such altruism has been largely invisible and ignored, and also different in kind. It is evident mostly in their work to support their families, in their bravery to save strangers, and especially in the male deaths in the "saving professions" (600 p.a. in the police, about 90 p.a. among firefighters in the United States); in the "death professions" – mining, logging, deep-sea fishing etc.; in some suicides, we do not know how many, for many men are worth more dead than alive; in the military deaths of men who gave their lives for their country: this averages out at 6,500 p.a. for the United States over the last century and 1,000 p.a. for Canada. Male altruism is expressed in profoundly different ways than female altruism.

The problem here is not only the widespread failure to recognize and problematize the very high rate, and the large numbers, of violent male deaths; it is also the failure to recognize and appreciate the immense altruism behind so many of these deaths.

Chapter 6

Power

Gender relations are power relations. This is the conventional wisdom, following the earlier understandings that class and race relations are also power relations.

The proposition is usually interpreted as meaning that men have power over women. This statement may have some validity in some parts of the world where gender cultures and traditions are highly segregated, and where equal rights are not universally recognized and respected. And it is probably also true in the vapid sense that all relations, interpersonal and intergroup, are power relations. As Samuel Johnson said: "no two people can be half an hour together, but one shall acquire an evident superiority over the other".

We might interrogate this proposition with its negation, which has perhaps equal, or even more, truth value. Gender relations are *not* power relations. And they are *not* like class or race relations. In gender relations the (alleged) vertical hierarchy of sovereign power is cross-cut by the horizontal egalitarian relation of love power. We need to appreciate not only the vertical axis of the oppressors to the oppressed (with men and women in both these categories) to the horizontal axis of mutuality and love. This last has been largely neglected by activists on both sides of the gender wars and the battle of the sexes. And this has been a huge failure, a defeat of common sense on the altar of identity politics, camouflaged by the rhetoric of justice, fairness, equity and female powerlessness. Not that women are not victimized and oppressed – but so are men. To prioritize the one over the other is poor scholarship and poor politics.[1]

Our gender relations are cross-cut by other power lines and fault lines: class, especially in the U.K., race, especially in the U.S., religion, especially in Ireland and the Middle East and Asia, and language, especially in Canada. There are many other fault lines, and lines of conflict from ethnicity and nationality to politics. Heraclitus, one of the early Greek sages, opined that: "All is war."

Gender relations are not just power relations: they are far more complex with powerful women as well as powerful men, powerless men probably even more than powerless women, and gender relations intersected by class, race, language and love relations. Clearly men do not have all the power. Indeed men constitute the vast majority of the least powerful people in the western democracies. And women are far from powerless, in politics, business, academia, the media, the

---

1   It is politically correct to assert that we should not engage in competitive victimization. It is also unrealistic, since the victimization of women has been publicized for over 40 years, while the victimization of men has been ignored. We need equal understanding before we can proceed – a level playing field, as they say – and we are far from that.

home... . Finally, while we all no doubt need "empowerment", i.e. more power and autonomy over our own lives, in general men are far less powerful than women: at work, at home, in prison, in the education system, in the welfare system, in poor health and early deaths: many at work, and many at war. Many men are powerless.

The most unfortunate achievement of feminism has been to portray women as victims of men, and to hide and ignore the enormous casualty figures of men. The benefits to women have been enormous. The costs to men have been high, not so much because of feminism, but because of the missed opportunities to create a more just society for everyone, not just for women e.g. to care as much about crimes against men as we do about crimes against women, and so on in health, education and welfare. The recognition of this failure to value men has cost old-style feminists something in reputation, and perhaps cost Hillary Clinton her election to the presidency. The contrast with the new-style Sarah Palin, the former beauty queen and now Governor with five children was certainly marked.

Power: its production, allocation and distribution – its use and abuse – how to get it and how to keep it – has been perhaps the central theme in world history. Plato, Machiavelli, Hobbes, Spencer, Darwin, Marx, Freud, Foucault have all addressed these issues from their own distinctive viewpoints; and gender factors into these concerns.

Plato's concern with the ideal *polis* and politics in *The Republic* i.e. that the best, the wisest, should rule in a meritocratic system was eventually followed by Erasmus, who advocated that the prince should pursue virtue. But in *The Prince* (1517), Machiavelli advocated ruthlessness in his advice on how to stay in power. In *Leviathan* (1651), written during the English Civil War, Thomas Hobbes recommended absolute rule, a "mortal god", to prevent another civil war – without it there would be, in his famous phrase, "a war of all against all." Herbert Spencer (1851), on the other hand, regarded war as a useful instrument of human progress contributing to "the survival of the fittest" – an idea that Charles Darwin (1859) borrowed while discussing the universal "struggle for survival." Freud too recognized the universality of conflict describing Man: "homo homini lupus": man is a wolf to man (1985:302).

However it was Marx and Engels who had the most influence on the world stage of power politics. They presented a detailed analysis of power in *The Communist Manifesto* (1848).

> The history of all hitherto existing society is the history of class struggles ...
> Society is more and more splitting up into two great camps, into two great
> classes directly facing each other: Bourgeoisie and Proletariat. (1974:79–80)

They argued, as Engels (1845) had done in an earlier work, that society is maintained by violence and the threat of violence. "One capitalist always kills many" wrote Marx (Bottomore and Rubel, 1965:150). And Marx and Engels advocated and predicted "the forcible overthrow of all existing social conditions. Let the ruling classes tremble at a Communistic revolution" (1974:120).

Marx and Engels were already out-dated, despite their later fame. The power of the ruling classes had already been challenged. The American revolution transferred power, by war, from the imperial power, Britain, to the new nation. The French Revolution abolished the monarchy by decapitation, and destroyed the traditional aristocracy on the guillotine. Meanwhile slave revolts across the United States and the Caribbean challenged the power of the slaveholders, resulting first in the independence of Haïti and eventually influenced the abolition of slavery. At the same time the franchise was steadily extended to include broader sectors of the population and eventually to universal adult suffrage at the beginning of the twentieth century in the U.S.A., Canada and the U.K.

In 1948 the U.N. Universal Declaration of Human Rights stated in Article 1: "All human beings are born free and equal in dignity and rights," and so inspired the Rights Revolution of the second half of the twentieth century. This included the nationalist and decolonization movements in India, Africa, the Caribbean, Asia and around the world, dismantling old empires, eventually even the Soviet Union (1989). These transfers of power were achieved with varying degrees of violence and are still in process.

In the United States the Civil Rights movement and the Black Power movement, symbolized by Martin Luther King and Malcolm X, both of whom were assassinated, transformed race relations, and were ably supported by Presidents Kennedy and Johnson. Similarly the Women's movement transformed gender relations. So dramatic have been these transformations that Barack Obama was elected President in 2009, though Hillary Clinton was the early favourite.

Power "to do" implies freedom. Power "over" implies responsibility and perhaps oppression i.e. lack of freedom. Many of the theorists of power espouse this "sovereign" model of power: rule over. But as in Newtonian physics, such power tends to generate resistance, revolt, conflict, revolution, social movements. Capitalist power generated worker power, the union movement, new political parties and reform or revolution. White power created Black power and the Civil Rights movement. Patriarchal power created the Women's movement.

Michel Foucault did discuss the vertical axis of power: domination vs. resistance, most notably in his discussion of society as a prison, the Panopticon of Jeremy Bentham in his well-known *Discipline and Punish* (1977). He also qualified it, seeming to find this axis too simplistic. He insists: "Power is everywhere; not because it embraces everything, but because it comes from everywhere ... power is not an institution, and not a structure ... it is the name one attributes to a complex strategical situation in a particular society" (1978:93). This is a useful insight for gender relations, given their variability in society as a whole and even from family to family. The powers of sex, money, physique – the power to earn the money and the power to spend it, the power of leisure, knowledge, myths, beauty, organization, guilt, minority status, and the power of love ... they are all part of this complex strategic situation. This theoretical framework, asserting the multiplicity of sources and types of power, seems more realistic (but also more elusive) than the conventional binary model of traditional gender studies.

Where men's and women's rights are equally respected and recognized, as is generally the case in the developed world, the hierarchy of formal power is relatively few powerful men and women at the top, and an increasing number of increasingly powerless men and women down the slippery slope from top to bottom of a social pyramid: the triangle model of sovereign power – and resistance.

bell hooks, for instance, has written eloquently about the common struggle of black women and black men against racism; but, she adds, such men and women may not be united against male sexism: indeed black men may be sexist (hooks, 2004). To which I would add that black women may be sexist too (e.g. Alice Walker and Terry McMillan). In all cases, gender relations are cross-cut not only by race and class lines, but also by love lines.

Power is a complex idea – and reality – for a number of reasons: the many types of power (political, economic, military, ideological, physical, sexual, and social, or "soft" power), the degrees of divergence/convergence between these types of power, the personal-social distinction, the direction of power (top-down, bottom-up), the locus (self, family, company, state etc.), the legitimacy of power or otherwise, and so on. Basically, therefore, power is a resource, along a continuum of more to less, with many different dimensional types.

Generally speaking, we tend to conceptualize power structures in two rather contradictory ways. Some see power differentials and inequality as unfair, oppressive, discriminatory in a democratic age; others see them as a function of differential skills, hard work, interests and ambitions in a meritocratic age. These world views are often described as the conflict vs. consensus or radical vs. conservative paradigms. But whether we think inequality is fair or unfair, just or unjust, will depend partly on the degree of inequality as well as our commitment to the ideal of equality. Americans are more committed to the ideal of liberty than equality, Scandinavians and the French are more committed to the value of equality. All this is reflected in tax rates and health care as well as the inequality of distribution of income. Within North America, however, right-wing parties and the wealthy tend to favour liberty, left wing parties, unions and minorities tend to favour equality. And both compete for the women's vote with candidates and policies which have systemic consequences (see below).

The former world view, both personal and political, emerged out of Karl Marx's work on class and class conflict, and the necessity of violence to emancipate humanity, to abolish the class system and to establish universal equality. The latter world view emerged out of Durkheim's theory that society is held together by common values and mutual organic interdependence (not violence). Society, the body politic, mirrors the body physical in the interdependence of our body-parts. The former tend to be dissatisfied with society, and to desire change; the latter to be satisfied and to desire stability.

As with class relations so with race relations and then, in sequence, gender relations. The Women's movement has picked up the rhetoric of the class struggle and the race struggle and developed its own rhetoric in the fight for justice. Yet the concept of power is ambiguous. We struggle for power, yet negative associations attach to power. We might say that someone is power-hungry or over-powering, he's on a power-trip or he's a control freak, and Lord Acton's phrase expresses the downside of power: "All power tends to corrupt." Paradoxically, negative connotations also attach to the *lack* of power: powerlessness is not a goal, nor is impotence. We seek empowerment i.e. power, as individuals and collectively with interest groups, identity politics and a sense of grievance and victimization. This tends to re-define power in more positive terms, hence the replacement of the word power by empowerment: a switch in emphasis from status (bad) to process (good).

The simple and binary model of gender epitomized by the phrase "patriarchal power", whatever its validity in the past or even today in some parts of the world, is certainly inadequate as a model or a framework for gender relations in Euro-America. Indeed it is misleading and dysfunctional, despite its political value in misandry.

Class relations and race relations are part and parcel of gender relations. Gender relations are only one facet of power relations, and all (or most) countries are the sites of multiple and overlapping power conflicts. Power is everywhere, as Foucault remarked, and intersectionality is everywhere as a result. Men and women may conflict over differential rights and responsibilities, but they will also be allies on the politics of race or class, language or religion. Allies and adversaries switch sides as their interests and values coincide or collide.

The war against women and the war against men and boys, as argued by some, must be contextualized in a multiple conflict model of the real world. Men and women fight about some issues, symbolically in politics, law and economics rather than physically; but the internal conflicts are equally significant: men against men, and women against women in fierce ideological debate.

Labour and management conflict, with strikes, lock-outs, sometimes sabotage and violence, with men and women on both sides, opposing each other. Federal politicians will likely conflict with state/provincial/county politicians who in turn often conflict with municipal politicians over political boundaries, laws, roads, taxes etc. The five stakeholders in universities (staff, students, faculty, administration, government) all fight each other over duties, responsibilities and scarce resources; and the battles within battles persist as student leaders disagree with each other, faculties and departments compete, staff unions negotiate, and so on. Men and women are on both sides of all these issues. Similarly Muslim men and women unite against Islamophobia, and black men and women fight together against racism, but both may divide over sexism, male and female. And so on.

Yet it is not all conflict. Men and women often, perhaps usually, like, respect, admire and even love each other. The love lines cross the fault lines of gender, colour, class, language and religion all the time.

The egalitarian (horizontal) theory of love and the two male and female supremacist (vertical) theories of gender – the complementary and contradictory dualisms of the models of gender – can be synthesized as a *diagonal* theory. Men and women are not the same: they often have different values and interests; but nor are they opposite: they often have similar values and interests. They are not totally side by side nor one on top of the other: they are more on the diagonal, and constantly switching sides and places and living multiple identities. Relations are fluid diagonals, with multiple power lines and love lines criss-crossing each other.

It is probably opportune to recall that neither men nor women are the most oppressed populations in Euro-America. These would include, surely, the mentally or physically handicapped, many racial and ethnic minorities, the Native People, the ugly, Gypsies, the obese, the very poor, the imprisoned... . All these populations suffer immense discrimination and prejudice in our cultures. They are not powerless as individuals nor as groups; but power is a function of numbers and organization and "voice"; and minority populations across vast continents have organizational problems, and little time or energy and few resources to spare, after struggling for survival, to mobilize for equality.

The world is not an equal place, not between men and women, nor between men and men or women and women; not between anyone. But how we see our worlds determines how we see gender. Conversely, how we conceptualize gender influences how we see the world.

The cover of *Ms* magazine (Jan.-Feb. 1992) expressed all this very succinctly: Rage + Women = Power. This formulation is too simple, since organization is also important; but, more importantly, this constant effort to stir up rage among women and against men in general is very much part of our current problems. Whatever the benefits wrought by feminism – and they have been considerable – the opportunity costs and downstream consequences of misandry and the definition of men as villains and women as victims have also been considerable – but little discussed.

The power paradigm is quite different from the gender paradigm. In this view the main variable is not gender but power. The more powerful dominate the less powerful. Marx and Engels asserted that: "Political power ... is merely the organized power of one class for oppressing another" (1974:105). Feminists simply substituted gender for class and equated men with the bourgeoisie and women with the proletariat, with the same theorization of exploitation and oppression. (Ironically, as we have seen, these early feminists were usually both white and middle-class and, not surprisingly, ignored the intersections of race and class, unfortunately.)

In any event, the binary model can be replaced by the multiple conflict/identity model of power.

Patriarchy Revisited: The Cyclops Syndrome

The U.S. Declaration of Independence asserted that: "We hold these truths to be self-evident: that all men are created equal ..." The first Women's Rights

Convention, held at Seneca Falls in 1848, echoed and critiqued this declaration with a Declaration of Sentiments:

> We hold these truths to be self-evident: that all men and women are created equal . .
>
> The history of mankind is a history of repeated injuries and usurpations on the part of man towards woman, having in direct object the establishment of tyranny over her.

In his famous speech after the Battle of Gettysburg (1863), Abraham Lincoln defined democracy as "government of the people by the people for the people."

Some feminists have defined this same democracy as patriarchy: government of men by men for men. Their point is all the more poignant when we remember that women did not have the vote at the time of Lincoln's speech, and nor did Blacks and nor did all males. It is even more poignant as we realize that almost 8,000 men were killed at Gettysburg. This is not government *for* men. This was government in which men sacrificed themselves, or were sacrificed, to preserve the union and to abolish slavery – or not, depending on which side they fought. Indeed the Civil War (1861–5) killed over 600,000 American men, 10 times more Americans than the six year Vietnam War, and 200 times more than Pearl Harbor and 9/11. These are "injuries and usurpations" and "tyranny" over men by men – in ways unimagined by Seneca Falls and ignored, forgotten or not realized by later misandrists – who were and are beneficiaries of these immense sacrifices.

The clearest and cleanest statements of the patriarchy model have come from Valerie Solanas and Redstockings in the 70s, as we have seen in Chapter 4. This view persisted into the 90s. Kate Bornstein argues that: "gender is no different a form of class oppression than the caste system in India or apartheid in South Africa" (1995:105). (Having visited South Africa during apartheid, I find her comparison not only absurd but insulting.) She adds:

> In the either/or gender class system that we call male and female, the structure of one-up, one-down fulfills the requisite for a power imbalance ... It's an arena in which roughly half the people in the world have power over the other half. (1995:107)

She explains her view: "it's not men who are the foe so much as it is the bi-polar system that keeps men in place as more privileged" (1995:106). And the *Encyclopedia of Feminism* defines patriarchy baldly as "the universal structure which privileges men at the expense of women" (Tuttle, 1986:242).

The solution to the alleged problem of patriarchal oppression is, of course, a capsize of the system: a revolutionary transformation of the society. Germaine Greer's *The Female Eunuch* was one of the early works of the second wave. Her concluding chapter on revolution outlines some of the tactics she sees as necessary for the future, and she discusses some of the feminist manifestos of the time. But what she emphasizes most is the implementation of a new set of feminine i.e. *superior* values:

> If women understand by emancipation the adoption of the masculine role, then we are lost indeed. If women can supply no counterbalance to the blindness of male drive the aggressive society will run to its lunatic extremes at ever-escalating speed. Who will safeguard the despised animal faculties of compassion, empathy, innocence and sensuality? (1971:114)

Compassion, empathy, innocence, and sensuality is Greer's list of the feminine virtues which will save humanity, men included, from blind, aggressive, lunatic males. This is the revolution? Such hostility to half the world is not a great start, nor very compassionate! Nor is such blind, lunatic stereotyping. This mimics Redstockings: "Our humanity is denied." It is not surprising that most women do not identify as feminists. This is not equity politics.

The moral superiority of women has been argued from Elizabeth Cady Stanton to the present. In a speech in 1848 demanding the suffrage, Stanton observed: "In my opinion he [man] is infinitely woman's inferior in every moral virtue" (Gordon, 1997:100). Infinitely inferior – tactless, perhaps, but certainly direct. The Italian sociologist and educator, Maria Montessori, reiterated this theme early in the last century:

> Perhaps ... the reign of women is approaching, when the enigma of her anthropological *superiority* will be deciphered. Woman was always the custodian of human sentiment, morality and honor (in Gould, 1981:107; emphasis added).

Now women are re-defined (by Stanton, Montessori, Greer, Redstockings, Montagu, etc.) as the superior gender. Therefore they should rule. As the T-shirts proclaim: "Girls rule. Boys drool."

The advantage of this binary model of power is that it is simple. Everyone can understand it. And to change the old patriarchal system all that women have to do is reverse the model, empower women, put women on top, perhaps without the violence and oppression which, being male characteristics, will somehow magically whither away – and there we are, paradise on earth. It is an enchanting hope.

At the Fourth World Conference on Women in Beijing in 1995 Hillary Clinton insisted: "If there is one message that echoes forth from this conference, it is that human rights are women's rights and women's rights are human rights, once and for all" (*Time* 25.9.95). Certainly women's rights are not universally recognized in much of the world. Hillary Clinton is right on this. But nor are men's. A *First World Conference on Men* would be most valuable. Men's rights are also human rights: men have rights to longer lives, healthier lives, safe workplaces, equality in educational outcomes, their children, their right to life rather than execution, to legislation enforcing zero tolerance for violence against men, and to freedom rather than high incarceration rates in conditions that would be unacceptable for pets ... in a word, they have equal rights to seats in the lifeboats of the "Titanic."

Some writers refer to patriarchy as "phallocracy," a sexist equation of a type of government with the penis. But it is this lack of respect for men, while demanding with "rage" respect for themselves, that so alienates so many women and men from feminism. And if patriarchy is phallocracy, what is matriarchy?

Two California feminists define patriarchal power as "cockocratic." Perhaps amusing, but also aggressive, obscene and provocative misandry. They define cockocratic as derived from Cockocracy, which means "the state of supranational, supernatural erections, the place/time where the air is filled with the crowing of cocks, the joking of jocks, the droning of clones, the snivelling of snookers and snudges, the noisy parades and processions of prickers: pecker order" (Caputi and MacKenzie, 1992:80). (There is better work on patriarchy e.g. Walby, 1990).

The imagination boggles. What next? prickocracy? peckercratic? dongocratic? even J. Tocracy ... the poetic muse casts its magic spell. So patriarchy is weinerocracy or sausagearchy? This is for the more culinarily and gastronomically inclined. For the more medically moved we propose testicolocracy; for the more populist, ballsocratic: a beautiful double play on the masculinity of Socrates, yet another "dead white male."

While I don't have the nerve to be quite as rude and crude as these misandric feminists, what would be the female equivalent of cockocracy? This could be defined, to parody the earlier definition of patriarchy, as: "the state of supranational, supernatural secretions; the place/time where the air is filled with the nagging of hags, the bitching of bitches, the whining of witches... ." Do I make my point? This sort of male-bashing so thinly disguised as humour merely expresses the venomous loathing of men which it also fosters – as this little role reversal above will serve to clarify, I hope, as well as to condemn.

Indeed such slurs are all the more surprising in that it was precisely the early feminists who protested so vigorously and so convincingly against sexist humour and the degradation of women, against the objectification and genitalization of women, against double standards, and against misogyny. What so many feminists once protested, so many feminists now practice – and often the same individuals. Applying the "shoe on the other foot" theory again, there is no way that women would find contemptuous remarks about them so amusing.

Indeed double standards being what they are, invisible to the believers, some feminists now engage in exactly the same sexist processes which their predecessors once so sternly condemned in men. And struggles for power, liberation, rights and justice seem very different, depending on our identifications and lenses: male or female, rich or poor, and our ethnic, religious or linguistic backgrounds.

For feminists the feminist lens is self-evidently the best lens: it sees clearest, so to speak. It sees the (negative) situation of women most clearly. All else is irrelevant. A classic example of this is the Canadian Panel on Violence against Women which specifically adopted what it called:

> a feminist lens through which violence against women is seen as the consequence
> of social, economic and political inequality built into the structure of the society
> and reinforced through assumptions expressed in the language and ideologies of
> sexism, racism and class. (1993:3)

A measure of how much we take feminist ideology for granted is that there was no public outcry about the absurdity of this statement. Yet imagine the outcry if the authors of a Federal Task Force or a Royal Commission had explained that "Of course we use only a Christian lens in our work" – or a Jewish ... or a socialist ... or a conservative ... or a masculist perspective! One wonders which lens a feminist would use to see violence against men. (Actually, we already know this. The Canadian panel ignored it. Not their problem, perhaps.) Yet obviously the two problems are closely linked, and the violence against men is also a consequence of ideological systemic "inequality" and "ideologies of sexism, racism and class." Actually the members of the Panel forgot that "ideologies of class and race" also oppress men, and they ignored the ideology of misandric sexism. The Canadian Panel converted social science into fundamentalist dogma: the one true faith. The whole exercise cost $10 million of taxpayers' money and missed the point anyway, since it was using the wrong lens, and could not see that domestic violence against women *and* men spring from the same source: a few violent individuals, and that we need to penalize both, not demonize men. And how useful it would have been to consider women's violence against men and their own children (discussed earlier and also below), and to ponder the far lower rates of violence against women than men.

This is the *Cyclops Syndrome*: using only one eye and, with a limited range of vision, blind to much of the action.

The anthropologist Elsie Clews Parsons said years ago: "Wisdom in ethnology, as in life, lies in having more than one approach" (1936:479). While she was talking about methodologies, the same applies to lenses: the more the better. A pink feminist lens shows all the world in shades of pink. A blue masculist one shows it in shades of blue. There are black and white lenses, Jewish, Christian and Muslim lenses, red socialist lenses and rainbow lenses. Identity politics is about the choice of lenses, and all I am saying is that a feminist one is a choice which, in the matter of gender, needs a complement. How much wiser to use many lenses, rather than just the one. Better to have binocular vision than monocular feminist vision.

The hegemony of the male is axiomatic in much sociological thought. As sociologist Michael Kimmel puts it: "Everywhere we look – politics, corporate life, academic life – men are *in power*" (1992:162. His emphasis). But Kimmel does *not* look everywhere. He could look at the doorways or in the parks and see the homeless, the streets where the beggars beg, the prisons where about two million of his fellow American men are imprisoned, the hospitals where men die younger than women, the legislatures which protect women but not men from violence, the courts which give away their children, the televisions, the newspapers and text books where men are caricatured, the battlefields where the men are killed defending the country, and the cemeteries where men are buried, so often dead by suicide or work or homicide or war. Kimmel should look down, look around, look more carefully. This failure to see is part of the problem.

There are powerful men, of course, and powerful women. Indeed one of the interesting questions is why there are not more women in national politics in the G8, and in the F500 corporations. Increasingly it is becoming clear that it is because so many women do not want these jobs. The costs are too high (Pinker, 2008).

That said, hegemonic women are an increasingly large and powerful sector of the population globally, not only in the developed world; and their power can be expected to increase, given the educational disparities which have now persisted in the U.S., Canada and the U.K. for about two decades.

Hegemonic Women

In the demonizing of the hegemonic male, the hegemonic female has been forgotten, or ignored; yet most of my students really want to be hegemonic themselves. Indeed the rapid mobility of women in North America is astonishing, as is the shift in sex roles, especially for women, over the last 50 years. The last century has witnessed the most massive, rapid and peaceful transfer of power from one population to another in history: a transfer engineered by those who had the power – men.

This transformation has been universal and systemic, so we will consider the systems of politics, income, business, education, and law, and note some of the changes, and also how women are, in some instances, privileged. These considerations are necessarily brief, just snapshots, but they may illuminate a reality other than the conventional wisdom.

Politics

Hillary Clinton was a candidate for the U.S. Presidency in 2008, and Sarah Palin for the Vice-Presidency in under 80 years since women were enfranchised. As Clinton remarked, when her mother was born, women did not have the right to vote. The speed of change under "patriarchy" has been remarkable.

Many great political leaders have been powerful women: Queens Hatshepsut and Cleopatra of Egypt, the Empress Wu Zetian of China, Isabella of Castile, Queen Elizabeth I of England, Catherine the Great of Russia, Maria Theresa of Austria to name a few.

In more recent, and more democratic times, Margaret Thatcher was elected Prime Minister in 1979 in the proverbially conservative U.K. – and for three consecutive terms – and only 55 years after women were enfranchised. Women have been elected or appointed Heads of State in over 35 countries, often more than once. In the G7, Canada, the U.K., France and Germany have or have had female heads of states. The U.S.A., Italy and Japan are the minority, the anomaly, the exceptions.

The Inter-Parliamentary Union monitors the representation of women in parliaments, both lower and upper houses (if there are two, as in the U.S., the U.K. and Canada). As of 30 November 2008, 24 of the 180 countries surveyed, had elected 30% or more to the lower house. Rwanda had the highest proportion (56%) followed by Sweden (47%) and Cuba (43%). Proportions in the G7 were: Germany 32%; Canada 22% with 34% in the Senate; Italy 21%; the U.K. 20% with 20% in the House of Lords; France 18%; the U.S. 17% and 17% also in the Senate; and Japan 9%. Several countries had no women elected: Belize, Micronesia, Nauru, Oman, Palau, Qatar, Saudi Arabia, Solomon Islands and Tuvalu. The IPU also presents data going back to 1997 which show substantial increases in representation. At that time the proportions were: Japan 5%; France 6%; the U.K. 10%; Italy 11%; the U.S. 12%; Canada 18% and Germany 26% (www.ipu.org. Accessed 10 Jan. 2008). In several countries, therefore, representation has doubled or almost doubled.

Various measures have been proposed to address the gender imbalance in many countries. They include improved mentoring of potential candidates to increase self-selection, changes to the party selection processes, improvements in the legislatures themselves and, most important, shifts from the "first past the post" system to some form of proportional representation. The greatest barrier however is probably the ambition gap: men want these jobs and sacrifice for them, in politics as well as business; women, not so much. This may be the wiser choice in terms of longevity, and a less work-obsessed life-style (and death-style).

The question arises: in whose interests do politicians govern? It is axiomatic for radical feminists that men govern in men's best interests; it is axiomatic for social democrats that governments govern in corporate interests; it is axiomatic for nationalists that governments govern in the national interest; and finally it is axiomatic for many men that they govern in women's best interests.

Women have been Presidents or Prime Ministers of a long list of countries, including Bangladesh, Bermuda, Canada, Dominica, France, Guyana, India, Ireland (two), Israel, Indonesia, New Zealand (two), Nicaragua, Norway, Pakistan, Panama, Philippines, Sri Lanka (two), Switzerland, Turkey and the U.K. And in Africa: the Central African Republic, Rwanda, Burundi and Liberia. More names and countries are added every year: in 2001, the Philippines and Indonesia. In 2002, Helen Clark was re-elected for the second time in New Zealand, having succeeded Jenny Shipley, South Korea elected its first female PM and the Acting President of Montenegro was female. Beatrix Merino became PM of Peru in 2003, and Vaira Vika-Freiberger was re-elected President of Latvia, and Anneli Jatteemaki became PM of Finland. In 2005 Yulia Tymoshenko became President of Ukraine, but resigned soon afterwards; Angela Merkel was elected the first female Chancellor of Germany, and Ellen Johnson-Sirleaf was elected President of Liberia: the first woman elected head of state in Africa. Then in 2006 Michelle Bachelet was elected President of Chile, and Portia Simpson-Miller was elected

Prime Minister of Jamaica, and in 2007 Pratibha Patil became the first female President of India, and Cristina Fernandez de Kirchner was elected President in Argentina, succeeding her husband. In 2009 Sheikh Hasina Wajed was sworn in as Prime Minister of Bangladesh, for the second time.

At the time of writing, women rule in over adozen countries, with their numbers and power steadily increasing. This has been steady progress since the election of the first female Prime Minister, Sirimavo Bandaranaike, in Sri Lanka in 1960; she ruled for three terms. And it is very rapid progress considering that few countries had extended the franchise to women before 1920.

Income

The increase of women in the full-time labour force, facilitated by the invention of the birth-control pill, legalized abortion and the plummeting drop in the fertility rate, has resulted in massive increases in women's income and, as a consequence, a proportionately massive shift in the domestic (and public) balance of power.

Newsweek ran a lead article back in 2003 pointing out that 30% of working wives earn more than their husbands (Tyre and McGinn, 2003). These husbands include numerous categories: the retired, the unemployed, students, presumably the incarcerated, the disabled, as well as stay-at-home dads and those husbands employed part-time or full-time at lower salaries. In any event, this increasing shift in the balance of economic power is likely to be permanent and to increase over time, due both to the educational shifts and also to the changing labour market which advances the female-dominated service sector while the male-dominated primary and manufacturing sectors are in decline and/or outsourced.

Similarly in Canada 29% of wives earn more than their husbands – almost triple the 11% who earned more in 1967 (*Gazette* 24.8.06).

The conventional wisdom is still, as pontificated by *Newsweek*, that "the average woman's wage still trails a man's (78 cents to the dollar)" (Tyre and McGinn, 2003:46); but this is misleading. The most obvious component of the wage gap is because a higher proportion of men are in the full-time labour force than women, and a higher proportion of women than men work part time. Beyond that the average wages for men and women in the full-time labour force, same occupations, same levels of education, are unequal – primarily because women work fewer hours/wk and fewer wks/year than men. This is not discrimination. This is the market. The 78 cents myth so widely promulgated seems to imply a 22% earnings gap due to male sexism, prejudice and discrimination, and has therefore been a useful tool in uniting women as a political force. Yet it is a myth. (U.S. Census Bureau, 2007:411).

Furthermore recent analysis of the 2005 U.S. Census data indicates that women are forging ahead of men in wages in New York, Dallas, Los Angeles, Chicago, Boston and some other cities. In Dallas women aged 21–30, of all education levels, made 20% more than men, and 17% more in New York – in large part because of higher education levels. Also they are less likely to be married, and more likely to be childless (or child-free, in the new lexicon) than suburban and rural women. Nationally, however, that group of women made only 89% of the average pay for women, for reasons suggested earlier; although interestingly wages are much more equal for Hispanics (97%), Asians (95%) and Blacks (92%) than for Whites (87%) (Roberts, 2007).

Similarly in Canada my indignant female students are largely unaware that for over a decade the female to male earnings ratio for single never-married earners has been 100% ± ½% (Statistics Canada 1995. Cat. No. 13-217). True, this is counter-intuitive given the high female enrolments in such love-interest rather than money-interest degrees as Fine Art, Art History, English, French Literature, History, Sociology and Anthropology; but the data stands – albeit largely unpublicized. It is children and different values about work/life balance which open up the wage gap, not (widespread opinion to the contrary notwithstanding) gender discrimination.

Business

Catalyst, which is the leading research organization reporting on the status of women in business, offers in its annual report "U.S. Women in Business" (2008) a pyramid: Women constitute 48% of the labour force, 51% of management, professional and related occupations, 15% of the board seats in the Fortune 500 Companies (F500) and 2.4% of the F500 CEOs. Thus women constitute a slim majority of the management occupations, and are over-represented compared to their numbers in the labour force. Their representation on boards has increased over 50% since 1995, when they held only 9.6% of the seats. And they are CEOs of 12 F500 companies, up from six in 2002: doubling in six years. This constitutes under-representation at the top, but also over-representation in the broad occupational arena, a fairly rapid rate of change at the top as younger businesswomen work their way up.

Catalyst, however, has commented in earlier work on the slow rate of progress towards parity, discussed the "barriers to advancement" notably "gender-based stereotyping, exclusion from informal networks, and a lack of role models." In their study of the Canadian Financial Post 500 (FP500), Catalyst notes the persistence of the "old boy network" and the tendency of male directors to select their clones for their boards (2008a).

Researchers might emphasize either the under-representation at the top and a slow rate of change, or the occupational over-representation and a rapid rate of change. This is an issue of politics and perception: the interpretation of data can be controversial.

Two further points: there is considerable evidence that many women have made autonomous choices to drop out of the "rat race," to choose different work-life balances than men, and to prefer staff to line careers (e.g. human resources to finance) (Morris, 2002; Sellers, 2003; Belkin, 2003; Tyre and McGinn, 2003;

Pinker, 2008). Indeed an examination of the differential enrollment rates in university departments indicates that many men and women have different goals in life, values and even interests e.g. selections of maths, computer science and engineering versus fine arts, social work and library science.

Both perspectives: male discrimination and female choice require consideration; but the most intriguing Catalyst finding is that those companies with the highest percentages of women corporate officers in both the U.S. and Canada had much higher returns on equity and total returns to shareholders than those with the lowest percentages of corporate officers. In any event, these are hegemonic women in business. It seems that women in business are good for business and profits.

Two examples: Carly Fiorino was CEO of Hewlett-Packard and ranked Number 1 on the Fortune Most Powerful Women list for six consecutive years with an annual income of $15.6 million in 2003, until she was forced out. But she lifted H-P up from number 28 on the Fortune top 50 in 2002 to number 14 in 2003. Pat Russo at Lucent earned more: $38 million – more than most of the supposedly hegemonic men – and more in one year than most men earn in their rather short lifetimes (Sellers, 2003).

The Health System

Men's health is notoriously poor. Some blame men for their lifestyle choices (Murphy, 2002). Some blame the system. Some blame both.

- Men's life expectancy in our target nations: the U.S., Canada and the U.K., is 5–6 year less than women's. In the U.S. in 2005, life expectancy at birth was 75.2 years for men, but 80.4 years for women: a longevity gap of 5.2 years. The life situation was far worse for black men. While overall life expectancy was 77.8 years, for black men it was only 69.5 years: 6.8 years less than black women, 8.3 years less than the American average, and a massive 10.9 years less than white women (Kung *et al.*, 2008: Table 8).
- The death-rate (age-adjusted) in the U.S. is 40% higher for men than for women; but for black men it is 57% higher than the national average and 88% higher than that for white women. And the death-rate for blacks is 29% higher than it is for whites (Kung *et al.*, 2008: Table 1) In terms of power – the power to live – male to female is as black to white.
- Men have higher death rates than women from 14 of the 15 leading causes of death (Kung *et al.*, 2008: Table B). The one missing is Alzheimer's disease: men do not live long enough – they are already dead.

The National Vital Statistics Reports from which this data has been collected are excellent sources for understanding men's health; but they are also, implicitly, an appalling description of men's health and an implicit indictment of government policy.

Three paradigms on health and death are helpful in understanding these issues: the personal, the cultural and the systemic. The Men's Health Network (MHN) based in Washington is the primary, if not sole, source for general information and activism on behalf of men's health. In terms of personal self-care, at which men are not proficient, MHN notes that a higher proportion of men than women have no personal physician, have no health care coverage (mostly because of the types of jobs they have), and they make only half the number of visits to physicians for preventive care, compared to women – and by that time it is often too late (www.menshealthnetwork.org).

This apparent failure in self-care is partly a consequence of the traditional male values of stoicism and self-reliance going beyond R.W. Emerson to the warrior ideal. It is partly a consequence of the fact that many men will lose their jobs if they make the required number of visits to physicians for preventive care: you don't turn up for work, you're fired. And if the worker is not fired, he is likely to have his salary docked, which the family needs. Male nurturance is often less about the emotional support of the family and more the financial support – so the man does not always take the time (and money) off, and his health suffers.

The cultural paradigm is also relevant. Men not only have the most dangerous jobs with the highest mortality rates (and excellent pay), as we discussed in Chapter 5; they also have the deadliest hobbies. Accidents happen. Such recreational activities as mountaineering, parasailing, ice-climbing, free climbing, bungee-jumping, BASE jumping, race care driving, scuba-diving, zorbing ... all are no doubt exhilarating, but also potentially lethal. Men not only tend to have more dangerous jobs and recreational life-styles, they also have less healthy life-styles. Men drink more, smoke more, use illegal drugs more, and start all of these usages at younger ages than women; they also have poorer nutrition – when older they stack up TV dinners like pancakes. They do tend to exercise more; but they also have similar obesity rates to women. Finally, crime is a particularly lethal way of life (Courtenay, 2000). The life-styles create the death-styles.

The third circle of health is the health system sustained by government. Its efficiency and level of availability largely influence mortality rates for both men and women. In the United States an Office on Women's Health (OWH) was established in 1991, with Regional Branch Offices and Departmental Offices. A proposal to establish an Office on Men's Health, recognizing the much shorter life spans of men and the much higher death rates, was rejected by the "male-dominated" Congress in 2005. Men were then "added" in an ironic twist to the OWH as an appendix. This was not so much a victory as an insult. While medical pundits recommend that men behave more like women in terms of personal care and life-styles, many fail to recognize the political and systemic nature of health care (e.g. Courtenay, 2000). Political decisions are not being based on clear and present health needs – despite the very high economic costs of all these potential years of life lost.

Indeed if federal policies were to be based on health *needs* and justice, as opposed to squeaking wheels, chivalry and blindness, the health priorities would target men, and especially black men, and especially low income black men since the poor live shorter lives than the rich.

In Canada, with similarly inappropriate priorities, the federal government followed suit and established the Women's Health Bureau in 1993, later re-named the marginally more inclusive – but still exclusive – the Bureau of Women's Health and Gender Analysis – which still omits men and men's health. Their website lists the four health policy initiatives of the Bureau – three of which only discuss women while the "Gender-based Analysis Policy" ignores the comparative data listed above. Remarkably, the website says nothing about differential life expectations, nor mortality rates. In fact, therefore, the Gender in "Gender-based" still means women only.

Then in 1996 the federal government established five Centres of Excellence for Women's Health, with a sixth added later (www.cewh-cesf.ca). Useful as they are for women's health, not one has been established for men's health.

It is not just that the federal government clearly does not care about men's health, but equally clearly, the "equity feminists" who have for so long demanded the level playing field do not care either; but also, *men* do not seem to care either! The combination of male and female misandry in their different political and medical forms means, again, that men pay a high cost for their gender – a point that the "Gender-based Analysis Policy" section of the Bureau should have noticed.

Governments, corporations, the medical establishments which co-operate with these Centres and Bureaus, the legislators, and health professionals – if they avert to men's deaths at all – so often blame men, rather than the system which they (men included) have built: a system which privileges women while excluding men, who are already marginalized and dying young.

Responsibility for this misallocation of resource no doubt rests squarely on the shoulder of the legislators who enact the legislation and the women who demand it; but also on the academics who ignore men's health needs. A recent text on Canadian health has one chapter on women's health, but not one on men's health, and the index on "women" is 14 lines long, but there is absolutely no mention of "men" in the index (Armstrong, Armstrong and Coburn, 2001). A more recent text by two of these authors on health care in Canada has six lines in the index on women, referring to 28 pages of text, but again, not one line on men (Armstrong and Armstrong, 2003). Again, a standard Canadian text on the sociology of health has four chapters in a section titled "Women, Family and Health" (Bolaria and Dickinson, 1988). No men. These exclusions and omissions of men are both startling and misandric. Men's ill health, health problems and deaths are invisible – to legislators, feminists, sociologists and the medical profession. Men are, again, the invisible and throw-away sex.

The result, of course, is a continuing high number of male deaths, and high male death rates, from a number of causes – all within a society which does not seem to care, takes minimal political, economic or medical action to reduce the high male death rates, and places its resources in women's much lower death rates.

Perhaps men will wake up to this misallocation of resources. Or perhaps men don't care. We'll live and die our lives as we like.

The Education System

The education system largely fails boys and men, just like the health system. This has been widely recognized in the United States; less so in the U.K. and Canada. *Newsweek* recently cover-paged "The Boy Crisis: At Every Level of Education, They're Falling Behind. What to do?" (Tyre, 2006). C.H. Sommers published "The War against Boys. How Misguided Feminism is Harming our Young Men" (2000). A series of works, mostly by psychologists have begun to relate "The boy crisis" to a range of adversities including suicide rates, alcohol and drug use and violence rates – all of which are much higher for boys than girls, and for young men than young women – and depression too, and have offered their experience and recommendations both for inside and outside school (Kindlon and Thompson, 1998; Pollack, 1998; Gurian, 1997, 1999).

The data is compelling, and the "crisis" begins early due at least in part to the earlier physical and psychological maturation rates of girls. In the U.S. girls are surpassing boys in standardized reading and writing tests, from grade 3, and the gap widens over the years; and boys are 33% more likely to drop out of high school than girls (Tyre, 2006). In Canada 14.7% of young men have failed to complete high school by age 20, compared to 9.2% of young women: 60% more (McMullin, 2004:220). Failure to complete high school is therefore not a male problem as such, but it is *disproportionately* a male problem. The question is why? The *Newsweek* article is titled: "The Trouble with Boys" (Tyre, 2006). More accurate would be: "The Trouble with the Education System."

The situation is similar at university, where the inequality is as striking as the change. In the U.S. in 1960, men constituted 66% of those graduating with Bachelors degrees, 68% of those with Masters and 90% of those with Ph.D.s. By 2004 this distribution had been reversed (thanks in part, no doubt, to the largely male professoriate). Men constituted only 43% of those graduating with Bachelor and 42% of those with Masters – below parity. These gender gaps of 14% and 16% are substantial and show few signs of being closed. Men did earn the majority of doctorates, 55%, and 5%± is usually accepted as parity (U.S. Census Bureau, 2008:183, 523). By 2009, however, the male numbers will probably have slipped lower.

The situation is virtually identical in Canada (Statistics Canada, Cat. No. 81-229; Nicoriuk, 2004).

More specifically, while Engineering schools are still mostly male, Medical schools, Dental schools, Veterinary schools and Law schools are now mostly female. The gender capsize from secondary school to university has enormous implications for both sexes, families, the economy and society in general.

In the U.K. the University Admissions Service (UAC) raised the alarm, noting that 56% of the applicants were female in 2007, up from 54% 10 years ago – thus creating a 12% gender gap, similar to the gaps in the U.S. and Canada. Authorities expressed concern that young men were either boycotting university or had not achieved the academic credentials sufficient for application, or both. A spokesman for the UAC affirmed: "There could be a range of reasons why this gap occurs. More research needs to be undertaken in this area to fully understand this trend" (http://news.bbc.co.uk (15.2.07)). A statement so stunningly banal is worth quoting. The gap itself is more than 10 years old, evidently; why has it not been researched already in the U.K.?

There is a range of reasons why the education system is failing so many boys and men. The following list represents – not a consensus, there is no such thing on this topic – a summary of explanations suggested by different authorities. We might bear in mind that both males and females drop out – and to that extent our secondary school system fails members of both sexes, as does the university system; the point is that the education system fails males more than females. It also fails on the basis of socio-economic status, race and ethnicity; but that is another story, and even these intervening variables do not negate the gender gap. Some of the reasons for the higher male drop-out rates are given below, but are differentially applicable at the secondary and tertiary levels of the system.

Hate

It is well known that many boys often hate school; that schools hate boys is not so well known. Boys are often boisterous, noisy, trouble, restless, bored … the antithesis of what a good student should be: quiet, clean, tidy, respectful, and enjoying her school work. Girls are the default mode from kindergarten throughout. As one author remarks: "Often boys are treated like defective girls." Another noted that schools are "biologically disrespectful" (Tyre, 2006:46, 47).

Money

Why the higher male drop-out rate? Simple! It's the money. Boys and young men can earn good money in high wage, low skill jobs, at least for a while. Brawns not brain nor literacy are required in unskilled or semi-skilled labour. It is a short-time policy, but young men are not well-known for deferred gratification.

Unionization

The unionization of primary and secondary schools, and universities, has resulted in improved conditions and higher pay for teachers, but it has also shifted attitudes from a vocation to a profession, from a status to a contract, and to limited duties. This shift has contributed to a decline in extra-curricular activities, especially sports, and vocational dedication. Yet sports were and are one of the few aspects of education which many boys enjoyed! This decline and/or removal of sports and hobbies from the informal curriculum also removed an incentive for many boys to attend school, and to enjoy it if they did. The unionization which benefited teachers did not necessarily benefit boys.

Learning Disabilities

Boys are 2–4 times more likely to suffer from learning disabilities: autism, dyslexia, Aspergers, ADD, ADHD and emotional or linguistic disabilities. Those students with learning disabilities are a low priority within the education system, which is itself a low priority within the financial system. More male students are allocated to Special Ed. classes, and tend to be allocated less, rather than more, financial resources – indeed even less than is intended. Some research indicates that some resources allocated to L.D. students are in fact transferred to support services for regular students (Millet, 2004). It is not surprising, therefore, that such students tend to drop out.

Medicalization

Boys are increasingly being medicated for being who they are, boys. They may be correctly tested and diagnosed for a specific medical condition, but often doctors do not have the time to run batteries of tests on each child and will, apparently, take the parents' word for it, following advice from the school authorities. Yet the children may simply be unusually active, or totally bored and acting-out as an attention-getting device or malnourished or unhappy because their parents are getting a divorce or fighting etc. Such medicalization is also presumably humiliating: one is not "normal." And some children are prescribed both stimulants and anti-depressants simultaneously. Some students benefit. Some do not. But boys are far more medicalized than girls.

Criminalization

In the past, teachers and principals disciplined their charges, often physically, which is now illegal, or with detention, which would now require extra hours with pay for teachers, according to union collective agreements. Expulsion is now rarely a viable option. Today the principle punitive option is to call the police. This is not necessarily imprudent, but it does criminalize the education system and the boys who tend to be the major offenders – not surprisingly, given their dislike of school. Some schools have metal detectors for guns and knives. Violence is always a possibility – Columbine most infamously in 1999. Indeed the presence of armed security guards in some high schools make school seem like the prison that many boys think it is. And the banks of surveillance cameras reinforce this reality. The criminalization of discipline problems, however necessary this may be in some circumstances, is likely to minimize boys' love of school.

Feminization

Kindergarten and primary school have always been feminine environments, with the majority of teachers female. This seems to have worked well for boys for decades. But increasingly education researchers have realized that boys and girls require different teaching styles, disciplines, rewards etc. Some recommend separate classrooms, some separate schools, some more male teachers as role models for the boys, more contact sports, higher pay to attract more male teachers etc. One example: as a treat my step-son's class was taken to the ballet! For him, this was a punishment. He would rather have gone to a baseball game. Neither *Anne of Green Gables* nor *Black Beauty* are boys' favourite reading! (Sommers, 2000).

Misandry

Any culture which systematically demonizes men, referring to them collectively as male chauvinist pigs, oppressors, rapists, the death sex, and so on ... which attends primarily to male negativities while ignoring male positives ... which angelizes women's positives while ignoring their negativities – is likely to have negative impacts on the self-concepts of boys and men. We have addressed this issue in Chapter 4. As with the other factors discussed in this list, the precise impact of the culture of misandry, like the culture of divorce is impossible to calculate. Intuitively it just seems probable that these negative cultural values will be internalized, at least by some young men, and will become self-fulfilling prophecies.

Absent Fathers and the Culture of Divorce

About 40% of marriages contracted now and in the recent past are expected to end in divorce or separation (and some others in death) with custody of the children, if any, almost always awarded to the mother. It is estimated that about 40% of boys in the U.S. are growing up without their biological fathers; but however the mothers may feel about the fathers, the fathers are necessary for their sons – and their daughters. Psychologists suggest that a boy without a father is like an explorer without a map (Tyre: 2006:51).

The culture of divorce (itself due to a range of factors from changed legislation, more accepting attitudes to divorce, higher expectations of marriage, women's increased role in the labour force) has probably harmed rather than helped the children of divorce. The degree of harm varies no doubt; but it relates not only to the initial trauma but also to the frequency and intensity of parental alienation syndrome – which often systematically alienates the children from the non-custodial parent, usually the father (Cartwright, 1993). To the initial absence is added the hate: both with negative effects and affects on boys and girls.

Fathers may be absent for many reasons: divorce, death, work, prison, addiction; or because, after divorce, the mother denies visiting rights or relocates with the children, which also prevents contact. Yet the broader problem of absence is the absence of *both* parents at work. Increasingly children are raising themselves (or not) or being raised by paid strangers and their similarly situated peers. From the education data, girls are succeeding better than boys.

Male Values

Some argue that boys and to some extent men's values are antithetical to school and to education. School is not cool; and the attitudes to school learned in school may persist to university. Some teachers are concerned that boys identify more with Beavis and Butthead and Bart Simpson and Dennis the Menace, Trailer Park Boys, James Bond, video games, hockey, soccer – anything other than school-work. They talk about their anti-intellectualism, though this is a cultural variable.

All these explanations for "the boy crisis" indicate that schools must become more "boy-friendly" if they want to retain them and train them, and if we want boys to go on to university. Otherwise the waste will continue to drain our resources, the economic costs of lost opportunities will rise, and marginalized boys and young men will find destructive outlets for their energies. This is a "school crisis."

The Legal System

The legal system is largely about men, both as law-enforcers and law-breakers; but, as my lawyer once informed me, any relation between law and justice is purely coincidental. This is not so much a comment on the whimsies of juries or judges, but a matter of historical record. There have been great lawmakers in the past: King Solomon, Solon of Athens, the Emperor Justinian – but there have also been great injustices: the Slave laws, the Penal laws in Ireland and England, Jim Crow in the U.S., the caste laws in India, the Nuremberg laws in Germany, the Apartheid laws in South Africa, and laws which discriminate against women in some parts of the world and also, laws which discriminate against men.

Legal systems are not always about justice, but institutionalizing the interests of the law-makers, in terms of race, class, gender, religion or political party or other identities. Long ago, Marx and Engels criticized the law from a class perspective. In *The Communist Manifesto* (1848) they affirmed: "Your jurisprudence is but the will of your class made into a law for all" (1974:100). Justice is not blind, but biased. And Engels noted in 1845 that:

> Because the English bourgeoisie finds himself reproduced in his law, as he does
> in his God, the policeman's truncheon which, in a certain measure, is his own

club, has for him a wonderfully soothing power. But for the working-man quite otherwise. (1969:253)

The "wonderfully soothing power" of the club enforces the interests of the powerful bourgeoisie who make the law.

Similarly Alexis de Tocqueville (1964/1840) criticized the American legislation which legalized the slavery of blacks and the expropriation of Indian lands. He cautioned against what he called "the tyranny of the majority" which institutionalized such deep injustice against so many.

These criticisms of law by class and race were simultaneously supplemented by feminist critiques by gender. Harriet Martineau noted:

> The question has been asked, from time to time, in more countries than one, how obedience to the laws can be required of women, when no woman has, either actually or virtually, given any assent to any law. No plausible answer has ... been offered; for the good reason that no plausible answer can be devised. (Hoecker-Drysdale, 1992:63)

Since then, laws have been enacted to respond to the injustices of class, race and gender. The (predominantly male!) legislators in the G7 countries, and to varying degrees in most of the world, have transformed the legal landscapes. The U.N. Universal Declaration on Human Rights (1948) initiated the principles for these reforms, and the pendulum began its swing. Affirmative action legislation, sexual harassment legislation, maternity legislation and abortion legislation, work with flex-time, part-time and contract options, subsidized day care, child allowances, equal pay for equal work requirements and, more controversially, equal pay for work of equal value (more controversial because of debates about how value is measured other than by the free market), zero tolerance for violence against women legislation – all this has had a profound impact on the changing status of women, and the creation of a (more) just society.

But has the pendulum swung too far? Men's rights activists assert that the justice systems discriminate against men in multiple domains, and need to be reformed.

The list of concerns is long and gender inclusive and well-known, referring to systemic injustice towards minorities and the poor, men as well as women, but also specifically, men – in the administration of both criminal, civil and family law.

To argue that the legal system and the justice system fails men is *not* to argue that it fails all men all the time, but rather that it is unfair to many men in many ways: ways that we perhaps are unaware of, or have not noticed. One caveat, again: we can only raise the issues, sketch some of them. Readers may wish to pursue them in more depth. So herewith a few examples linking the individuals on the one hand and the system on the other.

In the criminal justice system, the prison population is about 95% male across North America and Europe. That is a problem. Crime is expensive in terms of human and economic costs. "Crime pays," it is said; and it can, in the short run, usually, and for the individual; but for society, the costs are high. Why crime is a male empire has often been discussed; nature and nurture and their combination both have their proponents, as do individual choice and societal generation. The male villains have already been discussed; it is how we treat them that is the issue here. This too is a problem.

Incarceration rates vary widely around the world, evidence both of the differential criminalities of the population: the people in some countries are more law-abiding than others, and also of different penal philosophies and ideas about justice. The U.S. has the highest incarceration rate in the world: 724/00,000 in 2006, 5 times higher than the U.K. at 143/00,000, but France is lower still at 88 and Finland has the lowest incarceration rate in Europe at 66. And this surely reflects not only different crime rates and penal philosophies but also attitudes to men, and to humanity generally.

Prisons have been described as universities of crime, and revolving doors with recidivism rates, often for more serious crimes than the original, of about 70% in three to five years. Almost everywhere in Europe and North America the prisons are over-crowded, and rape, sex slavery and homicide are serious problems, and the expenses are horrendous. Prisons not only often destroy the inmates, physically or psychologically, but they break up families, leaving children without their fathers, leave the wives without the income, the ex-cons often unemployable because of their records and their sons likely to follow in their fathers' footsteps. Incarceration is no doubt sometimes necessary, notably for career criminals; but its high failure rate, to deter men from offending and then re-offending, indicates the need for reform and re-evaluation where incarceration rates are very high. Prisons are necessary, but they destroy men and society.

Miscarriage of justice is another problem affecting mostly men. In the U.K. notorious cases included the Guildford 4, convicted for IRA bombings which killed five people, but released after 15 years; the Birmingham 6 convicted for killing 21 people in two bombings, and released after 16 years; the Bridgewater 4 were convicted of the murder of a paper-boy; three were released after 17 years and the fourth died in prison.

In Canada the most notorious case was that of Steven Truscott, who spent 48 years in jail for a murder he did not commit. The Association in Defence of the Wrongfully Convicted has to work hard, and the roll-call of the men includes Milgaard, Morin, Johnson, Marshall, Parson and Driscoll.

In the U.S. the Innocence Project was founded in 1992 and is a network of law schools, journalism schools and defense attorneys dedicated to exonerating the innocent, based mostly on DNA evidence. So far the Project has overturned the convictions of 227 Americans, 17 of them under sentence of death. The average duration of their sentence was 12 years, for a total of 2,724 years served by innocent people in maximum security prisons doing hard time. Almost all are men. About 70% of them are from minority groups. Their website lists a number of factors involved in these false convictions: eyewitness misidentification (the most common factor), forensic science misconduct or error, prosecutorial or police misconduct or error (often due to overzealous selective perception and tunnel vision), false testimony of informants (snitches), false accusations (e.g. rape) and incompetent lawyering.

Neither racism nor poverty nor sexism are mentioned as factors, nor is mental illness nor low I.Q. The Project notes that freedom is just the beginning of a new set of problems. Many states offer no compensation for false convictions; families have often disappeared or disowned him; jobs are gone and he has acquired no work skills in those 12 lost years, and the world has changed. The ex-con is free, innocent, alone often, impoverished perhaps and perhaps suicidal (www. innocenceproject.org. Accessed 19.1.09).

The Duke University lacrosse team scandal is a fascinating example of the almost universal assumption of male guilt and female innocence. In March 2006 the team was celebrating a victory at the house of one of the team captains, and they had hired two strippers. Three days later one of them said that she had been raped by three of the players. The DA assumed they were guilty. So did the police, the president of the university, who suspended the team for two games and forced the coach to resign, and many of the faculty who wrote a letter condemning them. It was a classic case: female against males, poor against rich, black (the dancer was black) against white.

The case continued for over a year before all three were declared innocent and the prosecutor, Mike Nifong, was disbarred, and 38 students filed suit against the university, the hospital and the police.

The draft: gender-selective conscription is the most widespread and destructive form of discrimination – yet we are so accustomed to its normality, because of its necessity, that we do not see the injustice and the double standards. We are more sensitive to the injustices against women far away: clitoridectomy, female infanticide etc. than to the injustices against men closer to home.

Gloria Steinem, for instance, addressed the American Sociological Association in 2006 and claimed that violence against women kills six million lives a year. Where she got that figure from, I don't know – the same figure as the Holocaust. But given that violence against men, by both men and women, kills far more men, the total for men – and the grand total for both sexes – must be even higher. Steinem ignored that, the Cyclops syndrome, which itself is symbolic violence against men.

The three strikes law sent one man to prison for 25 years for stealing some razor blades, and another faces 63 years for selling marijuana and carrying a gun. Yet the sentence for hijacking is 25 years, and for second-degree murder is 14 years (*Economist* 5.6.04; *New York Times* 12.9.04)

Ironically, the "get tough on crime" policies simply generate tougher criminals and higher crime rates. And our legal systems continue to put men away into horrendous conditions as if they were garbage. We need to re-think men, and our policies towards them.

Family law is equally prejudicial against men. This is illustrated by the sad case of Darrin White. His marriage fell apart. His wife was awarded sole custody of their three children. He was told to vacate his house within 48 hours and ordered by a judge to pay his estranged wife *twice* his take-home pay in child support and alimony. He committed suicide (Laframboise, 2000). So his children lost their father, his estranged wife lost her income, but no word on the judge who probably lost a promotion.

One sad story does not prove a point, only illustrates it. It may be an exception. But Fathers 4 Justice was founded in the U.K. and is now international working for fathers' rights. Some of the contested issues are about money (for child support and alimony, including the validity of of pre-nuptial agreements and/or divorce contracts, the duration of child support etc.), the adversarial legal system (which raises costs and ill-feeling) as opposed to mediation or compulsory arbitration, the penalties for non-payment of dues and the prevention of visitation (high for the former, low for the latter), paternity fraud (DNA must be tested within three months of birth in the U.S.A.), after that the non-biological putative father is responsible, not the biological father, who in any case may not be known. The mother cannot be compelled to divulge the name when asked.

Parental Alienation Syndrome is the systemic alienation of children by the custodial parent, usually the mother, from the non-custodial parent. This occurs to a greater or lesser degree after most, but not all, divorces – not surprisingly, perhaps, since the parents are usually alienated from each other. The consequences for the children, however, can be dire. To the negative consequences of loss of their father due to divorce are added more negative consequences due to alienation. Much depends on the age of the children and the degree of alienation and the amount of contact. In the end, however, if and when the children grow up, renew contact with their fathers, hear their stories and check them out, they may turn against their mothers (Cartwright, 1993).

In a recent case in British Columbia, the court decided that a doctor had to continue to pay "child support" to his 23–year-old daughter to help her through medical school: $22,000 (*National Post* 15.1.05). In New York another doctor donated sperm to a friend and is now being sued by the mother for child support for the boy, now 18 until he is 21. To complicate the issue, the putative father was not allowed by the judge to test the DNA to determine if he actually *is* the father, because of alleged "traumatic effects" on this 18 year old (*Seattle Times* 1.12.07).

In England and Wales 160,000 children are affected by divorce every year. Half of the 61,000 court-ordered contacts were broken in 2002, and 40% of fathers have lost all contact with their children within two years. A High Court judge went public to effectively agree with Fathers 4 Justice that the family law system is biased. He cited the case of a man, "a wholly deserving father" who had given up a five year battle to see his daughter, whom he had not seen in two years, after more than 43 court hearings before 16 different judges (*Economist* 10.4.04).

Certainly it must be difficult to distinguish right from wrong, justice from injustice, in assessing the relative rights of children, women and men, and to synchromesh these with their respective duties and responsibilities. By any standards this is a legal system which is failing men and failing justice.

Women as Victims

The systemic victimization of men in some domains of power should not blind us to the victimization of women. We have discussed this in the contexts of war, suicide, homicide and accidents, less so in the contexts of the health, education and legal systems. Furthermore, victim feminists have also explored the victimization of women at length.

No doubt victim theory applies more viciously to women in developing or less developed nations than it does to women in the G7. Not that these women do not have problems, as we know, but clearly they are nothing like so severe.

Civil wars are particularly horrific for women and children, and increasingly cruel, with the recruitment of child soldiers and the systemic deliberate rape of women. Bosnia, Liberia, Sierra Leone, Congo, the Central African Republic, Darfur in Sudan, Colombia – the reports from NGOs, peacekeepers and medical authorities are horrendous. In Bosnia, thousands of women were raped. In Darfur, an NGO reported over 500 cases of rape in five months. An estimated 70% of rape victims in Rwanda were HIV infected. And so on (*Economist* 21.2.09).

Sex-selective abortion is problematic. About 10 million female fetuses were aborted in India over the last 20 years by women wanting sons (*Time* 23.1.06:8).

Bride-burning in India, "honour" killings, stoning for adultery, trafficking in women and sex slavery, perhaps genital mutilation (though this is disputed), restricted educational opportunities, a well as domestic physical violence – these are all atrocities primarily affecting women.

Increasingly such atrocities are reported internationally in the press, as well as by UNESCO, WHO and UNICEF and other organizations like Amnesty International, Human Rights Watch etc. Globally, the increasing empowerment of women is monitored, measured and reported annually by the U.N. Human Development Reports.[2]

---

2   One of the difficulties in discussing the victimization of men and women is grasping the sheer brutality and suffering of it all – from the millions of battle deaths of young men in war, for which they often volunteer, to the cruelty of contemporary slavery and slave traders, to the strange cultural norms for westerners of the lotus, suttee, tooth-removal, clitoridectomy and more. A second difficulty is appreciating that while some cultural norms are evidently patriarchal in the worst sense of oppressive: acid-throwing, bride-burning, honour killings, some others – which may seem equally oppressive to us outsiders – are sometimes the autonomous choices of women: the lotus, suttee and clitoridectomy for instance, just as hara-kiri or seppukka was the individual choice of Japanese men, not women. The lotus, suttee and hara-kiri have now been outlawed by the respective governments of China, India and Japan.

Closer to home the list of grievances is long, and reported frequently:

- Violence against women
- The 70 cent dollar
- The double load
- Sexual harassment
- The pink ghetto
- Gender apartheid
- The glass ceilings, walls and escalators
- Wife-battering and intimate homicides
- The poverty of single mothers, and the deadbeat dads
- Unequal pay for work of equal value
- Political under-representation and misrepresentation
- The objectification of women in advertising
- The absence of day care facilities
- Unequal representation at the top

For some, this constitutes a war against women, as we have seen. For others, patriarchy is long gone and it is time to lose victim feminism and embrace power feminism (and maybe men too) (Badinter, 1989; Wolf, 1993; LaFramboise, 1996 etc.).

What we need now is a new feminist theory of "success feminism" or "glory feminism" – in which the extraordinary successes and achievements of women are acclaimed, and their continuing successes are highlighted as I have tried to do earlier. Positive self-concepts are much more useful for women – and men – than the self-concept as victim. Yet almost all my female students are totally convinced that they are victims of male oppression. They also remain largely unaware both of female hegemony and of female villainy, which we need to address in the interests of negating stereotypes. This is the "moral" paradigm to parallel the men as villains paradigm.

The anthropological norms of cultural relativism, that people from one culture cannot or should not judge the practices of another, for that is cultural racism, have been challenged by feminists and others for their pacifism, for failure to support women's rights and to be activist against abuses of human rights. They in turn have often been described as cultural racists by indigenous activists, and told to mind their own business. Some have remarked on television that the cosmetic surgery practices of American men and women, from labiotomies to rib or toe removal to augmentation and reduction surgeries are not much different.

Women as Villains: Negating the Stereotypes

This positive stereotyping of women as "angels," as nurturing, kindly, "sugar and spice," and morally superior – and as victims of men – has been a cultural norm for ages. And the negative stereotyping of men as "bastards," rapists, villains and criminals and morally inferior has neatly complemented the former by polarity. This theme of the moral superiority of women ante-dates second wave feminism by more than a century, so we cannot just blame second wavers, nor women, for this.

Long after Stanton and Montessori declared the "anthropological superiority of women" the American anthropologist Ashley Montagu picked up and developed this theme in his book *The Natural Superiority of Women* (1952). Montagu anticipated some of the later even more misandric authors with a string of binary oppositions. His male/female comparisons are clean and clear, judgemental and morally hierarchical – converting sugar and spice nursery rhymes into putative social science:

> Woman is the creator and fosterer of life; man has been the mechanizer and destroyer of life ... Women live the whole spectrum of life; they do not think in terms of achromatic black and white, Yes and No, or in terms of the all-or-none principle, as men are inclined to do ... Women love the human race; men behave as if they were, on the whole, hostile to it ... *It is the function of women to teach men how to be human* (1968:157–9. His emphasis).

This is about as achromatic, black and white, all-or-none as it gets, surely! And an early definition of men as sub-human.

It is no part of my mandate to demonize these angelized women; but it is part of my mandate to indicate that this moral bi-polarity: woman/good and man/bad is unrealistic, despite its popularity and prevalence among both men and women. This bi-polar Manichean ideology does have the utility of simplicity with only two categories: male bastards and female angels; "destroyers of life" and "creators of life"; but it is not realistic. A more complex two by two table could accommodate not only male bastards and female angels, but male angels and female bastards. All the quadrants could quickly be filled, but probably not in quite the same ways.

The de-bunking of the myth of women as angels, goddesses, nurturing and morally superior has been initiated not with a "backlash" by the proverbial AWMs (angry white males) but with memoirs by women themselves. It is women who have negated the construction of women as victims and proclaimed themselves as, if not villains, then certainly neither sugar nor spice nor necessarily nurturing nor empathetic – perhaps ambitious, mercenary, sexy or whatever – just human beings – amazingly similar in many ways to the men whom they might love.

One of the first to challenge the stereotypes of the female was Xaviera Hollander's *The Happy Hooker* (1972) in which she described her occupational choice as autonomous, her sexual activity as enjoyable and lucrative, and her men in positive terms. Her book was a best-seller, but her views did not coincide with feminist orthodoxies.

The conflict lines were being drawn. Not that all sex workers have been equally happy, male-positive or fortunate – so much depends on whether one is a street-walker or an expensive call-girl. In her own memoir, Evelyn Lau described her unhappy childhood, and her difficult times with drugs, street life, prostitution – and her hatred of men: "ALL MEN ARE THE SAME … God I hate men. I hate life" (1989:283). Not a great choice of profession if you hate men; though the hate may have evolved from the profession. On the other hand, the Hollywood prostitutes and party girls in *Once More with Feeling* (Parrent, 1996) seem relatively satisfied with their lifestyle choices, until early retirement. Most got into it for the easy money, and some found that the money came at a high price. In any event, the open discussions of these stigmatized and even illegal activities offer realistic portraits of not especially angelic women.

More recent memoirs include Kathryn Harrison's *The Kiss* discussing her long affair with her father, Laura Tanenbaum's *Slut* and Elizabeth Wurtzel's *Bitch: In Praise of Difficult Women*. Wurtzel noted an important dimension of power, ignored by such eminent writers on power as Max Weber, Bertrand Russell and Gloria Steinem: sexual power. "These days," she wrote, "putting out one's pretty power, one's pussy power, one's sexual energy out there for popular consumption no longer makes you a bimbo, it makes you smart" (1999:11).

At the micro-level, women's nastiness to others has become a matter of pride in *Cosmopolitan*, where women boast in the occasional specials of "Cosmo Confessions" of the nastiest things they have done, usually to ex-boyfriends or to rival females. There is nothing "sugary" about these women, nor do they exemplify an "ethic of care," nor are they "nurturing." Many of the confessions are imaginative and amusing rather than simply gross or malicious, but any chivalrous male with romantic illusions about the purer sex reading these stories would soon find his illusions endangered. What is so intriguing is the pride the women take in their revenge. Their significant others may call them "sugar" and "sweety" and "honey" (although the prevalent metaphor today is thermal rather than gastronomic: "hot") – but some women identify and define themselves quite differently: tough, bitch, slut.

The appropriation and re-evaluation of such traditionally female-negative terms as bitch and slut is an interesting and important reversal of values. It is epitomized in the T-shirt slogan: "Good girls go to heaven. Bad girls go everywhere". Indeed this Nietzschean transvaluation of values is a defiant rejection of the usual stereotypes. Some women are now revelling in behaviour that others would hide, and that many of both sexes would blush to affirm. The confessional literature, whether by Catherine Millet (2003) (who described her remarkably rich and varied sex life in Paris) or Harrison, Wurtzel, Lau or Hollander, may be an advance in terms of de-bunking stereotypes, but somehow it does not seem like moral progress. Similarly the sociological literature on women, crime and violence is no doubt realistic; but we might prefer the illusions, and the rosy pictures of women painted by novelists,

Hollywood, television and various feminists. If we merely add women behaving badly to men behaving badly, we may debunk the stereotypes and become more realistic, but we might just be normalizing and encouraging incest, prostitution, sluts, bitches and promiscuity: an interesting cost-benefit calculation.

The exercise of political, economic and moral power is familiar terrain in the sociology of power; but the practice of sexual power, or more crudely (to quote Wurtzel) pussy power, is virgin territory, somewhat incompatible with the angelization, deification and romanticization of women. But it might be regarded as realistic, and as a viable use of one's assets. Nancy Friday's *The Power of Beauty* discusses beauty as another such asset in her life. Thirty years after the protests at the Miss America Beauty Pageant in Atlantic City, the power of beauty and sexuality are being asserted by the new post-feminists or anti-feminists. The wheel has turned full circle.

Indeed the entire culture of women as morally superior and as innocent victims is being negated – with correlative implications, perhaps, for the re-evaluation of men. And new work is coming out on female villains.

The recent *Global Report on Trafficking in Persons* by the U.N. Office on Drugs and Crime might also de-mythologize and de-sacralize women, or some of them, anyway. We cannot demonize men or women by the actions of a minority. The UNODC states not only that most of the victims of human trafficking, which it says should be more accurately described as "enslavement", are women (79%) – "which we knew" – but: "Female offenders have a more prominent role in present-day slavery than in most other forms of crime." "In some parts of the world, women trafficking women is the norm" (UNODC, 2009).

The new critique of the old patriarchal and feminist moral binaries began for men with the heroism of 9/11 and the positive re-evaluation of men, and for women with women's confessional literature, but also with greater attention to, and concern with, female villainy and violence. Perhaps we are beginning to destroy the stereotypes of both men (negative) and women (positive) simultaneously and arrive at something approaching realism and humanism.

Female Violence

Bitches, sluts, traffickers, queen bees, sexual predators, psychic violence ... and all these contradictions to the popular stereotypes of women as the weaker sex, the better sex, as victims and life-giving – all these new portraits of women are drawn by women themselves. This is not a backlash against feminism but a liberating challenge to a stereotype, and a more complicated reality than the old binary gender opposition.

The ultimate challenge to the old model of gender relations is violence, and especially the unsavoury topic of murder. Violence is not a male monopoly. There are seven types of female serial killers and mass murderers. These include the Black Widow killers, the Angel of Death killers, the power killers, the sado-masochistic killers, the robbers, the child-killers and now the homicide bombers and terrorists. An alternative classification, for men as well as women, is by motive – which overlaps with type: Gain, Jealousy, Revenge, Elimination (in sexual triangles), Lust (in rape situations), Conviction (in mental illness) and Thrill (for the sheer joy of it). Finally the "battered woman" syndrome has emerged as a legal defence for homicide, either as self-defense or as a pre-emptive strike. Lane listed, rather morbidly, almost 200 female murderers and serial killers from around the world. This is not a complete list, obviously, but it included Léone Bouvier of France who shot her boyfriend. When asked: "Why did you kill him?" she replied: "I loved him" (Lane, 2006:68).

The Black Widow killers refers both to the spider, which kills its mate, and to the colour of funereal custom. Among the most notorious of these were Mary Cotton of England who poisoned four husbands, her mother, her sister-in-law and countless (perhaps 10) children and step-children. She was hanged in 1873. Initially these mass murders were committed for the insurance monies, later – nobody knows (Klein, 2003; Lane, 2006).

Nannie Doss (1905–65), originally from Alabama, killed four husbands, two children, a granddaughter, her mother, two sisters and a grandson by poisoning them with arsenic. She was not suspected ever, until 1954, when her last husband died the day he was released from hospital, after 23 days there, suffering from stomach pains. The autopsy revealed the arsenic. She made money on some, but not all of the murders, but explained the spousal homicides to investigators: "I was looking for the perfect mate, the real romance of life" (Grieg, 2006:12–14).

Belle Gunness was an early black widow killer. She and her husband initially collected insurance money on her home which burned down, twice, and her store, once, then her husband suddenly died and the grieving widow was able to collect on two life insurance policies. Her second husband also died tragically; fortunately his life was also insured. She never married again, but began advertising for suitors, with money to invest in her farm in La Porte, Indiana. Unfortunately one day in 1908 her house caught fire. Three bodies were found in the house, and 14 more, mostly in the hog pen, including her foster daughter. She escaped and is thought to be the first female serial killer in the United States (Grieg, 2006:15–7).

In Los Angeles Helen Golay (77) and Olga Rutterschmidt (75) were dubbed the "Black Widows". They habitually befriended homeless men, took out insurance policies on their lives, murdered them, and were sentenced to life in 2008 (*Gazette* 16.7.08).

Second, the Angel of Death Killers: women who murder in the comfort zone of their hospital or nursing home. These include nurse Beverley Allitt, who murdered four infants in her care and injured nine others from 1991–3 in England. Suffering from Munchausen's Syndrome by Proxy, she is now serving 13 life sentences in a top-security mental institution (Klein, 2003:199). Nursing homes, boarding houses and hospitals are archetypal sites of nurturing; but Dorothy Fuentes ran a boarding house in Sacramento where she poisoned eight men and women for their social security benefits, and was arrested in 1987. Genene Jones, a pediatric nurse, murdered about 40 infants in Texas in 1981–2 (Pearson, 1997). In Austria four female nursing assistants at Vienna's largest hospital were accused of killing at least 42 patients in 1988 and 1989, and suspected of many more before that. They were only discovered by accident when a doctor heard Waltraud Wagner, the leader of the team, boasting in a bar. All were found guilty and sentenced to various terms of imprisonment (Lane, 2006).

Former nurse Kristen Gilbert was accused of four murders and three attempted murders (all men), in a Massachusetts hospital between 1995 and 1996 (*National Post*, 21.11.00). And Lucy de Berk, a Dutch nurse, was found guilty of killing three children and an elderly woman, and of three attempted murders in a hospital between 1997 and 2001. She was acquitted of 11 other murder charges and sentenced to life (*National Post* 25.3.03). Even so, Dr. Harold Shipman killed far more people in England. He was found guilty of 15 murders, suspected of having killed over 200 other people, sentenced to life and committed suicide in jail in 2005.

Jack the Ripper is notorious for having killed five prostitutes in London in the 1880s. Jane Toppan was convicted of poisoning almost 100 patients in a Connecticut nursing home soon afterwards. She stated: "This is my ambition: to have killed more people, more helpless people, than any man or women has ever killed" (Pearson, 1997:146).

An interesting aspect of female violent crime is its invisibility – partly because women commit less violent crime, of course, but also partly because we turn a blind eye to it, or explain it away.[3] Everyone has heard of Jack the Ripper; but who has heard of his contemporary, Jane Toppan, who killed so many more people.

Third, the power killers. Lord Acton famously wrote: "All power tends to corrupt. Absolute power corrupts absolutely." This tends to be true of women, no less than men. It is a characteristic of power, not of gender. Particularly notorious was Ilse Koch, known as The Bitch of Buchenwald. Koch was the wife of the commander of a Nazi concentration camp. Psychotic and sadistic, she engaged in torture and murder, once shooting 24 prisoners in one day, adorned her house with the shrunken heads of prisoners, had skins made into lampshades, and more. Her husband was shot for fraud in his own camp by the Nazis, but she was acquitted. After the war she was arrested, sentenced to life and she committed suicide in prison in 1967, having expressed no sorrow or remorse for her crimes (Twiss, 2002:156–65).

---

3   The second interesting aspect of female homicide is how well defended in law these women are. Farrell has described the 12 defense available to women but not to men: first, the underlying presumption of innocence, then the PMS defense, the battered woman defense, the postpartum depression defense, the mother defense (mothers don't kill their children, so may not be suspected for decades), "the children need me" defense (which does not work for fathers), the "my child, my rights" defense (11% of all U.S. babies are born to drug-abusing mothers, and many die as crack-addicted infants) and so on. Farrell cites examples (1993:254–83).

More recently Elena Ceausescu, the wife of the President of Romania, was shot by firing squad in 1989 after a rule of violence, corruption and abuse. Again, Biljana Plavsic, former Bosnian Serb President, was virulently anti-Muslim, an apologist for ethnic cleansing, and charged by the ICTY, the International Criminal Tribunal for the former Yugoslavia, with crimes against humanity and genocide. The latter charges were dropped after plea-bargaining, and she was sentenced to 11 years which she is now serving in Sweden (BBC News 27.2.03; 28.2.03).

Further back in time, some of the most notorious women include the first century Romans, Valeria Messalina and Agrippina the Younger, Elizabeth Countess Bathory of Hungary (1560–1614), the Empress Tz'his of China (1835–1908), Queen Catherine the Great of Russia (1729–96), and Queen Ranavalona of Madagascar (c. 1785–1863).[4]

Political power conveys enormous power; but so does knowledge of poison, possession of a gun, ownership of a nursing home, work in a hospital, autocratic power in a nation or a prison, and physical strength. Women are rarely mass murderers or serial killers (nor are men), but in 2006 Jennifer Sanmarco shot and killed six workers at a postal sorting office in California, before fatally shooting herself (*NYT* 2.2.06); and police in Mexico arrested Juana Barraza, the notorious Mataviejitas or Little Old Lady Killer – she was fleeing from one murder scene and is suspected of murdering 10 other elderly women (*NYT* 27.1.06).

Fourth, the sado-masochistic killers: Karla Homolka of Canada, Myra Hindley, the Moors murderer in England, and Rose West also of England. All three women worked in tandem with their husbands (Homolka and West) or boy-friend. Karla Homolka and her husband Paul Bernardo, tortured, raped and killed two young girls in 1991, and also killed her own sister. They also videotaped the murders (Pearson, 1997:182–200). In the United Kingdom, Myra Hindley and Ian Brady,

---

4   Messalina (AD 26–48) and Agrippina (AD 16–c55) were contemporaries and rivals in Rome, and would have known each other. Messalina was the first wife of the Emperor Claudius, until he had her killed for her violence and infidelities, and Agrippina was his fourth wife, until she (probably) poisoned him to put her son Nero on the imperial throne – until he had her killed for plotting against him, attempting incest with him, and her own history of homicide (Klein, 2003:35–55). It is Messalina and Lucrezia Borgia whose names have reached down the ages as the epitome of feminine evil; but in fairness, Caligula (Messalina's brother), Nero and Lucrezia's brother Cesare Borgia were far worse.

Elizabeth Countess Bathory enjoyed almost absolute power on her estate in Transylvania. Wealthy, highly intelligent and a famous beauty, her particular enjoyment was torturing her servants and local peasant girls to death, by various means – 650 of them according to her records. Complaints eventually reached the Hungarian Parliament and the Holy Roman Emperor, the Archduke Matthias II. After an investigation, the Countess' castle was raided, several bodies were found, and the Countess and some of her servants were arrested, tried and found guilty. She was walled into her cell and died in prison (Twiss, 2003:109–118). But the crimes of the sadistic Countess pale against the crimes of her near contemporary and near neighbour, Prince Vlad the Impaler (1431–76) of Wallachia, now Romania.

the "Moors Murderers" were convicted of three murders and suspected of two others, which were later confirmed, in the early sixties. Hindley died in prison (Klein, 2003:163–76). Also in the U.K., Rose West was convicted of murdering eight women, and two of her own children, in the 70s and 80s. Arrested in 1992 with her husband, who committed suicide in prison, she is still in prison (Klein, 2003:126–39; Grieg, 2006:57–61).

Fifth, the robbery killers, often gangsters like Ma Barker shot by the FBI after a crime spree in 1936, Machinegun Molly (Monique Sparvieri), shot by police in Montreal in 1967, and Bonnie Parker, who was shot to death with Clyde Barrow in 1935. Aileen Wuornos, convicted of the murder of six men for their money, and sometimes their cars, was executed in 2002. The film "Monster" portrayed her as something of a victim – which is the chivalric as well as the feminist norm for portraying (and excusing) female crime.

Sixth, the child killers are exemplified by Waneta Hoyt. She was charged with murdering five of her six children between 1964 and 1971. Her lawyers attributed these deaths to SIDS, then relatively unknown, and she was acquitted; but in 1994 she confessed and was sentenced to life (Klein, 2003:114–25). Marie Noe eventually confessed to killing eight of her 10 children by smothering them. By going to different doctors and different hospitals – and different insurance companies – she avoided detection for years, and the deaths were attributed to SIDS. The Allitt case in the U.K. and the Hoyt case in the U.S. however inspired journalistic attention and she was sentenced to 20 years probation in 1999. Susan Smith drowned her two sons in her car in South Carolina in 1994: she strapped them in, drove the car into a lake, and said they had been kidnapped by black males (Pearson, 1997). Andrea Yates drowned her five children in the bathtub in Texas in 2001. Her husband, whom she called right away, explained that she was depressed, and blamed her doctor and the hospital for the murders (*Time* 2.7.01:25). In Germany a woman has been charged with killing nine of her new-born babies born between 1988 and 1999 (*New York Times* 3.8.05).

Two other well-known American cases should be mentioned: Lizzie Borden, who undoubtedly killed her parents in Massachusetts in 1892, probably for the inheritance. But two victims at the same time does not classify as mass murder nor serial killing. Likewise Brenda Spencer, who killed the principal and the janitor of her school one Monday morning in 1979, and then shot and wounded nine children and a police officer. She famously explained :"I just started shooting. That's it. I just did it for the fun of it. I just don't like Mondays" (Smith, 2003: Klein, 2003).

Finally, terrorists now include female suicide bombers who have killed so many in India, Sri Lanka, Israel, Russia and Iraq: a relatively new and stereotypically unexpected phenomenon. Terrorists have been known to disguise themselves as women, but for women to deliberately kill others has surprised many with unrealistic stereotypes, and has required new security standards.

The German Baader-Meinhof gang, also known as the Red Army Faction, was responsible for 30+ murders in the 1970s and 1980s. Particularly notorious was Brigitte Mohnhaupt, who served 24 years in prison after being convicted of involvement in nine murders and expressed no remorse.

The new wars are still fought primarily between men and men, but increasingly, as civilians are targeted by female bombers, they have become Hobbesian wars of all against all. These days we have to re-think women *and* men.

Certainly women do not murder so many people as men do, and only the most exemplary female murderers have been mentioned here but most men and most women do not commit murder. The current stereotyping of men as "the death sex" (Miles, 1991), and of violence as "the foundation of our concept of masculinity" (Neroni, 2003:58) is both inaccurate and misandric.

In the United States, 26% of intimate homicides were committed by women: 442 men were murdered as against 1,252 women (U.S. Bureau of Justice Statistics, Homicide Trends, 2002:1–4). So while female intimates were three times more likely to be killed by men, women nonetheless murdered over one-quarter of these intimate victims.

Furthermore about 17% of known serial killers in the United States have been women; and at least 25 have been arrested and convicted from 1972 to 1997, including many of those mentioned above (Pearson, 1997). Serial is defined as more than three victims and solo operators.

Similarly in Canada 594 murders were committed in 2007: 432 were men and only 162 were women; 90% of the accused were men, but 10% were women. In terms of "spousal violence" (spousal defined as married, common-law, separated or divorced), 51 women were murdered and 13 men: women committed 20% of these killings (Li, 2008).[5]

One of the first to discuss women as villains was Anne Jones in *Women Who Kill* (1981); but despite the title, the book was basically exculpatory of women, suggesting that on the rare occasions on which they were driven to kill, it was usually in self-defence or in defence of the children – or, they may have been innocent. Even a more recent research report "Moms Who Kill" explains that post-partum depression and depression "can escalate to dangerous levels" and to murder. The bottom line, as with Jones, is that it's not their fault. Men, on the other hand, "far more frequently" "kill their children out of vengeance and rage against the other parent" (Levy, Sanders and Sabrow, 2002:64). Apparently this is their fault and they are not depressed – the authors do not address the issues of divorce, loss of wife, children, home and income simultaneously, as well as parental alienation; nor do they present any data at all. The research seems to reflect (and reinforce) the familiar dichotomy of women as

---

5   I asked my students to guess what percentage of spousal homicides were committed by men. The consensus was about 96–8%. When handed the latest statistics of 20% committed by the women they were surprised, horrified and then defensive. "Yeah but they must have had a reason: self defence or to defend their children … abused when young etc." All too true, much as for men, plus angry, jealous, drunk or on drugs, or for the money, the usual unhappy list. But what is as surprising as the reflex defensiveness is the intensity of the belief in the bi-polar myth of women/good ("They don't kill unless they have to!") and men/bad.

victims (of depression) and men as angry, vengeful villains, again. This does seem to be ideology disguised as science.

Most women are not serial killers, of course, nor murderers – nor are most men, misandry to the contrary notwithstanding. Nonetheless many scholars have recently begun to focus on female violence.[6] The findings are disillusioning for those who assert that women are angels, and innocent victims, or assert, like Montessori and Montagu, the myth of female moral supremacy. Indeed the history of female villains – or evil women, in the new terminology – is long and bloody; not as long nor as bloody as the list of evil men, given the power differentials, but more surprising, given the stereotypes, and often surprisingly invisible – which is why the stereotypes persist.

A California social worker involved in the Fuentes case explains: "I was real naïve about evil. I kept it very far away from me" (Pearson, 1997:174). She may have been naïve about evil, but she was also naïve about women. So socialized was she into the binary ethic of women as nurturing angels, that she could not believe that a woman could murder people. She could not believe that women could be villains, predators, killers. A more humanistic, realistic and egalitarian paradigm could have saved so many lives.[7]

Conclusion

The relations between gender and power are therefore complex, elusive and ubiguitous; but it is as well to try to grasp them, or we are in danger of living in the unrealistic worlds of stereotypes or identity politics.

I have tried to make a number of points in this chapter: to critique the conventional feminist model of gender relations, the patriarchy; to offer a power model of intersectionality, relating gender to other variables; to emphasize a vertical model of power cross-cut by a horizontal model of love – which distinguishes gender relations from other types of intergroup relations; to emphasize the fragmentation and heterogeneity of both men and women as groups; and to recognize a complex power structure crossed by our three paradigm moral perspective. Men and women may be heroes, villains or victims, although the dimensions of each vary widely.

---

6   Such scholars include Sommers, 1994; Farrell, 1993, 1999; Langan and Dawson, 1998; Pearson, 1997; Jones, 1981; Levy, Sanders and Sabrow, 2002; Twiss, 2003; Smith, 2003; Klein, 2003; and the pioneers: Straus, Gelles and Steinmetz, 1980, who received death threats for their work. For an annotated bibliography of violence studies on both sexes, see Farrell, 1999:323–9.

7   This echoes the remark of a woman who escaped from the serial killer Ted Bundy (who killed over 30 women) but said: "He didn't look like a murderer." But he was. And what does a murderer look like? There is no "M" tattooed on the forehead. Our idea is that he is ugly and male. That the murderer might be charming (like Bundy) or female is part of the problem.

All this presents a more realistic evidence-based theoretical framework for thinking about gender than I was taught; and much of it today is still very biased against men.

To summarize these matters of power: certainly some men do have enormous power: political, economic, religious etc. – as do some, but fewer, hegemonic women. Equally certainly, the most powerless people are also men: homeless, addicted, in prison, injured, dying and dead: you're not too powerful if you're dead! And betrayed by our health and education systems, and crippled by family and criminal legal systems, and welfare systems, "stiffed" by the changes in the economic systems, and demonized in popular culture and by misandric feminists and pro-feminists. So there is a lot happening in the gender world: heroic men and women, victimized men and women and villainous men and women. The calculus of power, good and evil, suffering and donation, tax and dividend, is difficult and will be personal.

Chapter 7
Theorizing Men

Theorizing men is not easy, not only because there are so many men (about 3.3 billion) and of so many types (the first typology dates back to Plato, as we have seen) in so many cultures which value various masculinities, according to their needs (Gilmore, 1990; Connell, 1995) – but also because there are so many theorists who so often disagree with each other. The resultant of all this may be some confusion, but also some enlightenment.

So, while we cannot offer one grand theory of men and masculinity (or masculinities), we can at least review some of the main themes in the contemporary theorizing of men, consider the evidence and counter-evidence favouring (or not) these theories, and readers can decide for themselves how to juggle the various ideas, insights and perspectives for themselves.

The theorists on men usually divide into two opposed teams: those who are male-positive and those who are male-negative. The former tend to emphasize men's hard work, altruism, self-sacrifice not only for their families but also for their communities and their countries. The military, police and fire-fighters may be seen as heroes not because of their deaths but because of their volunteering and risking their lives for others. The latter tend to view men as violent, oppressive of women, sexist and misogynistic, homophobic, perhaps emotionally stunted, work-obsessed and so on. Some of these male-negative theorists have already been described as misandrists, though we noted the realities of both heroes and villains, which legitimize both perspectives yet also limit the validity of each.

The second division which overlaps with the first is between those who emphasize power, the hegemonic male, the patriarchal dividend etc. – notably Connell; and those who emphasize powerlessness, and men in crisis: the disposable male, the soft male and the wars against men and boys (in order, Farrell, Bly, Hite and Sommers). This is the binary model both of gender (male supremacism) and of masculinity (alpha to omega, high MQ to low MQ), and coincides somewhat with villains (as abusers of power) and victims (as having some commonalities with women).

The *moral* perspective on men: positive or negative, princes or pigs, and the *structural* perspective: victors or victims, on top or at the bottom, are both prevalent in the literature. There is certainly a middle ground not only in the masculinization of women and the feminization of men, but also in the post-modern critique of the binary gender system, and also in the personal emotional and loving relations that often cross-cut the political perspectives.

That said, some gender theorists emphasize the victimization of women, others the victimization of men. Some say misogyny is the problem, others say misandry is the main problem now, at least in Euro-America. Some complain about violence by men, others foreground the violence *against* men, not only physical but also systemic. Some declare that there is a war against women (Vallee, 2007; Faludi, 1992; French, 1992), while others insist that there is a war against men (Hite, 2004) and boys (Sommers, 2000).

Power and powerlessness, love and hate, equality and inequality, similarity and difference – these are some of the issues the theorists debate as they re-think men and women. Historically our thinking has developed along dialectical lines: from male supremacism to female (moral) supremacism in both first and second wave feminism. Given the thesis and the anti-thesis, we might be expecting an egalitarian synthesis very soon. But this third stage has not emerged yet, and whether the sides are still polarizing or are beginning to converge is not yet clear. What is clear, however, is that there are two sides – or more. This chapter is therefore in the nature of pulling things together, seeing if a synthesis is possible between these two polar lenses and between feminist and masculinist perspectives. (Of course a synthesis is possible, intellectually, but emotionally is another matter. Many people hold grimly onto their convictions, ideologies and identities as to truth and a lifeline.)

In this chapter we will review some of the principle recent theorists on men, in all their rich and varied colours and contradictions, compare some of the men's movements which have arisen in recent years, and finally attempt to effect a synthesis within these orientations, and a gender-inclusive synthesis with feminism.

Theorists

Here we will review seven contemporary theorists of men, who themselves see men through different lenses. There are others, of course, but the selection is not totally arbitrary: each has made important contributions. The seven are Robert Bly, Warren Farrell, Michael Kimmel, Lionel Tiger, Robert/ Raewyn Connell and Paul Nathanson and Kathy Young.

Robert Bly

The beginning of the men's movement is often attributed to Bill Moyers' wonderful interview with the poet, Robert Bly, and to the publication of Bly's book, Iron John in 1990 (Moyers, 1990:267–84). This was not the first book to discuss men in crisis, nor to attempt to define the crisis; but it was the first to be on the *New York Times* best-seller list for 30 weeks. The mytho-poetic movement which Bly founded was based broadly on a Freudian–Jungian approach to men.

Bly attributed the emerging men's movement to "grief" that emerged with the Industrial Revolution. "It sent the father out of the home to work, " and the father has been absent from the sons and daughters ever since (Moyers, 1990:267). The women's movement helped some men to notice their feminine side but, he added: "In the seventies I began to see all over the country a phenomenon that we might call the "soft male" ... They're lovely, valuable people – I like them – they're not interested in harming the earth or starting wars ... But many of these men are not happy. You quickly notice the lack of energy in them. They are life-preserving but not exactly life-giving" (1990:2–3).

Fathers may be absent in many ways: they may be lost to work, to drugs or alcohol, to prison, to divorce or separation, or to emotional aridity, or to death. But too many are absent in too many ways, and boys (and girls) are paying for it. He coined the phrase "father hunger" to describe this phenomenon. Boys do not know how to be men, so they may join gangs as a substitute family and peer group. Bly's own father was absent from his family through alcoholism, which no doubt sensitized him to the issue of father absence. Since then this concern with absent fathers, and the negative consequences of this, have been examined by others (Popenoe (1996), Blankenhorn (1996), Braver (1998) and, of course, Faludi (1999)).

Bly also discussed how the psycho-sexual development of boys differed from girls. Using mythology and Jungian psychology to make his points (rather than case studies, which raised some hackles) he suggested that boys suffer two deep wounds in childhood: first the separation from the mother from whom they had so long been a part, as they realize that the genders are different, indeed opposite. The boy cannot become (like) his mother, as his sister can: in time, she can walk in her mother's shoes, literally. Second, the separation from his father also as, in adolescence, the boys realize somehow that they have to establish their own independence and autonomy even from their own fathers. They have to break away. Hence the frequency and indeed necessity of the adolescent rebellions (of both sexes) which cause parents so much worry. These psychic wounds are clear in mythology, and were developed further by Robert Johnson (1998); it takes time for these (hidden) wounds to heal, and it usually takes a woman (who is sometimes unfortunately confused with the mother), and other men.

These theories of the "soft" male, the absent fathers and the wounded boys were of course criticized. As was his suggestion that single mothers can raise babies to boys, but cannot raise boys to manhood. They need male help. His solutions were twofold: to encourage male-male communication to help heal their common wounds or, in more usual terms, to deal with common problems; so he set up seminars, conferences and retreats in the woods – he was keen on a return to nature and the outdoors as part of the neglected male psyche and he founded the ManKind project. He insisted on the importance of male mentoring, not just at work, everywhere – from coaching to saying thanks to workers for a job well done: spreading joy, but also being substitute fathers to other men and boys.[1]

---

1   Hagan (1994), Kimmel (1995), Faludi (1991) and Whelehan (1995) are critical of Bly and the Mythopoetic movement. Barton's (2000) anthology is very positive.

The movement has been criticized for class, race and heterosexual biases in its constituencies, but it has also been praised for its contribution to those who participated in this "men's work." One researcher, Michael Schwalbe, explained: The men "didn't know what to do with criticism of them as men. This criticism seemed unfair in light of the support the men had given to women's causes and to individual women in their lives." He added that: "They wanted to feel better about themselves as men, to learn more about their feelings and psychic energies ..., to live richer and more complex emotional lives, and to experience the rare pleasure and mysterious power of communities" (Barton, 2000:143, 145).

Warren Farrell

Where Bly suggested that men were victims of absent fathers, the Industrial Revolution and psychic wounds, Warren Farrell offered an alternative perspective. Farrell described men as "the disposable sex". He has had an interesting career trajectory. He was on the board of the National Organization of Women (NOW) in New York City for three years and was much in demand, and well paid, as a pro-feminist speaker. As the years passed and his feminist friends divorced, he realized that he had been talking to women, rather than listening to men; so he started listening, and realized that men had another point of view. Men did not have all the power, hence the title of his book: *The Myth of Male Power: Why Men are the Disposable Sex* (1993) – in sum, how men are victims too. He reviewed men as the suicide sex, the imprisoned sex, the executed sex, the homeless sex , the victims of war, the victims of violence, the victims of their jobs – the "death professions" and "the glass cellar", the victims of double standards in legislation (homicide, violence, family and divorce, the draft), and finally the victims of ill-health and early deaths. He adds that: "Men's victimizer status camouflages men's victim status" (1993: 357). Indeed the misandric feminist obsession with men as villains and as victimizers of women (and men's obsessions with women's concerns, and votes) has camouflaged the equally important realities of men as victims and of women also as villains and victimizers, and of both as occasionally heroic.

Farrell defines himself as a humanitarian and an egalitarian, and he is particularly eloquent on the oppression of men. "We have long acknowledged the slavery of blacks. We have yet to acknowledge the slavery of males" (1993:70). The point is overstated and rhetorical, and black males might find it insulting, particularly since it was so often the white males who enslaved the black males in the slave trade and in slavery, and who so often still may be racist and discriminate against black males. To see the slavery of males, black and white, however, look down, not up, as suggested earlier. Both black and white males are slaves to societal demands of men and to their own self-concepts as providers.

Farrell does emphasize the beneficial contributions of feminism to social life (1993:13–4), but there have been costs to feminism – notably a gender-exclusive approach to equity. Farrell, like Bly, uses the language of wounds: "The wound that unifies all men is the wound of their disposability. Their disposability as soldiers, workers, dads." (1993:355). He concludes with proposals for an Equal Life Opportunity Commission, and fundamentally: we need "to go beyond women as sex objects and men as success objects to both sexes as objects of love" (1993:371).

Farrell's more recent work includes his *Women Can't Hear What Men Don't Say* (1999), which moves from male disposability, victim masculinism and his emphasis on the need for equal gender rights to a discussion of contemporary misandry and a plea for men to communicate their feelings and needs i.e. *not* to say "Yes, dear" – so often suggested as the requirement for a happy marriage. Finally he entered into a dialogue with John Sterba, self-defined as "a feminist's feminist" in the not-too-happily titled *Does Feminism Discriminate against Men?* (2008): not too happily because much of men's crisis or pain has more to do with men and ideals of masculinity than feminism, so it's a false question. In any event, the debate was a dialogue of the deaf, in the sense that both made their arguments but never attempted a synthesis or a consensus, unfortunately. The book is valuable as a clear presentation of opposite paradigms.

Both Bly and Farrell are clearly in the male-positive camp, and also are concerned with the "crisis": variously defined as "the soft male", "the disposable male" and "the silent male" with multiple causalities in the long and short term: the Industrial Revolution, absent fathers, societies' lethal expectations and male altruism, double standards, cultural and feminist misandry, male silence and stoicism.

Others see men very differently.

Michael Kimmel

Today a prominent author in Men's Studies is Michael Kimmel. Kimmel is Professor of Sociology at SUNY and the author or editor of numerous books, including *Manhood in America* (1996), *The Politics of Manhood* (1995), a critique of Bly, *The History of Men* (2005) and recently *Guyland* (2008). He is also the editor of the journal *Men and Masculinities* and national spokesperson for NOMAS: the National Organization of Men Against Sexism – male sexism that is. So he is a prolific writer and a very hard worker: extremely influential, and self-identified as pro-feminist.

Kimmel's general orientation is that men should be more like women. This is his solution to all, or most, of men's problems, and perhaps a popular one with feminists who teach the courses that use the books. Most women, however, do not identify as feminists (*Time* 9.3.1992:42; 29.6.1998:52), so pro-feminist men are in the interesting position of identifying with an ideology and a label that is rejected by most women. This is ironic. Perhaps feminists and pro-feminists should spend more time listening to women.

Kimmel was one of the first to emphasize the social construction of masculinities: "Masculinity is socially constructed, changing (1) from one culture to another, (2) within any one culture over time, (3) over the course of any individual man's life, and (4) between and among different groups of men depending upon class, race, ethnicity, and sexuality" (1992:166). This is useful, and I would add that (5) masculinity is also biologically constructed, (6) cultures tend to reinforce the biological gender variance, and (7) masculinities are remarkably similar the world over – including the variations by age, class and culture, as Gilmore (1990) has emphasized, and as the Adjective Check List and the dictionary definitions confirm.

Kimmel is deeply critical of some who address men's issues: "It is a strange dialect that speaks to the pain of men and not the pain men cause" (1992:170). Yet surely not so strange. The pain caused by men to women has been discussed for centuries, and in exquisite detail. The pain of men has been largely ignored, and still is.

Ideally, no doubt, books on gender would speak to the pains – as well as the glories and achievements – of both men and women. However the history of gender has been about "the pain men cause." It is certainly time to listen to men who are often stoic, and, as Farrell (1999) noted, often not communicative about their needs and desires. It is time to listen to black men (Eckholm, 2006; Merida, 2007; as well as Malcolm X and Martin Luther King), and low-income men in Mexico (Gutmann, 1996) and all sorts of men (Brown, 2005), and soldiers and men paralyzed – there is both pain and pride there, and love. Such men bear little resemblance to the men of misandric feminism and pro-feminists.

Kimmel characterizes contemporary men as "Wimps, Whiners and Weekend Warriors" (1996:291) – all cracks at Bly and the mythopoetic movement; and he portrays "many men" as concerned only "with the size of their bulges – from bulging wallets to bulging muscles to bulging crotches" (1996:331). Not only is this insulting, but we know he could make no such negative generalizations about any other group, not women, not blacks or Jews, not the disabled, not the genitals, only men. But perhaps these sorts of remarks cement his credentials as a certain type of bona fide pro-feminist. Yet critical thinking might suggest that women are also concerned "with the size of their bulges", from lips to breasts to hips. It is not PC to mention this, but Kimmel's sexism does him (and feminism) no credit. One can be pro-male as well as pro-female; indeed surely we should be.

In the Epilogue to *Manhood in America* he states: "American men remain bewildered by the sea-changes in our culture, besieged by the forces of reform, and bereft by the emotional impoverishment of our lives" (1996:330). Bewildered, besieged and bereft: the three Bs. Evidently there is little consensus between Bly, Farrell and Kimmel, all writing in the United States about men.

He concludes that: "The American manhood of the future cannot be based on obsessive self-control, defensive exclusion, or frightened escape… We need a democratic manhood" (1996:333). As if "American manhood" is currently based on this trinity! – and in this nation that virtually invented the ideology and eventually the practice of democracy.

NOMAS, according to its mission statement, is "committed to justice" and "working to make this nation's ideals of equality substantive." These are excellent goals, but to my mind Kimmel is both misandric and male-negative, and negates these goals. In the second edition of *Manhood in America* he did at least delete his Preface, which was mentioned earlier – but he added an even more misandric chapter. His contempt for most men, seems to have deepened over the decade. He writes lyrically and his prose sparkles, but the substance of his work seems flawed as he characterizes the changes in men since his first edition as "From Anxiety to Anger" (2006:216). Not to be condescending, but he is unintentionally quite funny as he describes his version of the new millennium man:

> We're pumping up and working out obsessively to make our bodies impervious masculine machines ... while we adorn ourselves with signifiers of a bygone era of unchallenged masculinity, donning Stetson cologne, Chaps clothing and Timberland boots as we drive in our Cherokees and Denalis to conquer the urban jungle. We sought to block women's entry into the military ... And we ran off to the woods with the mythopoetics, rallied at sports stadiums with Promise Keepers, and spent our leisure time in upscale topless bars ... (2006:216).

We who? What about "our" Old Spice and Subarus and mowing the lawn, and I don't think Montreal has any "upscale" topless bars. Oh well. The man is clearly very angry about American male anger.

Lionel Tiger

Professor of Anthropology at Rutgers, Lionel Tiger is most well-known as the author of *Men in Groups* (1969) and the concept of "male bonding" – in sports, the military and at work. He returned to the subject of men in *The Decline of Males* (1999). He argues that the decline really began, not with the rise of feminism (as Hise, 2004, suggests), nor with the structural changes in the U.S. economy (as Faludi, 1999, argues), but with the female contraceptive. The other processes accelerated but did not initiate the decline. He points to the following familial and societal changes over the last 50 years since the pill: the fallen fertility rate, the rise in the abortion rate, the increased number and proportion of single mothers, the increased female participation rate in the labour force, the rise in the divorce rate, the fall in "paternity certainty" and the rise in DNA testing of newborns and the increased role of the state in the family: welfare, child support, alimony, divorce courts, legislation of all sorts. Men have been increasingly marginalized in reproduction, and also from production, since the pill (1999: 27, 249). All this stems from the advent of the pill, which gave women control over reproduction and freed them from their biology for the labour market. From children to work in 50 years. Tiger adds that there really is a battle of the sexes based on their different interests, and that women are winning the war – although they may not be happy with the victory. There are battles over family, jobs, incomes and reputation, and men are not even aware of the battles or the stakes. Men have not organized themselves effectively. There is no national equivalent of NOW to articulate men's concerns or interests or to apply political pressure where needed (1999:9). Furthermore he suggests that men have already been replaced in the family by the state in a relationship which is not polygamy but "bureaugamy." Of feminism he remarked: "An ideology devoted to one sex won't suffice" (1999:259). But of course it did for decades, and still does for some.

Tiger does offer some recommendations for a child and family centered policies (1999: 259–66), but does not suggest that they would reverse the decline of males. A couple of points are worth noting: first, Tiger hardly considers other scholars who have advanced their own theories about men. There are no references to Bly, Farrell or Connell, and only passing reference to Faludi and to Kimmel, whom he accuses of "sentimental naivete" (1999:74) – but this is invective, not a critique. Nor did he discuss such man-killers as homicide and suicide which, on the face of it, seem like evidence of men in crisis. Furthermore, Andrew Kimbrell's (1995) recommendations for father friendly policies, as well as Glenn Cartwright's (1993) on Parental Alienation Syndrome, would be useful additions to Tiger's insights.

The decline of males, such as it is, is not just about the pill – an invention – it is what women did with it: swallowed it, reduced their fertility rates, entered the labour market, competed for jobs, increased their incomes, educational qualifications and the divorce rate, lobbied for protective special legislation, and shifted the balance of power. The pill made this possible, but the revolution in gender relations was ideological; and the etiology was not only the pill but also the decline of fathering as bureaugamy rose, the decline of the primary and secondary sectors of the economy, the rise of women's rights often at the expense of men's, the rise of misandry, and male democratic support of women's mobility and empowerment.

Robert Connell/Raewyn Connell

Raewyn Connell is a prolific author with at least 15 books in 25 years on a wide variety of topics. He (as he then was) established his reputation in Men's Studies with the publication of his well received *Masculinities* in 1995 and followed it up with *The Men and the Boys* in 2000 and *Gender* in 2002. Then he had gender re-assignment surgery and became Raewyn Connell.

Connell certainly deserves credit for developing and popularizing the field, already initiated by the psychologists Joseph Pleck and Jack Sawyer (1974), Warren Farrell (1974), and Pleck (1981), and sociologists Mirra Komarovsky (1976) and Jack Nichols (1975). Arriving so soon after Bly's popular work, and as attention was beginning to shift after the second wave from women to men, the alleged problematic cause of the wave, Connell was the 'right' man (i.e. pro-feminist) at the right time. In scholarship, as in sex, timing is everything.

The Men and the Boys is a collection of essays covering a wide range of topics. She describes the five prevailing approaches to masculinity: psychoanalytic theory, developed by Freud, postulates relatively fixed gender identities, biologically determined. Sex-role theory, articulated in functionalism and developed by

Talcott Parsons (and Margaret Mead), admits flexibility and fluidity based on socialization. Social constructionism shifted the emphasis to cultural determinism, based on detailed ethnographic research. Connell adds the Mythopoetic movement, which she dismissed as "pop psychology" and the Promise Keepers, dismissed as "extreme simplifications" – and both are described as "masculine fundamentalism: on a continuum from soft to hard, where hard is the militia movement and the Taliban" (2000:5–9, 58). One gathers that she did not like them. A sixth approach would be his own: pro-feminist and anti-male.

Connell asserts that gender relations are "projects" achieved within "gender regimes" of specific institutions and within the gender order of a particular society, which is itself within a global gender order. She is well known for her concept of "plural masculinities" which may be hegemonic or subordinate (including "sissies," gays, ethnic minorities, and high school drop-outs), but also protest, frontier, military and transnational business masculinities. The idea of multiple masculinities is useful and demolishes the idea that "men are all the same," endemic to so many writers on men from Solanas to Kimmel. This had been developed before by Plato, Weber, Hite, Bly and others, but Connell's exposition was timely. He rejected the idea of a "core" masculinity as essentialist, though we have seen it defined in dictionaries, the Adjective Check List as well as Gilmore's comparative research. Plus it is not clear how many plural masculinities there are, what their components may be, nor the boundaries between them.

Equally controversial, she insists that: "The world gender order is patriarchal, in the sense that it privileges men over women. There is a 'patriarchal dividend' arising from unequal wages, unequal labour-force participation, and a highly unequal structure of ownership, as well as cultural and sexual privileging" (2000:46). In his view, globalization – defined as imperialism and colonialism – has, through male violence, oppressed women and subordinate populations and created a hierarchy of masculinities (2000:48). Then, she says, the suffragettes "forced concessions from the state" resulting in two types of responses from men: backlash with Bly's work and the Promise Keepers, and pro-feminism with groups like NOMAS (2000:5–5). And she complains about "the toxic consequences of contemporary masculinities" (2000:66). This is not an equity theorist. All men are toxic? There are no beneficial consequences? No good men?

Men must change, she argues. "Men's gender practices raise large questions of social justice, given the scale of economic inequality, domestic violence, and institutional barriers to women's equality ..." She adds: "The list could go on ..." (2000:200). Sure, and it could be a different list too. Placing himself, as he then was, in a martyr role, he suggests that "Men who try to develop a politics in support of feminism ... are not in for an easy ride." But as a fighter for social justice he will "press on into the flames" (2000:204). And seemingly justice is defined by feminism, even though most women, at least in the States, do not self-define as feminists, and the criticisms of many neo-feminists, dissident feminists and critical feminists have all been ignored.

Connell can be interrogated from many angles: that the men he accuses of backlash also see themselves as fighting for justice; that men have knocked down most of the "barriers to women's equality" as the 2008 U.S. election proved; indeed most of the "inequalities" in the developed world are matters of choice, not discrimination; that some women are also violent, especially at home, and especially to their children; the suffragettes did not *force* concessions: the last century witnessed this peaceful transfer of power, as quite voluntary. This was not like the American, French and Russian revolutions.

Finally this whole theory of the "patriarchal dividend" is questionable, on a number of grounds. First, women are highly privileged in our world, not only with the "Ladies first" and "Women and children first" (which no one on the Titanic said was infantilizing), but in a battery of legislation protective of women. Second, while there are hegemonic men, who no doubt benefit from their hegemony, there are also, and increasingly, hegemonic women, who have perhaps benefited from their privileged status: call this the matriarchal dividend maybe. Third, Connell forgot the "patriarchal tax": the high costs men pay for being men e.g. no special protective legislation, systemic discrimination in the health, education, welfare and justice systems, especially low income and minority men, the draft etc. Indeed his chapters on education and health largely misrepresent the issues and distort the realities. In sympathizing with women as victims and oppressed, Connell largely ignores men as victims and oppressed (even Marx recognized both), ignores hegemonic women (Nobels, PMs, CEOs), ignores "toxic" women, the occasional villains, and ignores men's heroism, sacrifices and donations: the patriarchal donation.

All her fine research and struggles for justice are marred by her ideology and her Cyclops syndrome.

Connell calls for "Gender Reform," which is code for male reform. He called for a "democratic politics of masculine embodiment, a politics directed towards social justice and peace" (2000:65). But no-one argues with goals of justice and peace, though there could be some discussion about how to achieve them. No-one argues about "democratic politics" either. But all this is ideological camouflage for Connell's critique of contemporary masculinities and men.

Connell presented the keynote address to the American Studies Association in 2008, on the theme of "Masculinities and Modern Institutions." She selected for her epigraph a paragraph from Raymond Chandler's *The Little Sister* and titled his paper "A Thousand Miles from Kind" – not a positive note on which to start. The reference was to the police: "hard" – repeated three times, with eyes "like freezing water," "proud of their power, watching always to make it felt," with a stare "not quite cruel and a thousand miles from kind." This negative portrait of stereotypical police as typical of men is surely indicative of how ideology influences scholarship. She could have selected, not an old novel, but recent facts: the number of NYPD who lost their lives helping to evacuate total strangers out of the Twin Towers. This is beyond kindness. Kindness is helping old ladies (or gentlemen) across the road. It is not risking or sacrificing your life for others – as happens so often, as the bravery awards indicate. She could have selected education as an institution and Frank McCourt's wonderful *Teacher Man* as an example of "a thousand watts of kind," or a recent Nobel Peace Prize winner, or any number of wonderful men out there: philanthropists perhaps – but not a paragraph from a 1933 novel! The bias is transparent.

On these gendered (i.e. male led) institutions, she says: "If we want to change the way they function – to prevent war and genocide, to slow down global warming, to pursue social justice, or even to make a small increase in public understanding – we must address those gender issues." Like men make no efforts to prevent war and genocide? Want global warming? Hate social justice? Try to decrease public understanding? It is primarily because of *men's* efforts that war deaths declined so dramatically in the second half of the last century, that global warming is better understood (Nobel Peace Prize winner Al Gore), that global poverty has been reduced, etc. With Connell as with others, if we reverse her assertions, we are often closer to the truth.

Paul Nathanson and Kathy Young

Nathanson is an independent scholar in Montreal, and Young is a professor of history at McGill University. Together they have written two remarkable books: *Spreading Misandry: The Teaching of Contempt for Men in Popular Culture* (2001) and *Legalizing Misandry: From Public Shame to Systemic Discrimination against Men* (2006). These are outstanding works of scholarship which broke new ground in terms of their analysis of misandry in popular culture and in recent legal discussions.

In *Spreading Misandry* the authors review the various types of misandry in the public domain, mostly in film but also in cartoons, on talk shows or by film reviewers and in the press. The chapter titles clarify the main types: "laughing at" men as stupid (e.g. *Home Improvements*, *The Simpsons*) – and Helen Reddy talking about her belief in reincarnation: "I've been a man many times. That's what I'm trying to atone for now" (2001:27), and a listing of misandric joke books. This is misandry as funny. Then there is "looking down" on men, epitomized by Pulitzer Prize winning journalist Anna Quindlen: "It's not that I don't like men; women are just better" (2001:59). This is the theme in much commercial and public television – it's virtually a cultural norm now, acceptable as truth. "Bypassing men" follows logically from alleged female superiority, they are not even necessary or useful as fathers (as the Dan Quayle/"Murphy Brown" debate clarified). *Waiting to Exhale* (1995) and *Fried Green Tomatoes* (1992) are two of the many films in which men were bad or, if good, inadequate while the women were good and heroic, overcoming male obstacles together. The prototype was *Thelma and Louise* (1991). Violence against men, and/or their property (trucks, cars, clothes) is now heroic, laudable and liberating.

More dangerous to men in terms of these portraits of them (or us) as stupid, inadequate, useless and as deserving of vigilante violence, redefined as justice

– more dangerous because of the self-concepts they might develop of themselves, which is the teaching function of the media – are the portraits of men as not only *doing* evil, but as *being* evil. Hence chapters on "blaming men" and "dehumanizing men" for all the evil in the world. This is beyond misandric trivializing and into extreme sexism. At the same time as portraying all men as villains, a consequence in part of so many made-for-television movies which focus on women as victims (who become empowered, sometimes by violence), real female villains and murderers are often portrayed rather sympathetically. *The Burning Bed* (1984), *9 to 5* (1980), *The First Wives Club* (1996) are discussed in this context. Even in 1991 the *Newsweek* film critic Harry Waters was fed up with television's portraits of men as homicidal husbands, abusive lovers, alcoholic fathers, sadistic sons, psychotic doctors, sex-crazed hospital orderlies, even diabolical college professors – with the ABC, NBC and CBS titles listed (2001:141). There is nothing equitable here, but this is a response to market (primarily female) demand. Two of the most inhuman men imaginable are presented in "The Silence of the Lambs" (1991); and the Disney version of "Beauty and the Beast" (1991) argues that "maleness is associated, both metaphorically and literally, with beastliness" (2001:161). The beasts are what men are, in these misandric movies – which might be fair if balanced with female beasts, but they are not. It is the persistent polarizing of men as evil and women as good which is the pattern of misandry; and the authors advise that "Like misogyny, misandry is about hatred, not anger. And hatred is ... a culturally propagated movement" (2001:193).

In their last two chapters, the authors refer to "ideological feminism" as an umbrella term for misandric/superiority/radical/hierarchical/dualistic/essentialist/ militant and gender feminisms, as opposed to equity feminism – which cuts through some terminological discussion. (This equates with the "extreme" feminism of Boyd (2004), and the "gender" feminism and "misguided" feminism of Sommers (1994, 2001). Yet the sexism is largely invisible "because sexism has been defined exclusively in terms of misogyny" (2001:237). And if people recognize misandry – and in my experience equity feminists do, but misandric feminists do not – they have three strategies: "excusing it, justifying it, or trivializing it" (2001:243–7). Ironically, this is precisely what happened in reviews of their book, as the authors demonstrate in their review of the reviews in *Legalizing Misandry* (2006:329–339) – indirect proof that the reviewers did not finish reading the book.

Legalizing Misandry may be seen as the logical consequence in legislation and legal action of all this widespread misandry. The book is divided into four parts. Men on Trial discusses the McMartin Case in California in 1983: a fascinating case of false allegations about child abuse and satanic rituals, widely believed in an extraordinary example of moral panic, mass hysteria and the assumption of male evil, which extended to other cases over a decade. The female accuser who started it all, feeding into misandry, was later institutionalized as a paranoid schizophrenic. Also the well-known Lorena Bobbitt case (1993) who got off with castrating her husband, the Anita Hill-Clarence Thomas case (1991) and the appalling Marc Lépine case: he murdered 14 women at the University of Montreal in 1989. This was the worst mass murder by firearm in Canadian history. The number of women killed, the gender-polarity, and the consternation about "the worst" contributed to an orgy of misandry: the rhetoric of male violence, the tip of the iceberg, and a federal report "The War against Women." The horror was politicized. We are now more used to school massacres; but December 6th is now commemorated with ceremonies across Canada, and memorials to female victims of male violence. (Forget the male victims and ignore the victims of female violence.) Lépine then committed suicide. "It is not accidental in this misogynous society that men kill women," argued one women's studies professor (2006:60). Others saw this as an isolated act of a mad man – but the Lorena Bobbitt defence of "temporary insanity" does not fly with male villains, nor does paranoid schizophrenia. Ann Jones explained: "Men are evil. Women are good" (2006:492).

These four case studies introduce the body of the book in which the authors assert: "Our basic point is that ideological feminism is no longer merely a point of view adopted by a few pretentious journalists or ranting academics. It has become institutionalized. It has become law ... [M]isandry has been legalized – that is, misandry has taken the form of systemic discrimination against men" (2006:79–80). The second section is entitled "Rights on Trial," with chapters on women's rights v. human rights, and maternal rights v. paternal rights. The third, "Sex on Trial," has chapters on pornography and prostitution, sexual harassment and violence against women. Finally, the fourth section, "Society on Trial" has excellent work on ideological feminism v. scholarship, and misandry v. equality. A number of appendices follow, on such topics as child custody, affirmative action, the abuse of statistics, double standards and comparative victimology.

These two volumes are groundbreaking in their solid scholarship as well as their moral initiative in exposing and critiquing misandry, and in the effort to heal the rift, bridge the gaps, between the sexes. There are others out there trying to do the same thing, as we have mentioned earlier, so perhaps the pendulum is slowly swinging back to a humanitarian equity – or perhaps not yet. The authors are pessimistic (2006:326). The third volume, *Transcending Misogyny* should be out soon.

Men's Movements

Men's movements, focusing on men's rights and entitlements, are a relatively recent development, emerging mostly in the United States and principally in the last quarter of the twentieth century with various goals, methods and ideologies.

At the end of the nineteenth century, several models of men and masculinity were embodied in popular culture. While distinct, they were not necessarily mutually exclusive and reflected Victorian concerns with health, work, and moral virtue. The slogan *mens sana in corpore sano* (a healthy mind in a healthy body) summarized a common theme in this range of beliefs and values – a focus on the physical body as determinant of the mind.

Benjamin Franklin presented the model of the self-made man: self-made in terms of wealth and virtue, the former of which he embodied, and the latter he tried to embody. In the U.K. Thomas Carlyle praised the hero in his "Heroes and Hero Worship" (1841), and developed the so-called "great man theory of history." Both he and de Tocqueville were anti-democratic: both were appalled by the excesses of mob rule in the French Revolution, and de Tocqueville had coined the phrase "the tyranny of the majority" to protest both slavery and the Indian Wars. In this they anticipated Friedrich Nietzsche's advocacy of the Superman and individualism. All were congruent with Franklin.

The third model was formulated by Charles Kingsley, an admirer of Carlyle, who is regarded as the founder of Muscular Christianity, a movement which developed in England in the 1850s, migrated to the United States, and died out after World War I. The emphasis on health, fitness and sports was reflected most famously in Thomas Hughes' *Tom Brown's Schooldays* (1857).

Reflecting these different ideals, the same era witnessed the rise of many men's organizations oriented towards business, health, religion, and sports. These included the Kiwanis, the Shriners, the Lions, and the Rotary Club, the YMCA, the Salvation Army and other Christian groups, the Olympic Games (re-invented in 1896) and, soon afterwards, the Boy Scouts (established in 1908 in the U.K. and 1912 in the U.S.). During the early part of the century most of these organizations, events, or sports were either integrated, like the business groups, or developed separate organizations, as with the YMCA/YWCA and the Girl Guides (established in 1912 in the U.S. and 1922 in the U.K.), or separate "leagues" as with sporting events like the Olympic Games (women participated from 1912), Wimbledon and sports teams from the municipality to the university (Putney, 2001).

Countering Kingsley, Cardinal Newman promulgated the ideal of the gentleman, as we have seen. Meanwhile in the States, R.W. Emerson advocated self-reliance as the characteristic American male virtue. Rudyard Kipling made the same point with the poem *If* in England.

By the end of the nineteenth century, the models of the self-made man, the hero, the muscular Christian, the gentleman and the self-reliant, autonomous man, were all presented to young men as worthwhile goals.

After the extension of the franchise to women and then the tectonic shifts of the Depression, the rise of the welfare state and the New Deal, World War II, and the invention of the pill, with their cumulative transformations of society, the second wave of feminism rolled into western shores. The theme was "liberation" rather than the suffrage, as feminists argued that political equality had not brought economic equality. Society was re-defined as patriarchy, male dominance and male-oppression – and misandry began to raise its ugly head, as we have seen, evoking two responses: men's movements and male identity confusion.

Following this second wave, the men's movements emerged, although with partly contradictory approaches to men. In the United States, the modern gay rights movement was galvanized by the 1969 Stonewall riots in New York City, although there had been fledgling anti-discrimination movements in North America from the 1930s to the 1950s. In the U.K. the Wolfenden Commission recommended the legalization of homosexuality in 1957 and it was legalized in the U.K. in 1967 and in Canada in 1974. Lambda Legal was established in the U.S. in 1973 to combat sexual orientation discrimination. The gradual liberalization of attitudes, legislation and policy has already been discussed.

The men's movement also emerged from other concerns during the 1970s. The National Organization of Men against Sexism (NOMAS), formed in 1975, and associated with Michael Kimmel, "advocates a perspective that is pro-feminist, gay affirmative, anti-racist, dedicated to enhancing men's lives and committed to justice." Incorporated in 1985, the organization is "deeply supportive of men who are struggling with the issues of traditional masculinity" and "strongly support[s] the continuing struggle of women for full equality..." (www.nomas.org). In contrast to the John Wayne model of tough, stoic, laconic, traditional masculinity, the "New Age Man" is committed to women's equality and in touch with his emotions.[2]

In contrast to NOMAS, the National Coalition of Free Men (NCFM), founded two years later, is committed to equal rights for men. Its mission is "to foster compassion, respect and understanding for all men," and to look "at the ways that sex discrimination affects men and boys" (www.ncfm.org). Among its concerns are parenting and divorce, Selective Service Registration and the Draft, mental and physical health, education, domestic violence, reproductive rights and paternity fraud, negative media portraits, misandry and more. Although both organizations are concerned with issues of men's health, NCFM is principally concerned with men's rights, and the wrongs done *to* men, and the need to reform society. Warren Farrell is represented on NCFM. (NOMAS is principally concerned with the rights of women, gays and minorities, and the wrongs done *by* men.)

By 1980, then, the gay rights movement, the men's rights movement and men's support for the women's rights movement were all institutionalized, with different policies, aims and goals. Robert Bly arrived on the scene in 1990 with the publication of *Iron John*, founded the mytho-poetic movement and the ManKind Project. The Project runs 38 centers worldwide offering New Warrior Training Adventures to about 3,000 men every year offering to connect head and heart, to turn men from a material life to an interior life, and emphasizing such values as stewardship, responsibility, courage, integrity and masculine energy.

This movement was paralleled in the same year by the formation of the Promise Keepers (PKs) by the University of Colorado football coach Bill McCartney. The PKs were formed to create "godly men" and committed to keeping seven promises: "Honoring Jesus Christ;" "pursuing vital relationships with other men... to help him keep his promises"; "practicing spiritual, moral, ethical and sexual purity"; "building strong marriages and families through love, protection and biblical values"; "supporting his church"; "reaching beyond any racial and denominational

---

2   See the "Statement of Principles" by NOMAS in Kimmel and Messner, 2004:564; also the parallel recommendations of Farrell (1993:355–71) and Kimbrell (1995).

barriers"; and "influencing his world" (www.promisekeepers.org). The movement expanded rapidly with mass rallies at sports arenas across the country, culminating in 700,000 men gathering in Washington in 1997. The movement declined equally rapidly, due perhaps primarily to financial mismanagement, and although the PKs have not created a permanent political movement, they still organize rallies for men (Bartkowski, 2004).

In 1995, Louis Farrakhan and the Nation of Islam, which is very influential within the Black community in the States and the Caribbean, organized the Million Man March. Echoing the 1963 March on Washington led by Martin Luther King, this march called for Black unity, brotherhood, renewed commitment to family, community and nation, and urged participants to register for the vote. Black celebrities from across the States participated, and there was widespread support for the goals of the march. There has been no equivalent march anywhere else in the world on such men's issues.

All six of these men's movements assume that men are in some sort of crisis. However, there is little agreement on the type of crisis. For NOMAS, the issues are primarily women's rights, men's sexism and misogyny and the wrongs done by men, and the problem is traditional masculinity. For NCFM, on the other hand, the issues are primarily men's rights, systemic discrimination against men, misandry and the wrongs done to men. For the gay rights movement the problems are societal: homophobia and systemic discrimination on the basis of sexual orientation. For both the PKs and the Nation of Islam the focus is on the spiritual crisis of men, and although both seek personal rather than political transformation, and they are both faith-based, they are based on different faiths – which are not known for their mutual co-operation and affection – and different racial constituencies too. Finally the Mythopoetic movement does not address systemic discrimination against one sex or the other, foregrounded by some, nor a hypothesized spiritual crisis foregrounded by others, but rather a positive sense of a masculine self.

In sum, the men's movements today are plural, fragmented, contradictory in goals, values and aims, with no sense of common interests and no single national organization. As such though their personal impact may be considerable, their political impact and clout is fairly minimal, especially compared to NOW.

Simultaneously, the *Journal of Men's Studies* was founded in the U.K. in 1992 and *Men and Masculinities* in the U.S. in 1998. These were followed by *Psychology of Men and Masculinities* (2000), *Fathering* (2001), the *International Journal of Men's Health* (2002) and *Thymos: The Journal of Boyhood Studies* (2007). Apart from the journals, the number of books on men and masculinities by both men and women has increased exponentially in the last decade or so.

Men's studies have come of age – perhaps. Certainly more people are thinking about, and re-thinking, men from a range of theoretical and ideological perspectives, concerned variously with men's health and the health system, the education and legal systems, issues around divorce as well as custody and Parental Alienation Syndrome, the justice system (the high male incarceration rates and recidivism rates), high male suicide rates, accident rates and homicide rates, the homeless, misandry, and violence along with a general discussion of male values and culture. Some organizations, mirroring these concerns, have developed with these specific political goals. The Fathers 4 Justice (F4J) movement, for instance, emerged in the U.K. demanding recognition of fathers' rights after divorce, and has spread to much of the world. In Washington, the Men's Health Network highlights the high male death rate, the gender gap in longevity, and the lack of resources invested in men's health. The Innocence Project has been successful in overturning numerous false convictions, almost all male, many on death row.

Some universities now offer courses on men, yet Farrell has cautioned that the few courses in this area are usually "*feminist* men's studies." He adds that: "in feminist studies, women's disadvantages are often seen as men's fault; in feminist men's studies, men's disadvantages are seen as men's fault" (2008:8. His emphasis). He does not pull his punches. "Feminists call it sexism to refer to God as He; they don't call it sexism to refer to the Devil as He" (2008:8). He argues that the goal of men's studies is ultimately, gender transition: "The preparation of the sexes to change together and to replace mistrust with empathy" (2008:12). But we are not there yet. The assault on masculinity continues. Misandry is widespread. Yet he points out that (masculinist) men's studies can help both sexes understand each other better, and with empathy.

Towards a Humanist Synthesis

Clearly there has been little agreement on the theorizing of men, nor on the theorizing of men and women in relation to each other. The differences can be explained partly by ideology and partly by the criteria through which men are theorized. The various orientations can be categorized in two different ways: first, the contrast between feminist and masculinist paradigms (Table 7.1); and second: the contrast within the Men's Movements between the various orientations and perspectives (Table 7.2). No doubt all the authors are sincere, and there is data enough to substantiate all the feminist *and* masculinist positions; but we need to be familiar with all of them. They can all be useful.

Yet comparing the perspectives or common ground of (simplified) feminist and masculinist perspectives is only half the battle. Certainly there are many feminisms. Similarly the principal authors in Men's Studies divide sharply between pro-feminist (Stoltenberg, Connell, Kimmel) and – not anti-feminist but pro-male (which can be a difficult distinction, given the prevalence of misandry): Bly, Farrell, Tiger, Nathanson and Young, as well as Paglia, Sommers and others.

Humanists are doubtless concerned with the legitimate grievances and concerns of both men and women, and the degrees and types of victimization or marginalization. It seems clear that there are more hegemonic males than hegemonic females, both in economics and politics; but also more victim males than victim females. The distribution of status and power for men (if such a broad generalization will be permitted) is a U-curve. At both the hegemonic power end

Table 7.1   Feminist and masculinist paradigms

	FEMINIST	MASCULINIST
SOCIETY	· Patriarchy · Battle of the sexes · War against women · Oppressive and exploitative of women.	· A common struggle for survival. · If patriarchy is so oppressive, it's surprising women live longer! · Society a class/race/ethnic structure oppressive of men too.
WORK	Dimensions of inequality include · Systemic discrimination · Glass ceilings · Glass walls · Unequal pay · 70 cents $ · Sexual harassment · Under-representation at the top · Feminization of poverty · Double load	· Men work longer hours/wk and more weeks/yr. · Affirmative action and equity legislation privilege women. · Men are the slaves to capital (Marx). · 92-96% work fatalities are male. · Over-representation at the bottom:homeless, etc · Masculinization of poverty.
POLITICS	· Women under-represented. · Interests misrepresented. · Priorities (child care, shelters, equal pay) ignored. · Is government of men by men for men.	· Political power exercised for women eg. Equity, Divorce, Custody, Violence legislation. · Note rapid rate of change since 1920s. · Is government by men and women for women.
CRIME	·Men are the criminal sex.	·Women get away with murder. ·12 defences (Farrell).
VIOLENCE	· Violence against women a major problem. · Women live "in fear" (French). · Husband is greatest enemy. · Zero tolerance for VAW.	· Men 2x more likely to be victims of homicide. · Women much safer than men. · VAM institutionalized for fun and profit.

	FEMINIST	MASCULINIST
FAMILY	· Family a "concentration camp" (Friedan, Ch. 12). · Sex is rape (Dworkin). · "All men are rapists" (French). · Women are men's property. · Deadbeat Dads. · Divorce impoverishes women.	· Divorce and custody legislation favour women. · Men must pay, but women move, and restrict access with no penalty. · Monstrous Mums. · Parental Alienation Syndrome.
HEALTH	· Women's health at risk in male-dominated health establishment. · Inadequate research funding. · Doctors don't listen! · Overprescription of drugs and sedatives. · AIDS: 55% of victims (world).	· Men live 5.7 years less than women. · Death rate 46% higher. · CVD: 96% higher. · Cancers: 36% higher. · Suicide: 80% of victims. · Work accidents: 96%. · AIDS: 95% of victims (U.S.). · Men's health a national crisis.
BEAUTY	· Beauty a trap and a myth: a waste of time, energy, money, and futile.	· Beauty is power (Friday). · (So is motherhood). · A resource/capital (Bourdieu).
GENDER	· Women are victims. · Men are villains. · Men objectify women as sex objects.	· Men also victims. · Women also villains. · Women objectify men as success objects (Farrell).
POWER	· Power is male. · Women demand equality empowerment.	· Male power a myth (Farrell). · Equality with which men? The homeless, the addicted, suicide victims, homicide victims, the incarcerated? All predominantly male.

and also at the victim powerless end, the majority are men, and a minority are women. Most of the alpha winners and most of the omega losers are men. The curve for women is a bell curve: a minority of women at the top and bottom of the status hierarchy, and the majority in the middle.

Put the two curves together and we probably have a straight line, a level playing field, with men "dominating" both extremes, and women "dominating" the centre. The playing field may be level with respect to gender, but clearly it is not level with respect to race, ethnicity and, by definition, socio-economic status. There are winners and losers but they do not coincide with gender.

Are men hegemonic or in crisis? The answer is "BOTH." It all depends WHICH men we are talking about. Women say they want to be equal to men. Which men? The CEOs, PMs, and Presidents? Or the homeless, the beggars in the streets, the two million men in U.S. jails, the suicides? That said, the three errors of many feminists of both sexes has been to homogenize men as hegemonic, and to ignore the male victims; and second to homogenize women as victims and to ignore the hegemonic women – perhaps out of a desire to simplify the identification and demonization, perhaps out of tunnel vision, perhaps out of the triumph of identity politics and ideology over scholarship. In polarizing the hegemonic male and the victim female, these theorists have omitted two important stakeholders: the hegemonic females and the victim males – and, probably the majority of men and women who are neither hegemonic nor victims.

The third error of binary gender feminists (not all) has been to ignore the intersectionality of race and class with gender. The most victimized population groups in the United States are the black males, often self-victimized, the poor, and perhaps the indigenous people, though the casinos as engines of economic development have proved valuable. Similar considerations apply in other countries.

The rhetoric of justice, equity and empowerment ought to apply to all, not simply to one "tribe." Exclusionism is not acceptable as an ideology of social change, which should surely be based on a humanistic assessment of need.

These three paradigms: heroes, villains and victims, and these two perspectives on reality, and also realities: hegemonic (dominant, leadership, or oppressive) and crisis (also oppressed) are not all mutually exclusive, nor restricted to one sex. Men probably all belong in all these categories, sometimes simultaneously, sometimes sequentially, and may flip like light switches from alpha to omega and positive to negative as we, or our circumstances, change.

Men and women may be hegemonic and loved at work, but in crisis at home – perhaps vacillating between homicide and suicide. We may be creative, destructive and self-destructive simultaneously. We may be controversial, and see different images of ourselves reflected around us. In the 1970s and 1980s Dr. Henry Morgenthaler was arrested several times in Canada for providing abortion services, but he was never convicted in jury trials, and for some women he was a hero. In 2008 he was awarded the prestigious Order of Canada. Times changed. In

Table 7.2　Masculinist paradigms

Author	Theory of Men	Etiology	Recommendation/ Movement
Bly	Soft	Decline of fathers	Mentoring Mankind Project
Farrell	Disposable	Rise of Feminism Silence of men	ERRA: Equal Rights and Responsibilities Act (1993) NCFM Improved communication (1998)
Faludi	Stiffed	Changed Capitalism Loss of provider role Absent fathers	None
Tiger	Decline	The pill	Male friendly policies
Kimmel	Disfunctional	Socialization	Be more like women Democratic Man NOMAS
Stoltenberg	Violent	Rape culture	Male transformation
Connell	Hegemonic	Patriarchal dividend	Power equalization changed male culture
McCartney	Faithless	Materialism Individualism	Promise Keepers 7 Promises
Farrakhan	Traditional	Loss of role Dysfunction	Increased commitment to family, community, nation Nation of Islam

NB. Some of the (misandric) feminist theorizing of men has been discussed in Chapter 5, including Solanas, French, Dworkin, Greer, Steinem, Walker, McMillan and others. Not that all feminists are misandric, but not many are male-positive.

2008 Joe Horn was arrested in Texas for killing two thieves, and charged; a jury found him not guilty – others considered him guilty: hero or villain?

Bill Clinton is a classic example. The most powerful man in the world fell into a deep personal and political crisis after his dalliance with the pretty young intern, Monica Lewinsky: the simultaneous union of power and crisis. In his autobiography *My Life* Clinton explained his theory of "parallel lives." His father was killed in a car accident before he was born, and his step-father was an alcoholic prone to violence against his mother. His home life was therefore a secret life. Hence the parallel lives: the external public life, "filled with friends and fun, learning and doing" but "my internal life was full of uncertainty, anger, and a dread of ever-looming violence. No one can live parallel lives with complete success; the two have to intersect" (2004:149). Mistakes will happen. In a sense, Clinton saw himself as a long-term victim of his step-father, and his half-brother Roger even more so; and then a victim of the Republicans and Kenneth Starr. In the end, up to the date of his deposition, the "whole four-year $40 million investigation had come down to: parsing the definition of sex" (2004:802; cf. 775–6, 811). Hero, villain, victim simultaneously, to himself and to others.

As for the future, some believe that the past was male but the future will be female, and that the present is contested terrain between the two sexes. They see de Beauvoir's second sex becoming the first sex, with women's increased social mobility in education, occupations, income and power. Others foresee a more equitable, balanced and androgynous future as the grievances of victim feminism are alleviated and men's rights are recognized: a synthesis is possible. Still others, notably evolutionary psychologists and difference theorists reckon that biology will out, and that men and women are driven by different imperatives, values and goals. Despite no doubt increasingly equal opportunities and structures, women and men will tend to have different work/family balances.

Certainly so many men are omegas, losing out due to incarcerations, addictions, suicides, homelessness etc. Yet others argue that there is a renaissance of the traditional male, evident in the "dick flicks", the presidential campaigns of 2004 and 2008 with war heroes Kerry and McCain vs. Bush and Obama, the male heroism demonstrated on 9/11 and in Afghanistan and Iraq, the continuing popularity of fitness clubs, contact sports and even extreme fighting, as well as such magazines as Maxim and FHM. The pendulum is still swinging, as most women now refuse to self-identify as feminists, and men are being urged to "Man up!".

The future will no doubt be more complicated than the binary past, with more options to both men and women: men can be more feminine and women more masculine as roles and identities overlap. Among men, the balances and imbalances between alpha and omega, gay and straight, new sensitive males, emoboys, metrosexuals and traditionalists, and heroes, villains and victims – all these choices and options are open, and will be evaluated variously by men and women. Difference theorists argue that differences will persist. One world theorists think that roles and identities are already blurring and converging into androgyny, and that the overlaps and options will be greater for both sexes. Probably both are correct.

If the feminists were right, that what benefits women also benefits men, then perhaps the reverse is also true, that what benefits men also benefits women.

In any event, to achieve gender justice and understanding we will need to proceed together, issue by issue, leaving behind our tunnel visions, identity politics and coloured lenses. Hopefully this book will contribute to our mutual empathy, admiration and love.

Bibliography

Alger, Horatio. ca1870. *Helping Himself.* Cleveland: Goldsmith Publishing.

Alvarez, Lizette. 2009. "Army Data Show Rise in Number of Suicides." *New York Times.* 6 February.

American Association of Suicidology, 2008. *U.S.A. Suicide: 2005 Final Data,* Washington, D.C. www.suicidology.org.

Archetti, Eduardo P. 1999. *Masculinities: Football, Polo and the Tango in Argentina.* New York: Berg.

Aristotle. 1984. *The Complete Works.* Edited by Jonathan Barnes. Princeton University Press. Bollingen, Press.

Armstrong, Karen. 2005. *A Short History of Myth.* Vintage Books. New York.

Armstrong, Pat and Hugh Armstrong. 2003. *Wasting Away. The Undermining of Canadian Health Care.* Oxford: Oxford University Press.

Armstrong, Pat, Hugh Armstrong and David Coburn. 2001. *Unhealthy Times: Political Economy Perspectives on Health and Care in Canada.* Oxford: Oxford University Press.

Badinter, Elisabeth. 1989. *Man/Woman: The One is the Other.* Collins Harvill.

Bahramitash, Roksana. 2005. "The War on Terror, Feminist Orientalism and Orientalist Feminism: Case Studies of Two North American Bestsellers." *Critique: Journal of Middle Eastern Studies.* Vol. 14, No. 2:223–37.

Ballard, Dr Robert B. 1987. *The Discovery of the Titanic.* New York: Viking/ Madison.

Baron-Cohen, Simon. 2003. *The Essential Difference. The Truth about the Male and Female Brain.* New York: Perseus Books.

Bartkowski, John P. 2004. *The Promise Keepers: Servants, Soldiers and Godly Men.* New Brunswick, N.J.: Rutgers University Press.

Barton, Edward Read. 2000. *Mythopoetic Perspectives on Men's Healing Work.* Westport, CT: Bergin and Garvey.

Beard, Richard. 2003. *Muddied Oafs. The Soul of Rugby.* London: Yellow Jersey Press.

Bellafante, Ginia. 1998. "Is Feminism Dead?" *Time.* 25 June.

Belkin, Lisa. 2003. "The Opt-Out Revolution." *New York Times Magazine.* October 26:42–7, 58, 85–6.

Beowulf. 1999. Translated by Seamus Heaney. London: Faber and Faber.

Blankenhorn, David. 1996. *Fatherless America.* New York: Harper Collins.

Bly, Robert. 1990. *Iron John.* New York: Addison-Wesley.

Bolaria, B. Singh and Harley D. Dickinson. 1988. *Sociology of Health Care in Canada.* Toronto: Harcourt, Brace, Jovanovich.

Bolen, Jean Shinoda. 1985. *Goddesses in Everywoman: A New Psychology of Women*. New York: Harper.

Bornstein, Kate. 1995. *Gender Outlaw. On Men, Women and the Rest of Us*. New York: Vintage.

Bottomore, T.B. and Maximilien Rubel (eds). 1965. *Karl Marx*. Harmondsworth: Penguin.

Braver, Sanford L. 1998. *Divorced Dads: Shattering the Myths*. New York: Putnam.

Briscoe, Simon. 2005. *Britain in Numbers. The Essential Statistics*. London: Politico's.

Brod, Harry and Michael Kaufman. 1994. *Theorizing Masculinities*. Thousand Oaks, CA: Sage.

Brown, Ian (ed.). 2005. *What I Meant to Say. The Private Lives of Men*. Toronto: Thomas Allen.

Brylcreem Mandom Report. 2008.

Bullough, Vern L. 1979. *Homosexuality. A History*. New York: New American Library.

Burke, Edmund. 1986/1790. *Reflections on the Revolution in France*. Penguin Classics.

Buss, David M. 1999. *Evolutionary Psychology. The New Science of the Mind*. Needham Heights, MA: Allyn and Bacon.

Butler, Judith. 1990. *Gender Trouble*. London: Routledge.

Campbell, Joseph. 1972 [1949]. *The Hero with a Thousand Faces*. Princeton, N.J.: Princeton University Press.

Campbell, Joseph. 1988. *The Power of Myth*. New York: Doubleday.

Canadian Panel on Violence against Women. 1993. *Changing the Landscape: Ending Violence: Achieving Equality*. Cat. No. SW 45-1.

Caputi, Jane and Gordene O. MacKenzie. 1992. "Pumping Iron John" in Kay Leigh Hagan (ed.), *Women Respond to the Men's Movement*. San Francisco: Pandora.

Carlyle, Thomas. 1993 [1841]. *On Heroes, Hero-Worship and The Heroic in History*. Oxford.

Carnegie, Andrew. 1998 [1889]. *The Gospel of Wealth*. Bedford, MA: Applewood.

Cartwright, Glenn F. 1993. "Expanding the Parameters of Parental Alienation Syndrome." *The American Journal of Family Therapy*. Vol. 21, No. 3, Fall: 205–15.

Castiglione, Baldesar. 1976 [1507]. *The Book of the Courtier*. Translated by George Bull. Penguin Classics.

Catalyst. 2008. U.S. Women in Business. www.catalyst.org.

Catalyst 2008a. Voices from the Boardroom. www.catalyst.org.

Cawelti, John G. 1965. *Apostles of the Self-Made Man*. Chicago: University of Chicago Press.

Cawthorne, Nigel. 2004. *Witches. History of a Persecution*. London: Arcturus.

Chang, Jung and Jon Halliday. 2005. *Mao: The Unknown Story*. New York. Knopf.

Charles, Nickie. 2003. *Gender in Modern Britain*. Oxford: Oxford University Press.

Chesterfield, the Earl of n.d. [1774]. *Letters to His Son*. Edited by Oliver H. Leigh. New York: Tudor Publishing.

Chichester, Francis. 1967. *Gypsy Moth Circles the World*. London: Hodder and Stoughton.

Choi, Doug Sull, 2004. "Origins and Realities of Suttee in Hinduism." In Richard Warms, James Garber and Jon McGee, eds. *Sacred Realms: Essays in Religion, Belief and Society*. New York: Oxford University Press: 196–203.

Clinton, Bill. 2004. *My Life*. New York: Knopf.

Clodfetter, Michael. 2002. *Warfare and Armed Conflicts*. Jefferson, NC: McFarland.

Cohn, Norman. 1976. *Europe's Inner Demons. An Enquiry Inspired by the Great Witch-hunt*.

Colapinto, John. 2000. *As Nature Made Him: The Boy who was raised as a Girl*. Toronto: Harper Perennial.

Committee on the Status of Women. 1991. *The War against Women*. Ottawa: House of Commons Cat. XC 28–343/1-3.

Connell, R.W. 1995. *Masculinities*. London: Polity Press.

Connell, R.W. 2000. *The Men and the Boys*. Berkeley: University of California Press.

Connell, R.W. 2002. *Gender*. London: Polity Press.

Cose, Ellis. 1995. *A Man's World*. New York: Harper Collins.

Courtenay, Will H., 2000. "Behavioral Factors Associated with Disease, Injury, and Death among Men: Evidence and Implications for Prevention." *The Journal of Men's Studies*. Vol. 9:1:81–142.

Covey, Stephen R. 1990. *Seven Habits of Highly Effective People*. New York: Simon and Schuster.

Crawford, Maria and Rosemary Gartner. 1992. *Woman Killing: Intimate Femicide in Ontario, 1974–1990*. Final Report for the Ontario Women's Directorate and Ministry of Community and Social Services. Toronto: Women We Honour Action Committee.

Crompton, L. 2003. *Homosexuality and Civilization*. Cambridge, MA: Bellnap Press of Harvard University Press.

Cross, Gary. 2008. *Men to Boys: The Making of Modern Immaturity*. Columbia University Press.

Daly, Mary. 1975. *The Church and the Second Sex*. New York: Harper Colophan.

Daly, Mary. 1978. *Gyn/Ecology: The Metaethics of Radical Feminism*. Boston: Beacon Press.

Darwin, Charles. 1981 [1871]. *The Descent of Man, and Selection in Relation to Sex*. Princeton, N.J.: Princeton University Press.

Darwin, Francis. 1887. *The Life and Letters of Charles Darwin*. 2 vols. London: John Murray.

Dauvergne, Mia and Geoffrey Li. 2006. "Homicide in Canada, 2005." *Juristat* Vol. 26, No. 6. Ottawa: Statistics Canada. Canadian Centre for Justice Statistics. Catalogue No. 85-002-XIE.

de Beauvoir, Simone. 1989 [1949]. *The Second Sex*. Harmondsworth: Penguin.

De Crescenzo, Luciano. 1990. *The History of Greek Philosophy*. Vol. 1. The Pre-Socratics. London: Picador.

Denfeld, René. 1995. *The New Victorians: A Young Woman's Challenge to the Old Feminist Order*. New York: Warner Books.

Doucet, Andrea. 2007. *Do Men Mother?* Toronto: University of Toronto Press.

Douglas, Jack D. 1967. *The Social Meanings of Suicide*. Princeton, N.J.: Princeton University Press.

Douglass, Frederick. 1892/1962. *Life and Times of Frederick Douglass*. London: Collier-Macmillan.

Dowd, Maureen. 2005. *Are Men Necessary?* New York: Putnam.

Dreier, Peter. 2007. "The United States in Comparative Perspective." *Contexts*. 6:3:38–46.

Duncan, Jennifer. 2004. *Frontier Spirit: The Brave Women of the Klondike*. Anchor Canada.

Durkheim, Emile. 1966 [1897]. *Suicide*. London: Routledge and Kegan Paul.

Dworkin, Andrea. 1976. *Woman Hating*. New York: Dutton.

Dworkin, Andrea. 1987. *Intercourse*. New York: The Free Press

Dworkin, Andrea. 1988. *Letters from a War Zone*. London: Secker and Warburg.

Eaton, John P. and Charles A. Haas. 1986. *Titanic: Triumph and Tragedy*. New York: Norton.

Eckholm, Erik. 2006. "Plight Deepens for Black Men." *New York Times*. 20 March.

Elegant, Simon. 2007. "Where Coal is Stained with Blood." *Time*. March 12:18–20.

Elting, John R. 1997. "World War II." *Encyclopedia Americana*. Vol. 29:529–31.

Emerson, Ralph Waldo. 1997. *Essays and Poems*. Selected by Tony Tanner. London: Everyman Library.

Engels, Frederick. 1969 [1845]. *The Condition of the Working Class in England*. London: Panter Books.

Erasmus, Desiderius. 1985. *Collected Works*. Edited by J.F. Sowards. Trans. Brian McGregor. Toronto: Toronto University Press.

Esping-Andersen. 2007. "Equal Opportunities and the Welfare State." *Contexts*. 6:3:23–27.

Esposito, John L. 2003. *Islam*. Chantilly, VA: The Teaching Company.

Estes, Clarissa Pinkola. 1992. *Women who Run with the Wolves: Myths and Stories of the Wild Woman Archetype*. New York: Ballantyne.

Faludi, Susan. 1992. *Backlash: The Undeclared War against American Women*. New York: Doubleday.

Faludi, Susan. 1999. *Stiffed: The Betrayal of the American Man*. New York: William Morrow.

Farrell, Warren. 1974. *The Liberated Man*. New York: Random House.

Farrell, Warren. 1993. *The Myth of Male Power. How Men are the Disposable Sex*. New York: Simon and Schuster.

Farrell, Warren. 1999. *Women Can't Hear What Men Don't Say*. New York: Tarcher.

Farrell, Warren and James P. Sterba. 2008. *Does Feminism Discriminate against Men?* New York: Oxford University Press.

Fausto-Sterling, Anne. 1993. "The Five Sexes." *The Sciences*. March/April:20–4.

Fausto-Sterling, Anne. 2000. *Sexing the Body: Gender Politics and the Construction of Sexuality*. New York: Basic Books.

Fergusson, R., M. Mauser and D. Pickering. 2004. *The Penguin Thesaurus*. Penguin Books.

Fillion, Kate. 1996. *Lip Service*. New York: Harper Collins.

Firestone, Shulamith. 1970. *The Dialectic of Sex*. New York: Morrow.

Fisher, Helen. 1999. *The First Sex*. New York: Random House.

Foster, Merna. 2004. *100 Canadian Heroines*. Toronto: Dundurn Press.

Foucault, Michel. 1977. *Discipline and Punish*. Trans. A. Sheridan. New York: Pantheon.

Foucault, Michel. 1978. *The History of Sexuality*. Trans. R. Hurley. Vol. 1. New York: Pantheon.

Franklin, Clyde. 1991. *Men and Society*. Chicago: Nelson-Hall.

Fraser, Antonia. 1989. *Warrior Queens*. London: Viking.

French, Marilyn. 1977. *The Women's Room*. New York: Jove Books.

French, Marilyn. 1992. *The War against Women*. New York: Simon and Schuster, Summit Books.

Freud, Sigmund. 1977 [1910]. "Three Essays on the Theory of Sexuality" in *On Sexuality*. Penguin Freud Library. Vol. 7:31–169.

Freud, Sigmund. 1979. *Case Histories II*. Pelican Freud Library. Vol. 9.

Freud, Sigmund. 1985 [1930]. *Civilization and Its Discontents*. In *Civilization Society and Religion*. The Pelican Freud Library. Vol. 12.

Friday, Nancy. 1996. *The Power of Beauty*. New York: Harper Collins.

Friedan, Betty. 1970 [1963]. *The Feminine Mystique*. New York: Dell.

Friedan, Betty. 1981. *The Second Stage*. New York: Summit Books.

Friedman, M. and G.W. Friedland. 1998. *Medicine's 10 Greatest Discoveries*. Yale University Press.

Garber, Marjorie B. 1992. *Vested Interests: cross-dressing and cultural anxiety*. London: Routledge.

Garner, Cindy. 1994. *How are Men Like Noodles?* Kansas City: Andrews and McMeel.

Gartner, Rosemary and Bill McCarthy. 1991. "The social distribution of femicide in urban Canada, 1921–88." *Law and Society Review* 25:287–312.

Gates, Henry Louis Jr. 1997. *Thirteen Ways of Looking at a Black Man*. New York: Vintage Books.

Giddens, Anthony. 1992. *The Transformation of Intimacy: Sexuality, Love, and Eroticism in Modern Societies*. Oxford: Polity Press.

Gilmore, David D. 1990. *Manhood in the Making. Cultural Constructs of Masculinity*. New Haven: Yale University Press.

Gilmore, David D. 2001. *Misogny. The Male Malady*. Philadelphia: University of Pennsylvania Press.

Goffman, Erving. 1959. *The Presentation of Self in Everyday Life*. New York: Bantam.

Goldman, Todd Harris. 2005. *Boys are Stupid. Throw Rocks at Them*. New York: Workman.

Goldstein, Joshua. 2001. *War and Gender*. Cambridge. Cambridge University Press.

Gordon, Ann D. (ed.) 1997. *The Selected Papers of Elizabeth Cady Stanton and Susan B. Anthony*. New Brunswick, N.J.: Rutgers University Press. Vol. 1.

Gordon, Mary. 1993. "Raising Sons." *Ms.* November/December 45–50.

Gorman, Christine and Wendy Cole. 2004. "Between the Sexes." *Time*. March 1:38–40.

Gould, Stephen Jay. 1981. *The Mismeasure of Man*. New York: Norton.

Gow, Andrew and Lara Apps. 2002. *Male Witches in Early Modern Europe*. Manchester: Manchester University Press.

Gray, John. 1994. *Men are from Mars, Women are from Venus*. New York: Harper Collins.

Greenfield-Sanders, Timothy and Elvis Mitchell. 2008. *The Black List*. New York: Atria.

Greer, Germaine. 1971. *The Female Eunuch*. London: Paladin Books.

Greer, Germaine. 1999. *The Whole Woman*. London: Doubleday.

Grieg, Charlotte. 2006. *Evil Serial Killers*. London: Capella.

Guinness, 2000. *Guinness World Records 2000*. New York: Bantam.

Gurian, Michael. 1997. *The Wonder of Boys*. New York: Tarcher/Putnam.

Gurian, Michael. 1999. *A Fine Young Man*. New York: Tarcher/Putnam.

Guthrie, W.K.C. 1965. *A History of Greek Philosophy*. Volume 2. Cambridge: Cambridge University Press.

Gutmann, Matthew C. 2007. *The Meanings of Macho: Being a Man in Mexico City*. Berkeley, CA: University of California Press.

Hagan, Kay Leigh (ed.). 1992. *Women Respond to the Men's Movement*. San Francisco: Pandora.

Halberstein, J. 1998. *Female Masculinity*. Duke University Press.

Halpern, Sue. 1999. "The Pulitzer Prize-winner." *Mother Jones*. September/October: 37–39.

Hazlitt, William. 1952. *Essays of William Hazlitt*. Edited by Frank Carr. London: Walter Scott.

Heald, Suzette. 1999. *Manhood and Morality: Sex, Violence and Ritual in Gisu Society*. New York: Routledge.

Health Canada. 1987. *Suicide in Canada*. Report of the National Task Force. Ottawa. Catalogue Number H39-107.

Health Canada. 1994. *Suicide in Canada*. Update of the Task Force on Suicide in Canada. Ottawa. Cat. No. H39-107/1995.

Hicks, Joe and Grahame Allen. 1999. *A Century of Change: Trends in U.K. Statistics since 1900*. Research Paper 99/111. House of Commons Papers. http://www.parliament.uk.

Hise, R. 2004. *The War against Men*. Oakland, Oregon: Red Anvil Press.

Hite, Shere. 1981. *The Hite Report on Male Sexuality*. New York: Knopf.

Hobbes, Thomas. 1960/1651. *Leviathan*. Oxford: Blackwell.

Hochman, David. 2008. "Ford." *Reader's Digest*. May:132–7.

Hoecker-Drysdale, Susan. 1992. *Harriet Martineau: First Woman Sociologist*. New York: Berg.

Holland, Jack. 2006. *A Brief History of Misogyny. The World's Oldest Prejudice*. London: Robinson.

Hollander, Xaviera. 1972. *The Happy Hooker*. New York: Dell.

Holliday, Laurel. 1978. *The Violent Sex*. Guerneville, California: Bluestocking Books.

hooks, bell. 1984. *Feminist Theory: From Margin to Center*. Boston: South End Press.

hooks, bell. 2004. *We Real Cool. Black Men and Masculinity*. New York: Routledge.

Horrocks, Roger. 1995. *Male Myths and Icons: Masculinity in Popular Culture*. London: St. Martin's Press.

Hughes, Thomas. 1993 [1857]. *Tom Brown's Schooldays*. Ware, Herts: Wordsworth.

Hughes-Hallett, Lucy. 2005. *Heroes*. New York: Random House.

Inter-Parliamentary Union. www.ipu.org.

Johnson, Robert A. 1989. *He: Understanding Masculine Psychology*. New York: Harper and Row.

Jones, Ann. 1981. *Women Who Kill*. New York: Fawcett Crest.

Jones, David E. 2006. *Women Warriors: A History*. Washington, D.C.: Potomac.

Jones, Ernest. 1954. *Sigmund Freud: Life and Work*. Vol. 2. London: Hogarth Press.

Joyce, James. 1992 [1916]. *A Portrait of the Artist as a Young Man. Penguin*

Jung, C.G. 1966 [1933]. *Modern Man in Search of a Soul*. New York: Harvest.

Jung, C.G. 1976. *The Portable Jung*. Edited by Joseph Campbell. Harmondsworth: Penguin.

Jung, C.G. 1983. *The Essential Jung*. Edited by Anthony Storr. Princeton, N.J.: Princeton University Press.

Junger, Sebastian, 1998. *The Perfect Storm*. New York: Harper Collins.

Keegan, John. 1998. *The First World War*. Toronto: Key Porter.

Kempe, C. Henry. 1980/1961. *The Battered Child*. Chicago: University of Chicago Press.

Kenner, Linda and Antonia Van der Meer. 1995. *Why Can't a Man be more like a Cat?* New York: Dell.

Kimbrell, Andrew. 1995. *The Masculine Mystique: The Politics of Masculinity*. New York: Ballantine Books.

Kimmel, Michael S. 1992. "Reading Men: Men, Masculinity and Publishing." *Contemporary Sociology* 21:162–71.

Kimmel, Michael S. (ed.). 1995. *The Politics of Manhood. Profeminist Men Respond to the Mythopoetic Men's Movement*. Philadelphia: Temple University Press.

Kimmel, Michael S. 1996. *Manhood in America: A Cultural History*. New York: The Free Press.

Kimmel, Michael S. and Michael A. Messner. 2004. *Men's Lives*. Sixth Edition. Boston: Pearson.

Kimmel, Michael S. 2004. "Clarence, William, Iron Mike, Tailhook, Senator Packwood, Spur Posse, Magic ... and Us." in Michael S. Kimmel and Michael A. Messner (eds), *Men's Lives* (6th edition). Boston: Pearson: 565–79.

Kimmel, Michael S. 2006. *Manhood in America: A Cultural History*. Second Edition. New York: Oxford University Press.

Kimmel, Michael. 2008. *Guyland: The Perilous World where Boys become Men*. New York: HarperCollins.

Kindlon, Dan and Michael Thompson. 1999. *Raising Cain: Protecting the Emotional Life of Boys*. New York: Ballantine Books.

Kirmayer, Laurence J. *et al.* 2007. *Suicide among Aboriginal People in Canada*. Ottawa: Aboriginal Healing Foundation.

Kimura, Doreen. 1999. *Sex and Cognition*. Cambridge, MA: MIT Press.

Klein, Shelley. 2003. *The Most Evil Woman in History*. London: Michael O'Mara Books.

Komarovsky, Mirra. 1976. *Dilemmas of Masculinity*. New York: Norton.

Krakauer, Jon. 1997. *Into Thin Air*. New York: Anchor Books.

Kung, Hsiang-Ching *et al.* 2008. "Deaths: Final Data for 2005". *National Vital Statistics Reports*. Vol. 56, No. 10, April 24.

Kuntz, Tom (ed.). 1998. *The Titanic Disaster Hearings: The Official Transcript of the 1912 Senate Investigation*. New York: Pocket Books.

Laframboise, Donna. 1996. *The Princess at the Window: A New Gender Morality*. Harmondsworth: Penguin Books.

Laframboise, Donna. 2000. "Father's suicide becomes a rallying cry for fairness in court." *National Post* 1 April.

Lafreniere, Sharon, 2002. "Death in a Coal Mine." *Montreal Gazette* July 8. (*Washington Post*).

Lane, Brian. 2006. *The Encyclopedia of Women Killers*. London: Magpie.

Lau, Evelyn. 1989. *Runaway: Diary of a Street Kid*. New York: HarperCollins.

Lenz, Elinor and Barbara Myerhoff. 1985. *The Feminization of America: How Women's Values are Changing our Public and Private Lives*. Los Angeles: Tarcher.

Leonard, Lori. 2004. "Female Circumcision in Southern Chad: Origins, Meaning and Current Practice." In Richard Warms, James Garber and Jon McGee, (eds) *Sacred Realms: Essays in Religion, Belief and Society*. New York: Oxford University Press, 2004:288–94.

Levin, Jack and William Levin. 1982. *The Functions of Discrimination and Prejudice*. 2nd edition. New York: Harper and Row.

Levinson, Daniel. 1978. *Seasons of a Man's Life*. New York: Ballantine.

Li, Geoffrey. 2008. "Homicide in Canada, 2007." *Juristat*. Vol. 28, No. 9. Ottawa: Statistics Canada Cat. No. 85-002.

Machiavelli, Nicolo. 1950 [1517]. *The Prince and the Discourses*. New York: The Modern Library.

Mailer, Norman. 1966. *Christianity and Cannibalism*. New York: Dial Press.

Majors, Richard and Janet Mancini Billson. 1992. *Cool Pose: The Dilemmas of Black Manhood in America*. New York: Simon and Schuster.

Malory, Sir Thomas. 1969 [1485]. *Le Morte d'Arthur*. Two Vols. Edited by Jane Cowan. Harmondsworth: Penguin Classics.

Mansfield, Harvey C. 2006. *Manliness*. New Haven: Yale University Press.

Marcus, Geoffrey. 1969. *The Maiden Voyage*. New York: Viking.

Marquez, Gabriel Garcia. 2004. *Living To Tell the Tale*. London: Knopf.

Marx, Karl and Friedrich Engels. 1974 [1848]. *The Communist Manifesto*. Harmondsworth: Penguin Books.

Mason, Philip. 1982. *The English Gentleman: The Rise and Fall of an Ideal*. London: Andre Deutsch.

Mauss, Marcel. 1979. Sociology and Philosophy. London: Keagan & Paul.

McCloskey, Deidre N. 1999. *Crossing: A Memoir*. Chicago: University of Chicago Press.

McGraw, Phillip C. 2001. *Self Matters. Creating Your Life from the Inside Out*. New York: Simon and Schuster.

Mead, Margaret. 1949. *Male and Female*. New York: Morrow.

Menninger, Karl. 1938. *Man Against Himself*. New York: Harcourt, Brace and World.

Merida, Kevin (ed.). 2007. *Being a Black Man. At the Corner of Progress and Peril*. New York: Public Affairs.

Miles, Rosalind. 1991. *The Rites of Man*. London: Grafton Books.

Miller, Nancy. 1999. "Cosmo's Field Guide to Guys." *Cosmopolitan*. April:246–9.

Millet, Catherine. 2003. *The Sexual Life of Catherine M.* Trans. by Adriana Hunter. New York: Grove Press.

Moir, Anne and David Jessel. 1991. *Brain Sex: The Real Difference between Men and Women*. London: Mandarin.

Montagu, Ashley. 1968. *The Natural Superiority of Women*. (Revised Edition). London: Macmillan.

Montefore, Simon Sebag. 2007. *101 World Heroes*. London: Quercus Publishing.

Moore, Harold G., Lt. Gen. (Ret.) and Joseph L. Galloway. 2002. *We Were Soldiers Once . . . and Young*. New York: HarperTorch.

Moore, Robert and Douglas Gillette. 1991. *King, Warrior, Magician, Lover*. San Francisco: Harper Collins.

Morgan, Robin (ed.). 1970. *Sisterhood is Powerful*. New York: Vintage Books.

Morris, Betsy. 2002. "Trophy Husbands." *Fortune*, Oct. 14. Vol. 146:7:79–98.

Morris, Jan. 1974. *Conundrum*. New York: Harcourt, Brace Jovanovich.

Moyers, Bill. 1988. *A World of Ideas*. Vol. I. New York: Doubleday.

Moyers, Bill. 1990. *A World of Ideas*. Vol. II. New York: Doubleday.

Mundle, Rob. 2005. *Fatal Storm. The 54th Sydney to Hobart Race*. London: A. and C. Black.

Murphy, Barbara. 2002. *Why Women Bury Men. The Longevity Gap in Canada*. Winnipeg: Gordon Shillingford.

Nafisi, Azar. 2003. *Reading Lolita in Tehran: A Memoir in Books*. New York: Random House.

Nanda, Serena. 1999. *Neither Man nor Woman: The Hijras of India*. Wadsworth.

Nardi, Peter (ed). 2000. *Gay Masculinities*. London: Sage.

Nathanson, Paul and Katherine K. Young. 2001. *Spreading Misandry: The Teaching of Contempt for Men in Popular Culture*. Montreal: McGill-Queen's University Press.

Nathanson, Paul and Katherine K. Young, 2006. *Legalizing Misandry. From Public Shame to Systemic Discrimination against Men*. Montreal: McGill-Queens University Press.

National Commission on Terrorist Attacks Upon the United States. 2004. The 9/11 Report. New York: St Martin's Press.

Neroni, Hilary. 2005. *The Violent Woman*. Albany: State University of New York.

New, Caroline, 2001. "Oppressed and Oppressors? The Systematic Mistreatment of Men." *Sociology*. Vol. 35:3:729–48.

Newell, Waller R. 2000. *What is a Man?* New York: Regan Books.

Newell, Waller R. 2003. *The Code of Man*. New York: HarperCollins.

Newman, Amanda. 1999. *Women are from Venus, Men are from Hell*. Holbrook, MA: Adams Media.

Newman, John Henry Cardinal. 1982 [1852]. Edited by Martin J. Svaglic. *The Idea of a University*. Notre Dame IN: University of Notre Dame Press.

Nichols, Jack. 1975. *Men's Liberation*. Harmonsworth: Penguin Books.

Nicoriuk, Susan. 2004. *Where Have All the Boys Gone?* M.A. Thesis. Dept. of Sociology and Anthropology. Concordia University. Montreal.

Niebuhr, Gustav. 1998. "Southern Baptists Declare Wife should 'Submit' to her Husband." *New York Times* 10 June.

Nietzsche, Friedrich. 1985 [1885]. *Thus Spoke Zarathustra*. Trans. R. Hollingdale. Harmondsworth: Penguin Books.

Nietzsche, Friedrich. 1977. *A Nietzsche Reader*. Edited by R.J. Hollingdale. Harmondsworth: Penguin Classics.

Nietzsche, Friedrich. 1979. *Ecce Homo*. Harmondsworth: Penguin Books.

Nordland, Rod. 2006. "The Death of a Monster." *Newsweek*. March 20:44.

Nunau, Kate. 2006. "Feminist icon Steinem cautions sociologists against complacency". *The Gazette* 15 August.

Nussbaum, Martha. 1999. "The Professor of Parody."*New Republic*. 22 February (www.akad.se/Nussbaum.pdf).

Oakley, Ann. 1992 [1984]. *Taking it Like a Woman*. London: Flamingo.

O'Brien, Mary. 1989. *Reproducing the World*. Boulder, Col.: Westview Press.

O'Faolain, Julia and Lauro Martines (eds). 1973. *Not in God's Image*. New York: Harper Torchbooks.

Ogrodnik, L. 2006. *Family Violence in Canada: A Statistical Profile, 2006*. Ottawa: Statistics Canada. Catalogue No. 85-224-XIE.

O'Hanlon, Redmond. 2004. *Trawler*. London: Hamish Hamilton.

Ovid. 1967. *Metamorphoses*. Translated by A.D. Melville. Oxford: Oxford University Press.

Paglia, Camille. 1991. *Sexual Personae*. New York: Vintage Books.

Paglia, Camille. 1994. *Vamps and Tramps*. New York: Vintage Books.

Parker, Kathleen. 2008. *Save the Males*. New York: Random House.

Parsons, Elsie Clews. 1936. *Mitla: Town of Souls*. Chicago: University of Chicago Press.

Pascoe, C.J. 2007. *Dude You're a Fag. Masculinity and Sexuality in High School*. Berkeley: University of California Press.

Patai, Daphne and Noretta Koertge. 1994. *Professing Feminism*. New York: Basic Books.

Paul, Pamela. 2002. *The Starter Marriage and Future of Matrimony*. New York: Villard Books.

Pearson, Carol S. 1989. *The Hero Within*. New York: HarperCollins.

Pearson, Patricia, 1997. *When She was Bad: Violent Women and the Myth of Innocence*. Toronto: Random House.

Pinker, Susan. 2008. *The Second Paradox. Extreme Men and Gifted Women*. Toronto: Random House.

Plato. 1985. *The Collected Dialogues*. Edited by Edith Hamilton and Huntington Cairns. Bollingen Series LXXI Princeton University Press.

Pleck, Joseph H. 1981. *The Myth of Masculinity*. Cambridge, MA: The MIT Press.

Pleck, Joseph H. and Jack Sawyer. 1974. *Men and Masculinity*. Englewood Cliffs, N.J.: Prentice-Hall.

Pollack, William. 1998. *Real Boys. Rescuing Our Sons from the Myths of Boyhood*. New York: Random House.

Popenoe, David. 1996. *Life Without Father*. New York: The Free Press.

Popper, Karl. 1966. *The Open Society and its Enemies*. Princeton, N.J.: Princeton University Press.

Putney, Clifford. 2003. *Muscular Christianity: Manhood and Sports in Protestant America, 1880–1920*. Cambridge, MA: Harvard University Press.

Radford, Jill and Diana E.H. Russell (eds). 1992. *Femicide: The Politics of Woman Killing*. New York: Twayne.

Ramirez, Rafael L. 1999. *What It Means to be a Man: Reflections on Puerto Rican Masculinity*. New Brunswick, N.J.: Rutgers University Press.

Ranke-Heinemann, Uta. 1990. *Eunuchs for the Kingdom of Heaven*. New York: Doubleday.

Reeve, Christopher. 1999. *Still Me*. New York: Ballantine Books.

Reuther, Rosemary Radford. 1983. *Sexism and God-Talk*. Boston: Beacon Press.

Rich, Adrienne. 1986. *Blood, Bread and Poetry*. New York: Norton.

Roberts, Sam. 2007. "For Young Earners in Big City, A Gap in Women's Favor." *New York Times*. August 3.

Rojek, Chris. 2001. *Celebrity*. London: Reaktion Books.

Roiphe, Katie. 1994. *The Morning After: Sex, Fear and Feminism*. Boston: Little, Brown.

Ropeik, David and George Gray. 2002. *Risk*. Boston: Houghton Mifflin.

Rousseau, Jean-Jacques. 1963 [1767]. *The Social Contract*. London: Deut.

Salerno, Steve. 2005. *Sham: How the Self-Help Movement made America Helpless*. New York. Crown.

Salmansohn, Karen. 1994. *How to Make Your Man Behave in 21 Days or Less, using the Secrets of Professional Dog Trainers*. New York: Workman.

Sassoon, Siegfried. 1929. *Memoirs of a Fox Hunting Man*. Coward-McCann.

Sassoon, Siegfried. 1965 [1930]. *Memoirs of an Infantry Officer*. London: Faber and Faber.

Save the Children, 2001. *State of the World's Mothers*. 2001. www.savethechildren. org/mothers.

Schmidt, Michael S. and Maria Newman. 2007. "Jury Punishes Knicks." *New York Times*. 13 October.

Seidler, Victor J. 2006. *Transforming Masculinities*. London: Routledge.

Shneidman, Edwin. 1987. "At the Point of No Return." *Psychology Today*. March: 55–8.

Sellers, Patricia. 2003. "Power: Do Women Really Want It?" *Fortune*. October: 80–100.

Sheehy, Gail. 1977. *Passages. Predictable Crises of Adult Life*. New York: Dell.

Sheehy, Gail. 1998. *Understanding Men's Passages. Discovering the New Map of Men's Lives*. New York: Random House.

Siegel, Deborah. 2007. *Sisterhood Interrupted*. New York: Palgrave Macmillan.

Simon, Harvey B. 1999. "Longevity: the Ultimate Gender Gap." *Scientific American* 10:2:106–12.

Simon, Harvey B. 1999. "Can Work Kill?" *Scientific American* 10:2:44–6.

Sivard, R.L. 1989. *World Military and Social Expenditures*. Washington: World Priorities.

Slocum, Joshua. 1958 [1900]. *Sailing Alone Around the World*. New York: Collier Brown.

Smiles, Samuel. 1958 [1859]. *Self-Help*. London: John Murray.

Smiles, Samuel. 1875. *Thrift*. New York: Edward.

Smith, Adam. 1976 [1776]. *The Wealth of Nations*. Chicago. University of Chicago Press.

Smith, Jo Durden. 2003. *100 Most Infamous Killers*. London: Capella.

Sobol, Beth. 2006. "How Sneaky Women Get Their Way with Men." *Cosmopolitan*. October: 202–6.

Solanas, Valerie. 1971. *S.C.U.M. (Society for Cutting Up Men) Manifesto*. London: Olympia Press.

Sommers, Christine Hoff. 1995. *Who Stole Feminism? How Women have Betrayed Women*. New York: Simon and Schuster, Touchstone Books.

Sommers, Christina Hoff, 2000. *The War against Boys. How Misguided Feminism is Harming Our Young Men*. New York: Simon and Schuster.

Staff. 1995. "How To Be Great!" *Psychology Today*. Vol. 28:6:November/December:46–54, 62.

Statistics Canada. 1995. *Earnings of Men and Women*. Cat. No. 13-217.

Status of Women, Canada. 1991. *Living Without Fear, Every Woman's Right*. Ottawa. Cat. No. SW21-12/1991.

Steinem, Gloria. 1992. *Revolution from Within*. Boston: Little, Brown.

Stephenson, June. 1995. *Men are Not Cost-Effective: Male Crime in America*. New York: Harper Perennial.

Stoltenberg, John. 1990. *Refusing To Be a Man: Essays on Sex and Justice*. Meridian Books.

Surtees, C.S. 1860. *Plain or Ringlets*. London: Bradbury, Agnew.

Synnott, Anthony. 1993. *The Body Social: Symbolism, Self and Society*. London: Routledge.

Synnott, Anthony. 1996. *Shadows: Issues and Social Problems in Canada*. Scarborough, Ont.: Prentice-Hall.

Tannen, Deborah. 1986. *That's Not What I Meant!* New York: Ballantine Books.

Tannen, Deborah. 1990. *You Just Don't Understand*. New York: Ballantine Books.

Tavris, Carol. 1977. "Masculinity". *Psychology Today*. January: 35–9.

Tawney, R.H. 1964. *Religion and the Rise of Capitalism*. London: Unwin.

Tennyson, Alfred Lord. 1905. *The Complete Works*. London: Macmillan.

Thomas, David, 1993. *Not Guilty: The Case in Defence of Men*. New York: William Morrow.

Thompson, Mark. 2008. "America's Medicated Army." *Time*. 16 June:26–30.

Tickle, Phyllis A. 2004. *Greed*. Oxford: Oxford University Press.

Tiger, Lionel, 1999. *The Decline of Males*. Golden Books.

Trevor-Roper, H.R. 1984 [1969]. *The European Witch Craze*. Harmondsworth: Penguin Books.

Truman, Margaret. 1976. *Women of Courage*. New York: William Morrow.

Tuttle, Lisa. 1986. *The Encyclopedia of Feminism*. New York: Facts on File Publications.

Twiss, Amanda. 2002. *The Most Evil Men and Women in History.* London: Michael O'Mara Books

Tyre, Peg. 2006. "The Trouble with Boys." *Newsweek*. 30 January:44:52.

Tyre, Peg and Daniel McGinn. 2003. "She Works, He Doesn't." *Newsweek*. May 12: 45–53.

U.N. Department of Peacekeeping. http://www.un.org/depts/dpko/fatalities.

U.N. Development Program. 2005. Human Development Report 2005. Palgrave Macmillan.

U.N. Development Program. 2006. Human Development Report 2006. Palgrave Macmillan.

U.N. Development Progam. 2007. Human Development Report 2007/8. Palgrave Macmillan.

U.N. Office on Drugs and Crime. 2009. *Global Report on Trafficking in Persons*. www.unodc.org.

U.S. Bureau of the Census. 2003. *Statistical Abstract of the United States*. Washington, D.C.

U.S. Bureau of the Census. 2004. *Statistical Abstract of the United States*. Washington, D.C.

U.S. Census Bureau, 2006. *Statistical Abstract of the United States: 2007*. Washington, D.C.

U.S. Census Bureau, 2007. *Statistical Abstract of the United States: 2008*. Washington, D.C.

U.S. Department of Education. 2006. *Digest of Education Statistics, 2005*. Institute of Education Sciences. National Center for Education Statistics.

U.S. Department of Justice. 1999. *Violence by Intimates*. Bureau of Justice Statistics. Ref: NCJ-167237.

U.S. Department of Justice. 2005. *Crime in the United States, 2004*. Federal Bureau of Investigation. www.fbi.gov.

U.S. Department of Labor, 2008. www.bcs.gov.

U.S. Fire Administration, 2008. *Firefighter Fatalities in the United States*, 2007. www.usfa.fema.gov.

U.S. Mine Safety and Health Administration. www.msha.gov.

Vaillant, George E. 1995. *The Wisdom of the Ego: Sources of Resilience in Adult Life*. Cambridge, Mass.: Belknap Press.

Vallee, Brian. 2007. *The War on Women*. Toronto: Key Porter.

Veblen, Thorstein. 1953/1899. *The Theory of the Leisure Class*. New York: The New American Library.

Vincent, Norah. 2006. *Self-Made Man*. London:Viking.

Walby, Sylvia. 1990. *Theorizing Patriarchy*. Oxford: Basil Blackwell.

Walker, Lenore. 1979. *The Battered Woman*. New York: Harper and Row.

Wallechinsky, David. 2006. "The World's 10 Worst Dictators." *Parade.* 22 January.

Warren, Mary Anne. 1985. *Gendercide: The Implications of Sexual Selection*. Totowa, N.J.: Rowan and Allanheld.

Weber, Max. 1958. *From Max Weber. Essays in Sociology*. Edited by H.H. Gerth and C. Wright Mills. New York: Oxford University Press.

Weber, Max. 1976 [1904]. *The Protestant Ethic and the Spirit of Capitalism*. London: Scribner's.

Weiss, Michael and Cathy Young. 1996. "Feminist Jurisprudence: Equal Rights or Neo-Paternalism?" *Policy Analysis* No. 256. June 19. Washington: The Cato Institute.

Whelehan, Imelda. 1995. *Modern Feminist Thought*. New York: New York University Press.

Whyte, William H. 1956. *The Organization Man*. New York: Doubleday Anchor.

Williams, John E. and Deborah L. Best. 1990. *Measuring Sex Stereotypes. A Multination Study*. London: Sage.

Wingert, Pat and Evan Thomas. 2006. "On Call in Hell." *Newsweek*. March 20:34–43.

Wolf, Naomi. 1990. *The Beauty Myth*. New York: Random House.

Wolf, Naomi. 1993. *Fire with Fire*. London: Chatto and Windus.

Wollstonecraft, Mary. 1985. [1792]. *A Vindication of the Rights of Women*. New York: W.W. Norton.

Wong, Kate. 1999. "The Most Dangerous Occupations." *Scientific American*. 10:2:47.

World Economic Forum. 2008. *The Global Gender Report. 2007*. www.weforum. org.

Wurtzel, Elizabeth. 1999. *Bitch: In Praise of Difficult Women*. New York: Anchor Books.

Young, Cathy. 1999. *Cease Fire! Why Women and Men must Join Forces to Achieve True Equality*. New York: The Free Press.

Zobel, Allia. 1994. *101 Reasons Why a Cat is Better Than a Man*. Holbrook, Mass: Bob Adams.

Zorpette, Glenn. 1999. "Extreme Sports, Sensation Seeking and the Brain." *Scientific American*. 10:2:56–9.

Index

The books listed below include only those from which direct quotations have been taken. Tables are indicated by *italic* page numbers. Footnotes are indicated thus: 123n2.